ASPECTS OF INDEPENDENT ROMANIA'S ECONOMIC HISTORY WITH PARTICULAR REFERENCE TO TRANSITION FOR EU ACCESSION

Modern Economic and Social History Series

General Editor: Derek H. Aldcroft

Titles in this series include:

Aspects of Independent Romania's Economic History with Particular Reference to Transition for EU Accession

DAVID TURNOCK
University of Leicester, UK

Taylor & Francis Group

LONDON AND NEW YORK

First published 2007 by Ashgate publishing

2 Park Square, Milton Park, Abingdon, Oxon OX14 4RN
711 Third Avenue, New York, NY 10017, USA

Routledge is an imprint of the Taylor & Francis Group, an informa business

First issued in paperback 2016

British Library Cataloguing in Publication Data
Turnock, David
    Aspects of independent Romania's economic history with particular reference to transition for EU accession. – (Modern economic and social history)
    1. Romania – Economic conditions 2. Romania – Economic policy 3. Romania – Foreign economic relations
    I. Title
    330.9'498

Library of Congress Cataloging-in-Publication Data
Turnock, David.
    Aspects of independent Romania's economic history with particular reference to transition for EU accession / David Turnock.
        p. cm. – (Modern economic and social history)
    Includes bibliographical references and index.
    ISBN 978-0-7546-5892-4 (alk. paper)
    1. Romania – Economic conditions. 2. European Union – Romania. I. Title.

HC405.T98 2007
330.9498–dc22

2006100204

ISBN 13: 978-0-7546-5892-4 (hbk)
ISBN 13: 978-1-138-25963-8 (pbk)

Contents

Contents

List of Figures

List of Tables

List of Abbreviations

bln:	billion
dwt:	deadweight
GW:	gigawatt
GWh:	gigawatt hour
h:	hour
ha:	hectare
j.v.:	joint venture
km:	kilometre
m:	metre
mg/l	milligrams per litre
mln:	million
MW:	megawatt
MWh:	megawatt hour
n.a.	not available
n.ap.	not appropriate
pc:	per capita
ppm:	parts per million
ptp:	per thousand of the population
sq.km:	square kilometre
t:	tonne
th:	thousand
tln:	trillion
yr:	year

AEC	Atomic Energy Company of Canada
AFPO	Association of Private Forest Owners
AFPR	Association of Furniture Producers of Romania
APMSH	Agency for the Privatisation & Management of State Holdings (APAPS)
APPA	Forest User Groups (Asociații Proprietărilor de Pădure)
ARSA	Authority for Recouping State Assets (AVAS: Autoritatea pentru Valorificarea Activelor Statului)
ASP	Airport Shopping Park (Bucharest)
ATM	Automatic Teller Machine ('Bancomat')
ATR	Aero International Regional
BC	Business Centre
BDIA	Biodiversity-important area
B-I	Bucharest-Ilfov region
BT	Transylvanian Bank (Banca Transilvania)
BTC	Bucharest Public Transport Company (RATB)

CANDU	Canadian Deuterium Uranium Reactor
CAP	Cooperative Agricultural Producer
CBC	Cross Border Cooperation
CBD	Central Business District
CC	County Council
CCCF	Railway Construction Company (Centrala de Construcţii Căi Ferate)
CCH	Cellulose and paper combine (Combinat de Celuloza şi Hărţie)
CCI	Chamber of Commerce & Industry
CCIA	Chamber of Commerce, Industry & Agriculture
CDF	Comprehensive Development Framework (World Bank)
CEE	Central & Eastern Europe (including FSU)
CEFTA	Central European Free Trade Organisation
CFF	Forest Railways (Căile Ferate Forestiere)
CIS	Confederation of Independent States
CoE	Council of Europe
CPAPSE	Commission for Poverty Alleviation & Promotion of Social Inclusion (CASPIS)
CRP	Romanian Oil Company
DCMT	Danube Criş Mureş Tisa Euroregion
DCR	Democratic Convention of Romania (CDR)
DDBR	Danube Delta Biosphere Reserve
DP	Democratic Party (PD)
DUHT	Democratic Union of Hungarians of Transylvania (PUMT)
DUP	Detailed Urban Plan (PUG)
EADS	European Aeronautic Defence & Space Systems
EBRD	European Bank for Reconstruction & Development
ECE	East Central Europe
ECEAT	European Centre for Eco-Agro Tourism
ECECs	East Central European Countries
EEC	European Economic Community
EF	Environmental Fund
EFCP	Environmentally-friendly concrete plant
EIA	Environmental impact assessment
EIB	European Investment Bank
EMBO	Employee-management buyout
ENGO	Environmental NGO
EPA	Environmental Protection Agency
EPCE	Environmental Partnership for Central Europe
EU	European Union
EWP	Engineered wood products
FAB	Functioning Airspace Block
FAO	Food & Agriculture Organisation
FDI	Foreign direct investment
FME	Functional market economy
FPSME	Foundation for the Privatisation of SMEs

FSU	Former Soviet Union
GDP	Gross Domestic Product
GIS	Geographical Information Systems
Glulam	Glued laminated timber
GMP	Good manufacturing practice
GRP	Greater Romania Party (PRM)
GUP	General Urban Plan (PUG)
IBRD	International Bank for Reconstruction & Development (World Bank)
ICC	International Criminal Court
IFAD	International Fund for Agricultural Development
IFC	International Finance Corporation
IFET	Forest Enterprise for Logging & Transport (Intreprinderea Forestiere pentru Exploatare şi Transport)
IMF	International Monetary Fund
IMGB	Bucharest Heavy Machinery Enterprise (Intreprinderea de Maşini Grele Bucureşti)
IRIS	Integrated Railway Information System
ISPA	Instrument for Structural Policies for Pre-Accession
IT	Information technology
ITC	Information technology and communications
IUCN	World Conservation Union
JBIC	Japanese Bank for International Cooperation
JTA	Justice & Truth Alliance (AJA)
LCC	Large Carnivore Centre
LDGC	Lower Danube Green Corridor
LFA	Less-favoured area
LPG	Liquid petroleum gas
LSL	Laminated strand timber
LVL	Laminated veneer lumber
MDF	Medium density fibreboard
MHPPW	Ministry of Housing, Public Works & Planning (MLPAT)
MIG	Minimum income guarantee
MWFEP	Ministry of Waters Forests & Environmental Protection (MAPPM)
NAAC	National Agency for Agricultural Consultation (ANCA)
NAE	National Agency for Employment (ANM)
NAMZ	National Agency for the Mountain Zones
NATO	North Atlantic Treaty Organisation
NBR	National Bank of Romania
NDA	National Dwellings Agency (ANL)
NDP	National Development Plan
NFA	National Forest Administration (Romsilva)
NGO	Non-governmental organisation
NHDR	National human development reports
NIDP	National Infrastructure Development Plan
NLIP	National Land Improvement Company
NLP	National Liberal Party (PNL)

NPA	National Privatisation Agency
NPCDP	National Peasant Christian Democrat Party (PNȚCD)
NPP	National Peasant Party
NRRP	National Roads Rehabilitation Project
NSF	National Salvation Front
NTC	National Tobacco Corporation
NWC	National Water Company
OECD	Organisation for Economic Cooperation & Development
OSB	Oriented strandboard ('Tischlerplatten')
OSCE	Organisation for Security & Cooperation in Europe
OVR	Opération Villages Roumains
PAL	Chipboard
PEEN	Pan-European Ecological Network
Phare	Poland-Hungary: Actions for the Reconstruction of their Economies
POF	Public Ownership Fund
ppm	parts per million
PPP	Polluter pays principle
PPPs	Public–private partnerships
PPPy	Purchasing power parity standard
PRNU	Party of Romanian National Unity
PSAL	Public Sector Adjustment Loan
PSD	Party of Social Democracy
PSDR	Party of Social Democracy of Romania
PSL	Parallel strand timber
RA	Regie Autonome (Autonomous national company)
BTC	Bucharest Public Transport Company (RATB)
RCB	Romanian Commercial Bank (BCR)
RCP	Romanian Communist Party (PCR)
R&D	Research & Development
RDB	Romanian Development Bank (BRD)
RERP	Regional Environmental Reconstruction Programme
RHG	Reichswerke Hermann Göring
RIB	Romanian International Bank
RICOP	Programme of Industrial Restructuring & Professional Reconversion
RNB	Radici Nylon Bergamo
RSB	Romanian Savings Bank (CEC)
RT	Romtelecom
SAPARD	Special Action Programme for Agriculture & Rural Development
SECI	South East Europe Cooperation Initiative
SEE	South East Europe
SEECs	South East European Countries
SMEs	Small and medium-sized enterprises
SOE	State-owned enterprise
SOF	State Ownership Fund
SNCFR	Romanian State Railway Company
SWOT	Strengths weaknesses opportunities threats

TER	Tineretul Ecologist Român
TICDC	Training & Innovation Centre for Development in the Carpathians
TINA	Transport Infrastructure Needs Assessment
TNC	Trans-national company
TRACECA	Transport Central Europe-Central Asia
UK	United Kingdom
UN	United Nations
UNDP	United Nations Development Programme
UNESCO	United Nations Educational, Scientific & Cultural Organisation
UNICEF	United Nations Children's (Emergency) Fund
UNHCR	United Nations High Commission for Refugees
USA	United States of America
USAID	United States Agency for International Development
VAT	Value added tax
VOC	Volatile organic compounds
WHO	World Health Organisation
WTmO	World Tourism Organisation
WWF	World Wide Fund for Nature
WWT	Waste water treatment
AEPZ	Zărneşti Area Ecotourism Association (AEPZ)
ZUP	Zonal Urban Plan (PUZ)

Modern Economic and Social History Series
General Editor's preface

Economic and social history has been a flourishing subject of scholarly study during recent decades. Not only has the volume of literature increased enormously but the range of interest in time, space and subject matter has broadened considerably so that today there are many sub-branches of the subject which have developed considerable status in their own right.

One of the aims of this series is to encourage the publication of scholarly monographs on any aspect of modern economic and social history. The geographical coverage is world-wide and contributions on the non-British themes will be especially welcome. While emphasis will be placed on works embodying original research, it is also intended that the series should provide the opportunity to publish studies of a more general thematic nature which offer a reappraisal or critical analysis of major issues of debate.

Derek H. Aldcroft
University of Leicester

Foreword

Romania has just become a new EU member state and this may rekindle interest in a country that escaped in dramatic fashion from a rapidly-shrinking communist bloc in December 1989. It then seemed that an 'island' of Latin culture had been imprisoned within an alien eastern bloc as much by it's own primitive and 'sultanistic' leadership as by the Soviet embrace that had been so stifling and irresistible during Stalin's last years. The imperative of industrialisation was reinforced as a not wholly inappropriate meeting of minds between a domestic leadership striving to build a proletariat from a predominantly peasant society (with the eventual prospect of greater material well-being) and Soviet involvement in global power politics that required the utmost cohesion among the bloc's member states – unified perversely under the banner of a command economy shaped a decade earlier by the realities of impending world war and Moscow's doctrine of 'socialism in one country'. But under Ceauşescu it became an even more obscene fetish as production was driven forwards not on the basis of real consumption needs so much as a global 'dumping' programme sustained by bilateral deals that not infrequently involved the disposal of manufactures for less than the real cost of the raw materials.

Draconian policies to maintain a high birth rate and consolidate settlement in key villages were indicative of a mentality that treated Romania as a gigantic 'Lego' kit allowing the old dictator to pursue his obsessive 'labour of love': literally *building* communism as new integrated economic complexes with energy resources, power generation, local manufacturing capacity and housing – all under communist party control – exemplified by the little town of Anina (in the Banat Mountains) that bears the scars not only of more than two centuries of coal mining but also of Ceauşescu's 'meglamania' in conceiving an energy project in the 1980s based on low-grade bituminous schist. Incapable of spontaneous combustion, natural gas had to be brought in specially by pipeline to a power station built on a limestone plateau (specifically on Ceauşescu's orders to assure the necessary integration) that consumed part of its production in pumping of cooling water from the valley below. Even so, the first generating set was already being choked by ash when the revolution occurred: a technical problem that had not been anticipated and for which no solution could be found. Within months the quarries were silent and the workforce dispersed, while the new town of Anina (due to replace the old as the latter became part of the opencast quarry system) was still-born with its first apartment blocks unfinished to this day and only partially habitable.

The book tries to show how the aberrations of the 1980s – and the excesses of the communist era as a whole – must be drawn into the wider picture of a neo-Balkan state striving for modernisation after centuries of Ottoman suzerainty were relieved progressively by removal of Istanbul's trading monopoly under the Treaty of Adrianople in 1829, the end of Russian protection at the end of the Crimean War in 1856; followed quickly by great-power recognition of the union of the Moldavian and Wallachian principalities in 1858 (though still subject to Ottoman suzerainty) and finally independence confirmed by the Congress of Berlin in 1878. Economic growth accelerated, but the country had to rebuild after the First World War; now with strong Western support for a 'România Mare' that was more than doubled in size through the incorporation of former Habsburg and Russian territories (historically Romanian but products of the fragmentation of the so-called East-Central European 'shatter zone' by rival imperial systems). However the wider political context continued to be all-important and Romania was obliged to adapt to German hegemony in the region in the later 1930s (accompanied by some further territorial changes in 1940) as well as the Soviet takeover of the resulting totalitarian structures after 1944. It is therefore a fascinating but complex task to reconstruct a continuous programme of modernisation punctuated by repeated territorial and ideological changes to which the Romanians were obliged to adjust.

However the main thrust of the book rests with 17 years of transition (1990–2006) that have seen a once-unlikely transformation in Romania from an ultra-conformist Soviet satellite (notwithstanding the so-called 'independent foreign policy') to an enthusiastic EU accession candidate. In fact the origin of the book lies in a contextual study for post-communist restructuring that could not (for reasons of length) be contained within a single volume: hence a number of references to the author's 2008 (in press) publication by Edward Elgar. After the early years of neo-communist uncertainty, Romania has once again accomplished a radical ideological change observed at first hand throughout. The new president (former communist Ion Iliescu) took a conservative approach and gained popularity for cancelling the most hated laws of old régime while refusing to 'sell the country' to foreign investors. His dubious credentials were spelt out in banner headlines when he repeatedly used Jiu Valley miners as a private army to intervene in Bucharest against more radical reform movements championed by the modernising wing of the National Salvation Front and emerging centre-right parties. But although Iliescu stayed in power until the beginning of 1997 – and regained office during 2001–2004 – he was eventually forced to concede that a 'third way' between the capitalism of a neoliberal EU and the orthodox communism of pre-Gorbachev era was impossible.

So, while reform was extremely tentative in the early years – justified allegedly by the Romanians' desire for 'peace and quiet' after their buffeting by Ceauşescu's excesses (increasingly aberrational in the 1980s) – the direction of change eventually became unmistakable. A centre-right coalition committed Romania unambiguously to the EU project during 1997–2000 and the new orientation was sufficiently compelling by 2001 to command the support of modernisers in the Party of Social Democracy (PSD) – evolving from the conservative wing of the Salvation Front – who were then returned to power. But it was doubly fortunate that the unexpected defeat of Adrian Năstase (PSD prime minister during 2001–2004) in the presidential election run-off at the hands of the charismatic centrist Traian Băsescu (leader of the Democratic Party: one of the governing coalition partners during 1997–2000) should then inspire a realignment of finely-balanced parliamentary forces and deny a further term in office for the PSD, now heavily tainted by corruption in both ministries and local government where the activities of some party 'barons' had become notorious. Instead, the centrist Popescu-Tăriceanu government has done enough to raise standards in public life (with vigorous attention to the criminal justice system) and stimulate an economy – continuously in growth since 2000 – to satisfy critics in Brussels.

The book is based on wide reading as well as fieldwork, but I have not set out to reference every detail noted in the proverbial 'thousand and one' media notes from which the book has been built up and citations generally refer to the substantive literature on which the bibliography is based. Furthermore the references to EU 'Country Reports' – annual reviews (often highly critical) of Romania's progress in meeting the conditions required for accession are available on the Internet through www.europa. eu. int/comm/enlargement/index/htm and are not included in the bibliography. Four domestic matters concern first, the introduction of the new 'heavy'leu (each worth 10,000 of the old) that came fully in force in 2007 after a transition period. However, the old currency – which after all is part of the economic history – is retained for most calculations although dollar and euro equivalents are now very widely used (incidently all $ references relate to US dollars). Second, Ceauşescu's tinkering with placenames by adding the Roman names to two cities – hence Cluj-Napoca and Drobeta-Turnu Severin – is acknowledged in the first-mention of these places in each chapter but is not repeated throughout. Third, Romanian names for organisatione e.g. ministries, agencies and NGOs are anglicised along with the names of businesses (such as. the leading banks) that are frequently used (with the Romanian names or acronyms in brackets in the list of abbreviations). But the names (or acronyms) of other businesses are given in Romanian with some English translation. Fourth, while the traditional spatial units for Romania are the historic provinces, counties and communes, the large regional development areas now in force have been used retrospectively as in Figure 3.1 and Table 3.5. Finally for the sake of simplicity the present Yugoslav successor states (including Kosovo and Montenegro) are used retrospectively for the whole post-communist period: hence the references throughout to Serbia rather than the (smaller) Yugoslavia or Serbia & Montenegro.

I am indebted to many people who have helped in various ways with the project. Although the entire text is my responsibility I have incorporated notes on the wood processing industry and forest privatisation by Florin Ioraş of Buckinghamshire Chilterns University College. My numerous friends in Romania have not been involved specifically in this project but I am grateful for the fact that I have been able to obtain information and comment from time to time from Şerban Lacriţeanu, Nicolae Muică, Mirela Nae and Dan Platon in Bucharest as well as Remus Creţan in Timişoara, Rodica Petrea in Oradea and Vasile Surd in Cluj. Nicolae Muică has also been particularly helpful in obtaining hard copy of some materials not available electronically and I also grateful to him for his help and companionship in the field over many years in connection with various rural research projects that have been part of the 'stock' on which this book is based. My sincere thanks also go to Ruth Pollington who has drawn all the maps (some of them produced specially for this publication) and to my wife Marion who has helped to prepare the text for publication; not to mention her patience and support during several years while I have postponed the conventional routine of a retired academic. Finally my thanks to Derek Aldcroft as the series editor for his advice and encouragement as well as Tom Gray and Amy Corstorphine at Ashgate.

Leicester, August 2007

Chapter One

The Romanian State and its Economic Development to 1918

This chapter provides a brief introduction to the Romanian people and the state within its present borders with reference to the complementary natural regions and priorities in policy-making. But its main purpose is to examine the major issues and themes in economic development until the First World War. Although development proceeded throughout the early modern period it was not until independence was recognised in 1878 that there was scope for fiscal policies in support of national industry; bringing to an end a period of free trade that saw much of the country's small-scale manufacturing wiped out by imports from the Habsburg Empire. Industrial growth was crucial for a modern commercial agriculture by creating an expanding home market and absorbing the subsistence farmers, yet heavy protection for industry risked damaging foreign trade in agricultural commodities which was important as one of the principal sources of capital investment. Although the country was fortunate in having timber and oil as staple exports to generate capital for industrial growth, Romania was a still a predominantly peasant society in 1914 with land reform a key element in the political agenda following the revolt of 1907.

Introduction To Romania

Romania is one of the larger East Central European countries (ECECs) in terms of both area (238.4 th.sq.kms) and population (21.73mln in 2003). It lies in the southeastern part of this region (sometimes seen as a separate region of Southeastern Europe: SEE) although Romania likes to see itself as eminently 'Central European' and resists the Balkan label more clearly applicable to countries lying south of the Danube. It occupies a Carpathian-Danubian-Pontic territory of considerable strategic significance, underlined by the recently-identified north-south and east-west trending Eurocorridors. The landscape is dominated by the semi-circular sweep of the Carpathians that are part of Europe's Alpine structures, yet with a crest line generally below 2,000m the mountains are modest in relation to the Alpine-Himalayan chain as a whole. Comprising metamorphic and volcanic rocks, the semi-circular mountain chain has historically provided a good defensive line, albeit weakened by low-level through valleys associated with the Jiu, Mureş, Olt and Someş rivers; while the range is also quite narrow: 100kms in the Rodna and only 70km in the Parâng. Along with the structural and erosional intermontane basins and depressions (including Ciuc, Făgăraş, Gheorgheni and Trei Scaune which may be old lake basins) these considerations enhance the accessibility of the high ground and help to account for a relatively intensive pastoralism since prehistoric times. Erosion surfaces are an added benefit for high-level occupation and although there is some controversy over the extent of permanent settlement it is clear that population pressure in the eighteenth and nineteenth centuries gave rise to the colonisation of the mountain surfaces wherever subsistence farming was possible and legacies of this occupation are still very evident to altitudes of 1,400m (especially in the counties of Alba, Hunedoara and Suceava). The mountain regions maintain a strong complementary role in the economy by producing the bulk of the non-agricultural domestic raw materials, many of the most skilled urban-industrial communities and an active peasantry which still makes full use of the agricultural potential and often retains a mountain homestead as a base for seasonal employments in other areas.

Subcarpathian hill country consisting essentially of Tertiary clays, marls and sands complement the main Carpathian range especially in the east and southeast. This belt is never more than 30kms across and it is usual to find the upland terrain broken by depressions like those of Caşin-Tazlău and Vrancea. In a forested state the land was fairly stable but heavy cutting of the woodland since the nineteenth century, complemented by the spread of subsistence farming, has left the countryside prone to instability with landslides (and more occasionally mudflows) a constant threat. Within the Carpathian arc lies the Transylvanian Plateau: one of the major Tertiary lowlands of ECE although subsidence was not as persistent as in Pannonia to the west. The landscape is one of smooth slopes developed on clays and sandstones. While it is too dissected and unstable for intensive arable farming it is suitable for high density mixed farming communities with intensive fruit growing and viticulture at the contact with the plains. Much oil has also been found in these Subcarpathian structures. Settlements claim a particularly long history and offer much of ethnographical and touristical interest, resting on the notion of cultural continuity for romanised Dacian population that assimilated Slavic (and Magyar) influences without radical change. While continuity of settlement on the high erosion surfaces of the mountain core ('corona montium') seems implausible the Latin base to the language and culture cannot seriously be disputed.

The peripheral lowlands, areas of prolonged geological subsidence, provide the bulk of the agricultural resources and their network of markets – combined with the ports of the Danube and Black Sea – provided much of the capacity for communist industrialisation. The Romanian Plain in the south (extending to the Lower Danube) and the Tisa Plain in the east are capped by loess deposits, sometimes up to 40m thick and stand at 90–140m above sea level. Chernozem soils are highly amenable to intensive cultivation sustaining Romania's large wheat exports in the late nineteenth century. But drought is a hazard, particularly in Bărăgan and Dobrogea, and high yields have only been sustainable since irrigation systems were installed. The floodplains have been of limited agricultural use apart from grazing (though fishing and timber has also been significant) but the temptation to dyke, drain and irrigate the wetlands under communism for intensive cultures added to the risks of flood damage to the point where some areas have been restored to a traditional régime. The Danube delta is the newest landscape in geological terms: a complex of backwaters, sandbanks and floating reed islands with drainage by the three main distributaries of Chilia in the north (marking Romania's frontier with Ukraine), Sulina in the centre (the main navigation channel) and the Sf.Gheorghe in the south. Only one eighth of the delta constitutes dry land and none of this rises to more than four meters above water level, apart from the complex sandy banks of Chilia and Letea. Once again attempts to intensify land use have given rise to serious ecological complications.

Geopolitical Unity

While Romanians like to see their occupation of the Carpathians as the key to their survival (albeit with some assimilation of Slavic elements) since the Romanisation of Dacia, subsequent recolonisation of the low ground as far as the Danube and the Black Sea has given rise to the notion of geopolitical unity across the Carpathian-Danube-Pontic zone. However this notion was compromised by the Habsburg, Ottoman and Russian imperial systems bordering on Romanian territory, with the additional complication in Transylvania of Hungarian and German settlement of Medieval origin. Of course the imperial powers were unable to sponsor an independent Romania, given the strategic importance of the territories involved (although the Ottoman concept of suzerainty allowed home rule at the principality level) and while France and the UK encouraged modernisation through models for government and socio-economic reform these states were in no position to apply military pressure in the Danube region. Hence it has been difficult to secure enduring external support for self-determination for a large island of Latin culture that has – remarkably – survived over two millennia since the Romanisation of the indigenous Dacian population. Romanian independence was first achieved in the former Ottoman Principalities of Moldavia and Wallachia along with Dobrogea thanks to the consensus reached by the Congress of Berlin in 1878. The First World War led to a 'Greater Romania' that included the whole of Transylvania (along with Banat, Crişana and Maramureş) as well as Bessarabia and southern Bucovina; thanks to West European (especially French) support following the defeat of both Russia and the Central Powers. However this settlement was contested bitterly by both Hungary and the Soviet Union regarding former Habsburg and Russian imperial lands respectively. The Soviets demanded the return of Bessarabia in 1940 along with southern Bucovina and the Herta district (now comprising – mainly – the separate Romanian state of Moldova), while Hitler's arbitration in the same year split Transylvania in half. Although the partition was overturned by the Soviets after the war in Romania's favour, contested sovereignty was all too apparent through the polemics of nationalist parties in Hungary and Romania during the 1990s until the interest of both countries in CoE, EU and NATO membership brought a tacit acceptance of the status quo in the context of more enlightened ethnic policies. Romania is now poised to realise the historic goal of becoming part of a westernised Europe and the prospect of territorial stability has generated confidence for the necessary business of cementing relations across the once-disputed frontiers.

Modernisation: The Rural Base

There is no space to explore the political geography of the post-Roman era which saw autonomous communities fall subservient to external pressures. But the evolution of Romanian society was strongly conditioned by the power held by Hungarian lords and German burghers in Transylvania while the principalities of Moldavia and Wallachia, falling within the Ottoman Empire from the fifteenth century, combined autonomy with greater ethnic unity. The Turkish practice of appointing a succession of short-term Greek 'Phanariot' rulers after 1711 (rather than native princes) had negative results through their priority over personal wealth, but Bucharest became the largest and richest Balkan city by the end of the eighteenth century as the Phanariots required luxurious housing and services and consigned wheat to Istanbul (whose trade monopoly became ever more important after the Ottomans lost their southern Russian territories in 1783). However the Treaty of Kuchuk-Kainardji (1774) gave Russia a protectorate over Moldavia and Wallachia (complementing Ottoman suzerainty) in the interest of defending Christianity and this was sufficiently inspiring for Moldavian volunteers to accept Russian objectives as their own during the 1787–92 Russo-Turkish War. But despite some Russian success with the Porte in easing the burden of Phanariot rule, Russian influence in Moldavia seemed rather less progressive when the eastern part of the principality (Bessarabia) was annexed in 1812 as the price for ending their occupation. Meanwhile the Habsburgs had occupied Oltenia during 1718–39 and initiated the 'Partition of Moldavia' by taking Bucovina in 1775 (by 1782 both the Habsburgs and Russians had their agents in Bucharest). However there was an economic stimulus (despite Vienna's preoccupation with the challenges of the existing Habsburg borderlands) through a mutual interest in trade and an "inadvertent promotion of economic ties" between the Principalities and Transylvania (Lampe & Jackson 1982, p. 107) sanctioned by commercial treaties. Indeed Balkan commodity surpluses became increasingly valuable to the Habsburgs as the expansion of cereal growing in Hungary reduced the scope for livestock rearing.

Feudal Landowners

Feudal landowners ('boyars') were certainly much encouraged by a sharp increase in cattle, horse and pig prices after the start of the Napoleonic Wars. Evolving from acquisitive village leaders who took over the best village lands and gained great influence as the nineteenth century elite, they exploited the peasantry according to the Ottoman model, although demesnes were usually worked less intensively than in the Habsburg lands to the north. Ottoman officials and feudal cavalry were usually supported by lands granted by the sultan for life (without inheritance) but while there was no feudal jurisdiction over the peasants, it was common for these fiefs to be administered illegally as 'chiftliks' on which the peasants were obliged – out of economic necessity – to work as sharecroppers under terms which might be onerous enough to ferment national revolutions. The estates became more prominent in the Principalities when the opportunities to supply grain as well as livestock to Istanbul "encouraged boyars to attempt to secure rights to the agricultural production of villages" (Stokes 1987, p. 52) and they controlled the plains not through landownership so much as their rights to collect tithes. While demographic setbacks and insecurity combined with transhumance to prevent tight control of a sedentary population in the eighteenth century, the nineteenth century reality was quite different thanks to more ordered government and a resumption of population growth. The boyars then gained clear access to power when the Ottomans replaced the Phanariot Greeks with native princes in 1821. Labour requirements were raised before the end of the eighteenth century while in 1815 settlement on boyar land became a privilege (rather than a right) and tithes were raised from a tenth of the production to a fifth. The Ottoman trade monopoly was removed under the Treaty of Adrianople (1829) and an expanding cereal surplus found its way to Central and Western Europe, albeit with continued dependence on sharecropping. Russian protection produced an era of enlightenment under the Count Kiselev who sought to enhance the political control of the centre over the landed interests and drew up constitutions in the form of 'Organic Statutes' (1831) that legally restricted peasant smallholdings to a maximum of two-thirds of the estate land. However, production continued to focus on small-scale operations because peasants disliked working as estate labourers and resisted official surveys that might reduce the land available; while the owners (or the merchants renting their lands) "were apparently more interested in maximising their short-term cash income than in organising production for long term" (Lampe & Jackson 1982, p. 223). They would rent additional estate land ('prisoare') to peasants (without survey) through contracts requiring payment in cash or kind rather than feudal labour services (increased by the codification of tasks in such a way as to take far longer than the customary 12 days). This exploitative arrangement facilitated a monetisation process and was very rewarding to the owners who "used not only the threat of surveying but also the growing peasant demand for land to increase rents sharply' (Ibid, p. 223). Thus, capitalist farming was introduced on the basis of neo-feudal obligations that made labour extremely cheap. While there was some mechanisation on the estates the process was limited by the fact that the labour was not supplied by rural proletariat but rather by a "peasantry of subjugated smallholding sharecroppers" (Stokes 1987, p. 54).

Gradual Reform

In 1848 a provisional government contemplated peasant emancipation as well as the provision of more viable holdings for which the estates would be compensated. But the reaction that followed the arrival of Ottoman forces saw a revision of land rights in favour of the boyars in 1851, paving the way for greater use of peasant labour on estate reserves – though this 'second serfdom' also saw the peasantry encroaching on estate land so that cultivation on peasant-worked land increased faster than on estate reserve land. This facilitated a growing grain output, albeit with low yields given the technology employed and the recurring drought conditions. In 1858 the boyars became landlords ('moşieri') while Prince Cuza's 1864 reform formally abolished feudalism and gave the peasants two-thirds of the estate land with the aim of creating an independent class of small proprietors. But this so alarmed the landowners that they mounted a successful coup against him; yet the peasant holdings were small and the prohibition of a land market prevented any evolution towards viable family farms.

Meanwhile the landlords obtained legal title to the remaining land (necessarily the best one-third!) and subsequently enlarged their estates through the secularisation of monastic lands. Both peasants and landlords could access state land but even so the average peasant holding declined from 1896. Furthermore, when leasing more demesne land for sharecropping a curious legal formality tied the contract to unpaid labour on another portion of the estate. And as landlords leased estate management to agents by competition, contracts had to ensure greater profits and so they became more onerous for the peasants. This was especially the case after 1895 when cereal prices stagnated in the face of North American competition, and when the flagging latifundia system was taken over by rapacious Jewish estate managers ('arendaşi') seeking the cheapest possible peasant labour, with adverse consequences for public health through long hours of peasant work and the virtual absence of protein in the diet. In 1904 the Liberal government sanctioned peasant cooperatives to compete for sharecropping leases but the system did not make significant progress because only rarely could the cooperatives compete with the managers. Owners actually preferred wage labour by landless Romanian peasants and seasonal Bulgarian, Macedonian and Serb migrants (the latter also prominent in Bulgaria and Hungary) but most failed to create a stable basis for capitalist farming since they entered world markets not "as profit-seeking farmers but as tribute-seeking rentiers" (Stokes 1987, p. 55) while German and Hungarian farms still secured greater efficiency. It was only after the First World War that the system was revised in favour of wider peasant proprietorship and heavier state taxes.

The Habsburg Lands
In this area – extending southeastwards after the Ottomans were pushed into retreat in 1699 – the Romanians managed to counter the ensuing ideological offensive through the support of the Uniate Church. At a time when Vienna was locked in a struggle with the nobility over centralisation, the Habsburgs singularly failed to win over the Romanian peasants to Catholicism. Although Horea's revolt in 1784 was firmly dealt with - at a time of revenue crisis on feudal estates just as Habsburg tax reforms were being perfected (Verdery 1983, p. 344) – the Hungarian nobles received only symbolic compensation for damage to their estates. Reactionary lordly attitudes in Transylvania were again apparent in the run-up to the 1848 revolution for Transylvania's diet rejected emancipation in 1846 – even with the support of the most commercialised estates producing sugar, oil and alcohol – when the opposite was being widely advocated across Hungary as a whole. With limited mining and manufacturing, this 'no' to agrarian capitalism kept the peasants on the land and delayed improvement even after a Transylvanian Agricultural Society was belatedly established in 1844 (Ibid, p. 357). In other words, in a complex situation that saw ethnicity interwoven with a process of state-building and economic change, Romanians were not without support in Vienna and they reciprocated with support for the emperor against the Hungarian nationalist revolutionaries of 1848. Feudalism was dismantled during 1848–54 but economic change came slowly except for small islands of modernity based on the more compelling mineral resources, as if there was a cynical acceptance of backwardness by a regional elite that maintained a high social and political status through control of a dependent peasantry. Ethnic relations were further complicated

when the Magyars settled for dualism through the 'Ausgleich' (compromise) with Vienna in 1867 allowing for a Hungarian civil service and industrial establishment in Budapest (built up from eastward-moving capital) along with a consolidation of colonialism in Transylvania.

Hungarian Supremacy in Transylvania   There was improved access to commodity markets but the peasants had to work on the estates to pay compensation for their plots (rendered progressively less viable through partible inheritance) with further agricultural work through sharecropping. Informal methods predominated, including payment in kind to migrant 'Highlanders' for casual labour even on the largest Romanian farms (Verdery 1983, p. 240). Meanwhile the progressive influence of the Saxons was undermined by outside competition and intrusion into their commercial niche by Armenians, Jews and Wallachians although – with larger farms and smaller families – they could mechanise and pay their workers in cash (Ibid, p. 346). Not surprisingly they found it hard to decide whether to ally with the Hungarians or Romanians as the latter were "persuaded that a viable economy could be organised only on a national basis [whereupon] they sought to create a Romanian agriculture, a Romanian industry and Romanian banks" (Ibid, p. 220). They had most success in banking and credit because starting with 'Albina' in 1872, 274 banks – mostly small and agricultural – were established by 1914. Hungarian assimilation tactics could not succeed because, as a predominantly rural people with Orthodox and Uniate traditions, the Romanians were "protected from the assimilative power of the cities in the central industrial regions which served as foundries of Magyarisation" (Ibid, p. 223). Progressive Hungarian leaders like I.Tisza (premier during 1913–17) wanted to deal with Transylvania's Romanians – as the largest minority in Hungary – to bring them into the mainstream of public life and weaken their links with Bucharest. Yet there could never be compromise over the Magyar character of Hungary that barred proportional representation for Romanians at all levels of government. Since the transfer of the province to Romanian rule after the First World War, under the Treaty of Trianon, a large Hungarian minority has remained, especially in the east (Covasna and Harghita). Along with other Hungarian minorities in Serbia and Slovakia this provides the prime focus for ethnic politics in the Middle Danubian region where right-wing calls for a restoration of the pre-Trianon frontiers was potentially destabilising in the early 1990s.

Modernisation in the Romanian Kingdom (Regat) To 1918

Important political progress was made through the union of the formerly separate principalities with the ending of Russian protection after the Crimean War (1856) and the inspired decision of 1859 when Prince Cuza was elected in both Moldavia and Wallachia combined with Western support for the larger state as a bastion against Russian expansion. However Ottoman suzerainty continued until the country gained its independence in 1877 at the time of the joint Romanian-Russian intervention in Bulgaria, following the suppression of revolt by the Ottomans, and sovereign status was acknowledged by the powers at the Congress of Berlin in 1878.

The ruling prince Carol I now headed a kingdom ('Regat') and presided over more than three decades of modernisation before the First World War intervened. Prior to 1878 Romania had enjoyed considerable autonomy, but always with the Ottoman Empire as the suzerain power (balanced by Russian protection from 1829 until the Crimean War). Politically the country was in the hands of the Liberal Party that represented an oligarchic industrial community, with opposition from the landowning Conservatives. The Wallachian capital (Bucharest) – a Balkan trading centre defended by a line of monasteries planted on hillocks and bluffs on the northern side of the Dâmbovița floodplain that became the residence of Wallachian princes – permanently from 1659 – became the Romanian capital from 1862 and the seat of a centralised government that grew rapidly after independence. More organised urban growth followed the constitution of 1831 but expansion well beyond the confines of a tight knot of winding streets was facilitated only by new boulevards in the late nineteenth century and a revolution in building through technical innovation in the cement industry by the landowner Prince Bibescu who used the family fortune to introduce the rotating oven in 1908. Since the trappings of modernism rested on an enduring oriental legacy there was evidence of a patrimonial state where a certain degree of corruption and authoritarianism was evidently justified in the interest of nationalism. But at the same time a tension between modernism and traditional values was all too evident.

The Land: A Fundamental Issue

As already noted, Prince Cuza attempted to modernise landholding in 1864 by giving land to the peasants and abolishing their feudal obligations, but smallholdings were not viable as family farms and the peasants were obliged to enter into highly oppressive labour contracts (or sharecropping arrangements) in respect of the estates retained by the landowners. This was the social basis of a farming system that made Romania the world's fourth largest wheat exporter. The situation deteriorated with an increase in the rural population while the total area of peasant plots remained relatively stable. Holdings that averaged 4.6ha in 1864 were reduced to 3.4 by 1905. At the same time payment for farm work failed to keep up with prevailing price levels because the landlords came under pressure from falling cereal prices at the end of the century, with little scope for other farming enterprises once the Austro-Hungarian market was closed to Romanian cattle exporters in 1882. Some contemporary commentators like R. Rosetti and V. Kogălniceanu wanted to improve peasant access to land and introduce a more equitable labour contract system, but there could be no fundamental change because the state desperately needed the proceeds of the cereal trade to help modernise the country and accelerate industrialisation which was not only a strategic necessity but also – as was argued by C. Dobrogeanu-Gherea and S. Zeletin – a social imperative as the only long-term solution to rural overpopulation. Arguably there was a role for both policies with the poorer peasants leaving for the towns while the more successful peasant families, with access to cooperative rural credit, might compete for land through relatively intensive farming systems on smallholdings created by the banks in purchasing and sub-dividing estates (although Kogălniceanu's Peasant Movement of 1906 was always constrained by the lack of adequate tariff reform to open the Habsburg Empire to Romanian cattle exporters). In his review of the 1907 peasant revolt P. G. Eidelburg (1974) skilfully meshes together the long-term consideration of falling cereal prices and population increase with a stark choice between high tariffs to protect an infant industrial establishment or low tariffs that would stimulate cattle exports but simultaneously threaten Romanian industry through a flood of cheap imports.

Continued Peasant Subsistence

The logic of a clear split between efficient farmers and a surplus peasantry absorbed by urban-based industry could not be achieved at the time: indeed, the process of displacement was hardly complete at the end of the communism, to say nothing of the recession over the past 15 years. So capitalist farming facilitated by the 1864 reform was complemented by a major subsistence effort that was only partly displaced to marginal land. The late nineteenth century, with its economic restructuring complemented by population growth, saw much expansion of farming on the margins of the forests (indeed the erosion of the woodlands through the pressure to extend the agricultural area can be widely inferred from the placename evidence) and also on unstable hill-slopes of the Subcarpathians as the fertile river terraces were reserved increasingly for commercial farming. Subsistence farming was combined with a wide range of occupations in manufacturing and services that made pluriactivity a basic characteristic of the modernising Romanian village (Muică et al. 2000). Meanwhile, in Transylvania population growth continued in the mountain valleys, including the high platforms of the Apuseni, since the 'Highlanders' could seek outlets in the lowlands for their handicraft production and their surplus labour at harvest time. There was also better scope for stock-rearing in view of the large Habsburg market that was virtually closed to Regat farmers by high tariffs erected in retaliation for the protection of industry. Maximising the opportunities for seasonal grazing pushed vertical transhumance systems to their limits and also extended the use of steppeland grazing to areas east of Romania that had not yet been ploughed up for cereals. However this was becoming more difficult where the challenge included the use of sandy lands for fruit growing and viticulture.

Industrial Development

The Regat had considerable potential for industry by virtue of its agricultural raw materials, forest wealth and minerals (especially oil). As primary exports, these commodities could provide the wealth needed to import the equipment and technology needed to create the broad manufacturing base needed both for employment and production of strategic goods. Despite the virtual absence of coking coal and iron ore (available only to a limited extent in Transylvania where metallurgical industries developed in the Hunedoara and Reşiţa areas) a diverse industrial establishment was achieved. Industrial development in the early nineteenth century was slow but the village craftsmen and urban-based artisans were numerous. Attempts by the princes of Moldavia and Wallachia to introduce factory industry to their respective capitals – Iaşi and Bucharest – were frustrated by the backward war-torn environment for which monopolies and tied labour forces were inadequate compensation. The Assan milling, oil-pressing and distilling enterprise in Bucharest stood out as the most impressive mid-century development and one of the first to use steam power. Craft skills in the rural areas were of some significance when organised on a workshop scale to cope with orders from the towns. Thus the Kogălniceanu military clothing factory at Târgu Neamţ (1858) was grounded in the reputation of the area for woollen textiles fostered by the Neamţ monastery.

Fiscal Concessions

Granted in the 1870s after great damage had been done by free trade initially accepted in the agricultural interest, these grew into more comprehensive schemes to stimulate industry, including free building land, customs-exempt imported raw materials, concessionary railway freight charges and some production subsidies. Usually there were stipulations over the scale of mechanisation (to ensure a significant level of production), the number of employees (usually 20–25 minimum) and the training of native workers. Protective legislation encouraged the paper and sugar industries in 1881–82 and further legislation followed in 1886–87 for large-scale industry as a whole, plus a Mining Law in 1895 to open the oil industry to foreign investment. Further laws in 1906 and 1912 maintained conflict with the Habsburg Empire with tariffs averaging 20 per cent on finished and semi-finished imports that were certainly high enough to deter some European manufactures while creating "a climate in which entrepreneurs could believe investment in domestic industry would yield at least long-term prospects for satisfactory profit" (Lampe & Jackson 1982, p. 269). There was however the downside from overvalued exchange rates pushing up food prices and lowering demand for manufactures while pressure on industrial wages was backed by an emerging socialist movement. After good progress in the 1890s (a decade blessed for the most part by high cereal prices) momentum showed signs of flagging when living standards ceased to grow, the virgin cereal lands were fully occupied and world prices stagnated. Moreover the saturation of the home market suggested that an industrialisation policy based on substitution had largely run its course, though perhaps not in textiles where import levels were still high. In Romania, where 40 per cent of the seats in the legislature went to urban representatives backing protection, industrial growth to 1914 averaged 6 to 8 per cent over a period extending back possibly to 1880 (Jackson 1986, pp. 60–61). However it is possible that protection was too high since the cost of requirements like military uniforms, paper, transport equipment and drugs was increased. Low initial tariffs might have been sufficient (unless immediate provision of a national armaments industry was required) but there was a real problem in knowing just how high tariffs needed to be to have the desired effect through a lengthy sequencing scenario (Montias 1978, pp. 70–71).

Foreign Investment

This produced the fastest growth, most notably in the oil industry. Refining began in the 1840s but it was not until the Mining Law of 1895 that the state could lease to a third party the mineral rights on land the owner could not develop himself. 'Steaua Română' was transformed by British and American capital into the first foreign-owned exploration and marketing company with resources for deep drilling in the Câmpina-Buştenari area that doubled production in 1898, with greater success arising from a new discovery at Moreni in 1904. Româno-Americană was formed to provide competition in Western Europe with companies operating in Russia and this in turn brought Royal Dutch Shell into the picture. However until 1900, 80 per cent of Romanian oil came from hand-dug wells that might extend to 250m after three or four years work under hazardous conditions. Oil and lignite supplied boilers and powered the first electric generators supplying Bucharest in 1882, Iaşi and Timişoara in 1884, and Craiova in 1887. Early hydro schemes (21 by 1900 within the present frontiers) included a mixed hydro and thermal project at Sadu (near Sibiu) in 1896 and a relatively large project of 1.0MW at Sinaia in 1898. The very first project was implemented in 1889 near Bucharest: a 360hp station at Grozaveşti's Lake Ciurel, replaced by a thermal plant in 1912. But industrial growth was spatially restricted (Figure 1.1). In the main industrial area that extended from the Danube at Giurgiu to the Hungarian border at Predeal, Bucharest supported a wide range of activities (including engineering, textiles and food processing) while Ploieşti shared with Câmpina the oil refining and oilfield engineering business of the Prahova oilfields. Giurgiu had a ship repairing business and a sugar factory while Comarnic produced cement, with beer and clothing at Azuga and textiles and wood processing at Buşteni. A second cluster in Moldavia was based in the Siret valley from Paşcani to Adjud where the railway ran parallel to the river and raw material flows arrived from the Carpathian tributary valleys to the west, especially the Bistriţa and Trotuş: there was wood processing at Piatra Neamţ (also paper at Letea and textiles at Buhuşi) in the former with coal at Comăneşti and oil production at Moineşti in the latter. A third cluster covered the ports of Brăila and Galaţi with engineering and some processing of the cereals and timber drawn in from extensive hinterlands by rail and water transport. With over 77 per cent of all the country's employment in large-scale industry in these three clusters, the balance fell to scattered nodes like the provincial capitals, with textile industries, and Botoşani where flour milling was associated with an agricultural market close to Austrian Bucovina.

Transylvania

The province lacked the capacity to legislate for its own industrialisation and could only expand as part of the Hungarian periphery with local capitalists processing raw materials while the popular banks, organised on an, provided resources for a number of small enterprises. The more compelling raw materials attracted substantial investment as centres of national importance like the Anina-Reşiţa metallurgical and engineering complex first promoted under a Habsburg mercantilist policy for the Banat region in the eighteenth century (Graf 1997, 2000). Iron production at Hunedoara and coal mining at Petroşani attracted investment a century later. The non-ferrous ores (including gold and silver) of the Apuseni (Abrud-Zlatna), Banat (Oraviţa-Sasca) and Maramureş (Baia Mare-Baia Sprie) were of historic importance but with some late nineteenth century upgrading by outside capital especially in Maramureş, based on Neogene volcanic rocks with hydrothermal vein mineralisation deposits as well as a Mesozoic crystalline unit extending eastwards to the Rodna Mountains. The Ferneziu furnace – opened in 1782 and fed by ore from water-powered crushing installations upstream – was upgraded by a hydropower supply in 1895 (while electricity supply

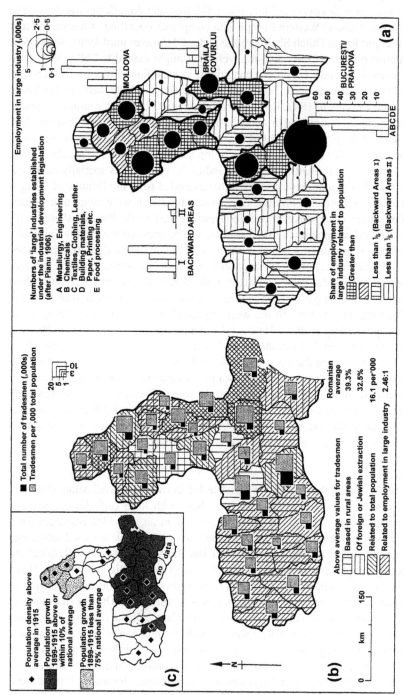

Figure 1.1 Industrial regions 1902

(a)
Employment in large industry (,000s)

Numbers of 'large' industries established under the industrial development legislation (after Pianu 1906)

A Metallurgy, Engineering
B Chemicals
C Textiles, Clothing, Leather
D Building materials,
   Paper, Printing etc.
E Food processing

MOLDOVA
BRĂILA-COVURLUI
BUCUREŞTI/PRAHOVA

BACKWARD AREAS
I   II

Share of employment in large industry related to population

Greater than
Less than 1/6 (Backward Areas I)
Less than 1/10 (Backward Areas II)

(b)
Total number of tradesmen (,000s)
Tradesmen per ,000 total population

Above average values for tradesmen
Romanian average

Based in rural areas   39.3%
Of foreign or Jewish extraction   32.5%
Related to total population   16.1 per'000
Related to employment in large industry   2.46:1

N
0   km   150

(c)
Population density above average in 1915
Population growth 1899-1915 above or within 10% of national average
Population growth 1899-1915 less than 75% national average
no data

in the Baia Mare area became more extensive with two 200hp gas engines in 1908 and two further generators in 1913). Modern Piltz furnaces were installed in 1902, followed by technology to produce sulphuric acid (1907) and a Herreshoff furnace for sulphur recovery (1911). Meanwhile the Pheonix sulphuric acid and chemical factory was built in Baia Mare during 1907-8 by the Weiser family, with a 30 year concession from the Hungarian state to valorise Ferneziu's sulphur dioxide gas, with the chemical fertiliser and copper sulphate production added in 1914. Smelting also spread east to Băiuţ in 1885 and rail transport was being complemented by overhead funicular systems for ore transport by 1918, whereas in Anina-Reşiţa and Hunedoara larger volumes of coal and ore sustained narrow gauge industrial railway systems (and the former developed. hydropower through an elaborate integrated scheme in the Bârzava valley that included scope for floating timber from the forests of Semenic). Railway systems were also used in Carpathian forests, with some diffusion to the Regat as well by 1914.

Tourism and Infrastructure

The development of tourism at Constanţa from the first bathing station of 1890 was indicated by the waterfront casino and the expanding suburb of Mamaia initiated in 1906 on the neck of land between Siutghiol Lake and the Black Sea. Meanwhile Romanian mineral waters were being placed alongside their more famous European counterparts thanks to their physical-chemical properties and therapeutic values. There were a number of Carpathian centres on either side of the frontier, especially in the vicinity of volcanic mountains. Before modern transport was available the reputation of some waters – initially distributed in casks and later bottles – was strong enough to attract invalids prepared to make lengthy journeys by 'diligence' from the nearest railhead. In the case of Borsec in eastern Transylvania, some visitors were prepared to travel from Miercurea Ciuc, Piatra Neamţ or Reghin before the railway arrived at Topliţa (only 20kms away) in 1909. However, most of the spas were relatively easy to get at: Felix near Oradea, named after Felix Helcher who – at the start of the eighteenth century – tried to capitalise on waters (likened to those of Buxton and Evian) that were later acclaimed by exhibitions in Paris (1869) and Budapest (1896). Buziaş – lying conveniently on the Timişoara-Lugoj railway and once regarded as 'Little Versailles' due to its Mediterranean-Continental climate and lush vegetation – offered waters with carbonic acid and carbon dioxide for the treatment cardio-vascular diseases, while nearby Ivanda village boasted waters with a stronger concentration of salt than those of Karlsbad (1899). Reference should be also be made to the appreciation of the healing potential of mud from the Amara/Balta Albă lake which attracted a worldwide clientele to the hotels built in 1872 and 1884. There were also therapeutic treatments for rheumatism and gynaecological problems involving the mineral waters and therapeutic mud of Lacul Sărat (six kilometres from Brăila) where a 40ha park was laid out; with further opportunities close to the Black Sea coast at Mangalia and Techirghiol. Finally, mountain stations were taking off. Such were the scenic and climatic attractions that both invalids and ramblers were happy to make a coach journey of 20kms from Sibiu to Höhe Rinne/Izvoru de Sus (now Păltiniş) at a height 1,452m where a resort established by Siebenbürgische Karpatenverein in 1892 accessed local forests and the Cibin gorges. As the townspeople of the Sibiu region started to copy the German community's love of hiking in the Cindrel Mountains the local resorts gained ground as centres of employment and the local spa Ocna Sibiului attracted its share of patronage from Vienna.

Infrastructure depended initially on the improvement of the Danube's navigation facilities, followed by extension of the continental railway network. On the Lower Danube shipping was frustrated by the Russians because after the Ottomans conceded navigation rights in the Black Sea (1744) they gained a stranglehold over the rivermouth by advancing their frontier across the delta to control all the river channels, a situation sanctioned by the Treaty of Adrianople in 1829 (though it constrained the exploitation of commercial opportunities arising from the end of the Ottoman trade monopoly in the same year). But international jurisdiction over the Danube became a possibility after the Crimean War when a European Commission (representing the Great Powers and Romania) was preferred to a commission of riparian states would have meant Habsburg dominance. It was originally formed in 1856 to clear the river of debris but an initial two-year lifespan was progressively extended and eventually perpetuated for an indefinite period (1883) as a major force for stability in the Balkans – although "the existence of an autonomous agency on Romanian soil was an affront to Romanian nationalism" (Frucht 2000, p. 215). It became clear that major works were needed and that one of the three main channels would have to be selected for improvement. But while the southernmost Sf.Gheorghe channel offered the shortest journey to the Straits, there was little settlement there at the time and provisional work carried out at Sulina (preferred by the shipping industry in general) seems to have been the determining factor. A remarkably successful canalisation of the Sulina estuary (initiated in 1858–61 and consolidated in 1878–81) provided a deeper channel over the coastal bar and set in train a series of projects that progressively straightened the whole river below Tulcea (1868–1902) and reduced its length from 84 to 63kms. While the total investment was probably greater than the cost of improving the Sf. Gheorghe channel (where the meanders were straightened out only during communist period, but with no intention of creating a major ship canal) work was undertaken gradually and could be financed from toll revenue.

Until the Congress of Berlin, Romania's access to the Black Sea rested on the Danube delta alone: this was a relatively well-urbanised area on account of the twin ports of Brăila and Galați (with relatively large food industries) and the smaller ports downstream: Isaccea, Tulcea, Sulina and towns on the Chilia channel: Ismail, Chilia and Cetatea Albă. However in 1878 Russian rule was restored to southern Bessarabia: lost when the victors in the Crimean War sought to remove her shared control over the mouth of the Danube. Romania was now compensated with the Ottoman territory of Dobrogea but was initially unimpressed with this relatively backward province, although a 'portage' railway had been built between Tchernavoda (Cernavodă) on the Danube and the Black Sea port of Kustendje (Constanța) in 1860. However the Romanians made a virtue out of necessity and converted the old harbour into the country's largest port. Rail access from Bucharest was secured by the extension of the existing Constanța-Cernavodă line across the Danube (by means of the Carol I Bridge designed by the Romanian engineer A. Saligny and built during 1890–95) to Feteşti and the continuation of the railway across the heart of the Bărăgan to the Romanian capital, already in contact with the Habsburg Empire at points close to Suceava in (1869), and Braşov and Orşova (1879); also with the Russian Empire at Ungheni (1875) and Reni near Galaţi (1877). Other railways subsequently radiated from Feteşti to Buzău (with a branch from Făurei to Brăila and Galaţi) and Ploieşti. These railways (along with the pipelines which were eventually laid alongside the track) carried the bulk of Romania's export staples: cereals, timber and oil. Constanţa offered a greater depth of water than the 7.3m available (by dredging) to Brăila and the combined land-sea route to the Straits was much more direct than the circuitous Danube waterway (even allowing for the works at Sulina). It is certain that additional interest arose from the desire for a trade route entirely under Romanian control, given the understandable ambivalence felt towards the European Danube Commission over the compromise of national sovereignty. Romanian Dobrogea was then enlarged in 1913 at Bulgaria's expense after a modest intervention in the Balkan War.

Conclusion

With substantial energy and raw materials, plus growing urban demand and stimulative legislation, Romania succeeded in developing significant clusters of industry but they were still complemented by a large force of rural craftsmen working part-time to supply local markets or, as in the case of plum brandy distillers or the producers of kiln-dried fruit, to sustain an itinerant commerce ('comerţ ambulant') serving the towns, especially Bucharest. Despite some urban growth in the county towns and a unified system of administration, education and health across the country there were massive contrasts between the rural areas and the capital city where canalisation of the Dâmboviţa opened the way for settlement on the floodplain and then on the terraces to the south, as at Filaret the terminus of the Giurgiu railway in 1869. Small gardens ('scuaruri') and lines of trees ('bulevardele de platbenzi') in streets and squares were complemented by some larger parks – Cişmigiu (17ha) in 1851–55; the Botanic Gardens (18ha) 1860; and Carol I Park (22ha) in 1906 – all of which was copied on a smaller scale in the main regional centres. Meanwhile rural living conditions remained rudimentary and the pressure of commercial agriculture meant that traditional rural lifestyles based on peasant self-sufficiency were increasingly difficult to sustain. Following the 1907 peasant revolt, radical land reform was widely seen as unavoidable but it was only with the outbreak of the First World War when the king gave a clear promise to the armed forces that this became inevitable.

Chapter Two

Modernisation in Greater Romania 1918–1945: Increasing the Role of the State

In the First World War Romania initially stood aloof with a stark choice between joining the Central Powers in the hope of regaining Bessarabia from Russia (a territory that was an integral part of Moldavia until it was ceded to Russia by the Ottomans in 1812) or joining the Entente in the hope of winning Transylvania; for despite assimilation (and a particularly aggressive Magyarisation policy in this province) Romanians remained emphatically in the majority. It was the latter strategy that was adopted but only belatedly. After joining the Entente in 1916, Romania shared defeat with Russia in the face of superior forces, leading to the German occupation of Bucharest while the Romanian government retired to Iaşi. Major German requisitioning followed, with pressure to cultivate oil and other industrial plants and to preserve food at factories in Bucharest, Piteşti and Craiova. The oil industry fell under German control and the Cernavodă pipeline was relaid to Giurgiu. But the Entente victory on the western front overturned the settlement with the Central Powers (involving major economic concessions as well as territorial adjustments of strategic importance) and the principle of self-determination produced a 'Greater Romania', doubled in size and rounded-off with a continuous strip of lowland along the edge of the Pannonian Plain including a chain of large market towns extending from Timişoara to Arad, Salonta, Oradea, Carei and Satu Mare. But this raised the critical matter of defending the enlarged territory against revisionist states, particularly Hungary: hence the basic foreign policy principles (formulated by one of the country's leading strategists) of avoiding both the domination of SEE by any single power and the vulnerability of isolation by seeking 'inclusion' as a European nation with full responsibilities in return for guarantees of territorial integrity at bilateral, regional and multilateral levels. Therefore good relations were cultivated with the western powers while the 'Little Entente' was established as a local alliance with Czechoslovakia and Yugoslavia: two other states with massive vested interests in the new political map. Meanwhile domestic policy would need to protect the unitary integrity of the state against autonomy or other steps towards fragmentation (Nelson 2004, p. 464). The chapter proceeds with brief review of the political structure and infrastructure followed by more detailed examination of agriculture and industry including the continued imperative of expanding manufacturing in the interests of both security and the relief of rural poverty. At the same time the sheer weight of the rural population called for policies to safeguard the countryside during an inevitably long transition towards a viable commercial farming structure. Although the run-up to the Second World War accelerated progress in some respects through the entente with Germany this would eventually prove disastrous.

Political Structure

The state continued to depend on oligarchic forces representing the urban-industrial interests of the Liberal Party but the old rivalry with the Conservatives was eliminated by the land reform of 1921 that destroyed the estates: under review ever since the revolt of 1907 the wartime experience made massive expropriation for smallholdings politically unavoidable. Instead a new opposition force emerged through a union of the Regat's National Party and Transylvania's Peasant Party in 1928 to create the National Peasant Party (NPP) that first gained power later in that year. But while this new force under I.Maniu sought a truly constitutional régime and protection of peasant interests, the stresses of the depression and Carol II's determination to secure total power effectively sidelined this moderating influence. Hence the clear impression of a divide between the 1920s, dominated by pre-war politicians, and the 1930s when the old parties splintered in the face of growing royalist/militarist influences and the resurgent power of Germany. Fascism came to the forefront, emphasising national over sectional interests but with avoidance of wholesale coercion and expropriation. It has been dismissed as an irrational response to problems of modernisation, attractive only to socially-marginal people and professionals inclined towards an authoritarian right-wing approach. But it retained an oligarchy to run the economy and perpetuated the ethos of a patrimonial state in the form of a royal dictatorship; collapsing through economic inefficiency and political corruption – as well as a grotesque ethnic policy (responsible for some 380,000 deaths among Jews and Roma through the Iaşi pogrom and wartime atrocities in Transnistria) – and ultimately military defeat.

Liberal rule comprised one full parliamentary term (1922–26) with a brief revival in 1927–28. But there is some continuity in economic policy through the first decade which included victories by the People's Party in 1919, 1920 and 1926 (with the latter success helped by a new rule giving half the parliamentary seats – and a proportion of the rest – to a party getting 40 per cent of the votes). Tremendous war damage meant massive reconstruction problems. The oilfields had been recklessly exploited during German occupation and much of the railway system could not operate due to the destruction of bridges and a general lack of maintenance. There was also a need for financial reconstruction complicated by the loss of gold reserves in Russia and the erosion of Reichsbank credits in Germany through inflation. And the integration of the new provinces acquired from Austria (Bucovina), Hungary (Banat, Crişana, Maramureş and Transylvania) and Russia (Bessarabia) posed massive administrative challenges – tackled by posting an army of 'Regateni' civil servants to the new provinces – not to mention the standardisation of the inherited infrastructure and the fiscal burden of Romania's allocation of the Austro-Hungarian debt. It was considered prudent to resist the urge to borrow abroad, although self-sufficiency – under the slogan of 'prin noi înşine' (by ourselves alone) – that delivered growth in agriculture, mining and manufacturing in the 1920s, may have been conditioned by the disaster of 1918 when the transfer of 3,000ha of state lands to the German 'Oel Länderein Pachtgesellschaft' was followed by ruthless felling of forests as well as requisitioning of crops and livestock and organised transfer of industrial plant. But loans would have been difficult to raise in any case because since the reluctance of the Liberals to settle outstanding debts (pending a revaluation of the leu through deflationary measures) complicated access to American and European capital markets. A higher value for the leu was achieved by the Liberals in 1927–28 when relatively good harvests generated substantial surpluses for export (for agriculture's performance was generally poor) but this new level proved difficult to defend. Export taxes helped to finance an industrial programme but the inefficiency of much of the country's manufacturing subjected the peasantry to rising costs while attempts to reduce the level of foreign ownership gave rise to heavy obligations in strong currencies and called for unrealistically high levels of saving.

Régime Change

Concern by the Regency Council (governing on behalf of the young King Mihai who succeeded his grandfather Ferdinand in 1927) that the tenth anniversary of Greater Romania would become an occasion for public discontent led to the installation of a NPP government during 1928–31. The party provided an effective opposition to the Liberals over the issue of foreign capital and negotiated a foreign loan of $100mln in 1928, earmarked largely for agriculture and infrastructure. The party's economic expert V. Madgearu thought protection for industry was justifiable only to provide an initial impetus and substantial tariff reductions in 1929 opened the way for larger imports of farm machinery. The oil industry was a great asset in terms of export potential and in a bid to increase foreign investment in exploration a Mining Law of 1930 gave foreign capital complete equality with domestic interests. However the cost of the loan was too great for farmers to get cheap credit and rural business was weakened by falling timber prices in 1928 (when Russia entered the market) while the collapse of wheat prices in 1929 (responding to New World production) eroded the benefits of the good harvests secured during the following two years, complicated by the onset of world depression. Even oil prices were disappointing while increasing production during 1924–27 could not always keep pace with export opportunities.

Meanwhile other events were threatening the country's stability. Although King Ferdinand decided in 1926 that his son Carol should not succeed to the throne on account of his matrimonial irregularities, the issue was highly contentious and Carol's position was strong enough for him to return from exile and claim the throne in 1930. While some NPP elements welcomed the prospect of a strong king as a unifying force at a time of depression – assuming that he was prepared to act constitutionally – Carol was resolutely opposed by premier I. Maniu. A strong fascist movement was also making its mark in Moldavia, defending Romanian cultural values against the Bolshevik threat and capitalising on the popular frustration that arose when upward mobility was constrained by depression (exacerbated by the substantial economic stake in the region held by the Jewish community). The violent anti-semitism of a new radical party – best known as the Iron Guard – culminated in the assassination of premier I.G. Duca in 1935. But equally significantly, the defeat of the NPP administration in 1931 was followed by a confusing series of government changes (including a brief return by the NPP in 1932–33) that provided the basis for a royal dictatorship firmly established in 1938. Parliamentary institutions were now closed and economic policy returned to Liberal principles with a strong emphasis on industries of strategic importance. Trade with Germany was boosted by a commercial agreement in 1935 that secured increasing amounts of Romanian cereals and oil at preferential rates in return for industrial equipment and munitions. Territorial losses in 1940 following the German-Soviet Pact forced Carol II's abdication in favour of his still-young son Mihai while the reins of government passed to Ion Antonescu: an effective leader who was inevitably drawn into supporting the Axis cause through the Soviet campaign (which regained Bessarabia and northern Bucovina and delivered a large occupied territory further east in Transnistria) until Mihai's coup against him in 1944.

Infrastructure

Oil provided ample energy resources although the abundance of oil residue for electricity generation restricted further development of hydropower: the 30MW installed during 1900–30 was largely accounted for by 16MW at Dobreşti (1928–30) and linked with Bucharest via Doftana. In his plan of 1933 Dorin Pavel demonstrated the potential for 550 new stations but this was not economically attractive until after 1945. There was considerable urban development, particularly in the middle-class suburbs of Bucharest complemented by the growth of commerce and tourism. Transport improved with the modernisation of the railway system complemented by the growth of airlines, road services and waterway links, including consideration of a strategic waterway connection that would have provided a link between the Baltic and Black Seas independent of Germany. This arose out of a powerful growth mentality in Poland after 1926 involving Gdynia port and the railway from Silesia; plus the need to cater for Polish exports to transit Romania and for Romanian exports to reach the Baltics, Germany and Scandinavia. But the technical and financial problems proved daunting at a time when Constanţa port was the primary Romanian concern. Moreover, the railways faced acute problems of standardisation through the inheritance of broad gauge in Bessarabia (converted by 1924) and the great variety of rails (with corresponding weight limits), locomotives and rolling stock. Meanwhile traction on the railways was provided by a new generation of steam locomotives and by railcars that were first produced in 1935 for branch line traffic and later in the decade in an aerodynamic form – modelled on the Hungarian 'Arpad' trains – for prestigious express services on the main lines.

New Railway Routes

Additional construction needed to integrate the new provinces but many schemes involved difficult Carpathian terrain and resources were quite inadequate for rapid progress, especially with new strategic roads as a complementary requirement.

Hence there were many exercises in prioritisation while achievements were relatively limited. Early attention was given to the short gap in the direct line between Arad and Oradea at Chişineu Criş in 1923. This was of great strategic importance in completing a link between the three countries of the Little Entente – from Stamora Moraviţa on the Romanian-Yugoslav frontier to Halmeu on the Romanian-Czechoslovak border. Extensions along the Black Sea coast to Mangalia and Tulcea were also achieved without great difficulty; likewise a number of small projects on the border in Banat and Bucovina and in the Bucharest area. A major disappointment was the failure to connect Braşov with Nehoiaşu across the mountains to the southeast. This would have given Transylvania a direct link with the Black Sea and reduced pressure on the Bucharest-Braşov line with its high summit at Predeal. But despite the construction of the longest tunnel in Romania at Teliu to reach Întorsura Buzăului in 1931 the unstable terrain of the Buzău Subcarpathians prevented further progress. Meanwhile in the Eastern Carpathians the Ilva Mică-Vatra Dornei line of 1938 provided a vital new connection between Transylvania and Moldavia, removing most of the need for elaborate transit arrangements through Poland and Czechoslovakia. A new link from Caransebeş to Reşiţa placed a former Hungarian metallurgical and engineering complex in more direct contact with Bucharest. But priorities had to be reconsidered in 1940 in the light of territorial losses, especially in northern Transylvania. A start was made on a new main line to Iaşi and a branch from Ţandărei reached the Danube to provide a potential springboard for an alternative route to Constanţa (since the existing bridge at Cernavodă was single track only). Doubling of track between Bucharest and Braşov was put in hand (with experimental diesel traction for the steep climb from Braşov to Predeal). And with the old routes through Transylvania compromised by the loss of territory to Hungary, the line to Sibiu was improved by a tunnel that avoided a sharply winding route through the Perşani Mountains. Even so several projects were not finished until the late 1940s like the coal railway through the Jiu defile to link Petroşani with Bucharest.

Agriculture and Rural Development

It is important to explain how the euphoria over land reform in 1921 (Evans 1924) failed to generate a lasting sense of rural contentment. In the first place land hunger was not fully overcome and despite some resettlement in the lowland – and the allocation of cereal lands for some hill communities – pressure on land resources remained heavy in the Subcarpathian districts. But the political situation has also been carefully examined for Romania through Verdery's (1983) study of the Transylvanian commune of Aurel Vlaicu near Orăştie where small farms not only absorbed much of what they produced but were further constrained in their exporting through the barriers arising from the government's lurch towards autarky and import substitution in order to maximise the growth of industry. It was not just a case of the state neglecting agriculture but "actively underdeveloping it" in preference for industrial growth because of "nationalistic designs to diversify the economy using protectionist methods in order to avoid what were considered the detrimental effects of monocrop export dependency" evident before 1914 (Ibid, p. 356). Despite the stimulus of urban markets to generate cash for limited modernisation (such as iron ploughs), peasants failed to consolidate and modernise due to high taxation on basic items of consumption and "their inability to earn enough in an agriculture whose prices the state depressed to support industry" (Ibid, p. 330): as proprietors they could no longer cut corners by 'covering weeds with dirt' as they had done when labouring on Hungarian estates before the war!

The inefficiency of much domestic industry caught the rural consumer in a price scissors between unrewarding prices for farm produce and rising relative costs for manufactures. Indeed, "the cycle of land circulation, low credit and high debt was on its way to proletarianising many peasants when the depression struck" (Ibid, p. 331). There was no government credit during the depression when the Romanian peasantry incurred the largest personal debt among the SEECs, though the moratorium imposed to check bankruptcy meant huge costs for the banks and also for the state which had to retreat from its policy of consolidation to create more viable farms: the popular banks reduced their loans (at a time when Bulgarian cooperative credit associations were increasing their assets by a quarter during 1932–34) but a large destitute population unable to find work in industry would have posed a major political risk and so the peasantry was granted a breathing space. Of course factory work was a great boon where it was available, while the cattle exports to Czechoslovakia were relatively buoyant and so enabled peasants to "utilise every corner of their ecological niche and survive on it" (Ibid, p. 314). Yet disillusionment among the peasants, as land reform was compromised by the rural poverty of the depression years, meant that the philosophy of agrarianism went into decline and the remnants were assimilated by the communist movement after 1945. At the same time, Verdery also sees an element of continuity with the fiscal pressures of the 1930s arising from "a Romanian state in partial collusion with merchants" (Ibid, p. 341) recalling the nineteenth century impositions by the Magyar state (along with its landowners and traders) and even those of the eighteenth century by feudal lords and Habsburg tax collectors. There was simply no viable basis for peasant farming and politicians of all parties (with the NPP differing from the Liberals only in their advocacy of foreign investment) had to generate more jobs in industry while seeking to hold the mass of the peasantry on the land in the interim.

Eugenics

At the same time the bulk of the population was rural and there was a political and strategic interest to maintain the nation's reproductive power (far superior to that of the urban population) through improvements in rural services. Eugenics gave a central role to the health of a nation and its development subject to laws of heredity and evolution (with biology the fundamental academic discipline: hence 'biopolitica' for the total eugenic state). It emphasised preventive health policies with a focus on hygiene and improved medical services, but it might also require a coercive approach (mixed Jewish-Romanian marriages were forbidden in 1940) embedded in a right-wing ideology confronting the liberal politics in the 1920s, though it did draw a positive response through the NPP's Public Health & Welfare Law of 1930: the most comprehensive piece of public health legislation of the inter-war period. I. Moldovan was the intellectual force behind the 1930 law and he made progress in Transylvania with his Hygiene Institute in Cluj and advocacy of mobile dispensaries. He sought central direction using doctors as elite technocrats, but with a decentralised system of implementation since his Gilău station was highlighted by the 1930 law as a model district health centre or 'plasă sanitară'. The model was demonstrated in other parts of the country such as Tomeşti near Iaşi. There were also mobile dispensaries to help mothers with small children through the distribution of health assistance, money, food and clothing. They helped reduce the high rural mortality rates and activity reached a peak in 1927 with 76.7th consultations and 53.4th home visits and almost regained this level after the depression through a network of 75 dispensaries, not all of which were operating at the same time. Hospital services were largely out of reach to the rural population. Using the place of death (home or hospital) as an indicator, Manuila (1932) demonstrated relatively high levels of hospitalisation – with hospital deaths more than a third of those at home – for urban dwellers (Banat, Transylvania and counties based on the large cities in the east: Cernăuţi, Chişinău, Galaţi and Iaşi) compared with little more than one per cent for rural dwellers. Surprisingly in this case Banat, Crişana and Transylvania recorded 0.22th hospital deaths compared with 93.74 at home (0.2 per cent) compared with 2.42 and 175.65 (1.4 per cent) in Bessarabia, Moldavia and Muntenia, though this may indicate a better rural nursing service in the west.

Rural Sociology

Another innovative strand of rural development arose through sociologist D.Gusti's 'Bucharest School' that attracted committed researchers on the basis of generous state support. The nationalist project sought spiritual as well as political and military unification: so the regions might be homogenised through culture. Urban culture was thought to have a foreign origin, hence "the unification strategy viewed the culture of the Romanian village as the only true authentic one, so providing the right model to follow" (Rostas 2000, p. 13). Each district had its own ecological and socio-economic profile and research in the inter-war years (inspired by the idea of settlement continuity and cultural tradition) delivered many studies of 'traditional' agriculture that still continue in the fields of ethnography and museum studies. Most impressive was the sociological programme dealing with sixty representative Romanian villages ('60 sate româneşti'). Economic profiles, intended as a basis for national planning, showed wide variations with some villages specialising in raw materials for textiles while others were concerned with fruit growing and viticulture or else had opportunities in forestry and manufacturing. Concrete actions followed some way behind the academic study but several Carpathian areas were selected for summer 'campaigns' that began at Fundul Moldovei (in Bucovina, near Vatra Dornei) in 1928 and then switched to Drăguş (near Braşov) in 1929 where over 100 people attended (Ibid, p. 8). Later in the 1930s two summers were spent at Şanţ near Rodna. Political overtones were particularly strong under the royal dictatorship (1938–40) when all college and university students had to perform 'voluntary' cultural work under a Social Service Act drafted with Gusti's assistance. There was a strong accent on public health (with an expanded role for doctors) as a preoccupation of some

3,000 'culture hearths' founded in 1939 to operate as local foundations (emphasising decentralisation and self-reliance). The rural movement provided the momentum for the Bucharest Village Museum to develop on the Colentina 'moors' during 1932–37 when the river was dammed to create a series of lakes with their adjacent parklands (notably the 52ha Herăstrău Park, doubled to 106ha in 1951): the project was first conceived during the Colentina floods of 1860, designed by the engineer N.Caranfil and implemented under mayors D.Dobrescu and A.Dobrescu with royal foundation funding. And there was an expansion of mountain tourism, facilitated by further forest road and railway building and the proliferation of chalets and refuges, along with the services of a Tourist Information Office (1937), equivalent to the old Astra organisation of 1872. However most tourist investment went to the seaside with growth at Eforie (Carmen Sylva) and Techirghiol to the south of Constanța, with the emphasis on medical treatment associated with the therapeutic mud already noted for Techirghiol. Mamaia was also expanding with the help of patronage arising from King Ferdinand's summer residence.

Industry

Romania "showed a remarkable will to stand on its own economically assisted by very substantial non-agricultural resources, notably oil and timber" (Radice 1985, p. 64). She was keen to use domestic resources rather then depend on foreign investment (at the expense of low living standards) but didn't coordinate effective plans "perhaps mainly because of the weaknesses of the administrative and fiscal systems" (Ibid, p. 64). However some inflow of capital was needed and it was unfortunate that "efforts to squeeze the money supply again in order to re-establish overvalued exchange rates had just begun to yield British and French loans when the depression struck in 1929" (Lampe & Jackson 1982, p. 589) whereupon the collapse of the gold exchange standard prevented any significant inflow of Western capital. When autarky was revised in favour of foreign investment and some improvements in agriculture, Romania did have the advantage of substantial oil exports that actually rose during the depression years, so industrial decline was quite limited (11 per cent of the 1929 level compared with 52 per cent in Hungary). But due to insufficient exploration oil production peaked in 1936 and compared with rapid industrial growth before 1914 the most optimistic estimate for 1913–30 is just two per cent per annum, rising to three in the 1930s (Jackson 1986, pp. 60–1). Rapid growth seemed to fade, perhaps due to problems in artisan/household manufacturing, and any spurt in the 1920s was largely a recovery from wartime decline. Nevertheless Romania's industrial establishment was large by most SEE standards given the wide range of raw materials, enhanced by the new territories, and the improving infrastructure.

Industrial Distribution

Industrial distribution (by production value) in 1929 shows a high concentration in five regions accounting for 66.9 per cent of the total compared with 11.0 per cent in four small 'outlying' centres with only 22.1 per cent for all the remaining areas (Table 2.1).

Taking individual sectors metallurgy, chemicals and building materials show the highest concentration with 93.5 per cent of the total employment in the main regions, 3.2 per cent in the outliers and only 3.4 per cent elsewhere (although Mehedinţi scored 84mln.lei for metallurgy and Someş 86 for chemicals). By contrast wood processing and food processing were much more widely distributed: for wood processing Câmpulung, Radăuţi and Starojinet in Bucovina together scored 581mln.lei; Argeş, Vâlcea and Muscel 350; and Maramureş and Năsăud 307. For food processing, Olt, Românaţi, Teleorman and Vlaşca attained 819mln.lei, northern Bessarabia 700, northern Moldavia and southern Bucovina 605 and southern Dobrogea 206. Figure 2.1 uses 1935 employment data that slightly weaken the impression of concentration. And polarisation is also brought out by statistics dealing with business as a whole (industrial and commercial firms combined) in the mid-1930s (Scărlătescu 1939). The survey deals with judeţ centres with a total of 803.4th businesses: 201.8 (25.1 per cent) fall to Bucharest followed by 17 centres with 10.0 or more (44.5 per cent): Chişinău 29.6, Timişoara 28.9, Arad 28.4, Cluj and Galaţi each 26.7, Ploieşti 26.2, Cernăuţi 26.1, Craiova 25.3, Brăila 23.3, Constanţa 23.1, Braşov 20.3 and Focşani 18.7, Balcic (12.9), Botoşani (10.9), Sibiu (10.2), Balţi (10.1) and Piteşti (10.0). The other 50 accounted for the remaining 30.4 per cent.

Table 2.1: Production in large-scale industry 1935 (mln lei)

Areas #	A	B	C	D	E	F
REGIONS	7944	11188	5853	1460	10704	10191
Bucharest	1597	8009	1210	424	1210	3178
Centre	1552	1498	2637	459	5436	1816
Moldavia	37	258	1142	22	1142	1209
Ports*	858	236	117	203	117	1449
West	3900	1187	747	352	2799	2539
OUTLIERS	382	246	250	41	250	1677
Baia Mare	255	160	19	12	19	110
Cernăuţi	97	70	147	20	147	1080
Dolj	15	1	41	7	41	326
Lăpuşna	15	15	43	2	43	161
OTHERS	323	367	875	67	552	3373
TOTAL	8649	11801	6978	1568	11506	15241

A Metallurgy; B Chemicals; C Wood Processing; D Building Materials; E Textiles; F Others
For the extent of the regions see Figure 1.2
* Brăila, Constanţa and Galaţi

Source: Scărlătescu 1939

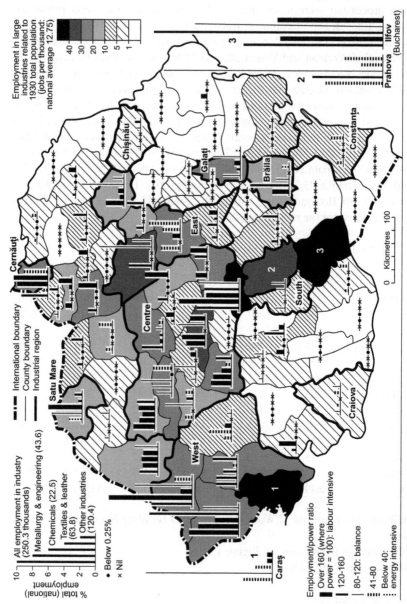

Figure 2.1 Industrial regions 1935

Employment in large industries related to 1930 total population (jobs per thousand: national average 12.75)

40
30
20
10
5
1

International boundary
County boundary
Industrial region

Ilfov (Bucharest)

3

Prahova

2

Chişinău

Cernăuţi

Galaţi

Brăila

East

Constanţa

Centre

Satu Mare

South

2

3

0   Kilometres   100

West

Craiova

1

Caraş

10
8
6
4
2
0

% total (national) employment

All employment in industry (250.3 thousands)
Metallurgy & engineering (43.6)
Chemicals (22.5)
Textiles & leather (63.8)
Other industries (120.4)

● Below 0.25%
× Nil

Employment/power ratio
Over 160 (where power = 100): labour intensive
120–160
80–120: balance
41–80
Below 40: energy intensive

Rural Areas

Rural areas can be brought into the picture through the contrasts in business revealed by the 1940 census; for manufacturing was a significant part of village life, although virtually all the participants played some role in agriculture as well. The distribution is also rather uneven since certain activities dependent on specific skills and raw materials, but wherever there were fruit surpluses brandy was distilled and widely sold on urban markets. Indeed it is possible that urban producers of spirits did some blending to combine rural production with a fine bouquet with neutral spirit distilled on a large scale. 94.4 per cent of Romania's 11,563 villages (a number that reflected the major territorial losses sustained in 1940) had fewer than 25 businesses and in many cases none at all. But there were 652 villages (5.6 per cent) with over 25 businesses (including 60 with more than a hundred) and the per centage was highest in Banat and Crişana with 14.7 per cent (with Arad and Timiş-Torontal most prominent) followed by 9.6 per cent in Transylvania (with the main focus on Alba, Hunedoara and Turda) only 4.0 per cent elsewhere. But everywhere there were some rural centres with significant commercial development to offer potential for a wider urban network. Unfortunately the potential (often reinforced by administrative status at the district or 'plasă' level) was largely dissipated by communist nationalisation and some transfers to regional centres.

Migration Flows

Despite the economic weakness it seems that longwave migration was restrained. The 1930 census found that 3.88mln persons (21.9 per cent) had moved from their birthplace, which would of course include many movements pre-1918 (Manuila 1932). Of this figure 83.5 per cent had moved within their region (55.6 per cent between counties) and only 16.5 per cent (640.2th persons) between the six historic provinces. When each pair of provinces is considered – a total of 15 – the main movements (combining the two directions) were between Muntenia (including Dobrogea) and Transylvania (including Banat, Crişana and Maramureş) with 24.6 per cent, Moldavia-Muntenia (19.8 per cent) and Muntenia-Oltenia (14.9). Intermediate values applied to five other pairs: Bessarabia-Moldavia (9.0), Bessarabia-Muntenia (6.7), Bucovina-Moldavia (6.2), Moldavia-Transylvania (4.7) and Oltenia-Transylvania (4.3) with the other seven transfers amounting cumulatively to just 10.1 per cent. All the regions showed a migration deficit except Muntenia (including Bucharest) with a surplus of +5.5 per cent. Oltenia recorded the greatest per centage deficit of -4.45 per cent although this was also the region with the lowest level of total migration (15.5 per cent). Thus there was a net transfer to Muntenia (largely the Bucharest area) but the total was only some 22,000 and so it would appear that most of the expansion in Bucharest came through natural increase and migration within Muntenia. Much of the expansion in the capital fell to the northern suburbs that extended towards the Colentina valley. The growth of substantial family housing in this area bears testimony to the growth of the middle class during the inter-war period. Meanwhile the migrants to the major provincial towns probably also originated within their respective regions.

World War Two

In the late 1930s Carol II strengthened his defences with a programme for strategic industries, including state support for rearmament through the Socomet cartel after 1936 (including the Concordia munitions plant located between Bucharest and Braşov). In the key mining area of Baia Mare modernisation was extended through electric generators and the partial dieselisation of underground transport; also flotation installations (at Baia Sprie and Băiuţ) to process crushed ore and further modernisation of the Ferneziu gold and lead refinery through new agglomeration plant and furnaces (while the Hungarian takeover later brought an expansion at the Pheonix copper refinery). But in the aftermath of depression the German embrace proved irresistible and Carol's attempts to maintain independence through his style of 'monarcho-fascism' was gravely weakened by events in Czechoslovakia in 1939 because of Československá Zbrojovka's one fifth interest in the Romanian munitions company Uzinele Copşa Mică şi Cugir (UCMC) plus a tenth of the Reşiţa metallurgical and engineering company: hence the German takeover of Czech interests "dealt a death blow to Romanian efforts at maintaining its military forces outside the German orbit" (Lampe & Jackson 1982, p. 518). The Nazi German company Reichswerk Hermann Göring (RHG) was also involved in Romania where "much was promised in the way of investment and little given" (Overy 1983, p. 289). A technical agreement provided for German investment and technical assistance to Malaxa and this set the pattern for Hunedoara and Reşiţa where RHG took over commercial and technical management through combining of the three units as Rogifer. In this way the Romanian metallurgical industry gained a new rolling mill and Siemens-Martin furnaces.

Armaments

The Germans were not keen on developing armaments in Romania although UCMC (controlled in the 1920s by Vickers) produced artillery and small arms while Avrig near Sibiu was concerned with shell filling and transport equipment. But when Romania began to use methane gas as a raw material for the chemical industry, the Germans eventually supported the trend as a useful contribution to the war effort through the advantage of having a source of explosives close to the southeastern front: a strong enough argument to counter resistance to the dispersal of German technology. Production of formaldehyde (needed for synthetic resins and explosives) at Copşa Mică in 1940 was followed by the 'Nitramonia' plant at Făgăraş for ammonia and explosives in 1942. A further plant was started nearby at Ucea de Sus (in a somewhat remoter, forested area to the southwest) but supplies of German equipment were cut off by the coup in Romania in 1944 and the works was then built to serve peacetime needs and opened in the 1950s with the name 'Victoria'. More widespread use of gas was envisaged through a pipeline to Braşov and Bucharest which, again, was not achieved until after the war. Meanwhile Industria Aeronautică Română at Braşov was controlled by an RHG subsidiary and retooled to produce Messerschmidt fighters in 1943.

The Oilfields

Great German interest was shown in the Romanian oilfields, where the most substantial defences were erected to protect 'Fortress Ploieşti' and its constellation of oil refineries from enemy bombers operating out of North Africa (Freeman n.d.). Following the economic agreement of 1939, Germany sought a modification to the 1937 Mining Law, which was eventually secured in 1942 to allow foreign exploration/ exploitation of entire structures; although there was still effective state control (including pipelines) insisting that all crude should be refined within the country. Indeed, by placing the wartime management of refining, transport and export in state hands – and leaving foreign interests little leeway for peacetime investment or expansion – West European and American oil companies were brought directly under Romanian government management. But the virtual nationalisation of Romanian oil operations from 1942 made it easy for the Soviets to create 'Sovrompetrol' in May 1945 controlling 36 per cent of oil output in 1947 (exporting two-thirds to the FSU). There was also some cooperation in farming because by the end of 1940 the Antonescu government agreed to broaden the 1939 agreement with Germany so that all Romanian agricultural exports would be geared to the German market, with a Ten Year Plan delivering set amounts at fixed prices. By 1942 the Ministry of Agriculture began to organise associations of peasants for joint production (without infringing private ownership rights) but success was compromised by the need to substitute eastern territories for what had been lost in Transylvania. Meanwhile German technical aid to Romanian agriculture was heading eastwards through officially-sponsored German-Romanian corporations pioneered by IG Farben in 1934 e.g. the Soya Corporation which trained farmers and guaranteed purchase at fixed prices. A purely German 'Südostropa' organisation promoted flax cultivation at fixed prices. However operations in Bessarabia suffered from the fact that it was not possible to replace the marketing network of small Jewish traders after it had been abruptly abolished.

Conclusion

Given the strength of feeling in favour of nation states it is hardly possible to see the inter-war arrangements as anything other than legitimate and progressive. As Verdery (1983, p. 349) points out, there was a yearning for inclusion through "autarkic efforts to become the economic equal of the world's more privileged nations". Where there had previously been the oppression of Magyarisation there was now a sense of national interest in economic growth even though it placed the farming population at a disadvantage. State security required rapid industrial growth for strategic and social reasons and this could not be generated by demand from a prosperous middle peasantry. Instead the farming population had to submit to a heavy tax burden to avoid heavy dependence on foreign capital that would distort the industrial structure. But in a democratic system only the ethnic minorities with minimal vested interests in the Romanian state would have sensed any discrimination or oppression. There was clearly much more government involvement and a growing consensus that this was the way forward, to the point where post-1945 central planning was in many respects anticipated with all its ideological dilemmas over democratic ideals and totalitarian systems. For despite the liberal-mindedness of the bourgeoisie the necessity to modernise under pressure made for strong central government under monopoly parties; raising the issue whether democratic government can work in developing societies. S. Zeletin defended the Liberals in his work on 'Burghezia română': democracy would have to take a back seat to a capitalist oligarchy: recalling C. Dobrogeanu-Gherea's earlier thesis in 'Neiobăgie' and validating the events of the 1930s. But as the social democrat S. Voinea pointed out "the Romanian bourgeois elite was too corrupt, too soft, too preoccupied with state favours and too dependent on tariffs to move Romania's economy forward quickly enough" (Chirot 1978, p. 51) while Gallagher (2005, p. 32) dismisses Carol II for acting as a Phanariot: a "disastrous role-model for a country needing inspiring leadership". Moreover, any effective strategy would require the political and economic support of a great power. Equally however a social-democratic approach would have to deliver higher wages; thereby threatening growth through rising consumption.

Chapter Three

The Communist Era of State Monopoly: Central Planning with a Descent to Sultanism

Introduction

Although Mihai's coup against Marshall Antonescu meant a break with the Axis and rapid clearance of the country of German troops (avoiding the horror of war on a front that would have advanced inexorably across Romanian territory) it accelerated the onset of Soviet domination which was hardly moderated in its severity by subsequent commitment to the allied cause for the remainder of the war. Despite the insensitivity of the Churchill-Stalin 'percentages agreement' – accepting, in advance of a peace treaty, renewed Soviet control of Bessarabia and northern Bucovina as well as an overwhelming interest over the whole of Romania at the end of the Second World War – it was probably inevitable that Romania would be consigned to an enlarged Soviet sphere of influence in the heart of Europe. The surprise arose through Stalin's decision – whether premeditated or pragmatic – to separate the Soviet sphere by the so-called 'Iron Curtain' and impose the whole edifice of Soviet autarky (elaborated in the 1930s for 'socialism in one country') on the entire tier of satellite states. So in defiance of understandings that revolution would not be precipitated Soviet mastery over Romania gave Moscow the opportunity of advancing the fortunes of an initially-insignificant communist party that was eventually brought to power through a rigged election in 1948 that was followed rapidly by Mihai's abdication. Although there was a precedent for state control of the economy – through nationalisation, the launch of the first Five Year Plan and the collectivisation of agriculture – nothing could have prepared the Romanian people for the highly oppressive dictatorship imposed by Stalin behind a facade of native leadership under Gh.Gheorghiu-Dej as civil society was systematically destroyed and replaced by a totalitarian system relying on expropriation, forced labour and terror in the context of a coordinated bloc subject initially to Stalin's personal interventions and increasingly, after his death, through the complementary institutions of Comecon and the Warsaw Pact. This chapter looks at the salient features of the state system that saw the Romanian government maximising its scope for autonomy but always with a preference for independent economic initiatives rather than social and political reform. This was probably well-judged in the 1960s and 1970s but it became apparent by the 1980s that the leadership was exploiting Moscow's coercive umbrella of communist totalitarianism to run the country as a uniquely idiosyncratic family business. The Soviet reforms of the Gorbachev era were highly unwelcome and the country was becoming increasingly isolated when both the Securitate and the armed forces refused to support the régime in the face of public defiance in December 1989.

The Roots of an Independent Policy

Leverage initially won through stability during the Hungarian uprising of 1956 was immediately invested in foreign and trade policy rather than domestic reform. Romania's independent line was clearly evident in the 1960s when Khrushchev sought a socialist economic commonwealth to rival the EEC, with a specific proposal in 1962 that Comecon should organise international specialisation, with supranational economic complexes as a possibility. With the US offering support from 1963 for communist states asserting their independence – and with further room for manoeuvre through Romania's attempts to mediate in the Sino-Soviet dispute – planning chief G.Gaston-Marin articulated Romania's quest for an independent economic policy. It was backed up by Gheorghiu-Dej's denunciation in 1964 of a supranational Comecon (threatening the country's quest for broad-based industrial development) and any attempted Soviet coup. Romania thus became the first bloc country to establish independent trading links with Western Europe – seeking technology in return for raw materials and low-cost manufactures under the planning of A. Bîrladeanu who was responsible for economic matters during 1960–65. Thus France and the UK agreed to deliver equipment for the Galaţi steelmill after the Soviets refused. But not all Romania's ambitions were satisfied. After purchasing a Soviet synthetic rubber plant (opened at the chemical complex in the new town of Gh.Gheorghiu-Dej – now Oneşti – in 1963) there was a desire to export highly resilient rubber using Firestone's technology for both the polyisoprene and polybutadiene types. 30,000t/yr of capacity was sought for each type as part of a shopping list involving 15 manufacturing plants of American provenance. The deal was agreed unofficially but foundered at the time of US bombing in North Vietnam that brought jibes from Firestone's competitors about 'selling the US down the Red River' (Floyd, 2005).

The Nicolae Ceauşescu Era

Romania persisted with her policy; resisting the strengthening of Warsaw Pact in 1966 and declining to scale down its links with Israel after the Six Day War, when other Warsaw Pact members put their relations on hold. Of course no excessive provocation of Moscow would ever have been countenanced and there was only limited relaxation at home despite the release of some 10,000 political prisoners in 1964. Indeed the Soviets may well have received disclosures by Romanian intelligence officers who posed as commercial specialists in their embassies in the west. However Romania certainly gained from invitations to join institutions generally closed to the Soviet bloc: the World Bank and IMF (1972); followed by preferential trading status with the EEC (1973); and MFN trading status in the USA (1975) at a time when Ceauşescu frequently made state visits to western countries. This young leader replaced Gheorghiu-Dej in 1965 and – behind a facade of anti-

Soviet dissidence – maintained rapid growth with enhanced authority for the party through a nationalist-socialist agenda combining Stalinism with perverse illiberal elements from country's Ottoman-Byzantine past.

Legitimacy was secured during the 'golden years' of the late 1960s with genuine solidarity during 1968–69 at a time of potential Soviet invasion in response to Romania's defiant stand over the Warsaw Pact invasion of Czechoslovakia. Ceaușescu saw Romania as 'independent within the Warsaw Pact': a developing socialist state linked with Africa and Asia and a bridge between East and West built out of opportunism during the Sino-Soviet dispute. But any hint of enlightenment ended with his 1971 visits to China and North Korea that exposed him to the Mao/Kim Il Sung model of cultural control: "a brand of communism that suited his character" (Gallagher 2005, p. 60). He then attacked western-style liberalism and pluralism as alien to Romanian indigenous traditions and backed the party's 'protochronists' extolling a 'pure' life divorced from materialism and not entirely at odds with the calls of the Orthodox Church for fortitude in the face of economic stress. By the 11th RCP Congress in 1974 Ceaușescu had completed the transition from being the spokesmen for a collective leadership (as he was in the late 1960s) to become not only a leader in his own right but an omnipotent ruler sustained by leadership cult in favour of 'Romania's most beloved son' surpassing even that of Stalin in its intensity (Fischer 1989, p. 160). Nevertheless he continued to find a welcome in the west and IMF agreements in 1975 (for $95mln) and 1977 ($64mln) were successfully finalised in 1976 and 1978 respectively. But by the 1980s Ceaușescu was exposed on the international front as a dangerous maverick by his boasts over nuclear armaments. Yet this was a minor matter by comparison with his domestic policies based on the corruption and nepotism associated with 'socialism in one family'. High growth rates were eventually undermined by gross inefficiencies that prevented any real prosperity for those outside the ranks of the 'nomenklatura'.

Policy Aberrations of the 1980s: the Climax of Sultanism
Economic policies became more irrational through the 'gigantism' of excessive capacities in oil refining, petrochemistry and steel production based on raw material imports (particularly costly in the case of crude oil after the world price rises of the 1970s) that were not recouped through the value of exports. Instead of allowing greater flexibility and liberalisation, central planning was strengthened in the last decade of communism with a continuing focus on plan fulfilment rather than profitability and more rigid plan-targets and subsidies for failing industries that saw "lagging and overly depreciated parts dragging down marginally productive ones" (Bacon 2004, p. 374). Although the large industrial 'centrals' gained some autonomy this power was used to extend the scale of their activity rather than to boost efficiency and profitability. The outstanding aberration in the 1980s was the obsessive prioritisation of paying off all foreign debts – achieved just months before the revolution. The issue arose out of the illusion of economic success during the 1970s that lasted "only as long as the West was willing to finance it through technology imported on credit" (Ibid). In late 1981 Romania needed IMF credit to meet debt obligations that in turn called for reduced trade and current account deficits – hence the régime's "centralised program of austerity which kept intact its nationalist priorities under the guise of 'reform'

in the new economic and financial mechanism" (Ibid). Romania's foreign debt of $10bln in 1981 (up to 30 per cent of GDP) was paid off by early 1989 thanks to a major reduction in imports while maximising exports to secure a $920mln surplus with EEC over 1980–82 alone; while gold and foreign exchange reserves were run down. Furthermore, investment in technical modernisation and renewal was curtailed: a grossly counterproductive strategy since western equipment could no longer be maintained and the country's competitiveness declined accordingly. There were deep economic imbalances "highlighted by the chronic shortages of energy and consumer goods, the utter neglect of public services and the paralysis of creative initiatives throughout Romanian society" (Isărescu 1992, p. 157). Energy savings, a decaying infrastructure – and more oppressive security – ruined the Black Sea tourist industry. The third IMF agreement of 1981 was cancelled in 1984 after $817mln had been disbursed.

Falling living standards were underlined by prices rising faster than wages and popular support was eroded. Yet Ceaușescu claimed that "my personal hobby is the building of socialism in Romania" (Tismaneanu 1990, p. 1) and the rhetoric of national communism was lined up with his obsessive treatment of the whole country as one great construction site. Prestige developments like the Danube-Black Sea Canal and the Bucharest 'people's palace' (that consumed a tenth of GDP at its peak) required contributions from all parts of the country in terms of lorry drivers and skilled craftsmen respectively; while rural 'sistematizare' concerned every village in the country (through the threat of total elimination in many cases). The population was also battered by coercive demographic policies. With rare exceptions abortion became illegal in 1966 and by forcing operations underground it is estimated that 11,000 women died over the following 23 years; not to mention the incalculable human costs elsewhere and the social injustice arising from the restrictions imposed and the checks introduced in the 1980s through gynaecological examinations in the workplace (Kligman 1992; 1998). Meanwhile AIDS became a major scourge through reuse of hypodermic needles for intravenous feeding and blood transfusions for malnourished orphans. Restrictions on the Orthodox Church in expanding urban working class areas deprived many people of spiritual leadership (a void that was filled to some extent by Protestant churches including Baptists and Jehovah's Witnesses). Policy towards the Hungarian minority veered strongly towards assimilation with reduced publishing in Hungarian, termination of virtually all radio and TV programmes in Hungarian by the mid-1980s, removal of bilingual placename signs and closure of some Hungarian education institutions. And while 'sistematizare' posed a threat to the entire population, one consequence was clearly perceived to be "the destruction of historic majority Hungarian villages and the forcible resettlement of their populations" (Chen 2003, p. 192). That the 'mămăligă' (maize pudding: a traditional food) did not 'explode' says much for the survival mentality adopted by the mass of the population and by the lower echelons of the party hierarchy who showed flexibility wherever they had the confidence to do so (Sampson, 1981). Some highly unorthodox networks were able to flourish in out of the way places – like Jina near Sibiu with its lucrative wool trade – but they were very much the exception (Stewart 1997).

Industry

Basic Characteristics

Under communism industry and construction advanced from 14.2 per cent of employment in 1950 to 25.5 per cent in 1965 and 43.8 per cent in 1980, by which time the growth rate was slowing down, while the share for services increased more slowly from 11.5 to 17.8 and 26.4 per cent and agriculture and forestry declined from 74.3 to 56.7 and 29.8. Industry's progress was underpinned by its high share of investment, averaging 50.0 per cent over the period while agriculture and sylviculture received only 15.4 per cent (Table 3.1). The economic turnaround was complemented by a revolution in settlement patterns as the urban population (including suburban communes) advanced from 23.4 per cent of the population in 1948 to 38.4 per cent in 1966 and 50.3 in 1984. The big push for heavy industry was evident through the expansion of existing units in the metallurgical, engineering and chemical industries fuelled by a greater domestic mineral output but more especially by huge deliveries of ore and coking coal from the USSR and to a lesser extent from other communist states in the region (while Romanian oil was initially sent to the USSR as war reparations). However as part of Romania's independent stand in later years mineral imports (including crude oil when the chemical industry outstripped domestic supplies) were drawn from a wide range of sources around the world and the geography of manufacturing became influenced much more by the ports: for example the metallurgical complexes at Galaţi and Călăraşi, the alumina plant at Tulcea, the shipyards at Constanţa and Mangalia, the oil refining and petrochemical complex at Năvodari and the fertiliser factory of Turnu Măgurele. The much improved infrastructure comprising main line railways, the 440Kv electricity grid and oil and gas pipelines enabled heavy industry – particularly engineering and chemicals – to reach most of the larger towns where brand new installations developed on greenfield sites (Figure 3.1). But in the early years most of the emphasis rested with existing complexes that built on existing expertise and capacity that switched from an Axis to a Soviet orientation and were gradually enlarged with new plant plus improvements in local electricity supply, rail transport, technical training and housing. Space does not allow a comprehensive review of all industries but before dealing with location policy and regional development in general some comments are offered on the growing preference for large units and the transport technology used in the exploitation of minerals and forests.

While acknowledging a substantial structural change in favour of more sophisticated branches, a critique of communist industrialisation would stress the very large size of many units. In 1975 82 per cent of industrial production and labour involved enterprises employing at least 1,000 and in 1989 the 1,075 such enterprises (51 per cent of the total number of industrial enterprises) accounted for 85 per cent of the output and 87 per cent of the workforce. Meanwhile those with over 3,000 employees were responsible for half the output and 53 per cent of the workforce whereas SMEs (with fewer than 500 employees) accounted for only six per cent of the output and four per cent of the workforce. Having no regard for the flexibility inherent in SMEs, 'gigantomania' was valued for propaganda purposes and also to

Table 3.1: Investment in the national economy 1950–89 by sectors

Sector#	1951–60 A	1951–60 B	1961–70 A	1961–70 B	1971–80 A	1971–80 B	1981–89 A	1981–89 B
Industry	6.66	53.8	18.56	46.5	55.45	50.5	112.39	49.0
Heavy Industry	5.79	46.8	16.56	41.4	46.27	42.1	98.36	49.0
Light Industry	0.87	7.0	2.00	5.0	9.18	8.4	14.02	6.1
Agriculture	1.40	11.3	7.74	19.4	15.84	14.4	37.93	16.5
Transport	1.57	12.7	4.50	11.3	15.03	13.7	31.12	13.6
Construction	1.89	15.3	7.13	17.9	18.48	16.8	41.76	18.2
Education	0.53	4.3	1.17	2.9	2.79	2.5	2.61	1.1
Health	0.22	1.8	0.47	1.2	1.03	0.9	1.13	0.5
Administration	0.11	0.9	0.37	0.9	1.18	1.1	2.29	1.0
Total	12.38	100.0	39.94	100.0	109.80	100.0	229.23	100.0

A Total investment per annum (bln.lei); B Percentage share
Agriculture includes Sylviculture; Transport includes Telecommunications and Distribution; Construction includes Housing and Local Services; Education includes Culture and Science; Administration includes Others

Source: Statistical Yearbooks (i.e. 'Anuarul Statistic' published annually by the National Commission for Statistics, Bucharest)

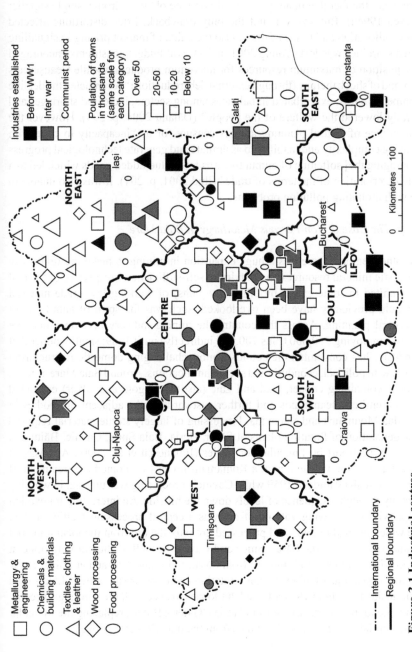

Figure 3.1 Industrial centres

Metallurgy & engineering

Chemicals & building materials

Textiles, clothing & leather

Wood processing

Food processing

Industries established

Before WW1

Inter war

Communist period

Poulation of towns in thousands (same scale for each category)

Over 50

20-50

10-20

Below 10

International boundary

Regional boundary

NORTH WEST

CENTRE

NORTH EAST

WEST

SOUTH WEST

SOUTH

ILFOV

SOUTH EAST

Cluj-Napoca

Timişoara

Craiova

Bucharest

Iaşi

Galaţi

Constanţa

Kilometres

0   100

maximise the influence of politically effective managers, given the ideology of state control and continued 'revolutionary' activity. However there were inefficiencies arising from the fact that many goods could only be obtained from a single supplier (Popescu 1994a). But size was not the only drawback. Price distortions affected resource allocation and terms of trade; also the value of market pricing in signalling relative scarcities was lost (Young 2001, p. 71). Soft budget constraints encouraged the acquisition of maximum resources for maximum production while Ceauşescu's own brand of shock therapy (through external debt reduction) "accentuated the decline in competitiveness, exacerbated imbalances among sectors, increased shortages and generally lowered the welfare of the people" (Dăianu 2004, p. 393). However the whole edifice of central planning attracts censure for its "incapacity to cope with increasing complexity and inability to assimilate and generate technological progress [encouraging the] softening of output towards low value-added goods which led to a steady deterioration of the terms of trade" (Ibid 2001, p. 204). It was also unable to cope with mounting pollution problems.

Mining: The Case of Non-Ferrous Metallurgy in Baia Mare

As in other regions, there was a huge expansion in mining to make the fullest use of domestic mineral resources and maximise self-sufficiency irrespective of the real costs (limited to some extent by efficiency gains) of working low grade material that would previously have been overlooked: such was the spirit of autarky built into central planning. Across the country the mining industry became a massive business employing 350,000 (plus 700,000 indirectly) until 1989: small wonder that the industry has constituted the country's most challenging domestic restructuring problem with political, economic and social ramifications. Around Baia Mare, mining the rocks containing copper, lead and zinc (also some gold and silver) expanded along the entire volcanic axis and further eastwards to the adjacent ore bodies in the Rodna Mountains and Bucovina. Processing of largely sterile material required a new generation of flotation plants at Săsar, Herja, Baia Sprie, Cavnic, Băiuţ and Borşa with transport by funiculars or lorries (Bălănescu et al. 2000). At Săsar, at the west end of the volcanic belt, a Romanian-Soviet j.v. adopted the treatment of concentrate with cyanide in 1959 while Cavnic's processing was unusual in working by gravity through a sequence of levels down the hillside. An interesting innovation to cope with the growing volume of ore was a central processing facility at Baia Sprie which opened in 1963 and processed not only the ore from the local mine but also material from Herja, Săsar, Şuior and Cavnic as well as the outlying mine at Turţ. Lorries were used to bring ore from Săsar, Şuior and Turţ and at Şuior, a new mine that opened just before the new flotation came on stream, a new 4.5km road system inside the adit in 1979 allowed 20t lorries to access all the workings directly. Meanwhile tunnels were driven from Herja ('Galeria Bulat', replacing the funicular that was initially installed) and Cavnic (from the new Boldut working).

Smelting and Electrification
Baia Mare remained the smelting centre and the nationalised plant of Ferneziu, with its established funicular link with Herja mine, was modernised with the standard

technology for the agglomerating plant, furnaces, refineries and foundries that are still working today; while copper smelting closed in 1976 in favour of the separate Pheonix plant where a new electrolytic copper refining hall opened in 1957. The power problem was solved in 1963 with the arrival of the 110Kv grid link with Cluj but until then local supplies were essential. A new thermal station opened in 1952 provided a unified system for the area, operating at 6.0 and 22Kw (but 35Kw in 1959) while 4.0MW of hydropower capacity was generated with the impounding of Strâmtori Lake in the Firiza valley in 1965 (needed primarily to improve the water supply and provide a recreational base). Finally, the scale of the business was such as to require specialised construction, repair and education facilities; while the labour crisis was initially overcome by drafting in peasants (assisted with housing until commuting by bus and train was better organised) while the use of political prisoners at Baia Sprie, Cavnic and Nistru during 1950-4 provoked an early strike through poor safety precautions. Across the country the mining industry became a massive business employing 350,000 (plus 700,000 indirectly) until 1989. But today it is sad to see the scale of the restructuring needed to bring the industry into line with the global economy.

The Timber Industry

The timber industry illustrates another remarkable aspect of Romania's own route to industrialisation. The industry desperately sought new stands of virgin woodland after the heavy felling of the war years and the additional burden of war reparations (linked with the Romanian-Soviet j.v. Sovromlemn). This opening up many of the hitherto-inaccessible areas of the Carpathians could not be done through a road system because there was no vehicle industry to produce the lorries and no fuel because oil was earmarked for reparations. The solution was an unprecedented expansion of narrow gauge forest railways during the 1950s, despite challenging conditions in areas of unstable terrain. Some 4,000 new wagons were built by the Toplet factory near Orşova, while a new fleet of standard 0-8-0T wood- and lignite-burning locomotives was built for the now-unified railway system 'Căile Ferate Forestiere' (CFF) by the Reşita engineering works while the inherited fleet of locomotives – originating mainly in Austria, Germany and Hungary – was gradually replaced, though a small number survived: although less powerful they were sometimes easier to handle on light, poorly-maintained track, as at Berzasca that received no standard locomotive until 1987. Indeed, until central repair shops were provided at Reghin in 1953, each forest railway system maintained its own workshops and much equipment was built on the basis of local possibilities e.g. trolleys for gravity working and simple railcars produced by converting cars or lorries. The total extent of the CFF was some 6,000kms in 1960 by which time virtually all plans had been achieved. But contraction then followed rapidly given a preference for forest roads, facilitated by the development of motor transport and the introduction of new network of processing units at central locations involving the production of furniture, chipboard/hardboard, plywood and veneer.

Regional Autarky

There was now more balanced forest exploitation through greater use of beechwood compared with the selective felling of fir and spruce: the proportion of beechwood in the total timber harvest rose to 15.6 per cent in 1955 and 26.3 in 1966 with the expansion of furniture and board production. This completed the transition from the small private sawmills nationalised in 1948, of which only a few were retained under the management of cooperatives or the state logging and transport company (usually in remote areas to meet a specific market, such as packing fruit). In the Eastern Carpathians this change had particular significance because Galați region (and subsequently Vrancea county) planned for the processing of its raw material within its own borders and therefore a comprehensive forest road programme was implemented to eliminate the funicular systems that crossed the main Carpathian watershed to join forest railways on the Transylvanian side and reverse the flow of timber to a new manufacturing complex in Focșani. Forest railways in the Milcov, Râmna and Râmnicu Sărat valleys were already supplying local processors, such as Gugești but the wood industry's planning institute argued for the superior efficiency of a unitary road system, extended from 98 to 533kms with secondary functions for mining and tourism. This plan was adopted in 1962. Elsewhere however road replacements were stopped by the oil price rises of the early 1970s and some 20 surviving rail systems were then retained as a fuel conservation measure until 1989. Now only two (Moldovița and Vișeu de Sus) are retained on environmental and economic grounds.

Location Policy

Concentration in the 1950s (backed by allocations of capital to a small number of regions) was accentuated by the nationalisation and consolidation of formerly scattered rural industries. This was followed by more constrained agglomeration after the counties were restored in 1968, leading to much labour-intensive manufacturing in the more backward counties. It has therefore been suggested that Ceaușescu was more sensitive over regional issues than Gheorghiu-Dej, although it seems more likely that by the 1960s it was necessary to limit migration and tap the remaining natural and human resources at source. Decentralisation was not allowed to undermine efficiency (beyond the weaknesses inherent in the system) because Ceaușescu remained keen for Romania to be a major regional producer of heavy industrial goods (Tsantis & Pepper 1979). Thus Slatina in the backward Olt county was in no way irrational as the location for a new aluminium industry since the town lay close to the country's largest cluster of power stations and was roughly equidistant between the alumina suppliers in Oradea and Tulcea (using domestic and imported bauxite respectively). Young (2001, p. 251) has also rationalised Romania's polarised regional growth through agglomerations (in Bucharest and the county centres) using the Perroux growth pole theory, Myrdal's cumulative causation theory (with polarisation and 'backwash' stronger than 'trickle down' and 'spread') and Marshall's theory of agglomeration economies. By contrast there was no sign of the regional economic convergence underpinned by the neo-classical equilibrium model with diffused growth unconstrained by development centres. However in

1977 the concentration of industrial employment in county centres was much greater in the old Regat – with 965,000 in the county centres and 296,000 in other towns – compared with Transylvania and the western and northwestern areas with 503,000 in county centres and 400,000 in other towns.

Gradual Convergence at the County Level
Development targets were spelt out in the broad terms of a commitment to greater equality until the 1981–85 FYP sought an annual industrial production value of at least 10bln.lei in each county. In 1985, 38 counties achieved this target while Călăraşi, Giurgiu and Mehedinţi failed with the poorest performer (Giurgiu) scoring only 4.8 per cent of the industrial production of the capital city (a county in its own right) and 9.4 per cent of the level of the second largest producer (Prahova at that time). In 1970 only nine counties had passed the threshold but the weakest county then (Sălaj) had shares of only 1.4 and 3.7 per cent respectively of the top two counties. Thus over 15 years there was a general upward trend in the value of production with a modest degree of 'catching up' by the weakest counties. This notion of gradual progress (in both senses) is confirmed by the 1975 situation, when there were 21 counties over the threshold and the weakest county (Bistriţa-Năsăud) scored just 1.7 per cent of the Bucharest output and 4.7 per cent of the next highest producer (Braşov); while in 1980 with 31 counties over the threshold and the weakest county (now Giurgiu) reached 3.0 per cent of Bucharest's level and 6.9 per cent of Braşov's. Economists highlighted the convergence by ranking the counties in terms of socio-economic status and identifying five clusters in addition to Bucharest (Dobrescu & Blaga 1973). However the statistics show only a partial convergence since Group Five's share of the total investment in the 1980s was only 70 per cent of the population share while Bucharest attracted investment 1.6 times its population; although the picture was one of near equality for the other groups (Table 3.2). When salaried employment is considered major differences emerge in 1989 with 486 jobs per thousand of the population in Bucharest and progressively lower figures through the groups to 255 for Group 5 implying much greater reliance on cooperative farm work (Table 3.3). However, although industry did not maintain its share in Bucharest and Groups 2-4 during the economic growth in the 1960s (pointing to over-concentration in some of the regions at that time) the growth in industry's share during 1960-89 is 26.2 percentage points in Group 5, 16.5 in Group 4, 11.2 in Group 3 and 8.7 in Group 2 while Group 1 shows a slight decline which may reflect the decrease in commuting across county boundaries. This would apply even more in Bucharest with the creation of the predominantly rural Ilfov Agricultural Sector in 1980.

Sector Distributions   The move towards greater equality can also be seen though the wider distribution of industry according to the strength of different sectors across the county groups. Average deviations from the mean declined during 1965–89 especially in light industry with food processing registering just 1.6 percentage points in 1989 compared with 4.3 in 1965); clothing (with comparable figures of 2.9 and 7.8) and textiles (5.0 and 13.9). But the trend was also evident for building materials (2.7 and 8.2), chemicals (4.7 and 11.5), engineering (6.3 and 12.3) and ferrous metallurgy (7.5 and 16.5); while fuels (12.0 and 14.2) and

Table 3.2: Investment 1950–89 by county groups. *first line*: percentage of the national total for each sector; *second line*: same values related to the group's population share

Group	Period	A	B	C	D	E	F	G	H	I	J	K
Bucharest	1950s	15.7	7.3	n.a.	n.a.	3.5	35.9	29.1	58.7	32.9	55.6	34.1
		2.1	1.0	n.a.	n.a.	0.5	4.8	3.9	7.8	4.4	7.1	4.5
	1960s	16.3	10.1	10.2	11.5	3.4	24.0	36.2	36.2	17.4	67.9	31.5
		2.1	1.3	1.3	1.4	0.4	4.4	4.6	4.6	2.3	8.7	4.1
	1970s	14.1	8.4	7.9	11.8	2.5	28.3	27.3	34.0	18.5	59.2	25.7
		1.6	0.9	0.9	1.3	0.3	3.1	3.0	3.7	2.0	6.5	2.8
	1980s	16.3	7.7	7.4	9.9	5.9	31.8	18.9	61.2	27.1	83.2	31.2
		1.6	0.8	0.7	1.0	0.5	3.2	1.9	6.1	2.5	8.3	3.1
Gp.One	1950s	27.3	25.3	n.a.	n.a.	11.9	17.9	17.5	10.5	16.8	10.2	21.6
		1.8	1.7	n.a.	n.a.	0.8	1.2	1.2	0.7	1.1	0.7	1.4
	1960s	18.3	22.2	20.8	15.5	12.8	15.1	13.0	14.4	12.3	7.1	18.0
		1.2	1.5	1.3	1.0	0.8	1.0	0.9	0.9	0.8	0.4	1.2
	1970s	17.0	20.2	21.1	14.6	13.2	13.6	11.8	14.9	13.9	4.5	14.7
		1.1	1.3	1.3	0.9	0.8	0.9	0.7	0.9	0.9	0.3	0.9
	1980s	15.5	20.2	21.2	12.6	14.0	10.4	8.5	8.9	12.5	5.8	13.7
		0.9	1.2	1.3	0.8	0.9	0.6	0.5	0.5	0.8	0.4	0.8
Gp.Two	1950s	24.8	25.3	n.a.	n.a.	27.7	22.7	27.8	11.0	23.4	13.7	21.5
		1.2	1.2	n.a.	n.a.	1.3	1.1	1.3	0.5	1.1	0.7	1.0
	1960s	26.6	29.0	29.9	25.8	27.1	22.4	23.0	16.7	35.6	9.5	22.4
		1.2	1.4	1.4	1.2	1.3	1.0	1.1	0.7	1.7	0.4	1.1
	1970s	26.2	25.8	26.9	18.5	26.1	26.8	32.4	17.8	21.8	11.6	22.4
		1.2	1.2	1.2	0.8	1.2	1.2	1.5	0.8	1.0	0.5	1.0
	1980s	24.5	22.1	22.2	21.4	23.4	28.2	43.3	11.7	15.9	3.5	21.9
		1.1	1.0	1.0	1.0	1.1	1.3	2.0	0.5	0.7	0.2	1.0
Gp.Three	1950s	19.8	22.1	n.a.	n.a.	31.0	11.2	12.1	7.2	13.3	8.4	11.7

The table below is printed rotated 90° on the page. Columns correspond to county-group / decade entries; the 23 data rows correspond to the categories A–K (each category shown as a pair of figures, plus a trailing value).

#	[Gp.Three] 1960s	1970s	1980s	Gp.Four 1950s	1960s	1970s	1980s	Gp.Five 1950s	1960s	1970s	1980s
1	0.5	0.3	0.6	0.3	0.5	0.5	1.5	n.a.	n.a.	0.9	0.8
2	13.1	7.8	17.3	12.9	13.3	13.3	24.5	19.7	19.8	20.8	19.1
3	0.5	0.3	0.7	0.5	0.6	0.3	1.0	0.8	0.8	0.9	0.8
4	14.4	7.5	20.2	13.4	13.2	14.3	24.8	18.7	23.9	23.2	20.5
5	0.6	0.3	0.9	0.6	0.6	0.6	1.1	0.9	1.0	1.0	0.8
6	14.8	5.1	19.3	7.8	14.3	13.4	23.1	19.3	24.8	24.2	20.1
7	0.7	0.2	0.9	0.3	0.6	0.6	1.0	0.9	1.1	1.1	0.9
8	7.0	7.9	9.3	8.2	8.3	7.8	16.6	n.a.	n.a.	6.3	5.4
9	0.4	0.4	0.5	0.5	0.5	0.4	0.9	n.a.	n.a.	0.4	0.5
10	11.1	4.9	11.0	13.0	9.6	10.5	16.7	18.5	12.8	10.6	11.7
11	0.6	0.3	0.6	0.8	0.6	0.6	1.0	1.1	0.8	0.6	0.7
12	9.8	8.8	14.7	12.8	9.6	10.3	18.7	22.3	12.1	13.4	13.2
13	0.6	0.5	0.9	0.8	0.6	0.6	1.1	1.3	0.7	0.8	0.8
14	11.4	1.5	15.5	6.8	12.1	10.7	17.6	19.6	16.8	17.1	14.9
15	0.7	0.1	0.9	0.4	0.7	0.6	1.1	1.2	1.0	1.1	0.9
16	4.1	4.1	4.3	4.5	5.2	4.5	10.3	n.a.	n.a.	2.7	4.7
17	0.3	0.3	0.3	0.3	0.3	0.3	0.7	n.a.	n.a.	0.2	0.3
18	3.9	2.8	6.4	6.7	4.8	4.6	15.5	9.0	6.5	7.3	8.0
19	0.3	0.2	0.4	0.5	0.3	0.3	1.0	0.6	0.5	0.5	0.5
20	6.9	8.4	10.9	7.1	5.6	6.7	14.7	14.1	8.2	9.0	9.0
21	0.5	0.6	0.8	0.5	0.4	0.5	1.1	1.1	0.6	0.7	0.7
22	7.0	1.0	9.7	3.6	4.4	5.5	16.4	17.2	7.6	8.7	8.8
23	0.5	0.1	0.8	0.3	0.3	0.4	1.3	1.3	0.6	0.7	0.7

A Total; B Industry; C Heavy industry (including Building Materials, Wood Processing, Paper and Glass/Porcelaine); D Light Industry; E Agriculture/Sylviculture; F Tertiary Sector Total; G Transport Telecommunications & Distribution; H Education &Science; I Health; J Administration; K Others. Constitution of Groups: Group One: Braşov, Caraş-Severin, Hunedoara, Prahova, Sibiu and Timiş; Group Two: Arad, Argeş, Bacău, Brăila, Cluj, Constanţa, Galaţi and Mureş; Group Three: Alba, Bihor, Călăraşi, Covasna, Dâmboviţa, Dolj, Gorj, Harghita, Ialomiţa, Maramureş and Neamţ; Group Four: Buzău, Giurgiu, Iaşi, Mehedinţi, Satu Mare, Suceava, Tulcea and Vâlcea; Group Five: Bistriţa-Năsăud, Botoşani, Olt, Sălaj, Teleorman, Vaslui and Vrancea. Sources: Dobrescu & Blaga 1973; Statistical Yearbooks.

Table 3.3: Salaried employment by county groups 1960–89

	1960			1970			1980			1989		
	A	B	C	A	B	C	A	B	C	A	B	C
Romania	178	38.6	102	252	42.9	73	331	46.7	58	345	47.6	55
Bucharest	365	43.9	92	557	32.4	68	515	44.2	47	486	42.6	43
Gp.One	225	56.4	50	325	62.0	31	399	54.2	38	402	54.7	36
Gp.Two	176	36.0	118	290	33.3	87	345	42.9	63	359	44,7	56
Gp.Three	137	37.9	76	233	36.4	60	307	45.2	57	320	49.1	57
Gp.Four	114	30.1	153	195	23.4	110	264	41.6	93	290	46.1	84
Gp.Five	81	19.5	295	136	24.4	209	226	37.6	90	255	45.7	87

A Jobs per thousand population; B Percentage of jobs in industry; C Light Industry (Textiles, Clothing, Leather and Food) as a percentage of heavy industry (Metallurgy, Engineering and Chemicals)

Source: Statistical Yearbooks

non-ferrous metallurgy (11.6 and 17.5) remained relatively uneven. There was least change for cellulose and paper (5.5 and 6.0) and wood processing (4.1 and 3.9: a slight widening). At the same time there was an inexorable trend towards heavy industry everywhere which can be seen in the declining weight for light industry (column C in Table 3.3) although excessively high values for heavy industry could not normally be sustained because of the inadequate opportunities for female employment: hence the recovery in Group 1 after 1970 (in Bucharest the tertiary sector was particularly well developed). The lower groups were more heavily preoccupied with light industry although there was no standard pattern for counties in each group despite a bias to light industry and maximum job creation. When heavy industry is compared with light industry on a simplified basis of metallurgy, engineering and chemicals against textiles, clothing, leather and food processing; counties with consistently high percentages for heavy industry (within a range of ten percentage points) are drawn mainly from Groups 1–2: (Braşov 82.0 – a figure that averages the heavy industry shares for 1960, 1970, 1980 and 1989, Brăila 65.0, Caras-Severin 91.1 and Prahova 77.1) but also Alba 76.8 and Neamţ 63.4 from Group 3 and Mehedinţi from Group 4 (in the case of Hunedoara from Group 1 with 83.8 and Maramureş from Group 3 with 73.4, there was an overall reduction thanks to some welcome diversification). Meanwhile, a large group of counties showing a steady increase in heavy industry of more than 15 percentage points (though still failing to reach 50 per cent* or even 40 per cent# in some cases) again features some Group 1-2 counties (Arad 47.6, Argeş 57.0, Bucharest 62.2, Cluj 58.2, Constanţa 55.6, Mureş 54.5, Sibiu 48.4 and Timiş 45.2) but includes more from Group 3 (Bihor 41.8, Dâmboviţa 69.9, Dolj 60.1, Gorj 61.0, Harghita 44.3, Ialomiţa* 24.0) and some from Group 4 (Buzău 53.4, Iaşi 50.6, Suceava* 37.7) and Group 5 (Botoşani# 22.4 and Vrancea# 28.8). Counties showing an increase greater than 30 percentage points included Bacău 40.1 and Galaţi 64.3 from Group 2; Covasna 32.3 from Group 3; Vâlcea 51.2 from Group 4; and Bistriţa 41.8, Olt 47.3, Sălaj 36.4 and Teleorman 47.5 from Group 5: the greatest advances here were achieved by Covasna (from 10.9 to 57.7 per cent), Galaţi (35.4 to 78.9), Olt (17.5 to 64.6), Sălaj (11.6-58.6) and Teleorman (16.2 to 61.3) which shows that the weakest counties were by no means restricted to the less-sophisticated industries with Galaţi attracting the country's greatest steelworks, Olt the sole aluminium smelter (as already noted) and Teleorman a large fertiliser factory. Yet at the same time, three counties saw heavy industry increase by less then 15 per cent, reaching a level that was still below 50 per cent in 1989: Ilfov/Giurgiu 41.5 and Satu Mare 47.5 from Group 4 and Vaslui 47.0 from Group 5.

Investment and Job Creation   Investment and job creation was a relevant issue since any policy boosting the position of the weaker counties might be expected to maximise employment through a higher level of labour intensity than was the case nationally – and with more emphasis on light industry Equally the more developed areas might be expected to experience a capital-intensive approach to increase productivity in towns under migration pressure. However these assumptions are only partially born out. Figures for the counties are available from 1965 and show an increase in employment of 2.12mln of which 1.34mln applies to heavy industry and 0.78 to light industry i.e. heavy industry jobs were 1.73 times greater than those in light industry, with a gradient from 4.88 in Bucharest to 2.31 in Group 1, 1.70 for Groups 2–3 (with Group 3 on 1.72 slightly above Group 2 with 1.68) and 1.21 for Groups 4–5 (with Group 5 with 1.22 slightly higher than Group 4 with 1.18). Meanwhile, a total investment of 1.90tln.lei means an average investment of 0.89mln per job but 1.25 in heavy industry and 0.29 in light industry. For heavy industry there is a gradient from 1.41 for Groups 1–2 (with Group 2 on 1.43 slightly above 1.40 for Group 1) 1.30 for Groups 3–4 (with Group 4 on 1.36 higher than Group 3 with 1.26) and 0.88 for Group 5. But Bucharest is even lower with 0.81, reflecting the privileged position of the capital in not attracting too much polluting industry. On the other hand Bucharest has a value for light industry that is higher than for heavy industry (0.98) which shows a logical desire for high productivity given a saturated labour market, but a gradient that runs from 0.29 for Group 1 to 0.25 for Group 2 and 0.24 for Group 3 then breaks down with relatively high investment for Group 4 (0.32) and Group 5 (0.27). Nevertheless any bias in favour of labour intensity in the weaker groups was not excessive.

Migration and Urban Development   Other evidence comes from migration and urbanisation (Erdeli 1998). Birthplace statistics for the 1966 census show movements of a far greater order than in 1930 with 30.9 per cent of the population involved (5.90mln) and 24.6 per cent of them (1.45mln) moved between a modified set of unofficial regions. The main flows were now between the South West (Oltenia) and a large South East region (20.9 per cent) and from North East to South East (20.0 per cent) with the Centre-South East at 16.2 per cent and Centre-West at 15.0. But the Centre and West also attracted significant flows from the North East and were in surplus overall (+1.18 per cent and +4.94 per cent respectively) along with the South East (+4.33 per cent). Migration figures were also published for the single year 1972 when 0.34mln people were involved. The same transfers are reinforced, particularly the flows from the North East (with its relatively high birth rate) to the Centre and South East. Thus long-wave migration shows a relative increase and net reception areas increased to include not merely Bucharest but much of Transylvania and the west. Migration can also be inferred from annual figures for the counties comparing the actual populations present with the totals inferred from rates of natural increase. Thus between 1966 and 1977 Bucharest and Groups 1-2 experienced a population growth of 1.69mln and an urban growth of 1.87mln, including net in-migration of 0.58mln from Groups 3–5 where population growth was only 0.90mln and urban growth 0.70. But between 1977 and 1989 the stronger regions grew by only 0.90mln (urban growth 1.18mln) with in-migration reduced to 0.28mln while the weaker regions grew by 0.70mln with urban growth almost double at 1.35mln.

It can also be demonstrated how the towns were growing faster on the whole in the more advanced areas (Bucharest and Groups 1–2) than those in Groups 3–5 until 1966 with a gradual turnaround thereafter. Of the 105 towns in Bucharest and Groups 1–2, 39 per cent grew much more slowly than the national average (i.e. below 70 per cent) for urban areas for 1912–66 while 38 per cent grew much faster (by more than 130 per cent of the average) but there were higher percentages in the below-average category during 1966–77 (59 per cent) and 1977–89 (52 per cent) and far fewer in the above-average category (13 per cent for both periods) – the others being within 30 per cent of the average. Meanwhile towns in Groups 3–5 with 61 per cent registering below average growth during 1912–66 saw that share fall to 54 per cent during 1966–77 and 36 per cent for 1977–89 while the percentage of their towns growing much faster than the average rose progressively from 15 per cent during 1912–66 to 19 per cent for 1966–77 and 33 per cent for 1977–89 (highlighting the rapid expansion of the county towns). Finally when 12 indicators of development (covering urbanisation, employment, investment, services and infrastructure) are combined and weighted according to population there is a fairly steep gradient from 1.49 in Bucharest to 0.74 in Group Five for 1989, although the gap was even greater in 1970 from 2.55 in Bucharest to 0.49 in Group Five (Table 3.4).

Agriculture and Rural Development

Central planning required fairly direct state control over agriculture to ensure an increased production at price levels acceptable to the state. But following the Soviet experience, the logic of restructuring peasant agriculture purely on the basis of state farms – which would have required huge resources for the necessary planning, coercion, administration and inputs – was restricted to a limited network based on existing experimental farms and expropriated private estates including former royal domains, subsequently enlarged by ad hoc transfers of some of the better land in the hands of collective (later cooperative) farms. In this way the typical state farm would comprise a considerable number of units with a fragmented distribution across a large area of land. In later years state farms were grouped into larger trusts with a degree of autonomy in negotiating sales including exports. With a full-time salaried workforce they made a key contribution of food and agricultural raw materials to the towns plus substantial exports. They also enjoyed priority in investment that paved the way for intensive livestock units from 1960s with their unsolved problems of liquid manure, although traditional methods were retained as in the case of one of the 14 units of the Şura Mică farm comprising pasture and woodland at an altitude of 1,250m at Crinţ in the Cindrel Mountains above Sibiu: this was concerned with the summer grazing of cattle and horses in partitioned pastures with its own sawmill and wild life management. The state farms were also prominent in viticulture, with an extensive revamping of the business at Cotnari in Moldavia where the vineyards were extended from 600 to 1,300ha (and then to 6,000ha in collaboration with neighbouring cooperatives) and a new central processing facility was installed during 1964–68), with hydraulic presses and large fermenting vats – replacing five small separate vinification and storage units – while traditional three-four year storage in caves was retained.

Cooperative Farms

Cooperative farms (CAPs) were first established in 1949 and arose from individual peasant contributions of land and livestock ('associations' were a transitional form) with the element of coercion concealed by appeals to the essentially traditional nature of cooperation among smallholders (Kideckel 1982). This was a relatively simple way of controlling the peasantry, without the heavy investment reserved for

Table 3.4: Development levels by regional groups 1970–89

Group	Year	A	B	C	D	E	F	G	H	I	J	K	L	Ave
		Percentage shares related to population:												
Bucharest	1970	251	185	303	203	181	343	196	22	339	210	267	557	254.7
	1980	196	156	161	136	99	146	176	23	232	208	161	336	169.2
	1989	167	141	131	206	92	126	166	22	175	150	156	253	148.7
	Average	205	161	198	182	124	205	179	22	249	189	195	382	190.9
Gp.One	1970	135	133	178	108	145	120	121	121	113	124	133	100	127.6
	1980	126	121	154	97	123	107	114	116	110	115	114	96	116.1
	1989	120	116	136	94	116	107	107	110	103	119	113	100	111.7
	Average	127	123	156	100	128	111	114	116	109	119	120	99	118.5
Gp.Two	1970	106	106	106	121	115	95	106	107	111	120	103	74	105.8
	1980	107	104	109	120	113	93	106	99	117	110	100	93	105.9
	1989	196	104	115	101	106	98	106	95	124	128	102	101	107.2
	Average	106	105	110	114	111	95	106	100	117	119	102	89	106.1
Gp.Three	1970	80	85	73	91	81	101	83	119	64	79	77	54	82.2
	1980	80	91	78	95	101	96	87	127	70	80	91	62	88.2
	1989	84	93	83	86	97	98	90	125	73	75	91	77	89.3
	Average	81	90	78	91	93	98	87	124	69	78	86	64	86.6
Gp.Four	1970	62	76	57	75	65	81	78	99	57	66	67	46	69.1
	1980	71	80	67	78	83	93	79	103	70	70	83	65	78.5
	1989	78	84	72	86	100	91	82	109	80	71	82	72	83.9
	Average	70	80	65	80	83	88	80	104	69	69	77	61	77.2
Gp.Five	1970	51	53	33	50	39	69	61	74	29	58	45	28	49.2
	1980	60	68	56	82	69	86	67	87	54	64	76	50	68.2
	1989	70	74	68	66	82	87	70	104	70	70	82	51	74.5
	Average	60	65	52	66	63	81	66	88	51	61	68	43	63.8

A Urban population (excluding suburban communes); B Wage earners; C Industrial production; D Investment; E Professional school enrolments; F Hospital beds; G Retail sales; H Modernised roads; I Water distribution; J Postal items; K Television licences; L Telephone licences.

Source: Statistical Yearbooks

the industrial sector, since the more assertive elements among the former landless peasantry provided a highly-motivated leadership, while all the available labour could be recruited – without the need for formal engagements and salaries – against modest shares in the final production and the right to a private plot. The latter gave the peasant the incentive to work even longer hours to provide for the household and perhaps generate a margin for the free market. Nevertheless the logistics of cooperative management were such as to preclude successful implementation in some mountain districts, where considerable numbers of 'non-cooperativised peasants' remained after the CAP programme was declared complete in 1962. These mountain peasants had to accept production plans – effectively a quota system – but they did give access to cheap fodder and the state made pragmatic use of its contractual arrangements to ensure that it would gain more from the peasants that it would by undertaking the costly work of organising them into cooperatives. Additional outside support (though sometimes stimulative through higher prices – and collection facilities in the case of milk) tended to bring more demanding contractual obligations.

Rural Planning: 1960s–1970s

Although many peasants deplored the coercive nature of collectivism there was an element of pragmatism while the system also served as an instrument of rural planning and social policy. All rural dwellers had a place in the new order and an element of welfare arose when, for example, state loans for land improvement might be written off if the cooperatives failed to show a profit. On the other hand successful farms were required to pay in full for the services provided by machine-tractor stations, veterinary specialists and agronomists. Since young people no longer had any prospect of inheriting a family farm there were few barriers standing in the way of employment outside agriculture that the state was only too happy to encourage through commuting or migration. As regards the choice of farm enterprises there was always a tension between the state's interest in regional specialisation, to maximise surpluses for urban consumption and export, and the peasants' desire for subsistence and minimal involvement with a cash economy. Research was undertaken to establish the potentials, particularly with regard to climate and landscape types: lowland openfield systems (with some enclosures in the foothills); fruit-growing landscapes in the Subcarpathians; and mountain systems with small enclosed crop areas set among the open pastures and hayfields. Land improvement was highlighted: partly the tidying up of boundaries with adjacent farms (albeit with extensive open fields prone to erosion) but eventually from the mid-1960s through the use of chemical fertiliser and irrigation. Investment in fertiliser production grew only slowly until the later 1960s with a curious decision of neglect domestic production of nitrates in preference for phosphates based on apatites from the USSR and North Vietnam. The irrigated area was to the quadruple from 0.20mln.ha in 1960 to 0.80 in 1965 but western expertise was only belatedly sought and the available areas increased slowly to 0.73mln.ha in 1970, 1.47 in 1975 and 2.30 in 1980. Labour was an important consideration with regional development programmes invoked to ensure that there was an appropriate balance of enterprises operating under the cooperative umbrella to use labour all the year round.

'Acord Global'

By the late 1970s attention moved to economise in transport (linked with the heavy burden of imported oil) with greater attention to 'ecological plans' that would enable the needs of each town to be met to a greater extent from the production of the surrounding countryside. And American studies emphasised the importance of improved productivity while doubting the régime's willingness to stimulate the peasantry through higher living standards and welfare benefits and greater independence (Gilberg 1980): so fine was the line between encouraging the peasants to keep working while ensuring that they would not be perceived as wealthy by the proletariat. However, the 'acord global' provided for piece-work and in effect re-introduced share-cropping by allowing peasants to look after the entire seasonal round of cultivation tasks on designated plots with payment through a share of the harvest, but that state always denied any thought of 'convergence' between capitalist and socialist thinking and insisted that all land was to be seen as the nation's patrimony (and therefore subject to central planning) irrespective of the type of management. The scope for private transactions in respect of private plots on cooperative farms (and entire holdings in the non-cooperativised areas) was however reduced in the 1980s by the setting of maximum prices on free markets; elaborate registration procedures for livestock and more demanding state contracts that left relatively little for other forms of disposal anyway. The state also found ways of controlling at least a part of the output from private plots by requiring payment in kind for certain consumer goods or entering into contracts whereby peasants reared young animals supplied by the cooperative.

Rural Planning: 1980s

At a time of desperate effort to maximise exports and pay-off foreign debts, land reclamation created some entirely new agricultural landscapes through extending the policy wetland drainage from the Danube floodplain to the delta where the farmed area comprised only some 11,000ha in small 'gulfs' that had naturally silted up. In the early post-war years the communist planners were interested mainly in the reed beds to supply a new cellulose factory built at Brăila, but the use of heavy machinery damaged the root systems and production fell sharply. Some of the reed beds were then reprofiled to expand fish production (and compensate for the losses arising from floodplain drainage upstream). A total of 29 large basins (covering 50,000 ha.) were marked out for development during the 1970s with new species of fish brought into a controlled water régime. But results were disappointing through poor water circulation and a lack of compatibility between the new fish and the native species. Then during the 1980s a further 'şoc' was experienced through the drive to increase food production through the Danube Delta Management Project of 1983 seeking extensive polder development of the kind first attempted over 3,400ha on Tataru Island in 1938-40 and subsequently envisaged (though ultimately postponed) on a bigger scale in the 1960s: there would now be a total managed surface of 1,000sq.kms (520 for farming, 420 for fisheries and 70 for forestry). Work started on agricultural projects at Pardina (27,000ha) and Sireasa (7,500) and forestry schemes at Carasuhat (2,800ha) and Murighiol-Dunavăţ (2,500ha) with dyking, levelling, artificial drainage and concrete roads to access the future town of Chilia Veche with housing, services and a pig farm. Excessive use of pesticides in land reclamation made dairy products unsafe for export and further pollution arose from toxic waste stored at Sulina through enterprise encouraged the town's free port regime. Further dramatic change occurred through the quarrying of sand (for its mineral content) at Caraorman and the construction of an access canal from the main Sulina Channel. The Sf.Gheorghe Channel was shortened from 109kms to 70 during 1985–90 and work started on an elaborate dyke and trench system along the coast between Sulina and Sf.Gheorghe in a bid to stop the marine erosion of the coastline.

The state increased its production plan demands in 1984 through higher quotas for pigs (100kg every year from a private farm and every other year from each private plot) as well as sheep, poultry, milk, potatoes and fruit. There were also livestock registration procedures and price limits on the open markets. This reflected the role of agriculture in helping to increase exports to pay off all foreign debts and thereby remove the influence of global financial institutions over economic planning. There would be more attention to fertiliser and irrigation with the latter tied to artificial water storages (integrated with protection forests and further hydropower projects). A further inspiration was a far-reaching project to integrate state farms and cooperative farms within specific areas through unitary councils (CUASCs) that would coordinate agricultural production and processing. This was partly responsible for the resurrection of a settlement restructuring programme conceived in the light of the completed collectivisation programme to eliminate 'redundant' small villages that had no function in the socialist economy and consolidate settlement in viable units including an expanded network of small towns and a great increase in population density to reduce the cost of utilities and save 320,000–350,000ha of potential arable land.

'Sistematizare' or Rural Settlement Reorganisation
This began with a central commission for village reorganisation set up in 1965 to improve services while preventing the loss of farmland through ribbon development. Then a comprehensive planning programme started in the 1970s, inspired by the drive for greater regional equality arising out of the 1968 reform of local government. And this gave rise to the 1974 law for urban and rural territorial reorganisation to develop the countryside through a focus on the more viable villages while the rest would be gradually starved of investment (for example, by householders being prevented from making structural repairs to their properties). But momentum was lost in the late 1970s and the 129 new towns promised by 1980 never emerged (likewise the further 140 by 1985): the only promotion was a new lignite mining town (Rovinari) in 1981. No explanation was ever given but it may be that Ceaușescu transferred his attention to the Danube-Black Sea Canal and – after the 1977 earthquake – saw ways of making a lasting impact on the townscape of Bucharest. The belated relaunch in the 1980s took a more radical form through (a) a proposed reduction in the number of villages to 5,000–6,000 (grouped in 2,000 communes) – implying that 7,000–8,000 would be destroyed; (b) consolidation of settlement in three-four storey buildings for workers and intellectuals (with 50–90m plots) while farm workers would live in small blocks with four apartments or individual two-storey houses (with gardens restricted to 250sq.m) in contrast to the traditional cottages; and (c) urbanisation of

the countryside through some 550 new agro-industrial towns by promoting the most dynamic and centrally-placed communes (Sampson 1984). The number should not be taken too literally since 300–400 new towns were mentioned several times before a specific reference to 558 by Ceauşescu at a conference in 1988 (Deletant 1995, pp. 307–8). Nevertheless, the project was now clearly "distorted into a revolutionary scheme to transform the entire country in accordance with Ceauşescu's wishes" (Fischer 1989, pp. 253–4).

Although aspects of the programme were absolutely necessary – the improvement of services and the growth of non-agricultural employment (e.g. by means of branch plants) to stabilise the workforce and reduce long-distance commuting; also an expanded urban system to bring rural areas closer to the towns – the programme allowed little scope for local consultation and appeared destined for implementation over far too short a timespan (hence compulsory resettlement) with no realistic compensation for the expropriation needed to create civic centres – on which Ceauşescu kept a close eye through personal checking of all the plans (although much ground had already been covered in the 1970s). Each centre was to have its administration and party office, a cultural centre (dedicated to composing 'Hymns to Romania' – one of Ceauşescu's many obsessions), post office, school, health centre, sports ground, public baths and – in the new towns – a 100-bed hospital. However the package also included visionary references to the 'new man' and a fully modernised agriculture that would draft farm workers into apartment blocks without the need for access to their own hen coops, pig sties and storage space. Such a lifestyle was inconceivable to cooperative farm members whose experience with private plots was tied up with the ethos of the small mixed farm and immediate access to crops and livestock. Ronnas (1989) stressed the ideological nature of the programme but this ignores Ceauşescu's unrealistic conception of a new agricultural revolution at a time when the state was increasing its production plan demands though higher quotas (as already noted). Maybe Ceauşescu saw individual farms and plots as time-expired, with the historic compromise now to be revised over a short transition period to the state's advantage and taken to the ultimate extreme. On this basis peasants would be disciplined to accept a role in the modern CUASC-dominated agriculture with apartments providing a better basis for supervision and control than individual family houses. A further inspiration behind this integration of state farms and cooperatives within specific areas was the coordination of agricultural production and processing. Each unitary council would comprise a group of communes and an urban centre (existing or newly created): thus providing the key to the planned increase in the number of towns. The huge capital demands of the project were not published but substantial economies would arise from the minimal compensation payable to property owners for plots required for town centre facilities. Since the people involved would lose their owner-occupier status it became the key preoccupation for influential families to try their best to ensure that the site of their 'civic centre' was selected so as not to threaten their land.

The Radical Impact   The radical impact intended can be seen in Figure 3.2 showing the hinterlands of Carpathian towns existing in 1950 (distance basis) and their 'invasion' by new towns actually declared and others anticipated under the programme to achieve a reasonably balanced distribution (whereas earlier promotions were based 'ad hoc' on performance). However there is some reinforcement of earlier trends with the heavy urbanisation of the Prahova Valley in sharp contrast to the Buzău Valley – marginalised by the Ploieşti region and only promoted strongly by the newly reconstituted Buzău county after 1968 (but with Nehoiu the only realisation). Also the urban cluster in the Petroşani coalfield and the creation of new towns of Nucet and Petru Groza (now Stei) based on the uranium mine of Băiţa and a related mining and transport establishment that produced a new cluster in south Bihor when added to the existing towns of Beiuş and Vaşcău. Table 3.5 shows the 1984 pattern of hinterlands. Combining town and hinterland populations there were ten regions over 300,000, all dominated by the respective city: Bucharest 2,283.0, Iaşi 452.0, Timişoara 402.5, Cluj-Napoca 396.3, Craiova 374.8, Galaţi 356.3, Ploieşti 349.8, Constanţa 342.6, Braşov 336.7 and Bacău 303.4 with another 55 over 100,000 and only 21 smaller than 20,000. The average number of communes for each town was 11.5 but there were 71 with 15 and over, of which 12 had 25 or more: Craiova (25), Bârlad (28), Roşiorii de Vede and Târgu Mureş (29), Bacău (30), Iaşi and Reghin (31), Buzău (32), Urziceni (33), Râmnicu Sărat (35), Drăgăşani (37) and Bucharest (48) assuming that each commune would be oriented towards its nearest town.

In terms of the total population in the surrounding areas, urban hinterlands of over 100,000 were all in Moldavia and Wallachia with a relatively poor urban network: in the North East – Iaşi 141.9 (161 villages), Bacău 133.9th (184), Botoşani 127.7 (114), Roman 125.9 (118), Bârlad 118.5 (200) and Suceava 105.2 (68); in the South – Urziceni 135.2 (113), Piteşti 130.0 (189), Roşiorii de Vede 124.3 (91), Ploieşti 117.5 (106), Olteniţa 108.2 (58), Târgovişte 107.6 (96) and Videle 101.3 (84); in the South East – Buzău 153.3 (209), Tecuci 131.1 (76), Râmnicu Sărat 123.8 (194) and Focşani 105.9 (86); in the South West – Drăgăşani 123.0 (196) and Craiova 107.3 (133); and in Ilfov – Bucharest 321.7 (139) and Buftea 117.8 (73). Completion of 'sistematizare' would have reduced the units with over 100,000 population to 31 while boosting the smallest category (below 20,000) to 293. It was envisaged that the average number of communes per town would be reduced to only 3.7 although there would still be some large individual hinterland populations: Bucharest 100.2, Ploieşti 62.0, Iaşi 60.3, Bacău 56.6, Craiova 55.0, Radăuţi 54.3, Roşiorii de Vede 53.9, Piteşti 52.6, Târgu Mureş 50.9, Suceava 50.1, Vălenii de Munte 47.0, Bolintin 46.7 and Timişoara 45.8. On the other hand there were clusters of planned towns that seemed to be far too close together for efficient servicing. But no definitive list of proposed new towns was ever published and the table only anticipates some 400 (based on planning studies) rather than the 558 mentioned in 1988. Arguably this latter number was excessive and it is questionable if such a number of promotions to urban status would ever have occurred even with the continuance of a communist dictatorship.

'Sistematizare': Implementation   The programme fell behind schedule and of the 100 new towns expected by 1990 only 24 were declared late in 1989 (just before the revolution) (Ianos et al. 1989; Misiak 1993). There was considerable discussion in the scientific literature including much muted criticism, such as through the strong ecological slant adopted by geographers who were trying to get across their concerns about environmental damage at a time when overt discussion of these problems was

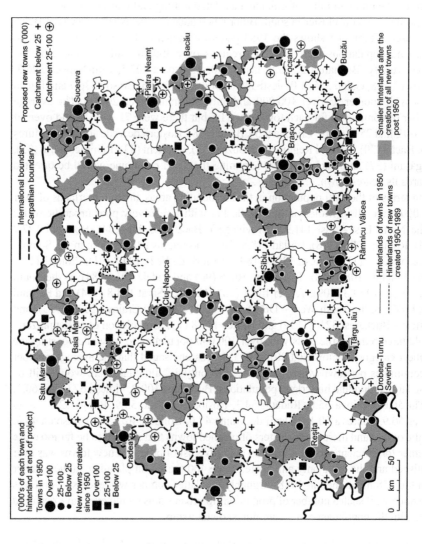

Figure 3.2 The rural settlement programme in the Carpathians

Table 3.5: **Rural reorganisation: population groups** *first line:* situation in the 1980s; *second line:* situation after programme completion

Region	A a	A b	B a	B b	C a	C b	D a	D b	E	F	G	H	I	J
									|← Towns and hinterlands →|					
Bucharest	1	13.7	5	186.3	1	135.2	1	2283.0	2	0	0	0	2	17.5
	6	79.1	20	674.5	1	55.1	1	2061.4	8	2	5	0	1	3.6
Centre	52	632.7	27	795.2	15	1070.8	4	979.4	45	19	21	4	1	7.5
	1	5.0	3	123.6	9	633.3	3	708.1	91	82	8	1	0	3.2
NorthEast	39	443.9	42	1101.6	15	1097.7	12	2236.1	31	1	10	14	6	16.9
	3	26.6	5	136.0	11	747.1	7	1227.8	99	70	25	4	0	4.6
NorthWest	44	546.7	36	1037.2	17	1164.5	8	1536.0	33	6	11	16	0	11.7
	3	33.5	7	204.5	7	467.8	4	877.3	91	70	21	0	7	3.6
South	32	402.6	48	1441.0	11	777.6	16	1855.6	37	9	7	14	0	10.7
	3	37.5	7	253.2	14	926.6	4	759.6	98	63	32	3	4	3.4
SouthEast	55	678.3	27	710.4	8	594.6	8	1920.8	26	5	10	7	0	14.1
	3	30.0	6	208.1	5	341.5	5	1153.4	92	81	11	11	2	3.3
SouthWest	41	509.0	32	846.6	9	645.3	10	1510.4	28	5	10	11	0	14.0
	2	25.9	22	728.1	5	338.6	4	670.5	82	62	19	1	0	4.1
West	29	345.0	27	805.6	5	298.9	6	1096.1	34	14	16	4	0	7.9
	21	237.6	69	2328.0	4	306.6	3	683.7	63	54	9	0	0	3.8
Total	293	3571.9	244	6923.9	81	5784.7	65	12830.1	236	59	85	70	22	11.5
					56	3816.6	31	8141.8	624	484	130	9	1	3.7

A Number of groups of below 20.0th; B Ditto 20.0th; C Ditto 50.0-49.9th; D Ditto 100.0th and over; a number of groups; b total population (th); E Total number of towns; F Hinterland population: groups below 20.0th; G Ditto 20.0-49.9th; H Ditto 50.0-99.9th; I Ditto 100.0th and over; J Average number of surrounding communes per group.

Sources: Map analysis and census data

officially discouraged. Study of soil, vegetation, drainage and relief – especially in unstable Subcarpathian country – pointed to a landscape mosaic with variations in potential (between brown forest and rendzina soils) that the authorities as well as the peasants needed to take into account. These studies painted a picture of great opportunity that could boost the viability of remoter villages after R.Rey (1978) first suggested a special authority for the non-cooperativised mountain zone to improve the rural services in each locality, such as in the Apuseni Mountains where electricity, water supply and surfaced roads could stabilise the population, along with agrotourism and handicrafts. Agriculture could also develop through a better fertiliser supply and 'minimaşini' to collect all the available fodder (Iacob 1980). Fish farming was widely advocated as an option for cooperative farms that would link with irrigated cereal production. However Ceauşescu's aim was initially to drive the programme forward in the lowlands. He decided to make Ilfov Agriculture Sector (situated around Bucharest) a showpiece (due for completion by 1992–93) for emulation by the rest of the country so that the whole national programme could be finished in 2000.

However, even with the help of loyalists in local government the only villages that had disappeared by the end of 1989 were Buda and Odoreanu (to make way for a reservoir), Dimieni (on an airport flight path) and Ciofliceni and Vlădiceasa in Snagov commune with its recreation complex for the nomenclature (Mihăilescu et al. 1993). Of course this was traumatic enough for the people involved, for they stood to lose everything: Deletant (1995, p. 295) states that no more than six months notice was given and while the maximum compensation was 80,000lei (two years of average salary) it was usually much less and nothing at all where the land was taken for agriculture, as at Vlădiceasa where people were charged 2,000lei if they did not demolish houses themselves. On the other hand symbolic compensation was paid for the housing area redeveloped in Snagov's Ghermăneşti village to provide state apartments for those resettled (Ibid p. 318). Meanwhile the viable villages were seeing much consolidation. Mihăileşti was endowed with 3,500 new apartments with drastic clearance of old property so that an increased population was accommodated on an area 180ha smaller, even allowing for a further 1,000ha needed for a 100mln. cu.m reservoir. The same scenario occurred at Bragadiru, Măgurele, Otopeni and 30 Decembrie. Services were poor: indeed this was also a widespread problem on the expanding housing estates on the edge of the city since facilities such as cinemas remained concentrated in the centre. There was no effective opposition within Romania – even the Orthodox Church was silent. However 'Opération Villages Roumaines' was launched in Belgium in 1988 by architects, archaeologists and journalists so that threatened villages could be adopted by communities in Western Europe who would offer material assistance and send protests to Ceauşescu. By May 1989 368 links had been forged by communities in Belgium, France and Switzerland. Mercifully however the whole project was scrapped after the revolution and some people moved back to villages that had been destroyed, notably Vlădiceasa.

Infrastructure: Transport and Power

Much investment was needed to build up the national airline and a large fleet of ships to handle much of the country's international trade (especially ores from outside the Soviet orbit). The national roads were largely surfaced and the beginnings of a motorway system were laid between Bucharest and Piteşti while the development of a national motor vehicle industry (involving cars, lorries and tractors) was a major achievement. The Danube navigation was already in existence but the delta seaway through Sulina was protected by a dyked channel progressively extended into the Black Sea to block the drift of sediment from the north. At the same time resources were dissipated in unnecessary public works including the Danube-Black Sea Canal (DBSC) and massive redevelopment in Bucharest. The DBSC was started during 1951–53 by 19,000 political prisoners and 20,000 other workers but was abandoned after Stalin's death and then revived by Ceauşescu (on a new alignment) after visits to Antwerp 1972 and Amsterdam/Rotterdam 1973 where he heard about the Europa Canal (Rhine-Main-Danube) project in Germany and saw the long-term implications for Romania. Work on the 64.4km canal started in 1976 and was completed two years late in 1984: a mammoth task excavating 300mln.cu.m of earth and laying 3.6mln.cu.m of concrete. In 2004 it was being used at well below half capacity. Meanwhile the railways played a key role under communism although there was only a modest increase in total route length from 10,853kms to 11,348 (1950–90). The era of network expansion was effectively concluded by a more direct route into Suceava, the Brad-Deva connection and the line from Vâlcele (north of Piteşti) to Râmnicu Vâlcea line started in the 1980s (and still unfinished) to provide a direct line from Bucharest to Sibiu and relieve pressure at Predeal. New lines were also needed in the coalfields of Oltenia but a surge of new branch lines in Moldavia may have arisen from the autonomy of the construction enterprise in Iaşi (though not, of course, without Ceauşescu's approval).

Railway Development

Railway development also involved the whole complex of track, control, traction and rolling stock provision that attracted heavy investment through the 1960s and 1970s. The welding of heavier rails accommodated faster trains (up to 160 km/h) with higher axle weights and capacity was maximised by improved control systems with scope for direct communication with train crews. Particular reference should be made to the progress in widening and electrifying track. In 1970 only 10.0 per cent of the network was twin-tracked and only 2.0 per cent was electrified, whereas in 1990 the proportions were 26.0 and 32.4 per cent respectively. In 1970 the Bucharest-Braşov line was double-tracked and electrified throughout while the single-track line from Craiova to Caransebeş and Reşiţa (double-track from Craiova to Strehaia) was very well-advanced, including the 24km diversion (Coramnic-Valea Cladovei between Drobeta-Turnu Severin and Topleţ, with ten tunnels and 21 viaducts) required on account of the Iron Gates hydropower scheme. This system was then extended along single track from Caransebeş to Timişoara, Arad and Curtici, where the first electrified cross-border link was opened in 1974: also the single-track coal-carrying lines Filiaşi to Petroşani and Deva; and Strehaia to Motru. In addition, work started on the single track lines from Braşov and Adjud to Ciceu and their continuation to Deda and Beclean. This meant that extra capacity could be made available without the need to double the track. But both doubling and electrification was undertaken on some lines e.g. from Bucharest to Constanţa and Craiova; and Braşov to Mediaş, Cluj and Beclean.

Traction Policy
After concentrating on steam traction through the early and middle 1950s, there was renewed interest in diesel locomotives by the end of the decade and traditional links with Switzerland were revived for a 2,100hp diesel electric prototype. Six locomotives were built in Switzerland followed by series production in Craiova under licence (1959), although speed was limited to 100km/h, fuel consumption was heavy and the lack of train heating called for special heating units in winter. Romanian-designed diesel hydraulics of 2,400, 1,250 and 7,000hp were built in Bucharest and introduced for secondary lines and light traffic from 1966 (some with train heating capacity) and by 1976 it was decided that a more powerful 4,000hp Romanian-designed diesel-electric locomotive would be built at Craiova under licence using American Alcoa engines. But as the greater capacity provided by dieselisation was fully utilised from the end of the 1960s, electrification at 25Kv began with the Predeal line and the choice of a prototype locomotive rested on Swedish (ASEA) technology. 5,100Kw units were built at Craiova under licence with some exports to Bulgaria, China and Yugoslavia: in the latter case there was some exchange with smaller locomotives built in Zagreb by Rade Končar from 1973. Steam locomotives handled only a tenth of the traffic in 1973 and their role was limited to shunting by the 1980s. The country also built new rolling stock for higher speed running (with a margin for export): coaches at Arad and wagons at Caracal, Drobeta-Turnu Severin and Paşcani, using various component suppliers including factories at Balş (bogies), Brăila (braking systems) and Buzău (axles). But little happened in the railcar field. A new initiative produced the 'Săgeata Albastră' (Blue Arrow) in 1959 to operate a prestigious holiday service between Vienna and the Black Sea. But the two trains – each of six units of which two were powered by Maybach engines – were restricted to limited operations with foreign tourists on the Bucharest-Constanţa line (although five cars – two with power – are still believed to be in store in Arad). Given the philosophy of long, heavy trains and the availability of old coaches displaced from main line service, only a few new railcars were built for branch line use.

Electrification
This was another massive achievement to underpin the progress with industry and urbanisation. Pavel's surveys were revived as a contribution to the Ten Year Electrification Plan (1951–60) which included a number of stations of intermediate size (totalling almost 100MW at Bicaz, Crăinicel, Moroieni and Sadu) before the major hydro projects of the 1960s: 960MW mainly on the Argeş and Bistriţa; followed by 2,130MW in the 1970s and 2,110MW in the 1980s: mainly on the Danube (Iron Gates I and II) and the Lotru-Olt basin. But thermal power was needed as well since the hydropower potential was not unlimited while investment costs were high and

there were long gestation periods given the complexity of the engineering work. Maximum use was made of coal, especially lignite: hence the eventual opening of the Oltenian field to supply the three large power stations of Craiova-Işalniţa, Rovinari and Turceni. Many smaller stations were also needed especially in the early years before the national grid was completed (this also explains why many small hydroprojects were implemented in rural areas – sometimes as accessory features at lakes impounded primarily for water supply purposes e.g. the 4.0MW capacity at Strâmtori Lake near Baia Mare in 1965, which like many other hydro projects meant the loss of housing as well as pasture and woodland. Natural gas was used in some stations (in Transylvania but at other locations served by the pipeline system) while oil was reserved as far as possible for the petrochemistry and transport. Soaring demand, inflated by inefficient use of energy (which, like all industrial raw materials, was not realistically costed) eventually required consideration of the nuclear option although progress was extremely slow. Soviet assistance in the 1960s was given up in favour of a deal with the Canadian Atomic Energy Agency concerning an entire nuclear power system using the CANDU reactor that was not only considered safe for an earthquake zone but required only natural uranium and heavy water that could be produced within the country. The first unit was to be built at Cernavodă during 1980–85, while heavy water would come from a new plant operating at Halinga near Turnu Severin (two modules were ready by 1989) and the fuel would be supplied by a natural uranium facility at Feldioara near Braşov (drawing ore from several domestic sources), with further processing in Piteşti. But the whole project came to a standstill in 1982 when American and Canadian credits were suspended and there was little further activity until the CANDU project was revived – and carried to completion – after the revolution.

Urban Development: Bucharest and the Black Sea Coast

The communist state made a radical impact on the towns through the somewhat incoherent development of factories and apartment blocks (Ianos 1994b; Ronnas 1992, 1994). Although much use was made of rural commuters (Ciotea 1979, 1980), many county centres saw reconstruction in their central areas as well as incremental growth through housing and industrial estates, although towns in Banat and Transylvania seemed to salvage more of their traditional urban landscape than those of Moldavia and Wallachia. Bucharest saw the growth of a constellation of large apartment complexes at Balta Albă-Titan, Drumul Taberei, Militari, Berceni and Pantelimon whose high density concrete buildings boosted the summer 'heat island' in the centre. Another irritant was the growth of much of the industry (totalling 215 units occupying 3,450ha and employing 700,000 workers) in the central area with serious pollution problems: especially dust and sulphur dioxide but with some emissions of ammonia, hydrochloric acid, lead, above the legal limit (since the available filter technology was not fully used). Pollution was aggravated by the low level of the city (below 100m) and lack of strong winds and green spaces. With a prevailing wind from the northeast the Obor and Budeşti industrial concentrations were to be acknowledged as mistakes, although not until after 1989. Some industry was located on the periphery (in a traditional market gardening area colonised by Bulgarian and Serbian immigrants) associated with the 'first line' rural settlements e.g. Chitila, Pantelimon, Popeşti-Leordeni and Voluntari that were outside the city limit and not subject to the migration controls imposed in the 1970s. Apartment blocks also appeared in villages close to the urban limits of provincial cities to accommodate migrants who could work in the city but were barred from living there e.g. Apahida and Baciu near Cluj and Dancu near Iaşi.

Radical Change in Bucharest

However, the most radical changes in Bucharest came in the last two decades of communism after Ceauşescu was moved by the excessive monumentality of Pyongyang which Romanian architects were sent to study after his own visit in 1971. Earthquake damage in Bucharest in 1977 provided many opportunity sites for redevelopment (Church 1979). On the periphery there was the new airport of Otopeni to the north, balanced on the southern side (near 30 Decembrie) by a port project linked with a Danube-Bucharest Canal that has yet to be finished. But there was a clearance at Văcăreşti for new accommodation linked with water sports on a new lake impounded in the Dâmboviţa valley. Unfortunately water soaked into the ground and undermined buildings: after the revolution people staked out their plots close to the lake wall and also made claims within. In the centre the Dâmboviţa axis was reconstructed to provide a sequence of basins (separated by dams) with clean waters on the surface and sewers below. This provided a line for the metro which developed from 1979 and permitted a substantial restructuring of in other forms of transport during the 1980s e.g. the tramway was reduced from 165 to 153kms and tramcars from 600 to 400; while the bus network was reduced from 420 to 240kms and vehicles from 1,500 to 720. Finally the Dâmboviţa project was the lauching pad for an intersecting 1.5km 'Victory of Socialism Boulevard' (120m wide): a project funded in 1981 but delayed until completion of the DBSC of 1978-84 (Cavalcanti 1997).

Ceauşescu's 'Casa'

Ceauşescu's 'Casa' was a particularly massive realisation of his conception of the 'civic centre' as a new heart for a socialist city and one that would typically require compulsory purchase (with minimal compensation) of substantial properties largely undamaged by the 1977 earthquake. In their place "the insertion of new blocks entirely out of scale with the old city's spatial framework established an urban chaos of great proportion" (Cavalcanti 1992, p. 283). A new boulevard led to a semicircular plaza with space for half a million people to gather in front of a new People's Palace ('Casa Poporului') built on a 6.3ha site on the edge of the hill of Dealul Spirei, a historic site previously used for the army arsenal and before that the Ypsilanti Palace (Curtea Arşă). The 'Casa' itself is 276m long with a facade 86m high and total area of 300,000sq.m. Ten-storey buildings lined the boulevard which also provided carriageways and sidewalks along with a central strip of 8.0m with fountains and two 8.4m green strips with fir, lime and oak trees. Forty thousand people were expelled from the periphery, while the loss of many historic monuments brought protests from prominent architects and historians (though some monuments were relocated:

for example the church from Mihai Vodă monastery was moved 225m to a site behind the new facade). Ceaușescu had plans for another new boulevard to extend towards the airport from a redeveloped Strada Galați but the revolution occurred before work could begin.

The Black Sea Resorts

The Black Sea Resorts were also greatly enlarged under communism (beginning at Mamaia in 1959) to produce a total of 15 'stațiuni' over the 70kms from Capul Midia to Vama Veche (Năvodari and Mamaia to the north of Constanța; Eforie Nord, Eforie Sud, Techirghiol, Costinești, Olimp, Neptun, Jupiter, Venus, Saturn and Aurora between Constanța and Mangalia; Mangalia itself – with a sanatorium based on local mineral waters; and 2 Mai and Vama Veche between Mangalia and the Bulgarian frontier). There is also a bathing station at Nuntași to the north of Capul Midia (associated with the Razelm-Sinoe lake complex). By the early 1980s there were more than 200 hotels (as well as sanatoria at Eforie and Techirghiol) and places for over 155,000 visitors (including 35.000 at Mamaia, 18,500 at Eforie Nord, 13,100 at Saturn, 11,900 at Eforie Sud and 11,400 at Venus): both Romanian nationals and travellers from abroad organised by the package-tour companies flying in their clients to the Mihail Kogălniceanu airport near Constanța. Meanwhile the inland spas continued to expand with new hotel accommodation at the leading resorts such as Băile Felix, Băile Herculane, Băile Olănești, Călimănești-Căciulata, Covasna and Sângeorz Băi. And while Romanians were in an overwhelming majority – given the many subsidised holiday opportunities through the unions – there was nevertheless a growing foreign element involving nationals from both Comecon and western states. This was also the case where touring was concerned, given the road improvements which saw the bulk of the national roads surfaced by the 1970s (although compulsory currency exchange was imposed in 1974 and private accommodation went out of bounds for foreigners the following year). However the tourist industry lost ground in the late 1980s with poor levels of service and increasing conflict between the needs of foreign visitors and the government's austerity programme. There were many customer complaints with the limited availability of evening entertainment a particular issue.

Conclusion

It is hardly possible in a short work to explore the reasons for the collapse of communist Romania, especially since the national scenario can hardly be separated from the events occurring throughout the region and the question could well be approached through the anomaly that saw Moscow repudiating Stalin's excesses (through Khrushchev's 'dethronement' speech) while maintaining the irrationality of a system perfected to drive Soviet investment to Siberia in the run-up to World War Two. Perhaps western-style pluralism was unpalatable at a time when the untold Soviet wealth in hydrocarbons seemed capable of sustaining a competitive economic and political system until American pressure demonstrated to Gorbachev that the show was over. Yet his declaration of independence for the erstwhile satellites seemed hollow until the Poles stumbled over an exit strategy and the rest became history. The Ceauşescu régime had appeared impregnable as the only one in the region that combined "totalitarian and sultanistic tendencies" (Duran 2000, p. 6) i.e. the domination of civil society by a state under unrestrained personal rule. Rather than meet the challenges of the 1980s with a reform programme on the Hungarian model, his last years brought a period of extreme austerity (per capita GDP fell after 1984) combined with a high level of centralisation and preservation of a revolutionary spirit linked to his distorted personal priorities. Despite strikes in Braşov in 1987 and some discontent within the party in the run-up to the 14th Communist Party Congress held in November 1989, change was ruled out and the liberalising trends in other communist countries were deplored. Yet the following month the régime collapsed amidst rumours of an organised coup that have yet to be vindicated. But all parties cannot have been unaware of events in the region and in the end it only required a little confidence by spontaneous protesters, first in Timişoara and then in Bucharest, and hesitancy by the authorities to set events in train. However earlier heavy-handed suppression of reformist tendencies – with all critical currents stifled by the Securitate on which Ceauşescu was completely dependent during 1985–89 – made for a conservative trade-off between moral credibility and experience for the post-1989 political elite. Romanians could look further back to more progressive government but a lengthy period of stock-taking seemed inevitable. And economically the country was left in a very poor condition for re-integration into global structures.

Chapter Four

The Political Context of Post-Communist Economic Restructuring: The EU and NATO

As the discourse moves on the transition which the is main theme of the book, a whole chapter is devoted to the political context for the economic changes accompanying the radical shift in foreign relations away from the old Soviet bloc to the resumption of a close association with Western Europe. As already noted, western links underpinned Romania's modernisation from the end of Ottoman suzerainty until the onset of the communist era that ushered in a relatively brief but formative phase of separation at the behest of Moscow. Romania's contested national space and its location in the strategically sensitive Carpathian-Danube-Black Sea zone – close to the Middle East and the Caspian hydrocarbon province – has made for a keen interest in geopolitics – evident both before and since a communist period when such discussion was obviously taboo (all the more so in view of the abusive way in which Bessarabia was annexed by the Soviet Union in 1940 and again in 1944). Nevertheless Romania was rather slow to join international organisations (apart from the EBRD in 1991). She joined the Central European Initiative in 1996 (after it been started by Austria, Hungary, Italy and the then Yugoslavia in 1989) and CEFTA in 1997, six years after its initial launch. More importantly, after a few years of indecision under governments frequently identified with neo-communism, Romania abandoned any notion of a 'third way' and gave top priority to the twin goals of EU and NATO membership. They were already contemplated when the centre-right government took power in 1998 but they quickly became explicit and have dominated the political scene ever since.

Despite frustrating delays, NATO membership was achieved in 2004 and this book has been completed in anticipation of EU accession at the beginning of 2007. This political orientation has a crucial bearing on the economy both directly, in shaping the ideological approach to a market economy dominated by private enterprise, and indirectly through perceptions of the country's stability and reliability – crucial for foreign investment – arising from its international relations and membership of global organisations. The role of the EU is absolutely fundamental since a critical test of fitness for membership is a 'functioning market economy' (FME) which has required a massive reorganisation, considering that in 1989 the private sector was insignificant, and while privatisation started before EU membership became a key priority the process has been driven forward in recent years by the need to open up all economic sectors including banking, energy and transport to competition linked with private enterprise. The EU also requires social reform to ensure equality and inclusivity so that, once again, the political agenda has been internationalised and some early aberrations – notably an aggressive nationalism projected by reactionary 'protochronists' conditioned by the Ceauşescu years – have been marginalized (albeit with some difficulty) by the modernisers who now control the centre-left as well as the centre-right. The final section of this chapter therefore considers inter-ethnic relations with particular reference to the Hungarian and Roma minorities.

Membership of the European Union

Despite the appeal of a self-indulgent 'protochronism', many Romanians felt that after the wasted years of the early-1990s (discussed in Chapter Five) they had little choice but to respond to the challenge of building economic strength to gain security through EU (and NATO) membership at a time when these organisations were ready for enlargement deep into the former Soviet sphere of influence. Romania signed a trade agreement with the then EC in 1973 before significant assistance arrived through Phare in 1990 (adding up to €1.2bln in the course of the decade). Rather than ignore Romania as what Chen (2003, p. 201) has referred to as "a sadly decrepit irrelevance" with potential for an anti-western backlash, Europe (and the USA) has accepted a moral obligation towards a Latin nation in the Slavonic-Turkish borderlands on the edge of Europe. Romania is by no means a liability given its large size and strategic position which make it an important player in the Danube-Black Sea region; yet progress has been conditioned not only by a weak economy struggling to cope with the forces of globalisation but also by daunting social problems arising from the 'mineriada' syndrome (successive interventions by reactionary Jiu Valley miners as instruments of political pressure and intimidation) and ethnic problems concerning both a marginalised Roma community and a Hungarian minority linked with contested sovereignty over Transylvania which has made for traditionally-strained relations between Romania and Hungary. However, a commercial and economic cooperation agreement with the EC was signed in 1991 followed by additional accords for textiles and wine. A European association agreement in 1995 anticipated the removal of many customs tariffs by 2000 and an application for full membership was made later in the year. Exports to the West were booming by 1996 when more than half Romania's trade was conducted with the EU (especially Germany, Italy, France, UK and The Netherlands). And in the same year the Hungarian treaty cleared the way for serious consideration of both EU and NATO membership.

A minimalist view was expressed when Phinnemore (1998) raised doubts about EU capacity for enlargement beyond a first wave of front runners, with negative implications for Romania given her heavy demands on structural funds and lack of strong backers (though Romanian membership would be in Hungary's interest). The 'Copenhagen criteria' drawn up in 1993 required institutions to guarantee democracy (including judicial and administrative capacity and human rights applied across civil society as a whole and with respect to minority groups, especially the Hungarians and Roma) and FME to cope with competitive pressures and the process of economic and monetary union. The accession process was formally launched in March 1998 at a meeting of foreign ministers from 15 member states (10 ECECs and Cyprus) and negotiations continued until the end of 2004 (with a change of government at the end of 2000). Romania presented the first version of its national programme for adoption of the 'acquis' in March 1998 and revised it in 1999. The accession process began in 2000 on the recommendation of the Helsinki meeting in 1999. From the outset Romania was concerned by EU visa requirements perceived as discriminatory and unhelpful for business links and other activities relevant to integration. But they remained in force for the Schengen area until 2002 because of inadequate border control as well as insufficient internal control on immigration. Romania started imposing restrictive financial requirements for exit visas (funding up to $100/day – up to $500 – plus medical insurance and a return ticket). Meanwhile visas stayed in force in UK 'until borders are placed under strict control' and asylum applications fall significantly, although in 2005 Romania promised to take stronger action against illegal immigrants and criminals who have to be repatriated.

Accession partnerships were formed in 1998: setting out priority areas and providing policy instruments through the extension of Phare (the main programme for building institutions and enhancing economic and social cohesion) from 2000 through the Instrument for Structural Policies for Pre-Accession (ISPA), dealing with environment and transport, and a Special Accession Programme for Agriculture & Rural Development (SAPARD). Following an increased absorption of Phare funds in 1999 when the Regional Development Agencies were set up under the law of 1998 (a significant move towards decentralisation), annual pre-accession funding for 2000-6 was set at €260mln for Phare, €240mln for ISPA and €150mln for SAPARD: a total of €650mln out of a total transfer of EU money of €1.3bln/yr. With information and know-how disseminated through Euro-Info Bucharest and a network of regional offices, such as Euro-Info Baia Mare (for the counties of Bihor, Maramureş, Sălaj and Satu Mare) and 250 sub-centres, these funds provide the opportunity for 'learning by doing' (EPICSDS 2000, p. 107), although assistance was not always used efficiently due to inadequate absorptive capacity (linked with difficulty in securing co-finance which usually had to be borrowed from banks). EU money is also difficult to access, even after an award has been made, when applicants fail to understand all the conditions. Political factors could get in the way of a judicious allocation, highlighted by enquiries from EU ambassador J.Scheele over the failure to implement improvements to infrastructure in Bucharest (arising from feuding between premier Năstase and the General Mayor – T.Băsescu, then leader of the opposition DP – that made the government disinclined to place funds at his disposal). Following accession (scheduled for 2007 as early as 2002) some €11.0bln is available for Romania during the first three years (2007–2009) of which €6.0bln will cover economic modernisation while €4.04bln will be for agricultural support (0.73bln for market measures; 0.88 for direct payments to farmers; and 2.42 for rural development – all phased in gradually with growing absorption capacity) with 0.80bln for domestic policy.

Against the financial injections Romania has had to cope with the contradictory requirements of association "when they (the EU) call for trade liberalisation and specialisation according to comparative advantage, while maintaining a managed protection of sensitive products" – like clothing and steel, but especially agriculture, where "protectionism bears more heavily on the weaker partners" (EPICSDS 2000, p. 105). Moreover "the unpredictability of the EU import restrictions on agricultural goods often means losses even for companies that have exported agricultural products to the EU and have started developing their business": hence losses in dairy products, live animals and other sectors (Ibid, p. 106). Iancu (2000, p.6) was more forthright in referring to "a flagrant contradiction between the economic and social realities of Romania and the economic policies practised under the pressures exerted by IMF and by other international financial bodies". On the one side, the reports of the European Commission in the late 1990s rightly mentioned that Romania could not be regarded as an FME as it was not capable of coping with the competitive pressure and the market forces within the EU. On the other side, the enforcement of the association accord and the conditions imposed by the IMF in granting loans explicitly require that market forces should guide restructuring and orientate decisions of development and specialisation in keeping with the principle of comparative advantage. Paul (1995, p.32) referred to "a cynical paradox" in the international treatment of ECE as a whole, for although the international community wanted the region to integrate into the capitalist world economy, western countries were slow to open their markets to ECE production while opposing limited forms of protection in this area.

Meeting The Copenhagen Criteria

The EU's 1997 Luxembourg meeting agreed on annual 'Country Reports' from the end of 1998; also on 'Accession Partnerships' as the key feature of an enhanced pre-accession strategy 'mobilising all forms of assistance to the candidate countries within a single framework' to meet the Copenhagen criteria. It was stated by the Commission in July 1997 that Romania did not satisfy these criteria and the following year Romania was judged the most backward of all candidate countries, with a second consecutive year of economic decline since the recovery from depression in 1993. The EU has been seen as 'too soft' on Romania through its preoccupation with formal membership criteria while treating election irregularities with only muted criticism: a mechanistic approach that can create self-delusion over the adequacy of a strategy of 'plodding on' towards a goal that may in reality be decades away. But the EU has wisely taken the view that membership should not appear unattainable since it can encourage a frustrated population to toy with neo-fascism, as occurred in the 2001 election when the nationalist V.Tudor became the presidential runner-up. However "the policy of accession to the EU has given an impetus to a kind of over-optimism of the political elite and the public for accelerating their integration into the EU" (EPICSD 2000, p. 99). There has been reliance on centralised government decisions as a driving force – hence "political rhetoric rather than a true understanding of what integration entails" (Ibid, p. 100).

The European Agenda under the Democratic Convention: 1999–2000
It was clear from the start that while Romania was on its way to satisfying the political criteria of membership – with the country's standing set to improve through presidency of the OSCE in 2001 (coming hard on the heels of unequivocal Romanian support of the Kosovo war effort and the Balkan Stability Pact) – the economy would raise many difficulties. Eight large regions – conforming to the EU's statistical requirements – were endowed with regional development agencies and following the previous

'ad hoc' approach there was now more consistency over spatial problems, although the counties remained the highest order units of local government (Figure 4.1). Over social issues, the UNHCR concluded that Romania was no longer to be characterised as a refugee-generating country and that basic standards of human rights were respected. There was a lively and active press although the legal system was seen as needing reform because journalists continued to be sentenced for accusation of slander and offence to the authorities; there was excessive use of custody and pre-trial detention; and degrading treatment of people by the police especially Roma, children, homosexuals and prisoners. In 1999 efforts were acknowledged in the domain of child protection (especially the situation of children in orphanages) while the Jiu Valley demonstrations saw that "the government dealt effectively with public order while respecting the right to strike and demonstrate" (Country Report 1999, p.11). More was needed by way of "rooting out corruption, improving the working of the courts and protecting individual liberties and the rights of the Roma" (Ibid) and while conditions in the penitentiaries were slowly improving (with pressure reduced by the community service option of 1999) they were still below standard and overcrowded. Other criticisms arose over the consistency and capacity in the judicial system and administration, the independence enjoyed by the National Council for Combating Discrimination and the high level of corruption generally. In general terms the capacity of the public administration to implement and manage the 'acquis' was still found to be very limited in 2000, representing "a major constraint in the accession preparations" (Country Report 2000, p. 89). A great burden was imposed because "a group of large and inefficient firms have been allowed to survive with continued support from the state which has not been able to stop them building up very considerable arrears to creditors including workers, utilities and government" (Ibid, p.34). Romania could not be granted FME status, being unable to cope with the competitive pressures of the European market.

The European Agenda under the Năstase Government 2001–2004
Following Bulgaria's success in 2002, Romania made good progress with structural reforms and gained FME status in 2004, thanks to strong growth, low inflation, a small budget deficit (below three per cent) and rising country ratings. There were however shortcomings with regard to subsidies for loss-making industries, tax arrears and poor financial discipline through soft budget constraints; while Craiutu (2004, p. 9) also referred to "weak enforcement of market regulations, low transparency and stability of the regulatory framework". Criticism also highlighted the politicisation of the administration, government control over the judiciary and violence against journalists. Implementation and enforcement capacities were also considered insufficient with regard to border controls, drugs control and the fight against crime and corruption, considered 'severe and widespread' in 2004. Despite a National Anti-Corruption Prosecutor's Office in 2002 and a National Authority for Control, the government was not considered to have any genuine intention to fight corruption despite the negative impact on FDI. These organisations certainly failed to stop the misuse of public money. But concern expressed by the European Parliament and its rapporteur for Romania (Baroness Nicholson) over the alleged trafficking of some of the 60,000 children in the state's care resulted in improved standards in

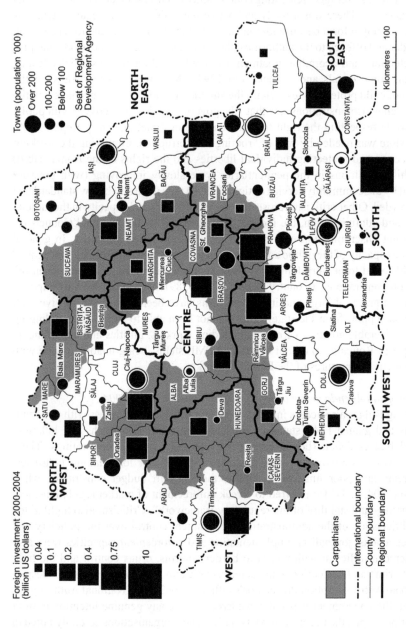

Figure 4.1 Development regions and counties – note towns are named only when different from the county name.

childcare institutions by a National Agency for Child Protection, with integration a national priority in 2001 when more children were placed in foster homes and small institutions (while 54 large care institutions were closed) and more accommodation was provided for homeless and abandoned children. Finally, environment was also a major stumbling block with investment of €20bln required over 20 years to meet EU standards, not to mention insufficient legal expertise at the environment ministry. Transition periods have been sought for all but four directives: 15 years for drinking water quality and urban wastewater; 10 years for landfill and packaging 10 years; eight years for the discharge of dangerous substances, integrated pollution prevention and volatile organic compounds (VOCs) from solvents; seven years for nitrates; five years for large combustion plants; and three years for VOCs from petrol and waste incineration. There was also concern over the Roşia Montană gold project's environmental impact assessment (EIA). It was not impossible that these deficiencies could invoke the safeguard clause of delayed entry where a country is 'manifestly unprepared in an important number of areas' by no means restricted to economics and the internal market.

The European Agenda under the Popescu-Tăriceanu Government 2005–2007
EU pressure was exerted over social legislation (for example, to remove the ban on adult homosexual relations); the independence of the civil service; and aspects of property restitution (given the exclusion of state schools previously owned by Hungarian churches and other buildings seized for official or NGO use, albeit with compensation through treasury bonds). Craiutu (2004, p. 9) also referred to "inefficient public administration and an ineffectual judiciary", the latter a particularly sensitive point after the Constitutional Court threw out the government's reform package for the judiciary in 2005. Meanwhile there was real concern in some quarters that Romania (and Bulgaria) would contribute poverty, corruption and clientelism, as well as the political immaturity reflected (as some saw it) by President Băsescu's support for the USA as well as on-going tensions between the president and his prime minister. Indeed, the EU sent an 'early warning letter' in June 2005 highlighting corruption especially among the border police service – likened to a mafia with officials open to bribery over inadequate documentation or exit (with €500 normally required). Despite dismissal of the Arad border police management in 2005 for irregularities, embarrassing incidents occurred on the Spanish border when Romanian buses were denied entry. There were also efforts to clean up the Anti-Corruption Prosecutor's Office in order to confront the power rings in the counties. Delayed accession until 2008 would not have been very damaging economically, but certainly would have been politically on account of uncertainty. However some Romanians would have favoured an even more gradual accession (banker Ion Tiriac suggested 2010) with resources directed to other economic sectors in the meantime. On the other hand Romania is getting €10bln of financial support over the first three years of accession – for agriculture support (€4.07bln including €2.42bln for rural development), cohesion and structural funding (€5.97bln) and internal policies and administration. However accession in 2007 was certainly President Băsescu's top priority (which has now been achieved) along with Romania's role in NATO and stability in the Balkans and Black Sea region, where Băsescu wants to see more EU and NATO support for

reforms in Georgia and Ukraine to remove totalitarian structures. However although Romania's influence in the region is increasing Russia's position in the energy market remains very strong and the presence of her forces in Transnistria must be taken into consideration.

A defining moment sees the modernists propelling Romania into the EU to take a unique opportunity for sustained economic development and 'catching up', equivalent to the 'big push' anticipated by Rosenstein-Rodan (1943). While Romania is contributing its large area and population and the prospect of a stable outpost beside a restless zone, there is no doubt that Romania needs the EU more than vice versa. Salaries are likely to rise by 1.9 per cent more than the rate of inflation in 2007 while property prices should remain quite buoyant and sustained growth faster than the EU average should come from higher saving and investment (over 30 per cent GDP) linked with FDI. However, openness to global economic space cannot itself ensure economic development and provide a substitute for an economic development strategy and also "a public policy geared to favour the development of human capital and infrastructure" (Dăianu 2002, p. 103). There could be losers among backward industrial sectors such as mining, chemicals and engineering that will mean higher accession costs. And possibly 1,000 food processing units (15 per cent of total sector capacity) will close due to poor hygiene and other failures in meeting standards; while working conditions will have to improve across the board. The national bank sees a great challenge over the next five years in reducing the size of the agricultural sector while boosting services, with a further critical period after 2010 to adopt the Euro. For all its hesitancy, progress over the 'acquis' will be quicker than longer-term restructuring to embrace progressive institutions crucial for responsible public policy and changed mentalities. Even if the economy can be turned around in the next few years Romanian GDP will only reach some 30 per cent of the EU average in 2010. Thirty-five years are needed for Romania (and Lithuania) to catch the weakest EU states: substantially more than Hungary, Poland and Slovenia (20–25 years) and the Czech Republic (10–15), though much less than Albania's 65–75 years! Such is the millstone carried through low technological efficiency and interrupted foreign investment during Soviet domination, which makes the European embrace fundamentally different from the subordination of Romania to the Soviets after the war (Carey 2004a, p. xiii). At the same time, it is likely that the 75 per cent confidence level in the EU (exceeded only by the church) and the lack of strong euro-sceptical currents includes an element of 'blind confidence' and over-optimism based limited information in 2004. Romanians were more sanguine by 2005: half believed that accession would bring short-term disadvantage through price and unemployment rises (hence lower living standards) but two-thirds saw longer term benefits. Meanwhile the government showed great energy in revamping the legal system (under justice minister Monica Macovei); effectively out-pacing Bulgaria on this critical issue. But the government also passed a law on religion laying down a demographic threshold (0.1 per cent of the population: 23,000) and a tiered system involving a 12-year wait for some faiths to achieve the highest status (seem as move to bolster the Orthodox Church over its recently-reconstituted Greek Catholic rival; not to mention Adventists and Jehovah's Witnesses). However Romania is in great need of an updated image which most Europeans still associate with Ceaușescu's communism and the social problems concerning orphaned/homeless children and the Roma community generally.

Membership of the North Atlantic Treaty Organisation

In parallel with the European project Romania sought membership of NATO as further insurance against Russian expansion. Indeed the NATO objective seemed the more achievable of the two and after applying to join in 1996, great efforts were made the following year to gain inclusion in the first wave of ECE membership (with the Czech Republic, Hungary, Poland and Slovenia) after a smooth change of government and the advantage – following the 1996 treaty with Hungary, after the 'Open Skies' agreement of 1991 – of Romania and Hungary sorting out their relations within the alliance. Apart from peacekeeping in Angola, Romania had already participated in the 1991 North Atlantic Cooperation Council – involving NATO, six Central European countries (including Romania) and the Baltic states – and the economic embargo against former Yugoslavia. She regained MFN status in 1992 (after Ceauşescu had given it up) and was also the first country in the region to sign up for the Partnership for Peace in 1994, with application for NATO membership in 1996 and subsequent support for military attacks in Serbia. It seemed important that NATO should expand while Russia was relatively weak, with a cooperative disposition evident through the NATO-Russia 'permanent consulting council' of 1997 and the subsequent 2002 NATO-Russia joint council that led to the accord ending the cold war. It was also suggested that Romania (like Poland) could be a pivotal member of the alliance not only because of active partnership in NATO programmes from the outset, with financial contributions pledged for all activities, but through a well-developed military infrastructure with transport systems offering fast deployment of troops in Central Europe. Romania also offered a substantial arms manufacturing capacity including Romtechnica and Aerofina (supplying missile components of interest to Iraq in 1994–96 and small arms to Rwanda via Yemen in 1997), although much greater integration would be needed. Romania also had good relations with her neighbours in view of progress on the Hungarian front on top of stability – if not enthusiasm – in dealing with Sofia and evident cordiality where Belgrade was concerned.

A strategic location was a strong card in Romania's favour given her position on the Black Sea and Danube, for while the river marks the boundary with Bulgaria and Serbia, the delta lies largely within Romania (including the Sulina Canal which is the main shipping lane). Commercial links with Western Europe first developed through use of the Lower Danube-Black Sea route into the Mediterranean with much capital invested – by both Romania and the Danube Commission – in building up the ports and improving the navigation; but most recently, in connecting the river directly by canal with the Black Sea port of Constanţa. At the same time Russia was still seen as a threat through the logic of expansion towards the Straits that would inevitably mean control over the Lower Danube: a threat that precipitated the Crimean War in the 1850s. The axis remains very important for navigation, with facilities improved by locks (combined with hydropower projects), now that the Rhine-Main-Danube Canal provides a connection between the Black Sea with the North Sea. There is also the potential for oil transfer by pipeline between the Black Sea and the Adriatic following the Danube and its tributaries for most of the way (Celac 1998). Being happy to cooperate with the Caspian zone on the basis of mutual respect, Romania has set up a regular ferry service between Constanţa and Poti in Georgia, reflecting EU support for a Europe-Caucasus-Central Asia Corridor (TRACECA) that will also comprise overland transport from Poti to Baku, a ferry from Baku to Turkmenbashi (Turkmenistan) and overland links with Uzbekistan and Kazakhstan. The Danube is also central to environmental policies for the region in view of the need to conserve wetlands following decades of investment in the dyking and drainage of the floodplain.

Negotiating Membership

The Madrid Summit of 1997 conceded that, with Poland to the north, Romania's inclusion would be strategically and geopolitically advantageous "as the southern anchor of a linchpin that would cement the security alliance territorially and strategically" (Leonard 2000, p. 529). Also a second NATO member state bordering the Black Sea [in addition to Turkey] "would be the West's best tool to help ensure regional stability" (Ibid). But her claims for full membership were supported initially only by the southern members: Greece, Italy, Portugal, Spain and Turkey. Against this there was the scepticism of the USA – also Germany and the UK – about the value of a member state on the southern rim. Moreover, Romania's economic and political difficulties raised questions whether the country could afford to participate in NATO exercises. However President Clinton went to Bucharest in 1997 to say Romania would receive primary consideration in a subsequent evaluation of candidates; probably in 2002 when Romania would need to demonstrate its capability to offer security to the alliance, accelerate progress in the creation of the institutions of a market economy and a stable democracy, and implement civil control over the army. At the same time, NATO would need to decide how far expansion could proceed. Rhein (2000, p.38) expressed the commonly-held view that expansion to the Pacific would make the alliance "unmanageable as a single legal and political area". However, it also seemed reasonable that Romania, along with Finland, the Baltics, Poland and Slovakia, might well mark the eastward limit of feasible growth.

Kosovo and '11 September 2001'

Failure in 1997 was a major disappointment for the Constantinescu presidency considering that the greatest restraint was shown in economic restructuring in order to maintain stability on the domestic front. But efforts continued, with broad public support, to endorse alliance actions while working steadily to enhance Balkan stability, control organised crime and illegal immigration – and continue restructuring while containing the reactionary force of 'mineriada'. There was a damaging incident in 1998 with the departure of the cautious finance minister D.Dăianu who insisted on financial rectitude (to protect the social budget) over a major project for helicopter building and procurement with the American company Bell Helicopters which President Constantinescu was very keen pursue to help get US companies into Romania: he thought that NATO would be impressed if Bell's had a $50mln controlling stake in the Ghimbav (Braşov) factory with capacity for export on top of the 96 helicopters that Romania would buy on national security grounds. But international agencies were not supportive and the deal fell through, although only after Dăianu had been sacked. Meanwhile, Romania contributed to a joint peacekeeping battalion in 1998 and permitted Hungarian troops to cross Romanian territory to reach Kosovo in 1999. But the situation after 11 September 2001 (not without significance for EU membership as well) provided an all-important opening for stronger ties with Washington: Romania became a coalition member over Afghanistan, opening up her airspace and eventually sending forces in 2002. And troops were sent to Iraq when the EU was divided on the issue (though domestic public opinion was not too strongly opposed) while Romania supported the International Criminal Court (ICC), with ratification in 2002 when the EU was clearly opposed; she also reached a bilateral immunity agreement in 2002, pledging not to surrender US citizens to the ICC. Again in 2002 Constanţa was used as a staging post for rotation of US troops operating in the Balkans. All this modified the attitude of the Bush administration leading to the invitation made at Prague in November 2002 for Romania to join the alliance in May 2004; a decision that offered some welcome 'balance' in the context of Hungarian membership of the EU scheduled for the same year.

Military reform has proceeded in accordance with the NATO membership action plan for force reductions from c.100,000 in 1998 to a planned 45,000 when membership was secured in 2004. Romania has also taken firmer control of her frontiers with a border security contract with French/German EADS, which is claimed to be on schedule despite renegotiation in line with proper tendering procedures. Two ITT air traffic control radar systems have been introduced by the Romanian Air Force for precision approach and landing. Links the USA have strengthened with a military presence at Mihail Kogălniceanu near Constanţa (where $20mln was spent in 2003) and Mangalia military port. The USA is placing an army headquarters in the region with forward deployment units comprising a Black Sea depot in Bulgaria and Romania to which brigade-size units (3,000–5,000 troops plus support) will be sent in rotation; reflecting the need to guard against threats in eastern Europe, the Caucasus and Africa. In 2005 an agreement was reached with the USA over forward operating sites – for use by US soldiers preparing for missions – not only at Mihail Kogălnceanu, but also at Babadag, Smârdan (Galaţi) and Cincu (Transylvania): the first case of the permanent stationing of US troops in a former Warsaw Pact country. This has helped to tie Romania to the US-UK-India-Japan axis dedicated to a peaceful China and prevention of despotic régimes, radical groups and nuclear proliferation in the Middle East. In an attempt to damp down irritation within the EU, much the agreement is wrapped up by bland references to access for American personnel, bases for Romanian troops under Romanian command and joint events involving NATO and Partnership for Peace countries. The American orientation has brought some help over flood protection from the USA Army Corps of Engineers helping over flood protection (linked with $5.0mln given to cope with flood damage in 2005) although there was much indignation over an American soldier dealt with very leniently in the USA in a case involving negligent homicide, aggravated by drink, in a Bucharest traffic accident. It came on top of earlier public criticism of support for the US over freedom from extradition to the ICC and reservations on the air strikes in Kosovo (whereas previously the USA always enjoyed great popularity as the potential saviour from communism). The US military has now arrived at Mihail Kogălniceanu – initially 900 men, working up to 1,500 – with Romania a potential launchpad for operations against Iran as well as the organiser of a forthcoming NATO summit.

Cooperation in SEE and Elsewhere

Reference should also be made to an informal political process for cooperation and security in SEE including the defence ministers of Albania, Bulgaria, Croatia, Macedonia, Romania and Slovenia – all Partnership for Peace members – and the NATO states of Greece, Italy, Turkey and USA. The headquarters for Multilateral Forces for Peace in SEE (SEEBRIG) moved to Constanța 2003. In 2005, in connection with zonal cooperation to diminish vulnerability to nuclear/ radioactive attack, Romania is establishing the first European centre for the management of undetected nuclear sources (providing support for the Balkans and Asia). This is linked with the US National Commission for Nuclear Activity and reflects Romania's strategic partnership with the USA. Romania is also becoming the Regional Meteorological Centre for SEE with the mounting of the meteorological radar at Bârnova, near Iași. This follows a lightning detection network installed for the first time in Romania in 2002 and is part of the new integrated national meteorological system (SIMIN) supplying specialised services for units of the national defence, transport and environmental protection ministries. The Băsescu presidency is giving priority to links with the US and UK in the interest of national security and a role for Romania as a bridge between Russia and Euro-Atlantic region. This may imply a shift away from France where the desire for a stronger 'European reflex' from Bucharest is backed by cautionary words that alliance with the US does not mean allegiance! However the embryonic Bucharest-London-Washington axis has evidently attracted some notice in China: not only did Băsescu make an early visit to the Chinese embassy but his communications and IT minister joined with his Hungarian counterpart to encourage China to get more involved in business with both countries. Romania also hopes to do business in Iraq and gradually regain part of the $2.6bln debt arising from construction work in the Ceaușescu era. Over 30 companies are now seeking involvement.

Relations with Neighbouring States and Regions

Hungary

This is a country of great importance because while it provides Romania with her window to the west the relationship is complicated by Budapest's commitment to the Hungarian minority in Transylvania: a community that dominated the Romanians politically before 1918 and has been resentful of its reduced status ever since. The complex historical legacy cannot be forgotten by either side, especially in view of Hitler's partition of Transylvania during 1940–44 and Soviet leanings towards autonomy that led to a Magyar Autonomous Region and thinly-disguised polemics over its subsequent suppression (in 1968) followed by Ceauşescu's policies of assimilation. It was always inevitable that Romania's progress with a Western agenda would require a rapprochement although this was frustrated at first by aggravated tensions in Transylvania in 1990, when Hungarians regained control of some of their institutions and provoked Romanians into launching the 'Vatra Românească' nationalist movement. Chauvinistic elements lobbied world opinion over the vexed question of autonomy while initially the West did little to discourage what was in effect an anti-Hungarian Bucharest-Bratislava-Belgrade axis at the start of the 1990s. Fortunately OSCE and CoE influence exercised a moderating influence leading to a strategic partnership with Hungary under the 1996 treaty of mutual understanding, good neighbourliness and cooperation signed in Timişoara. This has proved a model for the region, with a mixed governmental commission to oversee implementation. Military relations are good, with joint manoeuvres following the 'Open Skies' agreement of 1991. A Hungarian consulate was reopened in Cluj-Napoca in 1997, followed by an honorary consulate in Constanţa. The situation was also transformed by the consistent foreign policy developed substantially by Adrian Severin in 1997. The Romanian-Hungarian partnership is now seen as the core of the process of consolidating security in SEE, acting as a link in the Euro-Atlantic security architecture of which both countries are now members. But until Romania's position was secure, the Kosovo experience raised the spectre of Hungarians in Romania pushing for autonomy with NATO intervention if the Romanian unitary state reasserted itself. There was also some controversy over the Hungarian Status Law 2001 giving Hungarians in neighbouring countries 'certificates of nationality' (effectively national identity cards) to maintain cultural/linguistic identity and extend economic/social rights (medical and pension benefits and the right to work in Hungary for three months each year). Although designed to give diaspora elements some help through temporary work in Hungary that might deter them from migrating permanently, Romanians saw the extra-territorial nature of the law as a form of colonialism. Eventually ethnic Romanians were also made eligible for three-month work concessions (while the total number allowed to work temporarily was limited to 81,000 in 2002) and Hungary undertook not to assist ethnic Hungarian political organisations in Romania. Moreover identity cards were only issued on Hungarian territory to avoid encroachment on Romanian sovereignty. Consequently In 2005 premier Tăriceanu was able to meet his Hungarian counterpart (F.Gyurcsány) and agree that Romanian-Hungarian relations had moved beyond litigious issues to common European development projects.

Cross Border Cooperation (CBC)
Although seen initially by conservatives as a launching pad for Hungarian imperialism, progress with CBC is most marked on the Hungarian frontier where the elimination of tension has produced an investment boom in Banat (whereas by contrast Romania's North East struggles to attract investment and enterprise). It is a mature industrial region, for the expansion of engineering, supported by the iron and steel of Reşiţa, was reflected in urban expansion, early electrification, the growth of a relatively dense railway network and the emergence of food processing

industries (based mainly on the rich agriculture of the Banat Plain) before the First World War. The capacity of the Reşiţa metallurgical and engineering complex to act as a mother factory, stimulating a series of transfers of production to new locations, also indicates the high level of experience and skill. But it is also apparent that Habsburg colonisation of Banat involved diverse ethnic groups that greatly extended a cultural profile based on earlier contacts between Romanians and Hungarians. Although not the region with the largest non-Romanian population, Banat must be area with the largest number of different non-Romanian ethnic groups. And it is apparent that the emphasis has been predominantly on tolerance and mutual respect to the point where all contributions could be valued as parts of the region's economic and cultural identity. Nationalism has not significantly detracted from the positive role of ethnicity for the human resources of the region. Research on 'family strength in Romania' undertaken at Lincoln, Nebraska (Asay 1998) reports how the community in Giarmata ('German town') still retains customs associated with the former German inhabitants even though the present population is overwhelmingly Romanian. And it is this element of pluralism in the regional culture that links Romania with the core of Europe rather than with the Balkans with its struggles for more exclusive ethnic identities. There is also a certain momentum for international cooperation through the history of Banat and although the infrastructure has been damaged through the closed frontiers of communism (preventing direct journeys between Novi Sad, Szeged and Timişoara) the special relationship between Ceauşescu and Tito led to a measure of CBC through local traffic regimes and collaboration between enterprises.

The Danube-Criş-Mureş-Tisa Euroregion   On top of the increasing permeability of borders in general since 1989 is an encouragement for the development of further cross-border institutions concerned with all aspects of the life of the region. Modernisation is evidently facilitated through forwarding companies exporting into Romania from Hungary; facilitated by the growth of cross-border institutions (such as Chambers of Commerce & Industry: CCIs) encouraged by the existence of Euroregions (Batt 2002a, 2002b). This is bound to enhance the experience and efficiency of regional planning and promotion. However, the problems of restructuring are plainly complex and progress can only be sustained if a willingness to reprofile production and boost efficiency is complemented by an inflow of funds and know-how from international financial institutions and foreign direct investment. Romania's West Region has done relatively well with a range of new international links as well as intensification of contacts established in the context of the planned economy; while the development organisations established with help from the German 'Land' of Nordrhein-Westfalen have contributed momentum to the work of the larger region which began work in 1999. Regional strategies have now been elaborated to continue the diversification process – through light industry and ecotourism – while the concept of less-favoured areas (applied in the sense of high unemployment linked with the reorganisation of the mining industry in the Jiu Valley and three areas of Caraş-Severin) is a vehicle for additional financial assistance. The West Region should do well in the future in view of its human resources and infrastructure. There are signs that locations closer to Western Europe are finding it increasingly difficult to supply the labour required by foreign investors and the result may be a diversion of capital further south and east, as is already evident in Hungary. The region is evidently seen as attractive by young people in other parts of Romania, while migrants who have departed for Western Europe in recent years may in some cases be in a position to steer investments in this direction given their own awareness of Banat's stability and business record; not to mention the position of the region on the European transport corridors, including the Danube: offering local circulation by water through a revived Bega Canal to Timişoara which is the West Region's gateway city.

The Balkans

Under communism Romania necessarily maintained close relations with Bulgaria (her Comecon and Warsaw Pact neighbour) and the two 'non-aligned' socialist states in the region: Albania and Yugoslavia. There was particular cordiality in the case of Yugoslavia in the Ceauşescu-Tito era with collaboration over the Iron Gates navigation and power project as well as the engineering and petrochemical industries. But Romania's multilateralism also produced close links with Greece and Turkey. Hence there were no major outstanding problems to be faced after 1989: only the dilemma created by war in Yugoslavia. Although Romania felt obliged to support UN sanctions imposed in 1992, substantial quantities of oil were smuggled across the Danube. This was partly a small-scale affair involving private motorists (sometimes with specially enlarged petrol tanks fitted to their vehicles) transferring fuel to fishermen in villages like Pescari in the Moldova Nouă area who would then rendezvous with their Serb opposite numbers in mid-river during the night (Light et al. 2000). New petrol stations were opened in the area with a total capacity going way beyond normal local requirements and lax border security certainly helped to enrich the fishing communities judging by some dramatic improvements in the housing stock. But large-scale contravention arose through the close links between the petrochemical industries in Pančevo and Timişoara (Solventul). The Romanian government claimed it had no knowledge, which then implicated elements in the intelligence service standing to make fortunes by selling feedstocks at five times the market price.

Seeking Regional Cooperation

With peace now restored in the West Balkans following the violent break-up of Yugoslavia and chaos in Albania, Romania has done her best to help stabilise the region knowing that this will strengthen her own security and also accelerate the flow of foreign capital. However, while committed to the Balkan stabilisation process Romania clearly wants regional cooperation within the mainstream of Euro-Atlantic evolution. And she is not alone in retaining greater faith in wider European institutions than in organisations confined to the region. Cooperation also arises through the Southeast European Cooperative Initiative (SECI) was launched in 1996 to strengthen regional cooperation, economic development and political reform as the basis for integration into European and broader Western structures particularly with regard to border structures, energy and environmental protection (Clement 2000, p. 82). This is not primarily an assistance programme but a means of coordinating region-wide planning, although there is economic and financial assistance to support the modernisation of the local private sector and increase the involvement of the private sector in regional economic and environmental efforts. The initiative includes all the countries from Croatia and Romania in the north to Greece and Turkey in the south (though Croatia is only an observer-participant). Since 1996 there have been ministerial conferences on stability, security and cooperation; while in 1998 Albania, Bulgaria, Macedonia, Romania and Turkey – later joined by Greece – agreed a multinational Balkan rapid reaction force. Since the Kosovo War of 1999 this stability framework has been strengthened and SECI is now situated within a wider initiative known as the Stability Pact for Southeastern Europe, embracing Albania, Bosnia & Hercegovina, Croatia and Macedonia along with the two (then) EU candidate countries of Bulgaria and Romania. Serbia initially rejected the offer of observer status but later became a full member along with Moldova and Montenegro. The aim is a shared cooperation strategy for stability and growth in association with the EU although there are no independent financial resources or structures for implementation.

A Regional Environmental Reconstruction Programme RERP was launched in January 2000, to improve environmental monitoring and project preparation and enhance regional cooperation of the kind currently evident at Lake Ohrid and Lake Prespa. There is also emphasis on raising awareness among civil society and realising priority national and local projects such as the reopening of the Danube shipping lane which was initially scheduled for 2000 (after the Pact's Economic Development Working Group approved the RERP) but was actually delayed until 2002. Romania's economic losses through the Kosovo War – estimated at $2.0mln daily – were incurred largely from the interruption of trade through the blockage of the Danube at Novi Sad: over 100 barges and 15 tugboats were stranded to the north, while 60 vessels were left on the lower river with commodities for Hungary, Austria and Germany. There were also losses at Constanța due to reduced transit, while extra rail transport was needed between Drobeta-Turnu Severin and Hungarian ports to avoid the Serbia so that Romanian boats stuck north of the blockage could be reloaded. Transport modernisation is another important outcome, with much importance attaching to the Calafat-Vidin bridge between Romania and Bulgaria which offers an alternative route to Thessaloniki. It is longer than the usual way through Serbia and Macedonia – and is generally in a poorer condition – but there is an urgent need for an alternative, including measures to upgrade road quality and security (to cut down on bribery) and a joint Bulgarian-Romanian customs régime to reduce border waiting time. It seems that agreement has been complicated in the past by the question of finance since the route is seem as a particular benefit to Bulgaria, in view of Romania's preference for a second bridge at Giurgiu or else a crossing at Turnu Măgurele which is also convenient for Bucharest. The new route is part of a coordinated group of projects (supported by the EIB) that also include the Bucharest-Constanța motorway; the Bucharest-Constanța and Bucharest-Giurgiu railway upgrades, the Constanța LPG facility and work concerned with Danube ecology and navigation.

A Danube Cooperation Process was also promoted in 2001 as a joint initiative of Austria and Romania, launched at a meeting of foreign ministers in Vienna in May 2001. This creates a political impetus for cooperation not just in environmental/biodiversity and navigation matters but also through CBC and cultural programmes lining up with EU regional policies. Austria and Romania cooperated by hosting preliminary meetings in 2001 in anticipation of a summit in 2002 after the cleaning-up in Serbia. Romania also took the initiatives of hosting – at Mangalia in July 2000 – an international seminar on the reconstruction of security and confidence in the Balkan region, organised by the Institute for Political Defence Studies & Military History (Romania) and the Institute for National Strategic Studies of the Washington National Defence University. Romania also participates in the Organisation of Black Sea Economic Cooperation that started in 1999 – with a Black Sea Trade & Development Bank and coordination centre – after the initial framework cooperation in 1992. She also supports an Inter-Balkan & Black Sea Business Centre established at Thessaloniki (Greece) in 2000 to assist business in the region, with networking across a region extending from Albania, Macedonia and Serbia to Bulgaria, Turkey and a bloc of former Soviet republics: Moldova, Russia, Ukraine and the three Caucasian republics. Cooperation with the Caucasus (and Central Asia) is also developing through TRACECA. Romania was involved with a somewhat smaller grouping of countries from this area when the first meeting of the Association of Chambers of Commerce & Industry of the Black Sea Region was held in 1997. Finally Romania is also associated with a Private Enterprise Partnership for SEE established by IFC to provide technical assistance and advisory programmes for private sector development, especially through PPPs.

The East

Romania's eastern border extends over 2,070kms and seems destined to be the EU's longest external border after accession. It is estimated that some 4,500 policemen will be needed for border control, which includes land borders with Moldova and Ukraine as well as the Black Sea coast, and substantial funding has been provided (€560mln in 2004) to reinforce border security with Moldova and Ukraine, as well as Serbia. In 2002 in return for automatic visa access to the EU (apart from non-Schengen states) Moldovans and Ukrainians were no longer able to enter Romania freely. Indeed visas were required for citizens of Ukraine (as well as Russia and Turkey) in 2004 and were imposed on Moldova in 2007. However there is a balance to maintain. The EU and NATO need to be much involved given the danger from separatist movements in South Ossetia and Transnistria, the prevalence of organised crime including drug smuggling and the danger of mafia groups taking power. On the other hand Romania is poised to play a Black Sea role with Bulgaria and Turkey and there is certainly potential for progress with Georgia, Moldova and Ukraine expressing 'western' options. CBC activities are modest by comparison with the Hungarian border but Romania has ethnic minority interests across the Ukrainian border in Herta and Slatina, north of Dorohoi and Sighet respectively, and transport links have been improved in both cases by roads and bridges and (in the latter case) by local rail services. A bilateral treaty with Ukraine was signed in 1997 while negotiations over land and sea border delimitation were completed in 2003 with resolution of the Serpent Isle dispute – significant in the context of Black Sea oil and gas reserves – in Ukraine's favour. In 2007 a new bridge over the Tisa between Sighet and Slatina (Solotvino), where the population is 60 per cent Romanian, was inaugurated by the two presidents and a substantial amount of traffic has passed with the frontier issue now reduced to financial matters relating to visa charges and local taxes. Although visa formalities are in force Romanians living in the border area can obtain visas valid for a year (with no limit on the number of visits) at a cost of $20 –half the usual amount, which is good business when food and cigarettes are much cheaper in Ukraine and €purchases worth up to €175 has to be brought home each time!

Romania does not have a common frontier with Russia which narrows the scope for disagreement but relations remain soured by the dispute over 90t of gold (from the Romania's central bank) that disappeared in Tsarist Russia during the First World War; while other irritations arise from the lack of Russian investment (perhaps a matter of ambivalence in view of the element of Russophobia arising from the economic stake of Lukoil in Romania, including control of the Petrotel refinery) and custom regulations affecting Romania's trade that have to be seen in the context of a huge imbalance since Russia exports to Romania 18 times what it imports. Debts arising over the Soviet-era Dolinskaya iron ore enrichment project are also unresolved. These difficulties have frustrated a new basic treaty with Russia to follow after the 1991 treaty at the end of the Soviet era. Negotiations with Russia over a friendship and cooperation treaty 'continue' but while the two countries could certainly do various things together, such as arms production for sale to third countries, policy is driven by Băsescu's ideas for Black Sea democracy that may have to struggle for fulfillment given that the EU seems to have little to offer both V.Voronin's Moldova and Yuzenko's Ukraine, both tilting towards the CIS. Although Russia is taking a positive attitude towards Black Sea ferries and the proposed energy grid, the sensitive situation could encourage her not to comply with the Conventional Forces in Europe Agreement and keep forces in Transnistria, Abkhazia and South Ossetia. Meanwhile there are prospects for economic cooperation through organisations such as the Association of Chambers of Commerce of the Black Sea Region which held its first meeting 1997.

Moldova

Following the break-up of the FSU, Romania sought very close links with Moldova in anticipation of a possible reunion (as had occurred previously in 1918) but strong opposition from non-Romanian groups especially in the Turkish (Gaugaz) area around Cahul and the strongly Russified strip along the Nistru imposed an effective veto, especially in view of the Russian army occupation of the latter area that gives any government in Chişinău a primary interest in regaining control of its territory. Moreover independence gives Chişinău the status of a European capital, although the language – officially 'Moldovan' – is hardly different from Romanian apart from the Cyrillic script still found in parts of Transnistria. There has been substantial Romanian aid under a good neighbourly strategy that covers television, education and training. A Romanian government fund for relations with Moldova assisted economic projects like the Faleşti tubemill that opened in 1996 with cooperation from the Tepro mill in Iaşi, while an agreement on the Prut fishery was reached in 2004 on the occasion of 25th anniversary of the completion of Stânca-Costeşti hydro project. Indeed there is a continuing integration process evident in such areas as transport and telecommunications. There are quite regular high level meetings (Băsescu's first foreign visit was to Chişinău) and Moldova receives considerable political support e.g. over membership of the Stability Pact in 2000 and contacts with the EU (Baleanu 2000).

EU Activity in Moldova involves a delegation in Chişinău, with a special representative posted in 2005 to help resolve the Transnistria problem which has given rise to organised crime, corruption and the trafficking of drugs and weapons as well as women and illegal migrants. The approach is through political and economic reform to make Moldova a more attractive state for Transnistria to join and while this requires political and economic reform is also includes trade links with EU agreed in 2004 (with openings for Moldovan textiles and agricultural products while the home market remains protected for up to seven years). Since Yuzenko's election Ukraine has been keen to help prevent smuggling (including illegal Transnistrian exports through Odessa) by establishing a joint Moldovan-Ukrainian customs post in the province. However the situation is highly complicated with the persistence of Soviet-era politics lacking real debate or pluralism and with the rural areas effectively 'blind'. The communist leader Voronin has recreated Soviet-style districts ('raions') with centralised local administration subordinate to national government in defiance of the CoE principle of independent authorities. With no possibility of free and fair elections, given the role of TeleRadio Moldova, Voronin's flirtation with the EU seems highly opportunistic especially since he appeared to be on the verge of joining a Russia-Belarus union until Russia's President Putin backed his rival Smirnov. The Transnistria problem remains difficult with the 1999 agreement for a Russian withdrawal effectively reversed by the 2003 'Kozak Memorandum' drafted by Moscow to legitimise a 25-year military presence and give Transnistria a veto over Moldovan foreign policy. Clearly if Moldova maintains close links with Brussels (and Washington) Russian troops in the province on a permanent basis will not be acceptable but the oppressive elite in Tiraspol (the Transnistian 'capital') remains obdurate. Indeed it now seems that Transnistria has given up on any deal with Moldova along the lines of a federation or confederation while Voronin has responded to Băsescu's appeals to Europe – not to forget a country that was handed over the Soviet Union in 1940 – with polemics castigating Bucharest for the neglect of its entire northeastern borderland (presumably reflecting alarm over the danger of further out-migration if Moldovans gain entry to the EU through the issue of Romanian passports – assuming this does not contravene EU immigration policy).

Ethnic Issues on the Domestic and International Fronts

Although not always seen as a conventional political issue, the ethnic minorities have been central to Romania's progress in the international community since 1989. Despite the emigration of many Germans, Romania had a total minority population of 2.28mln (10.5 per cent) in 2002 – compared with 2.40mln (10.9 per cent) in 1992 – consisting of over 30 groups. However, all but eight involve populations of less than 20,000 that cumulatively account for 3.5 per cent of the total for all minorities. The larger groups in descending order are Hungarians (1,431.8th or 62.8 per cent), Roma (535.1th or 23.5 per cent), Ukrainians (61.1th or 2.7 per cent), Germans (59.8th or 2.6 per cent), Russians, including Lipovans (35.8 per cent or 1.6 per cent), Turks (32.1th or 1.4 per cent), Tatars (23.9th or 1.0 per cent) and Serbs (22.6 per cent or 1.0 per cent). With most groups there are few problems, although in the case of Jews (today numbering fewer than 6,000) there was not only discrimination in history, including a Romanian contribution to the holocaust (through the Iaşi pogrom in 1940 and subsequent atrocities in Transnistria) since the period immediately after 1989 saw "a guilt complex felt by some Romanians over their acquiescence or collusion with the communist régime exploited by the ultranationalists" (Dăianu 2004, p. 400) so that in 1990 the headquarters of the Jewish community in Braşov was attacked and in 1992 the government had to express its 'deep concern' over anti-Semitism, although the situation has since improved. However the aspirations of the Hungarians remain difficult to satisfy and this group is not only large but crucial for good international relations since the 'mother country' is a neighbouring state and also an EU member. Problems also arise in the case of Roma citizens for whom the official figure is way below CoE estimates of 1.5–2.5mln because the majority choose not to declare themselves. While many Roma elements are traditionally well-integrated, with the additional benefit of recent legislation, others have attracted EU attention to their marginalisation that is unacceptable in an inclusive society where human rights should be extended to all. However although minority rights promised after 1989 were not immediately delivered (due to concern that autonomy might encourage secession in the case of Hungarians) there have been many positive developments. The 1991 constitution certainly meets the international standard of minority protection, with a right to identity and to education in mother tongue, and integration into the European Council (1993). The ethnic issue has been handled with some skill and nationalism has been countered by a reduced perception of threat arising from access to the EU and the path to European integration. In this way the state has been strong enough to shoulder the risks of decentralisation.

The Election Law of 1992

The Election Law of 1992 gave minorities over-representation, though specific groups must get 5.0 per cent of the votes needed for a regular parliamentary seat (1,300–1,500 votes but varying from one election to another). Ethnic education is based on the 1995 legislation, revised by decree in 1997 and approved by parliament in 2000, repealing the requirement that geography and history should be taught in Romanian (provided Romanian names for places and persons are used). Provision comes in three categories: (a) mother-tongue education is provided in ethnic schools or departments for: Hungarians (2,437), Germans (273), Slovaks (41), Serbs (32), Ukrainians (20), Czechs (seven), Croatians (five), Turks/Tartars (four) and Bulgarians (one); (b) mother-tongue education is provided in Romanian schools for Poles, Roma and Russian-Lipovans; while (c) there are no facilities – but no claims either – in the case of Albanians, Armenians, Greeks, Italians and Jews. In line with the accession partnership (1999), amendments to the education law give national minorities the right to education in their mother tongue at all levels, with state universities even a possibility (Table 4.1). At present some five per cent of educational units teach in a minority language, usually Hungarian (though six other languages are involved, while a total of 15 minority languages are used in schools teaching basically in Romanian). Meanwhile a statute of 1991 on local administration, revised by decree 1996 and confirmed by the Local Administration Act in 2001, provided for the use of mother tongue in local government where a minority exceeds 20 per cent (with translators provided by the town hall if necessary). Also signage referring to placenames and public facilities is required, and councils use a minority language if councillors representing a particular minority account for at least a third of all councillors: this affects Hungarians (in 1,071 local government areas), Roma (112), Ukrainians (57), Russians-Lipovans (15), Turks (eight), Poles and Slovaks (six) and Tartars (three). In 1996 a Department for the Protection of National Minorities was set up, with a specific office for Roma while the Ministry for Public Information established state offices for inter-ethnic relations and for Roma communities. On the whole regulation until 1996 was merely 'adequate', while the years 1997–2000 created a sound basis for the education system and the use of minority languages within the administration. Thus the ethnic issue has moved a long way from the emotional to the pragmatic level but it can still be a highly sensitive matter and even among young students ingrained nationalist pride can generate intolerance. However nationalists routinely criticise new innovations – like the minority status law and its provision of a Cultural Autonomy Council, while there is much indignation (with calls for sanctions) over the criminality associated with Roma citizens abroad and traditionally biased attitudes persist towards HIVs and gays,

Hungarians

Hungarians everywhere have an understandable sense of nostalgia for the pre-1918 territorial arrangements that Romanians can scarcely even acknowledge as a historical fact for fear of offering some concession over sovereignty. Yet undue sensitivity inhibits mature consideration of the Hungarian minority's claim for autonomy and serves to fortify the platform of chauvinists in Budapest who are naturally resented by Romanians. The Hungarian minority is not poor and is not the target of discrimination; indeed the population is traditionally industrious and capable of sustaining its own SMEs and larger businesses. However, it is mindful of the better material condition of Hungarians in Hungary proper and seeks cultural autonomy notwithstanding the threat to sovereignty posed in the eyes of Romanians. Such a threat might well be diminished by concessions that Hungarian opinion would see as a positive contribution to softening the perceived injustice of the Treaty of Trianon that dismantled the imperial state. Pomogats (1997) sees a century-long struggle that must surely succeed in the long run. The origins lie in the Hungarian surrender of Transylvanian autonomy to Budapest in 1867: a mistake that Hungarians failed to rectify through decentralisation pre-1914. Romanians then failed to allow autonomy in the inter-war period (the Hungarian university in Cluj transferred to Szeged in 1919) but equally Hungary failed to grant autonomy for Romanians in North Transylvania in 1941 (when Cluj's Romanian university sought refuge in Sibiu). In 1946 the Hungarians gained their own university side by side with the Romanian institution that now returned to the city, but lost its separate existence in 1959 (whereupon the Hungarian scholarly elite began to emigrate to Hungary or the West with the tacit approval of the Romanian government). There was also a theatre, opera house and radio station opened in Cluj for Hungarians; along with Hungarian schools, newspapers, cultural groups and publishing houses were provided along

Table 4.1: Provision in minority languages at Romanian universities and high schools c.1995

County Town	University Provision	High School Provision
Alba Iulia		Hun
Arad		Ger, Hun, Slo
Baia Mare		Hun*
Bistriţa		Hun*
Braşov		Ger#, Hun#
Bucharest	Alb, Arm, Bul, Cro, Cze, Ger, Grk, Itn Rus, Srb, Slo, Trk, Ukr, Yid	Bul*, Ger, Hun
Cluj-Napoca	Cze, Ger, Hun, Rus, Slo	Ger*, Hun#
Constanta	Ger, Rus	
Craiova	Ger, Rus	
Deva		Hun*
Iaşi	Ger, Rus	
Miercurea Ciuc		Hun#
Oradea	Ger, Rus	Hun#
Satu Mare		Hun#
Sfântu Gheorghe		Hun#
Sibiu	Ger	Ger#, Hun*
Targu Mureş	Hun	Hun*
Timişoara	Cro, Cze, Ger, Rus	Bul*, Ger, Hun#, Srb
Zalău		Hun#

Other places (villages italicised) with high school provision: Aiud (Hun), Bălan (Hun*), *Band* (Hun*), Baraolt (Hun*), Carei (Hun*), Cehu Silvaniei (Hun*), Covasna (Hun*), Corund (Hun), *Crasna* (Hun*), Dej (Hun*), Gheorgheni (Hun#), Gherla (Hun*), Huedin (Hun*), *Joseni* (Hun), *Livada* (Hun*), Luduş (Hun*), Lugoj (Ger*, Hun*), Marghita (Hun*), Mediaş (Ger*, Hun*), Moldova Nouă (Srb), Nădlac (Slo), Odorheiu Secuiesc (Hun#), *Pecica* (Hun*), Petroşani (Hun*), Reghin (Hun*), Rupea (Hun*), Săcele (Hun#), Sebeş(Ger*), *Săcuieni* (Hun*), Salonta (Hun*), *Sânmartin* (Hun), Sighetul Marmaţiei (Hun*, Ukr), Sighişoara (Ger*, Hun*), Şimleu Silvaniei (Hun*), Sovata (Hun*), Târgu Secuiesc (Hun#), Târnaveni (Hun*), Taşnad (Hun*), Topliţa (Hun*), Turda (Hun*), Valea lui Mihai (Hun*), Vlăhiţa (Hun)

Alb Albanian; Arm Armenian; Bul Bulgarian, Cro Croatian; Cze Czech; Ger German; Grk Greek; Hun Hungarian; Itn Italian, Rus Russian, Srb Serbian, Slo Slovak, Trk Turkish, Ukr Ukrainian, Yid Yiddish
*dedicated section within a high school; # ditto in addition to a dedicated high school

Source: Buza & Ianoş 1997 p.7

with a theatre, opera house and radio station (all in Cluj). Soviet 'autonomous area' policies maintained a 'Magyar Autonomous Region' until 1968 but this did not amount to genuine self-government while Ceauşescu went on to undermine Hungarian educational and cultural institutions. Village 'systematisation' was seen as a great threat, although there was no radical implementation, but the dispersal of young professionals certainly denuded remoter Hungarian communities of talented people needed to defend their interests effectively. Meanwhile most Romanians could not understand how charges of discrimination could arise from legislation applicable equally to all Romanian citizens, although it was widely believed that restrictions imposed in 1973 on foreign visitors using private accommodation (limited to very close relatives) was a measure calculated to limit contact between Hungarians in Hungary and their kinfolk in Transylvania.

Revolution
Revolution brought reassuring noises from the NSF and Hungarians quickly regained control of their institutions (while some Romanians posted in Hungarian communities – through the 'stagiatura' system of labour direction for new graduates – went back home). However the rapid formation of a Democratic Alliance of Hungarians sent a 'disquieting message' to Romanians (Gallagher 1992, p.573) and when teaching in Hungarian was restored in Cluj-Napoca and Târgu Mureş at the beginning of 1990 there was resentment over the removal of some Romanian pupils from these institutions. This provoked an immediate Romanian counter-offensive through 'Vatra Românească' "playing on mistrust of Hungarian motives, fear of Hungarian revanchism, concern about an erosion of Romanian dominance in Transylvania and general unease about the economic future" (Dăianu 2004 p. 402). The movement attracted support from both professionals and Moldavian migrant workers who did not qualify for land restitution. Hence the 'vicious linguistic spiral' of 1989–95 when Hungarian pleas for autonomy were balanced by Romanian nationalist calls for reaffirmation of the country's unitary character. There were riots in Târgu Mureş in March 1990 when Romanian villagers were bussed in to 'stop the Hungarians taking Transylvania' (Rady 1992, p. 155). Further controversy arose with the autonomy plans of of the Democratic Union of Hungarians in Transylvania (DUHT) in 1993-4: J.I.Csapo's 'Statute of Personal Autonomy for the Hungarian Ethnic Community in Romania' was opposed by the 'Funar phenomenon', involving a prominent Romanian nationalist leader in local government in Cluj who entered national politics as a leading figure in the Party of Romanian National Unity (PRNU) sustained by the insecurity of semi-urbanised peasant workers. Funar was marginalised in 1996 but regained the position of mayor during 2000–2004 and orchestrated the party's parliamentary activities from the town hall.

The OSCE Contribution Of course the government's panderings towards nationalism initially ruled out the possibility of alliances between the DUHT and Romanian parties. But President Iliescu normalised relations with Hungary during 1995–96 leading to a basic treaty allowing 'adequate possibilities' for education in minority languages. An important role was played by Max van der Stoel (OSCE High Commissioner on National Minorities) as both the CoE and OSCE pushed the idea of minority rights during 1993–96 and Iliescu made integration into Euro-Atlantic institutions a priority. This arose out of CoE membership for Romania 1993 that provided for regular monitoring of human rights until early 1997. Thereafter further progress was encouraged by influence from the EU and NATO as well as NGOs such as the Princeton N.J.-based 'Project on Ethnic Relations' (with an office in Bucharest as early as 1991). Hence the centre-right Democratic Convention of Romania (DCR) brought the Hungarians into government in 1997 to boost EU/NATO prospects and foreign minister Adrian Severin built solid links with Hungary in 1997. However prime minister Ciorbea was over-hasty in agreeing to a discrete Hungarian section at the Babeş-Bolyai University in Cluj: a storm of local opposition caused the plan to be watered down to a Hungarian language institution elsewhere in Transylvania; an idea that resurfaced as a Hungarian-German 'Petöfi-Schiller' university from 1998 until the plan was formally rejected in 2006. A further stumbling block was the education law of 1995 stipulating that history, geography and civic education should not be taught in nominally independent Hungarian institutions; but after amendments extending the scope of minority languages (including the possibility of state universities for minorities), the 1999 'Country Report' recognised continued efforts to respect and protect the rights of the Hungarian minority.

DUHT Cooperation with the Party of Social Democracy (PSD) during 2001–2004
This brought further concessions for Hungarians – for example, policemen speaking minority languages were to be recruited where the minority exceeded 20 per cent; more consistent state support was given to churches; broadcasting facilities improved; and cultural facilities were provided through Hungarian language groups at the agronomic institute and music academy in Cluj as well as the Technical University and the Medicine & Pharmacy University in Târgu Mureş; also a Hungarian language department and chair at Babeş-Bolyai University in Cluj; and more industrial parks in minority areas along with school reorganisation and decentralisation. However the establishment of specific public universities with teaching in Romanian, Hungarian and German remained controversial. During the election in 2004, when there was a chance of a further centre-left PSD victory dependent on Hungarian votes, the independent newspaper 'Evenimentul Zilei' saw a pro-PSD DUHT trying to stifle other Hungarian groups in order to further its goal of Hungarian autonomy. Its leaders (including local power-broking 'bulibashas') were seeking rewards including jobs for their families while Hungarian vice-premier Marko Bela appeared to develop the pretensions of a media baron through his own TV station in Târgu Mureş. However the presidential election transformed the DUHT into supporters of a centrist alliance and although most people now think that relations between Hungarians and Romanians are better than before 1989, there are economic and cultural issues outstanding. More employment in Hungarian majority areas is needed to discourage the young from leaving their east Transylvanian 'reservations' in despair while a Hungarian university – refused on the grounds of multiculturalism – is needed for the many students from communities in eastern Transylvania who remain strongly traditional and do not associate with Romanians (indeed they are hardly bilingual). Rhetoric can still be provocative as in 2006 when Jozsef Csapo's Szekler National Council convened a rally in Odorheiul

Secuiesc to coincide with Hungary's national day (15 March) to declare autonomy for 'Szeklerland' with protection by a Szekler Legion ('Legio Siculis') as the prelude to a Kosovo-type solution. The Romanian nationalist leader V.Tudor threatened a counter-rally and the Romanian-majority Toplița area said it would secede from Harghita county (with its Hungarian majority). Fortunately President Băsescu defused the situation and Hungarian objectives were toned down to emphasise the 'ultimate' desire of autonomy for Covasna and Harghita counties and the minority Romanians in these counties now have a rival 'Forum Civic al Românilor' opposing autonomy for 'Ținut Secuiesc'.

Roma

The most intractable problem in the quest for a more cohesive society and labour market concerns the Roma, clearly marginalised but arguably as much through their own insistence on an unconventional roaming lifestyle as through active exclusion by mainstream society restricting them to the poorest residential areas ('mahalele'). The Roma outlook is based on a survival culture through a long history of feudal subjection bordering on slavery, but the interwar years saw a move towards integration and Roma newspapers started to appear: 'Glasul Romilor' in Bucharest and 'Timpul' in Craiova; while Roma personality G.A.Lazurica started a national 'Uniunea Generală a Romilor' in 1933. But progress went into reverse in 1941 when the Antonescu régime marginalised undesirable minorities and organised a massive deportation of Roma to Transnistria, copying the radical German Nazi wartime solution to 'Zigeunerplage' or Gypsy plague. Despite equality under the law, the Roma were neglected under communism through half-hearted assimilation: there was no specific education in their mother tongue, they did not benefit from land reform and no Roma union or independent organisation could be tolerated. Although there was strong pressure to settle, integration policies (for example, from 1977–83) were inadequately resourced and most Roma could do little better than take unskilled work in the factories and cooperative farms while occupying 'contingency housing' on the margins of settlement.

Revolution brought stress since many jobs were lost and an itinerant lifestyle was resumed in many cases. Many did not carry an identity card ('buletin') without which they could not obtain a job, claim social assistance and health/education benefits or vote while those who were successful normally secured only the lowest-paid jobs because they lacked professional training. "Their marginalisation by the society on which they live and their manner of obtaining the economic resources necessary for life are characteristics which set them apart as an anti-social ethnic group" (Costachie 1997, p. 112). Of course the Roma now comprise diverse elements, as noted by Voiculescu (2002) in Sângeorgiu de Mureș where there are four groups differentiated according to residence, dress, language (Romany, Romanian and Hungarian) and employments. Exclusion concerns those most committed to a traditional lifestyle with a poverty rate of 78.8 per cent in 1997 (revealed by household surveys for those identifying themselves as Roma): way above the average of 30.8 per cent for the total population, with Romanians slightly below this average and Hungarians even more so. A majority of Roma live in severe poverty: "finding fruit" in the summer while they "die of starvation" in the winter (Amelina et al. 2003, p. 183) when searching garbage dumps may yield a few dollars through the recovery of plastic crates, copper wire and scrap iron (meanwhile pursued by a dozen stray dogs, encircled by black flurries of crows, enveloped in the acrid stench of the refuse and stung by the winds of a Balkan winter). Their 'contingency' housing often lacks basic utilities: 70 per cent of households have no running water and 80 per cent cannot afford drugs. Half the girls are married before the age of 17 and the birth rate is double that of the general Romanian population (four times for mothers aged 20–24 and 25 times for those aged 15–19). In addition they often face discrimination by community elites and small minorities feel isolated with reduced solidarity within their communities and family networks. Some have emigrated – illegally or by taking advantage of relaxed visa formalities – to Poland and Western Europe to become beggars, black market workers or petty criminals (for example, through pickpocket groups) with consequent repatriation: arguably undermining Romania's prospects as potential foreign investors see in their own countries the worst possible representation of Romanian society. However some are well-integrated into Western business, like the Novacovici family with their summer palace in Buziaş (Timiş county) supported by a network of flower shops in Sweden.

Traditional leadership is manifest through the Cioabă and Rădulescu families in Sibiu. Indeed, Iulian Rădulescu – self-styled 'emperor of all Roma' – is looking for compensation for his deportation to Transnistria in 1942. However traditional leaders are not considered effective because authority is "rarely recognised beyond their extended families and the people who are keen to do business with them" (Barany 2004, p. 263). But there is a prospect of gradual change in ethnic values – with integration no longer equated with assimilation – and pressure from the CoE and EU for progress to a more inclusive society has stimulated a movement for Roma emancipation under the a Democratic Union of Roma (initially the Roma Party in 1992), the Roma Society and various cultural groups (like the Roma emancipation movement 'Aven Amentza' and the Organisation of Roma Women) while an overarching Roma Federation emerged in 2001. New organisations are often dominated by their leaders due to low membership, but they seek enforcement of anti-discrimination laws, better education and employment opportunities, more positive media portrayal (with more dedicated radio and TV) and more effective welfare policies. There have been successes in local government, though parliamentary seats are difficult to secure because the modest vote (reflecting lack of confidence in the electoral system) is been split between as many as five parties. Publishing has resumed through such innovations as 'O Glaso al Rromengo': a supplement to the Timişoara newspaper 'Baricada' and (although more are needed) a growing number of Roma journalists are enhancing the Roma image and influencing public opinion, perhaps through Roma-controlled media services including a radio station and a press agency as well as the newscast 'Rromano Lil'. With Phare support, a centre for ethnocultural diversity encouraged ethnic self-identification for the 2002 census while another organisation for social study and integration seeks to eliminate cultural stereotypes and all forms of discrimination partly through the mass-media.

Exclusion   The Roma generally lack claims to land and have often been pushed out of villages towards squatter settlements close to the towns. Indeed "the loss of agricultural employment had an especially negative effect on the living standards, social status and inter-ethnic relations of Roma in rural areas" where two-thirds reside (Barany 2004, p. 259), while stealing from private farms is not tolerated in same the way as theft from the old communist cooperative. Relations with mainstream communities are often difficult and many incidents have arisen. Some localised pogroms were reported immediately after the revolution but ten Roma homes were burnt in Racşa (Oraşu Nou commune, Satu Mare county) in 1994 where those responsible were forced to rebuild. Tension in Piatra Neamţ led the mayor at one stage to advocate a Roma ghetto under armed guard. As recently as 2002 right-wing ('Nouă Dreapta') elements sought to demonise the Roma in Deva and Sibiu through slogans daubed on buildings and in 2006 there were incidents in the Apalina area of Reghin in 2006 with 'racist' actions provoked by Roma infractions. Yet suburbs with a large Roma population like Ferentari in Bucharest, that outsiders associate with criminality, may actually be no worse than average (Dumitrache & Dumbrăveanu 1998, pp. 61–7). Further 'collateral' marginality may arise if investors steer clear of Roma areas or mainstream groups resent aid given to the Roma on the grounds that they should do more to help themselves. The worst ethnic violence occurred in Hădăreni (Cheţani commune in Mureş county) in September 1993 when an innocuous conversation between three young Roma men and a non-Roma women sparked a series of arguments and confrontations: a Romanian man was stabbed (and later died) leading to a pogrom in which three Roma were killed while 13 houses were burnt and five others ransacked. Police are alleged to have incited further anti-Roma violence after they arrived. Although several Romanians were jailed for murder and arson the sentences for murder were considered light – and were subsequently reduced with compensation (in one case) that was greater than the benefit a widow of one of the murdered Roma received. 2005 saw the conclusion of two legal actions: one by the Romanian authorities confirming an earlier decision that the Romanians responsible should to pay compensation and to have their houses seized in the process (although the houses have not yet been taken) and another by the European Court of Human Rights (started in 2000) required the Romanian government to pay €500,000 to the Roma victims. Meanwhile the National Agency for the Roma (replacing the Department of Roma Affairs in 2004) has been joined by the NGO 'Partners for Local Development Foundation' over community projects to improve relations (e.g. in health and education in 2005).

Government Actions include an Inter-Ministerial Committee for National Minorities in 1998 with a sub-committee responsible for Roma integration while the education ministry granted Roma reserved places for admission to teacher training and academic education in social administration. Special courses trained around 100 public officials recruited from Roma communities in Bucharest and in Buzău, Cluj, Dolj, Ialomiţa, Iaşi and Timiş counties (1999). The new government in 2001 established a national office for Roma (under the Commission for Human Rights, Religions and Minorities) and despite limited staffing and budgetary resources initially, this produced a government strategy in 2001 to tackle economic and social problems. And since 2002 Roma councillors have worked with each prefecture and county council, collaborating with the police and labour organisations to enhance integration in education and the labour market while reducing criminality. Education is critical because while marginality, with it's resulting tensions, is 'systemic' in many respects through traditional inter-ethnic relations (grounded in Roma exclusion) and fundamentally divergent value systems, it is also 'contingent' through inadequate qualifications and skills for competition in the labour market. Only 17 per cent of Roma children go to pre-school compared with 67 per cent for other children; and in 1998 44 per cent of the Roma population had not completed the basic eight-year schooling programme. Further barriers arise because Roma girls drop out of school very early and they are at risk from poor reproductive health; while Roma boys are disproportionately represented in the juvenile delinquent population. However some illiterate teenage women are going to school under a basic education programme initiated by the German foundation Friedrich Ebert Stiftung. Elsewhere, the Soros Foundation uses gold stolen from the Roma by Nazis to fund scholarships for Roma students (c.500 in 2001) in Romania and other ECECs, while some young Roma students have participated (with colleagues from other ECECs) in an intensive management course financed by the World Bank and the Ford Foundation of Roma. But more resources are needed: in 2003 George Soros gave $30mln to a Roma Education Fund (which now has a total of $43mln pledged) and followed this up by financing a World Bank Conference in Sofia (2005) to agree a 'Decade for Social Inclusion of Roma' across the region. It seems that the Roma are catching up, with employment rates rising from 39 to 48 per cent during 1996–2001 and earnings that reflect education qualifications and not ethnic discrimination. Indeed "if the health and schooling of Roma were to improve to the extent that employment prospects increase with human capital, they might move out of poverty without having to deal with discrimination in earnings" (Mete 2003, p. 43). Clearly labour market programmes must reach the unemployed Roma, but in general it may be desirable to target poor communities where Roma are over-represented in order avoid further marginalisation by singling-out the group explicitly (Ibid, p. ii). Sensitivity over limited ethnic autonomy prevents Roma-managed schools with bilingual education rather than Romanian-managed Roma segregated schools or Romanian majority schools lacking bilingual facilities. But while some progress is being made in education and levels of tolerance generally, Roma access to the labour market and social housing remains unsatisfactory in the opinion of the EU.

Housing Problems   The Roma continue to identify themselves prominently through their buildings but in the sharpest contrast to crude 'contingency housing' the more affluent Roma are now building 'palaces' with towers covered with zinc-coated plate as a sign of wealth. It is reported that since 1994 about a hundred of these Roma palaces have been built by the 'Coppersmith Gypsies' of Iveşti in Galaţi county alone – a distinct group appointing its own 'bulibasha' – and many have moved into this 'golden district', so-named after dealers in precious metals. Roma rococo has also run amok in Budeşti, south of Bucharest, where palaces built by coppersmiths investing in gold have tin roofs adorned with orbs, spikes and spears. However, when rich Roma families suddenly descended – in line with their spontaneous migratory tendencies – on Strada Constantin Diaconovici Loga in central Timişoara and erected 'palaces' without the required formalities the townhall insisted on their demolition, albeit with some diplomatic complications in the case of holders of double (Romanian-French) citizenship.

   Moreover incidents continue to arise when the authorities remove the 'contingency' housing erected by itinerant Roma groups in defiance of the local planning régime (as in the Chitila and Văcăreşti areas of Bucharest). Open-fire hazards have also been noted in the Ferentari suburb of the capital where non-payment of bills results in the majority of households lacking gas, electricity and sewage disposal (as well as employment). Such incidents provide a platform of populist politicians advocating debt cancellations where the utilities are concerned.

Social Risk

Ethnicity has relevance for the labour market which can best develop in a society that is fully inclusive and also, in the case of the Roma, for social security. There is unfortunately no space to discuss the poverty problem in depth but social risk has been a major government concern and while the Jiu valley miners have been the most volatile group, they were by no means the only 'losers' during transition. Polarisation was such that by 1997 the poorest 40 per cent of the population (including most of the Roma minority) had 16 per cent of the total income, while the richest one-fifth had 45 per cent. In 2000, 44 per cent of family members had a monthly income that did not exceed $50 compared with 49 per cent who had $50–100 and the remaining seven per cent who exceeded this level (Pavel 2001, pp. 99–100). Pay kept up with inflation only in the highest-paid sectors while it was badly depressed in the worst-paid sectors such as furniture, textiles and clothing, catering and public services including education and health where price inflation – and especially the hike towards European energy prices has been extremely burdensome. Minimum salary fell dramatically from 1989 and the proportion of earners who receive the minimum (or something close to it) increased sharply. But more crucially, salaried employment declined each year from 8.16mln in 1990 to 4.62mln in 2000 and 4.57 in 2002. Meanwhile per capita GDP, calculated according to Purchasing Power Parity standard (PPPy), fell from 32 per cent of the EU average in 1995 to 27 per cent in 2000. The unemployment rate initially fell from a high of 10.9 per cent in 1994 to 6.6 per cent in 1996 (due to the politically-engineered boom) climbed back to 10.4 per cent in 1998 and 11.8 per cent in 1999 (affecting 1.13mln people – a third of them young people). Although official rates are quite moderate by comparison with the transition states as a whole they mask the true picture because many families are underemployed on small farms. It is instructive to compare agriculture's position in the national economy when the high share for the occupied population is compared with the salaried workforce and the value-added (Table 4.2). It is also evident that modest social benefits provide little incentive for the unemployed to register or, in the event of qualification, to remain registered after receiving assistance for the maximum period of 18 months.

The main response to poverty has been through social aid ('ajutorul social') paid by local authorities from 1995 in return for work in the community; replaced in 2001 by a more standardised system of 'minimum income guarantee'. There are also heating allowances and higher rates of child allowance However, the best social policy is arguably the enhancement of incomes through more jobs – and also employment that pays higher salaries through the transfer of workers from low productivity state-sector jobs to higher productivity private sector jobs. At the same time some people showed considerable initiative in finding work; building on the tradition

Table 4.2: Major economic sectors according to salaries, occupied population and value added 1985–2005 (percent)

Year	Salaries			Occupied Population			Value Added		
	Agr	Ind	Ser	Agr	Ind	Ser	Agr	Ind	Ser
1985	8.7	46.8	44.5	28.9	37.1	34.0	15.5	59.0	25.5
1986	8.7	46.9	44.4	28.7	37.3	34.0	14.4	60.0	25.6
1987	8.3	47.3	44.4	28.5	37.4	34.1	13.7	59.8	26.5
1988	8.5	47.2	44.3	28.4	37.6	34.0	14.8	59.0	26.2
1989	8.3	47.5	44.2	27.9	38.1	34.0	15.2	58.1	26.7
1990	8.0	47.2	44.8	29.0	36.9	34.1	23.8	44.1	32.1
1991	8.0	48.1	43.9	29.7	35.3	35.0	20.1	40.4	39.5
1992	8.1	47.1	44.8	32.9	31.6	35.5	19.4	39.0	41.6
1993	8.4	45.2	46.4	35.9	30.1	34.0	22.6	36.5	40.9
1994	7.5	44.4	48.1	36.4	28.8	34.8	21.5	39.2	39.3
1995	6.8	42.5	50.7	34.4	28.6	37.0	18.7	35.6	45.7
1996	6.1	43.5	50.4	35.4	29.2	35.4	20.6	35.5	43.9
1997	6.3	43.6	50.1	37.5	27.2	35.3	19.6	33.5	46.9
1998	5.8	42.3	51.9	38.0	26.3	35.7	16.1	30.8	53.1
1999	5.0	41.8	53.2	41.2	24.4	34.4	15.1	30.9	54.0
2000	4.2	40.5	55.3	41.4	23.2	35.4	12.5	31.0	56.5
2001	4.1	41.2	54.7	40.8	23.6	35.6	15.0	31.4	53.6
2002	3.5	41.4	55.1	36.1	25.5	38.4	12.8	30.9	56.3
2003	3.3	40.3	56.4	34.7	24.8	40.5	13.0	28.2	58.8
2004	3.2	39.4	57.4	32.0	24.1	43.9	13.9	27.6	58.5
2005	3.2	36.6	60.2	31.9	23.5	44.6	n.a.	n.a.	n.a.

A new methodology for value added was introduced after 1998. According to this system, in 1998 the value-added shares would have been 16.2 for agriculture, 28.2 for industry and 55.6 for services.

Source: Statistical Yearbooks: Tables 3.9, 3.11 and 11.9

(especially in Maramureş) of taking up seasonal work away from home. Increasingly however this had translated into emigration – especially to Italy and Spain – illegally at first but more recently with the benefit of visa-free access to the Schengen area of the EU. With 'fruit pickers' able to travel to Germany in special coaches and return loaded with electrical goods, it becomes possible for higher (official) unemployment to bring about a reduction in poverty! Despite emigration unemployment rates have shown little change averaging 6.8 per cent during 1999–2001 and 7.8 during 2002–2004, with a slight increase in the number of salaried employees from 4.57mln in 2002 to 4.59mln in 2003 wiped out by a fall back to 4.47mln in 2004 with a recovery to 4.56mln in 2005.

Chapter Five

Post-Communist Economic Reform: A Chronological Approach

This chapter looks at the economics of transition: the restructuring process with particular reference to privatisation and foreign investment. It was absolutely essential to transfer responsibility for economic management to private enterprise, given that the revolution reflected the state's inability to cope with a popular desire for decentralisation and a focus on wealth creation. However a concern for social security – and the long-term survival of a substantial industrial establishment – has meant that the state could only divest itself of responsibility gradually and the process was highly contested politically during the 1990s. Foreign investment is also a critical matter in terms of integrating Romania with efficient, global capitalist systems and initial failure to realise its full potential in attracting participation by leading companies raised serious questions about the investment 'climate' of the Balkans in general and Romania in particular during the first decade of transition. The labour market is certainly an asset, although unemployment has been drastically reduced through emigration, both temporary and permanent; while the quality of the workforce is negatively affected by weaknesses in the education and health services. It will emerge that reform was not given a high enough priority under the first Iliescu presidency and the country's economic position was weakened as a result. Priorities changed quite radically under the Constantinescu presidency (1997–2000) with the adoption of a 'European' agenda but failure to maintain economic growth was a major set-back. However, a second Iliescu presidency maintained the momentum of reform and further continuity under President Băsescu from 2005 raised the annual inflow of funds to record levels; it also secured Romania's accession to the EU in 2007.

The First Iliescu Presidency 1990–96

Transition started with Romania at a disadvantage through the aberration of Ceauşescu's autarkic nationalist approach. Despite euphoria over the revolution there were serious economic difficulties because the central planning system had, understandably, not made contingency plans for its own demise. Building new institutions was a particularly painful process reflecting the mood for incremental change. The National Salvation Front (NSF) government secured their first election victory in May 1990 with a weak transition programme as the populist approach favoured by Iliescu ruled out the 'shock therapy' envisaged by prime minister P. Roman in a favour of a gradual transition based existing structures. The price distortions of communism that gave a legacy in low domestic transport and energy charges were left largely in place. There was certainly much popular apprehension over a market economy: following the great effort demanded under communism, people would not "sacrifice themselves [again] for the sake of future generations" (Nicolaescu 1993, p. 102). While the principle of free competition might be acceptable as an ideal, most people would hesitate to "replace government control with more seriously binding controls that are inflicted by market-related institutions" (Ibid, pp. 103–4). The NSF provided a comfortable home for former communists, especially elements from the state bureaucracy, state enterprises and trade unions that shared a resistance to change, and also gained willing allies among the peasants who, despite the trappings of ownership provided by land restitution, did not really behave as a private business community. Fearing higher taxes and lower net incomes (raising the spectre of landlessness), they did not want government control replaced by the vagaries of society governed by market forces and political parties seeking major economic reforms found the going hard. There was a presumption (fed to no small extent by government propaganda) that unfettered market forces would drive many small farms out of business and result in much larger capitalist holdings, perhaps controlled by the landowners who were expropriated after the First World War and whose claims might be accepted under the more generous restitution terms promised by the opposition.

A Philosophy of Gradualism

Under Roman's government trade liberalisation through 1990-1 gave scope for foreign direct investment (FDI) although it was not actually commended by the government until the election year 1992 – and only with enthusiasm when a centre-right government was launched in 1997. Yet there was pressure to boost imports of consumer goods after the deprivation of the 1980s (helped by an overvalued exchange rate) and prices rose sharply where controls were not in force. And any political will embodied in stabilisation measures "ran headlong into the lack of widespread knowledge about a market economy" (Isărescu 1992, p. 161). Limited income (pending a new tax system) meant that private and government spending had inflationary effects (despite credit ceilings); reinforced by wage rises (and a five-day working week) at a time of falling output, and accelerating growth in the money supply. There was provision for private business (through five types of company including limited liability companies), though domestic entrepreneurship was in short supply. But the restructuring of state-owned enterprises (SOEs) was not explicitly mentioned until the Roman government presented its programme in June 1990 and even then they only considered the transformation of state companies into autonomous organisations rather than privatisation. "Incapacity to cope with increasing complexity and inability to assimilate and generate technological progress led to a 'softening' of output towards low value-added goods which led to a steady deterioration of the terms of trade" (Dăianu 2001, p. 204). Later in the year – with sharply falling industrial production – reform had to be accelerated with a two-thirds leu devaluation and partial price liberalisation extending through 1991 (without compensation through wage rises). This upset conservative NSF supporters and precipitated the miners' demonstration ('mineriada') of September 1991 that removed Roman from the premiership. This helped to precipitate a split in the NSF with the conservative wing favoured by Iliescu forming the basis of the Party of Social Democracy of Romania (PSDR) and governing until the end of 1996 with nationalist support, while Roman's reformist wing spawned the centrist Democratic Party (DP) that ruled in alliance with the centre-right Democratic Convention of Romania (DCR) during 1997–2000.

IMF Assistance Compromised by Budgetary Deficits
Roman's successor, T. Stolojan, continued with gradual reform: for example a privatisation law provided a legal framework for employee-management buy-outs (EMBOs) and mass voucher privatisation but "economic reforms would continue to be highly dependent on the vicissitudes of Romanian electoral politics" (Bacon 2004, p. 376). There were growing tensions at the end of 1991 with an over-valued official exchange rate, artificially low energy and raw material prices encouraging over-consumption and insufficient FDI to compensate for low domestic saving. Hence there was much barter dealing, while capital flight and poor exports were important concerns. An IMF stabilisation plan was agreed in 1991 and action was taken early in 1992 with higher interest rates and exchange rate devaluation, but interest rates remained negative and the impending election of 1992 (a set-back for the now-divided NSF) prevented a consistent policy, while the IMF agreement had to be cancelled after $318mln had been disbursed. Radical restructuring was still resisted in favour of a gradual approach under a new premier (N.Văcăroiu) who mirrored Iliescu's reserve over economic liberalisation and his commitment to a state-led economy.

Production increased at the cost of heavy subsidies and a growth in the money supply (133 per cent in 1993), and rapid leu depreciation, though compensation through wage increases was more limited (especially in the case of the relaxation of price controls in 1994 when the leu became internally convertible with other currencies). Soft credits from the state banks could not stop the growth of inter-enterprise arrears and an accompanying economic blockage. Although they did not contribute to budgetary deficits they discouraged enterprise autonomy and undermined budget transparency at both the national and enterprise levels. The arrears culture was clearly seen through the huge losses incurred by the electricity utility Renel, increased by unused equipment for upgrading power stations. The government supporters who ran the company (with salaries that alone accounted for 1.0 per cent of GDP) could be relied upon to show tolerance over arrears accumulated by favoured customers. On the other hand there was a policy breakthrough during 1993–94 with decisive efforts to contain and reverse inflation through an interest rate 'shock' that also stemmed the flight from the leu (hence rapid remonetisation) and "aided the formation of a transparent foreign exchange market, thereby strengthening the potential of an export drive" and reducing the trade deficit (Dăianu 2001, p.208). Export growth headed off a decline in output of the kind that occurred in 1997 while allowing reduced subsidies to inefficient producers. This was the stage for a second mass privatisation in 1995.

Inflationary Pressures

Romania's philosophy of 'gradualism' (Shen 1997) was not soundly based and produced a 'stop-go' rhythm analyzed by Hunya (1998). Despite a period of improved trade and current account balances the overvalued exchange rate proved unsustainable and there was a relapse into inflation and rising external debt in 1995–96 with an import and consumer boom starting in late 1994, driven by highly import-dependent branches which fuelled inflation and brought remonitisation to a standstill. Exports remained uncompetitive and generally poor in terms of value-added (in the absence of radical restructuring) but did not expand significantly during four years of growth (1993–96), achieved partly by credit-financed expansion and expensive price controls (surviving until 1997) that served to widen the trade deficit. The burden of supporting loss-making enterprises soaked up potential investment capital and generated budget deficits financed by credits from the financial institutions. Indeed, financing the budget deficit (aggravated by losses in agriculture and the SOEs) by growth of the money supply to ease financial blockages meant that the IMF withheld credit on two occasions because of dissatisfaction over the progress of the agreed stabilisation programme: indeed none of Romania's five stand-by agreements with the IMF in the 1990s were completed. Rising prices for basic consumer goods in 1995–96 again demonstrated the danger of 'populist macroeconomics' and the need for privatisation to attract capital. A lack of consensus over economic reform strained the governing coalition and eroded public confidence in political parties generally but in late 1996, despite wages being allowed to rise with inflation, the balance began to swing decisively towards a better export performance to reduce the trade gap, moderate current account pressures and improve the environment for FDI.

The Restructuring Process

This was complicated in the extreme mainly through the lack of consensus at the highest political level about economic reform and in particular 'what makes privatisation desirable in the first place' (Negrescu 1999). Yet radical reorganisation of all SOEs would almost certainly have generated unacceptable levels of unemployment, given a limited social security system. Starting in 1990, many SOEs were organised into non-privatisable 'regies autonomes' (RAs) covering strategic branches of the national economy (including utilities and defence industries): there were around 950 by the end of 1992. They had 'patrimony' rather than equity capital and had total protection from the claims of creditors and the pressures of hard budget constraints. Naturally there was much lobbying among SOEs to obtain this status with 'no coherent criterion' to guide the decisions. Even when a legal basis for bankruptcy was provided in 1995 the RAs had a privileged status as fully-fledged commercial companies, but with complete protection from exit with an open-ended entitlement to budget resources. Meanwhile in 1991 a State Ownership Fund (SOF) was created to dispose of other SOEs that were treated as autonomous joint stock companies ('societăţi comerciale'); but again without any coherent criterion to separate the two categories. Meanwhile with regard to farming, a similar arbitrary distinction was made between the land of cooperative farms that could be used for restitution to former private owners and the state farm domains that remained intact. The SOF was modelled on Germany's 'Treuhand' with holdings sold to Romanian or foreign individuals and firms at an acceptable price. It was expected that a tenth of the SOF's equity would be disposed of each year. Despite assistance from EU Phare, the SOF only materialised at the end of 1991 with 5,900 companies and a capital of 45bln.lei and eventually grew through subdivision to 8,500 (of which around 80 per cent were SMEs with 20bln.lei capital). The SOF was complemented by five Private Ownership Funds (POFs) with a 70 per cent:30 per cent split respectively (later 60-40) between majority state capital to be retained in each company and a minority holding for distribution to the adult population through certificates (1992) and coupons (1995) exchanged for shares in chosen companies. Meanwhile the 1994 law on the capital market was followed by the National Securities Commission and the Bucharest Stock Exchange in 1995. The five private property funds (FPPs) subsequently became financial investment companies (SIFs).

Tentative Privatisation Measures
From the start there was a reluctance to contemplate extensive selling to foreigners and much political mileage was gained through brave declarations against selling the national patrimony; while the public as a whole was initially ambivalent over the principle of share ownership (Earle & Telegdy 1998). The SOF tried to make headway in 1993 with 40 selected companies (including the state airline Tarom and representative companies from all sectors of industry) but the initiative was constrained by the lack of an entrepreneurial class and inadequate markets and financial incentives, while Nicolaescu (1993, p.108) observed that "development of banking and financial intermediation institutions with foreign participation is an essential prerequisite of successful development of privatisation programmes". During 1993 and 1994 the emphasis was on pilot and spontaneous privatisation with a focus on EMBOs that accounted for 780 out of a total of 869 privatisations during these two years: 265 in 1993 (out of a SOF portfolio of 5,931 companies at the start of the year) and 604 in 1994 (from a portfolio of 6,291 companies – a larger number due to sub-division). Employees and management had what amounted to an unconditional entitlement with tribunals readily ordering the SOF not to sell if employees had asked to buy e.g. Bucharest's Ambasador Hotel. It was as if only insiders could benefit. Yet EMBO-ised firms rarely had working capital and there was both falling performance and rising indebtedness evident during 1996–97.

Mass Privatisation was launched when Romanians registered for their 30 per cent stake in July 1992; paying 100lei for a book of five vouchers (one for each POF), but the scheme was undermined by unintended speculation in voucher books as well as public apathy and inflation that prevented significant negotiation of shares. The government tried again in 1994-5 to deliver mass privatisation under World Bank pressure. It was still questionable whether the public would take the plan seriously and even with a downward revaluation of assets to encourage EMBOs the process failed to gain momentum by the end of 1994. A new initiative for 1995-6 covered 2,200 large companies and SMEs representing all branches of the economy and all parts of the country. 60 per cent of equity was available for allocation through non-transferable vouchers (worth $464mln). This involved an assault on the autonomy of the SOF through the sweeping responsibilities handed to the National Agency for

Privatisation (originally set up with a supervisory role though one that nevertheless generated endless disputes). It now launched a pilot project involving 22 SMEs in order to gain experience. After much initial confusion, over 2.3mln citizens invested their coupons during the last quarter of 1995 using computers installed in post offices, in anticipation of share certificates being issued by the end of March 1996. More than 70 per cent of citizens participated through investment funds, trust companies and citizens' associations. But the results were rather modest for even in the companies that did feature in the programme less than a fifth of the shares changed hands and the state almost invariably maintained a majority stake. In 1995 648 companies were disposed of (out of 7,602) – only half the target figure – and 1,388 in 1996 (out of 9,010). Although there were only 57 EMBOs, many contracts still went to insiders through certificates/coupons, perhaps supplemented by payments. This created core investors interested in the business, but typically with an overriding interest in protecting jobs by people with no resources for investment and no marketing expertise either. Nomenklatura elements were able to exploit influence over the SOF to obtain assets at symbolic prices.

The Results of Privatisation 1992–96   Altogether some 2,700 enterprises were sold (plus another 1,800 as EMBO deals, mostly with PSDR members as beneficiaries) but less than a hundred were large enterprises. The SOF was left with 613 (86.6 per cent) of its large companies (mostly in a precarious financial position and very difficult to sell) compared with 1,841 (74.9 per cent) of the medium companies (500–1,000 employees) and 966 (30.9 per cent) of the smaller enterprises. These surviving SOEs were autonomous but in the absence of hard budget constraints the state was obliged to cover losses that rose in sympathy with a lack of competitiveness. For social reasons the strategy of closing the least efficient plant in favour of investment in the more viable units was rejected in preference for modest lay-offs and retention of core establishments, sometimes with compulsory 'holidays' taken in rotation. Further pressure on the workforce arose when wage rises failed to keep in line with inflation, leading to strikes and demonstrations. At this time the socio-economic problems were linked with the Latin American model of a poor nation ruled by a small, rich and corrupt oligarchy. The IBRD in Washington tried to force the pace through a loan conditional on labour force reductions at three key SOEs: Republica (Bucharest), Sidex (Galaţi) and Tractorul (Braşov). In addition Sidex was to cease receiving subsidies from the state budget while the others were to make economies and start rationalising. The EU pointed out in 1999 how the experience of 1990–96 in failing to restructure (or close) large loss-making industrial companies – outrunning any controls by the public banks to impose financial discipline and evading bankruptcy proceedings – threatened any gains in macroeconomic stabilisation. At the same time, while the private sector share for GDP had risen from 16.4 per cent in 1990 to an estimated 52.0 per cent in 1996, the position in industry (35.0 per cent after 5.7 per cent in 1990) was way behind agriculture (91.0 per cent from 61.3), services (70.0 per cent from 2.0) and construction (65.0 per cent from 1.9). The private sector was also responsible for half the trade (0.3 per cent in 1990) and 42 per cent of investment (4.3 per cent in 1990). Yet commitment to a strong state industrial sector was confirmed in 1996 by the decree providing for full state control of the oil industry through Compania Română de Petrol (CRP) which sought to integrate the petrochemical industry with pipeline operators, distributors and fuel retailers. Foreign companies could buy into CRP only up to 49 per cent but few were interested in doing so.

Small- and Medium-Sized Enterprises

SMEs showed encouraging growth (Table 5.1). Outside help was forthcoming from the ROM-UN Centre that trained business consultants, while the Foundation for the Promotion of SMEs (FPSME) was created in 1992 to set up five centres for the development of SMEs and five centres for business incubation under a 1992–95 Phare programme. Also in 1992 a Centre for Business Excellence was founded by specialists from Washington State University and the Polytechnic University of Bucharest as part of the USAID Program for Management Training & Enterprise Development; while a Centre for Performance Management Improvement was established by the UK Know-How Fund; and an International Centre for Entrepreneurial Studies was provided by the Center for International Private Enterprise in Washington DC (affiliated to the US Chamber of Commerce). Meanwhile the Romanian CCI laid on trade fairs and exhibitions. And the banks gradually became more supportive. For example the Black Sea Trade & Development Bank, created in 1996 by the 11 member states as a regional development finance institution, identified four priority sectors that included SMEs along with energy and natural resources, transport and telecommunications. The first consulting centre was established in Romania in 1991, jointly funded by government and UNDP with contributions from the Dutch government and the British Know-How Fund. Various NGOs also provided SME consulting services, assisted by the International Management Foundation's Fund for Local Development Initiatives (Gherănescu 1996). The idea of private sector business associations was pursued by the International Centre of Business Studies at Bucharest University through a forum for associations in 1996 at the Black Sea Business Centre, Mangalia. It seemed that SMEs might become more prominent outside the main industrial centres if local authorities could improve their managerial skills and stimulate small business in remoter areas.

Special Financial Arrangements

These were needed in the opinion of the National Privatisation Agency (NPA) since Romanian banks could not cope for various reasons "including limited capitalisation, inexperience, collateral requirements and inflationary uncertainty" (Coclitu & Bratescu 1996, p.116). So the Federal Business Development Bank, supported by the Canadian International Development Agency, assisted the setting up of a fund – fully subscribed in 1994 with NPA as principal shareholder – to help SMEs access medium- and long-term finance. The Romanian-American Enterprise Fund was created as an American non-profit private corporation to encourage SMEs in Romania through transactions and investments for the promotion of know-how and Western business practices: the first projects included a new porcelain factory in Alba Iulia, expansion of an international garment company near Timişoara and the use of American technology to convert agricultural wastes into organic fertilisers.

Table 5.1: Small and Medium-Sized Enterprises 1992–2005

Year	Industry		Commerce		Other Services		Total		
	A	B	A	B	A	B	A	C	D
1992	19.1	15.1	79.2	62.6	27.3	22.3	126.5	12.3	30.9
1993	28.8	13,4	141.6	66.1	44.0	20.5	214.3	17.8	33.8
1994	31.0	10.9	213.4	75.2	39.2	13.9	283.7	20.1	41.3
1995	33.2	11.0	220.6	73.1	48.0	15.9	301.8	23.9	46.7
1996	30.8	10.0	225.8	73.0	52.8	17.0	309.8	29.1	48.3
1997	34.7	11.1	225.9	71.9	53.6	17.0	314.2	32.9	45.2
1998	37.7	11.9	221.8	70.2	56.4	17.9	316.0	37.8	52.8
1999	40.0	12.6	217.3	68.6	59.4	18.8	316.6	42.5	54.0
2000	40.7	13.3	202.7	66.2	62.6	20.5	306.1	46.9	55.9
2001	42.1	13.6	192.5	62.2	78.6	24.2	309.3	48.5	57.2
2002	45.9	14.6	177.6	56,7	89.7	28.7	313.2	50.7	55.9
2003	50.4	14.5	179.1	51.6	117.6	33.9	347.1	54.4	57.4
2004	55.0	14.0	191.1	48.7	146.4	37.3	392.5	58.2	57.5
2005	57.8	13.4	200.2	46.4	173.1	40.2	431.1	60.7	57.6

A Number (th); B Percentage all SMEs; C SME share of total employment in all enterprises; D Ditto turnover

Source: Statistical Yearbooks: Tables 15.8, 15.9 and 15.10

Enterprise was also assisted by the scientific support of the Phare programme while the World Bank provided a $150mln credit for Romania's private sector. Meanwhile to stimulate new enterprise the Ministry of Research & Technology coordinated a programme to provide low cost space (often by arrangement with local universities and other institutions) for fledgling businesses. Braşov featured in two pilot projects: a business incubator by the local SME Employers' Association in space available within the Roman and Tractorul factories and Transilvania University; and a Phare initiative for the training, retraining and professional guidance of the redundant workforce at the Electroprecizia enterprise in the satellite town of Săcele where specialists provided support to employees wishing to start a new business, seek a new trade or simply gain information about the labour market. Meanwhile a technological centre was set up within the Technical University of Timişoara.

Unsatisfactory Results

There were 546.5th registered SMEs at the end of 1996 – a modest number by the standards of other transition states – half had only a small turnover (below 50mln. lei) and half of those that exceeded a higher turnover of 1.0bln actually made losses, or profits below two per cent (effectively loss-making because of real expenses that were not tax-deductible). Moreover, 93.4 per cent of the SMEs had fewer than ten employees and "with very little start-up capital the entrepreneurs behind many of these companies focused their efforts on street trade, small service utilities and tourism" (Rusu 2001, p. 224). Growth was slow because the SME sector was blocked by difficult access to credit, high rents and taxation, excessive bureaucracy (even harassment indicative of discrimination against the private sector) and corruption as well as a continuing lack of management and market experience. There was also criticism over the lack of an information system providing banking, marketing, technical and other necessary information on starting-up and running efficient businesses.

The Constantinescu Presidency 1997–2000

Policy Overview

During 1997–2000 there was much greater political will to restructure and the change of government to a centre-right coalition was a good moment to launch reform because there was not only unconditional support from the international financial bodies and the EU but the population was ready to accept more radical change. But the new premier Victor Ciorbea was forced to retreat in Spring 1997 – at the first signs of resistance – in order to maintain social peace and hopefully win an invitation to join NATO at the impending Madrid summit. By the summer the first signs of the Asian financial crisis were apparent and this had a dramatic impact on share values and the investment climate. Hence the turbulence arising from Russia's economic crisis meant that the succeeding Radu Vasile and Mugur Isărescu governments faced a hostile domestic and international climate in 1999–2000 as well as difficult relations with the IMF that made for higher risk ratings and lower FDI. But this was not all, because the policy shock arising from price and trade liberalisation – will full convertibility of the leu in 1998 – led to much higher inflation than expected and this triggered a second recession (during 1997–99) through the massive contraction of real credit (especially the non-government component) that damaged the emerging private sector as sales fell.

SOE deficits also contributed to inflation while "poor fiscal management combined with controls on bank deposit rates to create a substantial credit crunch that brought investment to a halt" (Mete et al. 2003, p. 4). The sharp contraction of credit, with high interest rates, reduced the prospects for many SMEs and contributed to the fall of output. Thus "both policy-induced demand and supply shocks lay behind the plunge of the economy [into] the second transformational recession" (Dăianu 2004, p. 397). The situation was not helped by problems within the coalition as the finance minister sought a culture change through an improved tax collection rate from state companies (to halt the growth in arrears that accounted for 36 per cent of GDP at end of 1996) and a proposed property tax that would reduce the public debt to the IMF target level. But the National Liberal Party (NLP), one of the component parties of the governing DCR, opposed his plans while the financial position was further undermined by higher pay for the police and the military (to ensure loyalty at a time of labour unrest). The government was forced to cancel Romania's fifth IMF agreement negotiated by its predecessor in 1994 (which had attracted $94mln) but replaced it with a new agreement that failed the following year after attracting $121mln. It was ironic that a programme "designed to advance the process of reform in Romania actually wound up hurting the emerging entrepreneurial class and, due to the degree of austerity involved, encouraged the expansion of the underground economy" (Ibid). FDI accelerated and then fell back as policy ran into an impasse.

Policy Dilemmas Surrounding Dobrescu's 'Barometer'
Lack of resolve over wages undermined exports at a time when the exchange rate was appreciating. The poor export performance in 1998-9 shows weakness on the supply side of the economy with reduced competitiveness as real wage growth outstripped productivity growth during most of 1998. Autonomous state companies were a great embarrassment through paying high salaries and running up huge losses. The salaries of the electricity company Renel were 0.84 per cent of GDP in 1999 and the company losses were 1.0 per cent of GDP. Vasile blocked their bank account in 1998 but the measure was reversed due to unexplained pressures – with great damage to the government's image. Trade with the EU grew but it declined sharply with Russia, Ukraine and Moldova. Moreover exports became more concentrated on textiles and footwear (one third of all exports in 1998) with most of it involving sub-contracting arrangements with limited value-added in Romania. Machinery exports showed some strength but an abrupt fall in steel exports early in 1999 revealed the industry's difficulties in coping with falling world prices: traditional exporters were clearly vulnerable when restructuring failed to boost their efficiency. Meanwhile low labour costs could not prevent some lost ground on the domestic market through competition from cheaper and better quality imported products. Dobrescu's (1998) 'barometer' revealed the difficulties facing a restructuring programme involving further privatisation and the development of market mechanisms. While benefit would arise from efficient anti-monopolist measures and the fight against fiscal evasion while exports would rise through greater efficiency, there would be very high unemployment initially because of drive for higher productivity and consequently high social security expenditure. Wage increases – an inevitable part of a social accord for higher productivity – could fuel inflation and hence there would be no guarantee of a surge in FDI despite the prospect of progressive integration into Europe.

The Looming Banking Crisis of 1999
This arose out of three major interlinked threats and policy challenges: bad loans and reduced national bank foreign exchange reserves; persistently high real interest rates and bailouts in the banking system; and, most seriously, a risk of external payment default arising from IMF obligations. The figures are worth quoting in detail to indicate the scale of the problem. As summarised by Gallagher (2005, pp. 222–3) a new (sixth) agreement for a $547mln IMF loan in 1999 – granted in no small measure due Romania's assistance to NATO during the Kosovo campaign – required that another loan of $475mln be raised privately (at very high rates of interest given Romania's risk rating) to release the second tranche. Earlier in the year Romania had to pay some $610mln to service a foreign debt of $800mln incurred earlier in the transition; followed by an additional $480mln and monthly service payments of $156mln! Other estimates have pointed to total liabilities of some $2.9bln. It was remarkable that Romania was able to avoid default, thanks to a skillful balance of payments adjustment, along with leu depreciation and rises in inflation (c.55 per cent in 1999) and increased taxation, including cancellation of some concessions for

foreign investors and SMEs. Successful efforts were made to conclude privatisation deals at the end of 1998 e.g. Romtelecom (RT) and the Romanian Development Bank (RDB), with encouragement from the 1998 'Country Report' calling for substantial privatisation to establish credibility in international financial markets and attract FDI. And with the same report calling for financial discipline for SOEs, the government made efforts to close large loss-making companies with particular reference to the mining sector.

In view of the intense financial pressure the government effectively confronted the miners in 1999 and loss-making coal mining companies were drastically restructured, despite further 'mineriada' by union leader Miron Cozma in January and February and strong opposition by the PSDR and the nationalist Greater Romania Party (GRP) on the grounds of deprivation and unemployment. 113 mines were identified for eventual closure and the start of restructuring reduced losses by 43 per cent in the first half of 1999 compared with first half of 1998. Various pig and poultry farms were also closed in the context of the World Bank agreement. But the situation was not helped by the poor export performance in 1998-9 showing weakness in the supply side of the economy. Competitiveness suffered as real wages outstripped productivity growth but the decline was not halted by the real depreciation of the leu from the middle of 1998. In the first half of 1999 exports were 8.0 per cent lower than in the same period of 1998: a disappointing response to further trade liberalisation at the beginning of the year when export bans were lifted and many tariffs on industrial goods originating in the EU and CEFTA were lowered.

A Return to Growth

This was secured in 2000 under Isărescu's premiership when low domestic spending power suggested that the best strategy lay with exports, especially in the expanding German and Italian economies. This appeared to be the key for further growth over the following decade if the economic infrastructure could be improved, including international railfreight, and a new generation of technically advanced industries could evolve. Moreover, an exportable cereal surplus of 5.0mln.t (in the context of a total harvest of 20mln considered feasible) would help impoverished areas in the lowlands that paradoxically enjoyed the best land resources. So the vicious circle of economic decline and reduced investment/export barriers was replaced by a virtuous circle of lower deficits and interest rates (making for a lower tax burden), a competitive exchange rate, export growth and capital inflow and reduced inflation, with privatisation also playing an essential role. In part the export surge through price competitiveness may have been sustained by the delay in the adjustment of energy prices. Progress made way for agreement with the IMF in June 2000 on the extension of the standby arrangement and a resumption of official lending, although gains were fragile because of the limits to structural reform especially financial discipline. However this extension to Romania's sixth IMF agreement, started in 1999 with acceptance of tough measures for economic recovery, was destined to fail in 2001 and require replacement after $134mln had been attracted.

The Balance Sheet

Given its problems the government could claim some successes. By seeking integration and faster reform it had taken on board challenges eschewed by its predecessors and, with its 'back to the wall', had to take unpopular decisions without the advantage of a really cohesive administration with a well-defined economic strategy within a stable institutional framework. It was constantly exposed to external as well as internal criticism, thanks to the EU 'Country Reports' and was inevitably compromised – in a catch-up situation – by the absence or inadequacy of many of the institutions required to ensure the effective functioning of a market economy. Land and capital markets were not yet fully established, given the uncertainty about property rights and repeated changes in the legal and regulatory environment. But the share of the private sector in GDP reached 58.6 per cent in 1998 and remained broadly constant at around 60 per cent thereafter; albeit with a very important role through the SOEs and their strong economic links with many SMEs, while the grey economy developed rapidly to account for 30–40 per cent of GDP. Redirection of trade to the EU continued: $1,575 out of $4,265bln of exports 1991 (36.9 per cent) but $5,571bln out of $8,504 in 1999 (65.5 per cent); and $1,663bln out of $5,794 of imports in 1991 (28.7 per cent) but $6,277bln out of $10,392 in 1999 (60.4 per cent). However restructuring was more effective in some sectors than others and a slower reorientation, retaining more trade with Africa, Russia and the Caspian region may have been preferable (Dăianu et al., 2001). Crucially however, the appalling record over economic growth and constant disagreement within the coalition made a change of government inevitable. But at least a reform agenda had been set and no other responsible party could easily abandon it.

Restructuring and Privatisation

The Ciorbea government was keen to restructure through converting autonomous state companies into commercial companies e.g. RT, Radio-Comunicaţii and Posta Română in 1998. They also made an early start on privatisation so that 1,304 enterprises were disposed of in 1997 and 1,267 in 1998 (out of 5,554 available): predominantly SMEs apart from the largest cement producer and oil refinery. Almost the same number of companies was dealt with in the two years as in the previous four (when 2,571 companies had realised $1.13bln). There were some constraints arising from the abusive nature of the original state takeovers, delays in drafting sectoral development strategies and the limited capital resources of potential investors. There were also continuing complaints about lack of transparency including some from the DP that wanted more favours for its own clients: indeed it was this grudge against Ciorbea (plus his reliance on technocrats) that contributed to the strains in the coalition that eventually forced his resignation. Late in 1998 the government tried to force the pace (with the prospect of massive loan repayments due in the new year) through the aim of privatisation (or closure) of 49 prominent loss-making companies; while they also achieved a number of major successes in selling 35 per cent of RT to OTE (Greece) and 51 per cent of RDB to Société Générale (France) while Renault bought the Dacia car company. As a result FDI reached 5.4 per cent of net GDP in 1998 (a third of it due to RT alone) but the rate was still low in per capita terms due to the obstacle of macroeconomic instability.

Controlling the SOF and the RAs

Although already weakened by the 'reconquista' launched by the previous government through mass privatisation and wider powers for the NPA, it was natural for the new administration to seek even greater control because the SOF had previously shown favouritism in using the proceeds of privatisation to allot direct subsidies through non-transparent mechanisms while also depositing money insecurely e.g. in Columna Bank that had gone bankrupt. There was also a suspicion that the SOF was working slowly to keep itself in a job – although it could hardly stand out against the general culture and, arguably, it would best preserve its workplace (under the extreme pressure of 1998 for example) by coming up with good results! In 1997 the government decided on a full Ministry of Privatisation. It also corporatised some RAs to make them eligible for privatisation but the privatisation minister – from the leading coalition party: National Peasant Christian Democrat Party (NPCDP) – kept tabs on such former RAs to marginalise 'line ministries' controlled by other parties to head-off favouritism for insiders to which the DP was considered particularly prone. Privatisation of such national companies was still compromised by a government golden share (as in the case of RT) or by dedicated access for portfolio investors (rather than a strategic investor) in a bid to retain a competitive environment though the implicit barrier to a strategic investor was not altogether logical and the opposite strategy could have been advocated. Nevertheless there was a constant state of flux with RAs lobbying to retain their status while those that failed would often see the relevant government ordinance contradicted by amendment or parliamentary rejection! Plenty of ROs therefore survived, although again without any coherent criterion. In 1999 there was further pressure on the SOF when, under a new prime minister, line ministries got effective leverage over relevant corporatised RAs. This included special arrangements for tourism and agriculture (that should have been easiest for the SOF to deal with). It had been decided in 1998 that the tourism ministry would handle tourism privatisation, with 80 per cent of the proceeds going to a Tourist Fund, but the initiative was compromised when the ministry was downgraded to a National Agency for Tourism. Meanwhile in agriculture an Agency of State Domains was to dispose of the equity held by state farms while land would be leased rather than sold: again with 80 per cent of proceeds to an agricultural fund At this time of protracted dispute over restitution or compensation, the DP was lobbying over its own plan for a National Agency of State Farms.

Indifferent Results

Nevertheless, despite the culture change in favour of privatisation to conform to expert opinion and deliver funds to the state budget, there were still disappointments precipitating the removal of privatisation minister Sorin Dimitriu in 1998, although he claimed that political instability acted as a constraint and argued that privatisation 'against the clock', as required by the Vasile government, could be damaging and even catastrophic. The tempo certainly accelerated when R.Sârbu took over as head of the SOF in 1998 (after successful activity on the ground in Cluj-Napoca) and, with further decentralisation of privatisation negotiations to the counties, he was able to announce his intention of completing the entire programme by the end of the government's term. But some sales by auction realised disappointingly low values and many deals gave rise to litigation. He also stirred up bad feeling by keeping parliamentarians at arm's length in order to end 'trafficking in influence'; while the opposition were able to play on any transparency deficit and the sale of strategic companies for low prices. In 1999 as a whole 1,772 companies were sold (out of 4,330 available at the start of the year). This left 2,558 enterprises on the books at the start of 2000 and instead of disposing of all of them the total reached only 1,366 (with a very low rate – only 5.0 per cent in the first half of the year – to foreign investors). Moreover, a substantial number of contracts signed in 1998 and 1999 had to be cancelled because the investors could not honour their commitments. A major failing lay with the financial sector where government was dismayed by the performance of state banks in providing credit to the contracting non-government sector. Privatisation of two small banks was planned in 1998 followed by three larger ones in 1999, but progress only started with the RDB at the end of 1998 with Banc post following in 1999 – though the ailing Bancorex was closed and absorbed by the Romanian Commercial Bank (RCB), a quarter of which was eventually sold to EBRD and IFC in 2003. Needless to say methods of privatisation were constantly debated in the search for more flexible approaches. However over four years a total of 5,709 enterprises were privatised, taking Negrescu's (2000) figures for 1997-9 and those published in the newspaper 'Adevarul' (9 September 2006) for 2000. However, there are discrepancies between the two sets of figures since the Adevarul total of 8,824 for 1990–99 leaves only 3,113 for the period before 1997 when Negrescu's figures for 1997–99 (totalling 5,709) are deducted.

The Problem of Non-Viable Enterprises
Profitable companies were attracting interest from employee associations as in the case of the SOF holding in Multiprod (Zalău): a baking, brickmaking, furniture and milling concern with a rising share price. But a special effort was needed over heavy loss-making SOEs and others requiring substantial investment. Privatisation and new investment was often frustrated not only by bureaucratic delays but by union resistance to a high level of redundancy needed to raise productivity. In 1999, 551 large companies remained to be privatised by the SOF, representing about two-thirds of the total number of large enterprises in its portfolio at the beginning of 1992. It was evident that the high level of debts and arrears of large public companies was a major stumbling block because foreign investors were reluctant to take on the liabilities. Liquidation (and the selling-off of equipment) was contemplated for some smaller companies with huge losses where no interest could be found, such as Carpidarfil (Darabani) – formerly a branch of Uzinele Textile Moldova – with a share capital of 7.0bln.lei and debts of 5.0bln; also Hidropneumatica (Botoşani) with 8.0bln.lei capital and 15bln.lei debts. But this was not considered an option for very large companies.

In a bid to grasp the nettle five companies were singled out – Clujana (Cluj), IUG (Craiova), Nitramonia (Făgăraş), Roman (Braşov) and Siderurgica (Hunedoara) – with the intention of privatising or liquidating three of them. When this proved impossible agreement was subsequently reached with the World Bank over privatisation of 64 SOEs (thus greatly enlarging the original list) through a Private Sector Adjustment Loan (PSAL) attracting $500mln in two tranches and a Private Sector Institutional Development Programme. The entire exercise in restructuring and professional reconversion (known as RICOP) aimed at eliminating losses and reducing arrears by the end of 2000, with some dismissals. The list included many of the country's leading enterprises like Alro (Slatina), Antibiotice (Iaşi), Electroputere (Craiova), Romvag (Caracal), Sidex (Galati), Tarom (Bucharest), Terom (Iaşi), Tractorul (Braşov) and Upetrom I Mai (Ploieşti). Foreign consultants were appointed to advise on the best privatisation strategy, for instance the French Bank Paribas Corporate Finance won the competition to act as consultant for the aluminium companies Alro and Alprom (2000). PSAL objectives also included a privatisation plan for RCB, the Romanian Savings Bank (RSB) – with a special company to implement a managerial, operational and financial audit – and Eximbank, with a feasibility study from a consulting company. In the case of oil giant Petrom an investment bank was to handle the sale of the company to a strategic purchaser, while privatisation of a quarter of the gas distribution sector was scheduled for the end of 2001. These goals proved to be hopelessly optimistic but at least a new formula was now on the table.

A Radical Approach? Many in government thought that loss-making industrial giants should be broken up to eliminate unproductive sectors with large enterprises surrounded by a circle of SMEs to revitalise inefficient segments. Thus the Sidex privatisation strategy involved hiving-off accessories like apartments and houses, the canteen, cleaning services, the farm and greenhouse, a hotel and several villas, protection equipment, a rest and recovery complex, transport services and security. In this way some 6,000 people would leave the direct employ of the company during 1998–2000. Having been hived-off, the new companies would have one year of privileged relations with Sidex, acting as main shareholder of the new companies in order to control priorities and costs. Eventually repair work would also be hived-off to leave only the basic production flow by 2003. On the other hand some still questioned the wisdom of privatisation: while it might be the key to performance, buyers needed to be chosen with care and the advisability of forcing the pace seemed dubious under the prevailing (unattractive) economic environment. In the case of 'jewels' like the profitable aluminium companies there seemed to be no great urgency. But staggering losses were a driving force in almost all cases: at the end of 1998 Sidex was owed 1.1tln.lei by 625 clients but in turn it owed 6.0tln in debts to suppliers (including 1.0tln for electricity alone), tax funds and unpaid dividends. Indeed losses made by just 10 unprofitable state enterprises accounted for 7.5 per cent of the state budget.

Enterprises Outside the SOF Portfolio While some of the utilities – like RT – were restructured, there were still plenty of state assets in the defence, energy and transport sectors lying outside the SOF portfolio where only limited progress was made to convert them into commercial companies and overcome problems of obsolescence and over-staffing. The electricity company was burdened by an inefficient distribution system that consumed half the power generated and a poor collection record from customers; while financing the expansion of the Cernavodă nuclear power station had become a big political issue with leasing arrangements a possible way of safeguarding the infrastructure of the Romanian nuclear industry. Links between energy companies and their suppliers and customers were greatly complicated by some massive liabilities. Electricity generators owed money to coal producers that could not be paid because of larger sum owed by their consumers: one of them was Tractorul (Braşov) which in turn found itself decapitalised in 1997 with no money to buy raw materials and energy (though it had orders for 26,000 tractors) and sought a government guarantee for a $30mln credit to refloat production. Like many other companies, it had tried to finance itself through internal resources and the accumulation of arrears to suppliers and creditors. 172bln.lei of electricity debts by the alumina producer Ferom (Tulcea) forced a reduction in output (working with 60MW of power capacity out of the total of 2,000MW) and dismissal of 600 workers in 1998. Vâlcea furnished a particularly complex situation: Govora power station was owed 150bln.lei by the massive Oltchim petrochemical complex and another 87bln.lei by the local soda works, while it was itself in debt to the tune of 143bln to the Berbeşti lignite mine. To keep the debt as low as possible coal stocks were reduced from the usual 450,000t to 97,000t and contributed to a run-down of employment at the mine (producing the best lignite in Oltenia) from 9,800 to some 2,500 during 1997–98. As a result the 230bln owed to it was almost matched by its own escalating debts of 220bln. Vâlcea CC wanted to resolve the situation by having the mine take over the power station and the rail link, while the soda factory might be privatised and Oltchim supported by more government loans.

Small- and Medium-Sized Enterprises

The centre-right government thought the potential for SMEs in society was underestimated and they sought better credit arrangements in the hope that the sector would grow to contribute more than two-thirds of national GDP, sustain salary levels on a par with ECE generally and include a proportion of enterprises (5.0 per cent) with an innovative character and export orientation. The government also stated its intention of privatising SMEs with majority state-owned capital by the end of 1998 and undertook to facilitate the development of SMEs through a progressive profits tax with discounts for reinvestment; simplification of the permit system and book-keeping procedures; and a fund for SME development and environmental protection. Meanwhile CCIs were to improve the supply of information (including foreign funding possibilities), as well as training and liaison with national and local government and NGOs. There appeared to be good potential in rural areas for non-agricultural activities, given the acute shortage of craftsmen and tradesmen (barbers, carpenters, clock repairers, photographers, shoemakers, tailors and upholsterers) for many of the surviving practitioners were old and there was a lack of training through the education system and apprentice schools. Hence the potential for SMEs not just in urban centres but in village development through provision of an infrastructure and marketing system for various handicraftsmen generating large volumes of standard products appropriate for mail order firms distributing catalogues e.g. carpets, wooden bowls or painted eggs (though ceramics posed a problem for the American market because the glazes included a lot of lead which US standards did not allow). Help was again forthcoming from various quarters. Some NGOs provided consulting services, assisted by the International Management Foundation's Fund for Local Development Initiatives. Local centres were also assisted by the governments of various countries (Germany and Italy as well as Romania) and by programmes for training and technical assistance such as Phare, Know-How (UK) and USAID. Also helpful was a World Bank loan to fight unemployment through financial and technical support for people to start their own businesses and by counselling for small enterprisers (as well as labour market information enabling people to apply for specific jobs; training /professional re-entry courses; and support for economic agents in job creation).

SMEs were encouraged by the Ciorbea government to absorb unemployed people and they increased their share of labour but not their contribution to turnover. Most operated in light industry and were not prominent in wood and chemicals. As economic growth stalled, 80 per cent of SMEs substantially reduced turnover in 1997 or fell into a bankrupt state due to economic depression and high interest. While 71 per cent were profitable in 1996, the proportion fell to 47 per cent in 1998 and was destined to fall still further. Yet when Radu Vasile relaunched an SME programme in 1998 strategic objectives included an improved credit arrangement to achieve a share of two-thirds of GDP, with salary levels on a par with CEE. Moreover a proportion (5.0 per cent) of SMEs were to be innovators with an export orientation while all state-owned SMEs were to be privatised. Arrangements were made to introduce exemption from customs taxes for the import of know-how, machinery, equipment and raw materials in 1999; also a low profit tax rate (20 per cent) where new job creation increased staff numbers by a fifth or more over the previous year. Unfortunately the financial pressures of 1998-9 prevented implementation. Hence the balance sheet at the end of the decade was rather disappointing.

An Unpredictable Business Environment
During 1997–2000 SMEs (mainly in retailing and manufacturing) accounted for over half total turnover, a quarter of all exports and a fifth of all investment undertaken by enterprises. The share of employees working in SMEs rose from 33 per cent in 1997 to 47 per cent in 2000. Their share of turnover in 2000 was 56.1 per cent and gross value added 39.5 per cent. However, according to the 2000 'Country Report' (p.65), many SMEs faced economic difficulty given "the lack of a predictable business environment" and in particular constant changes in the legal framework for SMEs that was burdensome to individual enterprises. Government did not respond to the problems identified including administrative barriers. Although registration procedures were streamlined, SMEs still faced a maze of bureaucratic regulation resulting in "an oppressive and harmful environment in which firms do not flourish or choose not to participate in the formal economy" (Ibid, p.10). Suffocated by taxation they lacked the force for steady development and often struggled to get finance and management expertise. It was necessary to stop losses through inflation, corruption and fiscal aberrations; and instead to lower taxation while encouraging investment of profits and stimulating exports. The incorporation of the FPSME into the National Agency for Regional Development (along with the Romanian Development Agency)

was seen as a sign of reduced importance for SMEs given the insufficient funding available. There was corroboration from the Council (originally National Forum) of Private SMEs – founded in 1992 as an NGO representing 40,000 businesses through 41 branches – that of the 800.0th private SMEs registered only 401.5th produced a balance sheet for 1999 due to the poor business environment arising from the high bank interest rate and the continuing lack of a banking culture for SMEs; also difficulties in accessing foreign markets and lack of management training. Only 168.7th enterprises showed a profit. Thanks to a particularly sharp decline of units in commerce the total number of SMEs declined from 314.2 to 306.1 thousand during 1997–2000 (Table 5.1).

Sources of Assistance   FPSME organised a Phare-financed contest of business plans under the title 'Local Economic Development by Entrepreneurial Spirit', while Phare also helped with management training. Chicago Manufacturing Center (with a good record for updating and internationalising SMEs in USA) started working with Romania's national level CCI in 1998, which also launched a programme for closer communication between government and private companies to improve the business climate and stimulate exports. In 1998 there was also a drive to use school workshops for vocational training to provide the skilled labour for SMEs and it was suggested that SMEs should have access to space in the state sector and should enjoy tax concessions in respect of reinvested profits and fiscal incentives in special economic zones. A wide range of financial support was provided at this time, with most schemes focusing on specific parts of the country where the SME sector was particularly in need of development to reduce unemployment. In 1998 the Soros Fund for Economic Development began micro-financing with loans through Bancpost exclusively addressed to the small entrepreneurs in the economically less developed rural regions. The loan methodology was a combination between individual crediting and collective community responsibility; working with groups comprising the most respected members of the community. By 2002 3,200 one-year credits had been granted – worth over \$2.0mln, with an average credit of \$600 and a maximum of \$2,000. Many loans went to Iaşi county with others to Călăraşi and Dâmboviţa. They helped farmers to purchases seeds, fertilisers, machines and irrigation equipment; and they also supported handcraft workshops and services including rural tourism.

Regionally-Selective Measures   became common at a time of more 'joined-up' thinking over regional disparities, after the issue had been largely ignored in the early 1990s or dealt with on an ad hoc basis until the development regions were created at the end of the decade. In 1999 FPSME offered 10bln.lei for SME development in five pilot localities (Baia Mare, Buzău, Călăraşi, Miercurea Ciuc and Reşiţa) to include the development of institutions and there was also \$2.0mln from USA for SMEs in Caraş-Severin, Mehedinţi and Timiş adversely affected by Kosovo War. In 2000 the EC and the Agency for SMEs put €5.75mln at the disposal of companies doing business in Bucharest and also Argeş, Botoşani, Braşov, Cluj, Constanţa, Iaşi, Neamţ, Olt, Prahova, Suceava, Teleorman, Timiş and Vaslui. Also Phare support was provided through RSB credits (where this would constitute at least 15 per cent of investment value) in Botoşani, Braşov, Constanţa, Olt, Suceava, Teleorman, Sibiu, Timiş and Vaslui counties. And there were also RSB credits of up to DM100,000 from the Romanian-German Fund (Kreditanstalt für Wiederautbau) for projects in Bucharest, Braşov, Constanţa, Mureş and Sibiu. Micro-credits were available through the UNDP, the National Solidarity Fund and the Association for the Assistance of Entrepreneurs of Romania with centres in Alba Iulia, Braşov, Bucharest, Buzău, Constanţa, Drobeta-Turnu Severin, Focşani, Galaţi, Iaşi. Oradea, Petroşani, Ploieşti, Satu Mare, Târgovişte, Târgu Mureş, Timişoara, Tulcea and Vaslui. Credits could be used for equipment, rehabilitation of warehouses and storage places, raw material processing and trading of products, animal breeding and production/trade of handicrafts. Finally, the National Agency for Occupational & Professional Training declared that SMEs (and cooperatives) qualified for credit at advantageous interest rates from the Unemployment Fund via the Bancpost network. It should also be mentioned that as part of the restructuring of the mining industry launched in 1998 'less-favoured areas' were identified where new enterprises would benefit from tax

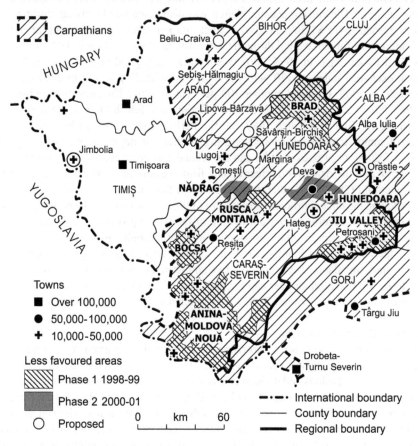

Figure 5.1 Less favoured areas in West Region

exemptions for up to ten years. The relevant areas in West Region are shown in Figure 5.1. Despite some pressure to extend the incentives to rural areas in need of further diversification (as requested by Arad county) the programme was restricted to mining areas, although the industrial restructuring areas identified in 2001 gave substantial assistance for SMEs.

The Second Iliescu Presidency 2001–2004

Policy Overview for the PDSR government under A. Năstase

Growth was maintained during this period at rates close to the 6.5 per cent level needed to achieve half the EU level in 2010. Strong exports brought a recovery in investment, with rising household consumption a factor in 2003, although questions were raised over labour flexibility, the extension of privatisation into the energy sector and improvements in the business environment (especially over corruption and bureaucracy). The current account deficit was also contained by rising remittances from abroad (over $1.5bln in 2002). Stock market values started rising after the withdrawal of foreign capital through the turmoil in Asian markets in 1997 followed by the Russian crisis in 1998: 2002 was a particularly good year with a Bucharest stock exchange index of 130 per cent compared with 39 per cent in 2001 and 26 per cent in 2003: it gained another 100 per cent in 2004. The consolidated budget deficit fell to 2.3 per cent in 2003 and inflation also fell, hitting single figures in 2004 for the first time since 1989, but the performance tended to be poorer than that of major trading partners suggesting further leu depreciation, especially in view of sharp wage rises in 2003 and the related consumer credit boom (sucking in imports); also the rising food prices arising from the poor 2003 wheat harvest. Carey & Eisterhold (2004, p.18) therefore commented that "unless financial discipline is imposed on the budget process the pressure of the central bank on the banking sector in general will become a constant feature of the way the system functions". There was a danger of populist macroeconomics in 2004 through unjustified public sector wage increases; also a looming crisis in social security with an ageing population and a 'stark imbalance' between the active and retired population. FDI increased but not to its full potential and per capita GDP reached $6,560PPPy in 2003, with a big disparity in earnings between $4,837 for women and $8,311 for men.

A Strong Reform Programme
The situation was somewhat surprising in view of the government's communist pedigree, but it's promises were modest: an enlarged tax base to include agricultural revenues, high pensions and dividends, a unitary VAT rate of 19 per cent, the phasing out of tax incentives for export; and a ceiling of 36 per cent on subsidy for the Bucharest metro. With the advantage of political strength, it also showed greater commitment to tight macro-economic policies than its predecessors, with stronger regulatory frameworks and financial system supervision that improved financial discipline for SOEs. The standby arrangement with the IMF – concluded in 2001 for a total of $431mln of which $273 was already received – reached a successful

conclusion (the first for 25 years) in 2003 with the final tranche of $159mln, delivered in the context of falling budget deficits (below 3.0 per cent of GDP), the elimination of losses from the energy sector and an ambitious privatisation programme. Premier Năstase was keen to enter into another IMF agreement almost immediately in order to keep economic policy on the right track and provide a guarantee in foreign markets that rules necessary for Romania's stability were being followed. A mission early in 2004 reached a standby arrangement to reduce inflation from 9.0 per cent in 2004 to 6.0 per cent 2005 and 5.0 per cent in 2006. 23,000 redundancies in the SOEs were agreed including 6,000 in railway sector and 7,000 in mining – plus 10-11,000 in other companies in the privatisation portfolio. IMF control seemed rational but risked inhibiting a domestic consensus over procedures for policy formulation. There was also interest in restitution by providing a fund (from parts of the government's holdings in RT, the national lottery and the national printing house) to compensate owners of properties abusively seized by communists that could not for various reasons be returned.

In Search of FME Status
With accession in 2007 looming, the EU was keen to maintain pressure and was reluctant to concede the ultimate economic prize of a 'functioning market economy'. The 'Country Report' of 2002 acknowledged progress but called for full and sustained implementation of planned measures. There was particular concern over environment because of inadequate administrative capacities (for legislative alignment and implementation) and financial resources for investment. The 2003 report was the best ever in view of favourable economic indicators with FME status linked with more decisive progress for 'vigorous and sustained implementation' of the reform programme, while the political situation was again reviewed positively as it had been since 1997. However, it also drew attention to disappointing collection rates for social security contributions and excise duties, the growth of tax arrears at enterprises undergoing restructuring and privatisation and the rapid growth of wages and private sector credit that was boosting imports. There were also references to the need for an independent judiciary, reduced corruption, improved human and minority rights (also relief for prison overcrowding and harassment of journalists and a more independent National Council for Combating Discrimination). In 2004, with the continuation of good indicators including much lower arrears, the government hoped for a good report to boost its election chances given the progress of privatisation in the energy sector and indeed it virtually crossed the finishing line with a concession from Brussels that Romania could be regarded as a FME provided that reform continued (implying that significant further reforms were still needed). Tension arose over the fact that Bulgaria had gained FME status in 2002 (as noted in the previous chapter). However Romania was fortunate that Brussels was tolerant towards the Năstase government's appalling corruption record with oligarchic domination a primary impediment to reform. Carey & Eisterhold (2004, p.17) declared that "the transparency and the public accountability which the EU will demand for Romania's entry in 2007 is nowhere evident".

Trade Policy in Support of Exports

Given the critical importance of sustaining a rise in exports, the government took a keen interest in trade, with the Foreign Trade Department subordinated directly to the prime minister in 2002. Exports were dominated by clothing, textiles and footwear worth €5,060mln (32.4 per cent): 2.3 times the share of imports, generating a surplus of €3,153mln in 2003. Exports of machinery and metallurgical products were worth €4,522mln (28.9 per cent) although in this case imports were much higher at €6,708mln (31.7 per cent). Export growth was impeded by slower growth in the Euro zone while competitiveness was affected by higher energy costs, with further pressure anticipated through the removal of concessionary levels of profits tax in 2004 (when a standard rate of 25 per cent would apply). Trade experts also referred to the low level of export credits provided by the banking system to export companies, especially in the agri-food sector. With some positive signs of export diversification into light machinery and electrical appliances in 2002, the government launched a financial plan in the following year to galvanise activity with an increase in Eximbank's capital by 500bln.lei to support agriculture (including export premiums for poultry, dairy, cereals, edible oil, vegetables and frozen fruit). With the Russian market posing considerable risks, despite its huge absorption potential, Eximbank then tried to encourage commercial relations through a guarantee system (85 per cent of the non-payment risk) at a time when Romanian trade centres were opened at the river ports of Rostov on Don and Samara to sell furniture, wine and mineral water (with the possibility of light industrial and chemical products to follow) supported by RCB and RDB. The Latin American market was also promising through its growing demand for trucks and tractors of the cheaper, stronger and less-sophisticated type that Romania could offer. Unfortunately ARO four-wheel drive cars sent to Colombia were found to have so many problems with the engine and gearbox that the export agreement broke down, while further problems arose over the quality of drilling equipment sent to Latin America.

The Contested 2004 Budget

In an election year the 2004 budget was a matter of much concern and the outcome of the balancing act was a deficit of 3.0 per cent of GDP (expenditure 33.1 per cent of GDP and revenue 30.1 per cent). This was not really appreciated by the IMF since it threatened both the inflation target of 9.0 per cent and a current account deficit below 5.0 per cent of GDP, unless the savings/investment balance of SOEs could be improved by 1.0 per cent of GDP through higher energy prices, faster restructuring (especially in mining and transport) and wage rises below inflation. But the government was keen to press ahead with major infrastructure projects, including motorway construction, and hence the compromise between the proposal of 3.7 per cent and the 2.7 per cent projected for 2003. Although inflation was falling, the impending election made it difficult to place pressure on welfare spending and public sector wage demands, while increased energy prices (seeking to reduce consumption) were deferred until after the election on the grounds of political expediency, thereby prompting further leu depreciation. Hence the IMF concern that domestic demand might increase the current account deficit 'already at the upper bounds of sustainability'. However while rises in credit and wages made for higher imports and a sharp increase in trade deficit – with the current account deficit of €4.4bln in 2004 widening by 43.9 per cent over 2003, with a trade balance of – €5.5bln – the rise in the Euro helped to maintain export competitiveness.

Restructuring and Privatisation

The private sector was now just over two-thirds of the total, although it fell slightly from 67.9 per cent in 2001 to 66.8 per cent in 2002 after a poor performance in agriculture. The government's action plan envisaged further privatisation to help reduce public debt – with a clear separation of the production, transport and distribution of energy – and made a particular commitment (which was not achieved) to privatise the RSB in 2001. There was commitment to reform and financial discipline as the ultra-cautious SOF was replaced by the Agency for the Privatisation and Management of State Holdings (APMSH) under the control of a minister for privatisation. Progress was accelerated by legal authority to sell at nominal prices (as little as a symbolic Euro in the 2002 law for accelerated privatisation) in return for commitments to invest, And there was a further change in 2004 with the transfer of 90 per cent of the 1,187 remaining state companies to a new Authority for Recouping State Assets (ARSA) with the primary task of administering privatisation contracts (i.e. monitoring the compliance of new owners). There was also an offer of transparent concessions allowing fair treatment for all investors and 'eliminating the arbitrary, subjective practices which can become sources of corruption'. In 2002 emphasis was placed on job tenders to stimulate offers to create 100-200 jobs. Meanwhile a 'White Charter' in 2001 provided for restructuring in energy and defence production and preparation for the privatisation of Petrom as well as electricity and gas distribution companies. A National Restructuring Fund (to be managed by the finance ministry or APMSH) was to take 60 per cent of the income from privatisation for new technology in companies being prepared for sale. And while the government was struggling to improve infrastructure, notably in IT, there was American help in making Romanian enterprises more attractive for investors through studies at Chimcomplex Borzeşti (Oneşti) with 2,100 employees and a large output of chlorine-sodium products and pesticides. Some assets were now divided like the catering and leisure organisation Socalp (Bacău) offered as eight separate units (a solution belatedly adopted at resorts on the Black Sea coast). The vast 'Free Press House' (the monumental Scânteia building in northern Bucharest, erected in the communist period) was broken up with the sale of the 'thousands of offices' within. Altogether the government disposed of 966 of the remaining 1,192 companies with annual figures of 211, 290, 307 and 158, according to the Adevarul data already referred to.

Privatisation Successes
Despite the spectacular failure to attract a single bidder for the state airline Tarom, some significant SOEs were disposed of in 2001 like the Agricultural Bank, Constanţa shipyard and the RAFO (Oneşti) oil refinery that left 1,673 outstanding at the end of the year; reduced to 1,342 in mid-2003 when 10 per cent were held by ministries and 90 per cent by APMSH (seeking to dispose of everything during the rest of the year so that the organisation could become a post-privatisation control body).

The situation was helped by agreement in 2002 with the World Bank over a further ($300mln) structural adjustment programme leading to the start of a second PSAL the following year with early success for the Hiperion (Stei, Bihor) mining and heavy industrial equipment producer and the stainless steel pipe maker Tubinox (Bucharest). Negotiations proceeded in several cases: some with foreign firms like the Swiss/Indian business of R.K.Goenka for the Corapet (Corabia) synthetic fibre plant and a combination of General Motors (USA) and Keg (Germany) for the vast electrical engineering complex of Electroputere (Craiova) while domestic interests – Interagro (Victoria) and Tender Group (Timişoara) – considered the Viromet (Victoria) phenol/methanol factory and the engineering works of Vulcan (Bucharest). Many deals did not succeed like Electroputere that had accumulated enormous debts of 1.21tln.lei in 2005, although in this case the sticking point was the government's insistence on keeping the whole complex together instead of disposing of individual sections (a strategy ultimately conceded in 2006).

Performance was, once again, well below target through reluctance to liquidate all the enterprises for which buyers could not be found. The matter was becoming crucial with continuing financial indiscipline through mounting arrears especially in the energy sector. The EU expressed concern over this problem since total arrears advanced from 4.0 to 4.5 per cent of GDP during 2003: sufficiently large to pose a threat to fiscal stability and external viability. Moreover labour was still flowing into unproductive sectors where workers were paid more than their marginal productivity. In the case of bus maker Rocar (Bucharest) – one of seven very heavy loss-makers remaining at the start of 2004; along with the metal fabrication works CMB (Bocşa), the logging firm Brafor (Braşov), the tube maker Republica (Bucharest), the heavy engineering works CUG (Cluj), the ball bearing manufacturer Rulmenţi (Slatina) and Contac (Tecuci) – the factory was notorious for its lack of competitiveness combined with a hard core of militancy that presumed on government orders in response to management failure to 'get closer' to European producers: essential if the plant was to survive as anything more than a spare parts producer. The situation was even worse since several 2003 privatisation contracts failed – the 'Landrover' maker ARO (Câmpulung) and Tractorul (Braşov). And the situation was not helped by conditions that APMSA felt obliged to impose e.g. insisting on buyers with five years experience in the manufacturing and supply of specific products – and an average annual turnover of $250mln over the previous three years – in the case of the huge Oltchim (Râmnicu Vâlcea) chemical complex.

The Sidex Scenario Fortunately some privatisations were highly successful like Sidex (Galaţi) – one of the great problem enterprises of PSAL – that was acquired by Mittal Steel in 2001 But how easily could the Sidex scenario be repeated? Arguably it needed "a global player in the respective industry, aiming at creating competitive advantage over global competitors by taking over emerging markets" (Dăianu 2004, p.405). Dăianu saw disappointments over OTE (Greece) with RT and Noble Ventures (USA) at the Reşiţa steelworks because these investors lacked 'global reach' as regional or niche players at best: hence "their managerial experience in reviving distressed companies was limited and their international network was not sufficiently expanded" (Ibid) with their Romanian assets offering a local competitive advantage but not a global one. There seemed a good chance of success with a Myo-O takeover of Tractorul that could benefit from their market knowledge as a dealer (as had occurred with the Bucharest farm machinery manufacturer Semănătoarea), but the deal fell through. And there were high hopes in the energy sector with sale of a 33.4 per cent stake in Petrom (plus investment to 51 per cent) to ÖMV (Austria) who succeeded in competition with ENI (Italy), Gazprom (Russia), Glencore (Switzerland), Hellenic Petroleum (Greece), MOL (Hungary), Occidental (US) and PKN Orlen (Poland). There were also offerings in regional electricity and gas distribution companies. The Banat and Dobrogea regional electricity distribution companies attracted interest from ENI (with Moldova and Oltenia to follow) while Enel (Italy), Gaz de France, Gazprom (Russia), Ruhrgas and Wintershall (Germany) were possible bidders for the two large gas distributors:Distrigaz Nord and Distrigaz Sud. All were politically sensitive companies and realistic bids were essential.

Small and Medium-Sized Enterprises

Further promotion efforts were made since there was really no alternative 'social safety valve' to generate new jobs and enhance export penetration. A ministry for SMEs was created and the first minister, Silvia Ciornei, acknowledged their importance. There were then 620,000 in Romania (97 per cent of all trading companies) but only 190,000 were profitable. Simpler incorporation and licensing procedures were announced. Customs exemptions were again allowed on machinery imports and the rate of taxation of profits was cut where new jobs were created. Later Ciornei referred to SMEs as the 'decisive leverage' for the development of the Romanian economy and the best way to lower the unemployment rate. They accounted for 44.3 per cent of employees and generated 67.1 per cent of GDP, yet taxation was irrational with access to funding ever more difficult. Although she also referred to market concepts in education and entrepreneur training centres, finance was certainly a major issue since local commercial banks were far more active in providing funds money for large enterprises: 23 per cent of their needs compared with just five per cent for SMEs, which therefore had to depend much more heavily – to the extent of 15 per cent – on family and friends. In addition, internal funds and retained earnings provided 65 per cent of financial needs of SMEs compared with 52 per cent for large enterprises. The share of loans going to SMEs was increasing – with over 3,000bln.lei of state/EU finance provided in 2002 for newly-launched SME projects (and the same in 2003) – but beneficiaries were still all too few. Lacking their 'dedicated' sources for risk capital with reasonable rates of interest, as well as training and consulting facilities for loan application, they were rarely taken seriously by banks.

Improved Financial Arrangements

To get around problems of collateral the minister wanted banks to give loans based on business plans with only the future receipts as guarantee; with more involvement by guarantee funds in the SME sector. A National Guarantee Fund for Loans to SMEs (2002) was hailed as a concrete expression of the government's SME policy. Further finance came from the Black Sea Bank for Trade & Development ($10mln to be distributed by Bancpost) while in 2001 EBRD offered $5mln to support modern techniques and production units through loans managed by the Transilvania Bank: the first bank in Romania to benefit from EBRD confidence to carry out a financing programme for SMEs under a contract signed originally in 1999. The following year EBRD provided a loan of €22.5mln through the same bank but also worked through RCB and Alpha Bank, with the latter also receiving €10mln to finance SMEs during 2003–2004. In 2002 Greece granted Romania €70mln in non-reimbursable funds as part of a Balkan reconstruction plan to foster SMEs covering energy, water, gas and the environment (also to finance hospitals, kindergartens and schools) and small credits were available from Romanian-American Investment Fund and the Romanian-German Fund (through Eximbank and RSB). Conditions naturally varied over maximum grant, pay-back arrangements, owner's nationality (usually Romanians only), beneficiary's contributions from own resources, maximum size of business (employees and/or turnover) and economic sector. Some funding continued to be tied to specific areas e.g. the Swiss government HEKS/EPER Foundation targeted Braşov, Covasna, Harghita and Mureş counties, while the International Fund for Agricultural Development was interested in the Apuseni Mountains and the World Bank supported mining areas. The latter also supplied micro-loans in 2002 for retraining military officers through business incubators; beginning in Bucharest with Bacău, Braşov, Constanţa, Craiova, Moreni, Oradea and Vălenii de Munte to follow.

Government restructuring in 2003 then eliminated the new SME ministry in favour of a national agency seeking a better business environment (with simplified procedures, coherent legislation including fiscal incentives and more consistent programmes) and access to finance. It transpired that a third of SMEs were unaware of non-reimbursable funding: €825mln was available 2005 and more later. Problems were revealed through financial blockage (with slow payment for work done at schools and sanitary installations) and lack of orders – hence 30,000 SMEs disappeared. Money owed by SOEs accounted for 40–45 per cent of the total SME debt. SMEs had to present guarantees when tendering for contracts from SOEs but the latter did not reciprocate with payment guarantees for the work done. The situation in Europe was certainly better for infrastructure, legislation, state administration, institutional mechanisms and banking systems to help with information, finance and services. So it was hoped that Romania would benefit from a forthcoming European Charter for Small Enterprises during 2004–2008. The situation at the end of the Năstase government saw Romania with only 22 SMEs/ptp compared with 57 in EU; with less than half the productivity of the EU and barely 15 per cent of the capital. With 60 per cent of Romanian SMEs in commerce (EU 25 per cent) and only 16 per cent in services (EU 30 per cent), their contribution to exports remained insignificant at only five per cent.

The Băsescu Presidency 2005–2007

Policy Overview for the Coalition Government of C. Popescu-Tăriceanu

As noted in the preface, the surprise victory of the centrist T. Băsescu in the 2004 presidential election over former premier A. Năstase paved the way to a realignment of parliamentary forces to deny the centre-left – heavily implicated in corruption scandals – a further term in office. This is the era that has witnessed EU accession and it will require ongoing attention to free society institutions, especially the functioning of the market and civil society. It will also require careful economic management despite the blessing of a rising trajectory that could peak at 8.0 per cent with greater efficiency and stronger market mechanisms. And while social justice is still high on the agenda with the pension problem a major issue, poverty is being eased by higher employment and foreign remittances. PSDR (now PSD) had already decided on a major taxation reform through a standard flat rate of 23 per cent in 2005, after deducting pension and private health contributions and mortgage interest. This meant eliminating a low band of 9.0 per cent as well as higher bands extending upwards 23 per cent to 40 per cent but since there were only 7.0 per cent of tax payers in these higher bands progressive taxation was considered inefficient (although socially equitable) whereas its abolition might reduce tax evasion and yield higher revenue. It was also important to 'rein in' the underground economy (with a 30–50 per cent share) as quickly as possible and compete with low tax régimes elsewhere. However while endorsing the flat tax concept, the Justice & Truth Alliance (JTA) between the DP and NLP opted for a lower rate of 16 per cent with personal allowances of 2.5mln (plus 1.0mln for each dependent to a maximum of 6.5mln) on monthly salaries under 10mln; tapering to zero for incomes above 30mln/month. Agricultural revenues are also taxed at 16 per cent (up from 15 per cent) while turnover tax doubled for SMEs (1.5–3.0 per cent) and dividends (5–10 per cent). The new rate also applied to corporation tax and so provided a boost for FDI.

Fiscal Reforms

In a bid to reduce speculation, a 10 per cent tax was imposed on property and stock market deals completed from April 2005 onwards, although critics argued that they could be harmful to 'maturing markets'. The government also stopped debt rescheduling for state and private companies in a bid to correct a situation where 27,000 SMEs and 415 large companies were owing money to the state budget including very large amounts in some cases: a handful of companies including Carom, CFR (the state railways) Pitcoal and Termoelectrica owed 23tln.lei (€586mln) between them. This raised the spectre of bankruptcy so that when Planet Leasing was placed under supervision with 128bln.lei owing there was consternation among customers fearing the loss of their cars! Further tax reforms were anticipated in 2006 with a reduced labour tax (possibly from 40 to 15 per cent) and lower social security payments to confront the underground economy and boost investment. However tax changes could increase the budget deficit in the short term, perhaps to 1.5 per cent instead of 0.5 per cent. Following the $400 loan negotiated in 2004 the IMF wanted to see the budget deficit cut from 1.2 per cent in 2004 to 0.5 per cent through tighter fiscal policies (freezing 2,500 education appointments and 4,500 other public sector jobs, reduced agricultural and mining subsidies and public sector pay limited to 4.0 per cent) to halt the current account deterioration, slow consumer spending and control inflation. They would even see a zero deficit potentially a viable option. Fortunately tax income for the first two months of 2005 was up 12 per cent perhaps because stiffer penalties encouraged SMEs to make their salaries legal by paying tax according to the true amounts. Meanwhile the sector was boosted by a new €200mln investment fund for SMEs with €10-100mln annual turnover: €50mln was expected from Société Générale (France) and €30mln from EBRD.

A Potential Economic Propellor for SEE?
Current growth is relying too much on a surge in domestic demand, reflecting high credit and wage growth, plus a culture of arrears and non-payment of taxes that is only just now being seriously addressed. There were substantial stock market rises in 2005 (commonly between a third and a half) and an inflow of funds triggered leu appreciation that posed a threat to exports: indeed the Central Bank had to buy €600mln in mid-February 2005 to contain a rising leu exchange of 38,000 per Euro (3.80 new lei). But after November 2004 the leu suddenly appreciated 11 per cent over the Euro (16 per cent for the dollar) – more than any other currency – making the leu the third most attractive currency for investors worldwide (after Polish złoty and Brazilian real). The rise followed (a) the national bank decision in November to reduce its role in managing the leu and (b) the lifting of the exchange rate anchor to meet the June 2005 deadline for capital account liberalisation. Hard currency reserves rose to €13.2tln in 2005. Convertibility has now been completed with Romanian residents able to open current and deposit accounts abroad, balanced by the option for non-residents to open lei accounts in Romania: the latter is a step in freeing Romania's capital account (previously held up by inflation) and could bring in some €2.0bln of hot money – with a consequent danger of leu appreciation.

Currency reform through redenomination was effected in July 2005 when 10,000 old lei became a single 'heavy' leu, although the two systems ran in parallel until the end of 2006. There are now four coins and notes for five, 10, 50, 100 and 500 lei. Money should stay on Romanian capital and real estate markets, but hot money is chasing too few stocks – new shares on the stock exchange are needed. A lower interest rate may also be needed to stop speculative capital (though this could boost an already buoyant domestic demand) – with further liberalisation to accommodate higher FDI inflows that reached €4.1bln of 2004 and €5.2bln in 2005. Meanwhile there is a danger of the economy overheating after growth in 2004, with a widening trade deficit as gains in competitiveness are overtaken by rises in credit and wages as well as a deficit in services. In 2004 imports of €26.3bln (+24.0 per cent) against exports of €18.9bln (+21.3 per cent) generated a €7.34bln gap and a rise in the current account deficit, which was likely to stay at 5.8 per cent in 2005 with tighter policy in 2006 perhaps reducing it to 5.0 per cent. Romania is vulnerable because half her exports come from outsourcing but, if properly managed, overheating could help Romania become the economic propeller for SEE (following China's example) with policies to develop the business environment. This will require Romania to develop her own success model – based on a mix of viable economic policies, educational/ management programmes and new technologies.

A Positive Outlook   follows 8.3 per cent growth in 2004 (the highest since 1989) thanks to a particularly good year in agriculture with 22 per cent growth. Current growth forecasts range from 4.0 to 5.5 per cent (2.0-4.2 per cent for household consumption) but to catch up appreciably on the more advanced countries of Europe will require 7.0 per cent sustained for 25 years and this is difficult to visualise with current levels of competitiveness. Inflation is still coming down from 14.1 per cent in 2003 to 9.3 in 2004 and some 7.0 per cent for 2005 for despite further energy price and excise rises, a proposed VAT increase from 19–22 per cent (9–11 per cent for the lower rate) has been resisted. Prospects for investment are good given the rising financial ratings that reflect the new government's reform commitment and low inflation, although there are constraints through institutional weakness, external imbalances, low prosperity and still a significant loss-making state sector. Fitch ratings have been influenced by a low budget deficit, investment growth through energy privatisation and progress towards EU accession, with all chapters concluded in early in 2005. Romania raised a €700mln by a 10-year Eurobond issue in 2004 followed by a €1.0bln 15-year issue in 2005. A World Bank loan of $475 was negotiated for transport restructuring ($225), modernisation of agricultural knowledge and information ($50), mine closures and environmental/socioeconomic regeneration ($120) and health sector reform ($80).

Foreign investors are pleased with the flat tax but consider the tax system as a whole too unstable and unpredictable: hence they seek an improved collection rate through full and fair enforcement, with a listing of debtors. They also deplore the toleration of illegal labour and look for an immediate anti-corruption strategy for public administration and judiciary reform. More broadly there is some concern over a lack of plurality of ideas on economic policy: the field is dominated by the central bank at a time (just five years from pre-Euro adoption phase) when the high lei exchange rate relies on the inflow of funds: if Romania were to become a net debtor things could change drastically. Other recommendations emerging from the Foreign Investment Council's 'White Book' on the investment climate are: bankruptcy proceedings without the procedural delays sought by unscrupulous entrepreneurs to further erode assets; reduced interest rate differences between lei and foreign currencies; and better regulation of financial and leasing companies. Amendment of the Labour Code is being undertaken because many bodies (including the EU, IMF and World Bank) think it is too strongly balanced towards employees with 240 articles on employer obligations and only 58 for employees; although naturally PSD and the unions do not accept that it is a priority matter. The aim is to reduce restrictions and costs (including the currently high employer social contributions) to ensure a more flexible labour market stimulative for TNCs, though not necessarily for SMEs where many workers see their best security in personal links with employers. It is certainly important to maintain a dialogue between government and business and work to improve competitiveness.

Problems of Institutional Weakness and Corruption   At the time of writing the situation is challenging but hopeful. The currency is appreciating but local experts discounted foreign speculation that the new leu could climb from the 3.80 level already noted to 3.15 at the end of 2005 and 2.80 in 2006. Standard & Poors ratings have moved Romania from the speculative to the investment grade with the upgrade in fiscal indicators and buoyant domestic demand (though the ratings are still constrained by institutional weakness, low prosperity, external imbalances and losses – albeit declining – in the state sector). Careful management of the capital inflow and domestic credit boom is needed. Further progress needs more policy predictability, sustained convergence with more highly-rated peer economies and solutions to governance problems. The national bank is helping with a cut in its overnight facility for surplus currency from 4.0 to 1.0 per cent in order to drive down interest rates on loans and encourage more capital into industry and less on consumption. Meanwhile, the budget creates problems for the IMF and the $400mln standby loan remains on hold after disagreement on public spending and the need for additional revenue to prevent overheating during 2005-6 following the new flat tax without the once-threatened VAT increase from 19 to 22 per cent, yet with a commitment to increase pensions by 6–8 per cent in 2006 (not to mention the costs of 2005's serial flood damage to increase the budget deficit). The government has come up with a 0.5 per cent tax on corporate assets that dismays a business community already paying such a tax to the local authorities (albeit at variable rates). Meanwhile the government chips away at the SOEs with 7,000 further job losses in mining (albeit at a time of falling unemployment). Fiscal evasion is being confronted in such areas as alcohol (€300mln), fuel (€600mln) and building work with an estimated evasion rate of 70 per cent in northern Bucharest alone. The fight against corruption is slow to produce results but court action has annulled the RAFO (oil refinery) shareholders' decision to convert $300mln debts to the state into shares: hence the state will now have precedence over other creditors in recovering the debt. Yet the business culture still attracts censure and former UK ambassador Q. Quayle has commented on a 'gang mentality' that informally brings together business with county and municipal leaders and raises questions over transparency. The subtle distinction between a tip and a bribe ('Bestechungsgelt' as opposed to 'Schmirgelt') is easily clouded over in a situation where bureaucracy can so easily become impenetrable.

Trade and Budget Deficits   The trade deficit rose sharply by €7.3bln (40.4 per cent) in 2005 to €20.3bln (while demand was rising and loans were now cheaper to obtain) and again by €14.9bln in 2006. In January 2006 RDB reduced interest rates on real estate and mortgage loans by 2.1 per cent on Euro accounts (down to 7.9 per cent) and 0.6 per cent on leu accounts (down to 8.9 per cent). The economy is helped by transfers from abroad that rose from €2.97bln in 2004 to €3.66 in 2005. And the government in trying to maximise income from taxation by cutting arrears, including pressure on football clubs and their wealthy owners. Hopes of substantial funds from further privatisation are not being fully realised with the two-year postponement over RSB (a decision now reversed) and the fourth failure over Electroputere privatisation while exports are suffering from the rising leu despite measures to limit foreign currency credits. The national bank is therefore raising its inflation forecast to 9.0 per cent rather than the 7.0 per cent planned and has run into trouble from the IMF that considers state sector wage rises are inconsistent with single figure inflation and also criticises the national bank for its concern over exchange rates rather than price stability. In fact there was a major dispute in autumn 2005 when a $400mln two-year standby loan agreed in 2004 broke down after two weeks of fruitless negotiation with the government rebuffing IMF recommendations on tax, public spending and monetary policy. The IMF claimed that Romania was risking weakened competitiveness, gross macro-economic imbalances, deteriorating education and health services and gaps in physical infrastructure while the government disagreed. This was all very unfortunate but it was not considered crucial since the EU requires merely a 'stable economic framework' rather than strict conformity with all IMF proposals.

While the IMF thinks that the 16 per cent flat tax has deprived the economy of €1.0bln (and wants VAT to rise in sympathy from 19 to 22 per cent), the government points to 150,000 'black jobs' and their respective salaries have come into the reckoning while a VAT rise would damage the government's reputation. The IMF says growth and productivity are falling with imports and external debt rising, but the government points to the special problem of flooding in 2005 whereas the previous year was good for agriculture. So for the time being the IMF agreement is derailed, but the door is open for further talks if the government revises its programme to favour growth rather than excessive consumption. Meanwhile the government was not 'out of the wood' where the EU was concerned, for the 2005 'Country Report' highlighted such matters as slow privatisation, the danger of unbalanced growth and a large budget deficit, the lack of labour market flexibility and low administrative capacity (through insufficient staffing and finance, arising partly though IMF pressure to freeze salaries). Another problem was low absorption of some EU funds amounting to barely a fifth of the €1.8bln available during 2000-5 underlining the need for applicants to have strong partners in commercial banking. It is very important that better use is made of post-accession finance that could total €31.5bln. The 'Country Report' also drew attention to the Agricultural Payments Agency and quality of veterinary services, industrial pollution, the piracy of intellectual property and the need for better control over the regional development fund.

However the economic situation at the time of accession was generally good because in spite of the worrying current account deficit, the debt level was considered to be sustainable given the massive inflow of funds that made for an appreciating currency. Indeed, the leu led the world in its performance against the US dollar; gaining 20 per cent to reach 2.6lei/$ at the time of the Erste privatisation of the RCB. Indeed it was thought capable of sustaining 2.5lei with a doubling of FDI following accession – on the basis of a large home market and low cost/qualified labour – plus a healthy flow of money sent home by Romanians working in Spain (about a quarter of total earnings: €2bln/yr). Romania was also attracting more favourable international ratings with 40 per cent of companies profitable in 2006 (a 10 per cent improvement on 2005). Romanians felt confident enough for unemployment to be banished as the overriding worry and replaced by low wages – albeit with a rising average from 750 new lei/month in 2004 to 1,100 in 2006 – outpaced by price increases; although in August 2006 prices fell for the first time since the revolution thanks to seasonal reductions for fruit and vegetables as well as relaxation for some consumer durables (including refrigerators and washing machines). However the stability of the coalition government remained a matter of concern with the 'final' rupture occurring between the Democratic and Liberal parties; requiring the replacement of the Democratic Party's ministers for home affairs, justice and transport, while the president had to win a referendum following his suspension from office by parliamentarians resenting pressure to divulge their sources of income. There are also continuing regional issues with growth in Bucharest (forecast at 7.0 per cent for 2007–2008) well above the national average of 6.4, although the weakest region – the North East is forecast to do a little better than the average (6.5 per cent) with a substantial hike in average monthly wages (68.2–68.9 per cent of the Bucharest rates) and overtaking the South East in the process (69.1 to 68.7). The poorest county – Vaslui – remains a source of concern with 10 per cent unemployment (very high for Romania where small farms provide social security for many underemployed families) and wages lower than other parts of the North East: construction workers receive 583 new lei/month compared with 711 in Iasi and 949 in Bacău (still below the national average wage of 1,100). There is also much 'black' labour in the country since employers cannot even afford the legal minimum of 390lei for a 170-hour month.

Restructuring, Privatisation and SMEs

The mining industry attracts further lay-offs – 5,000–7,600 for 2005 – with absolutely nil prospect of any early privatisation. The government is promising to make greater use of bankruptcy to reallocate resources by shutting down loss-makers although it remains to be seen if the necessary political will can be summoned. According to the Adevarul figures already discussed 76 state assets were privatised during 2005 and the first seven months of 2006 out of a total of 226 available, plus those added to the list since the beginning of 1999 when Negrescu (2000) stated that 4,330 were available at the time. Elsewhere the saga moves on with a desire to erase enterprise debts before privatisation. Another change is that future privatisation will not include fiscal benefits, such as applied to Petrom with royalties (presumably payable to the state) for exploitation of natural resources frozen for 10 years. Problems remain from earlier programmes: Electoputere, Tractorul and Rulmenţul in 2005 with threats of liquidation that were initially politically incapable of realisation. After four failed attempts, undermined in part by failure to cancel the mammoth debt burden, it seemed that only the most viable sections of Electoputere could be rescued. But in 2007 Al-Arrab came up with a token €2.3mln for the ARSA stake (62.8%) in addition to €117mln cover debts and provide thanks to the consortium's involvement in huge infrastructure projects in Saudi Arabia. But after valiant efforts by ARSA to maintain Rulmenţul and Tractorul of Braşov as going concerns, liquidation piece by piece became a reality as 4,000 workers were added to the list of local unemployed early in 2007: part of the problem being the high cost of upgrading (including redundancies) compared with greenfield projects. Nitramonia of Făgăraş faces a similar fate after the failure of privatisation in favour of S&T and Chemtrans (Austria). However debts have been cancelled in the case of 34 companies (including the Minvest and Remin mining companies) to avoid bankruptcy. There is a special case relating to 24 energy sector companies (mainly

Termoelectrica owing €0.9bln, including penalties) since energy costs are still too low – for social protection reasons – and company incomes are therefore compromised. Elsewhere progress has been easier, albeit with some delays. Arising from pressure linked with completion of a $413mln standby deal in 2004, IMF wanted RCB sold by 2006 (apart from the initial sale of 25% to EBRD and IFC that reduced the extent of government control). This was achieved with the sale to Erste (Austria); but not certain other targets linked with a €7.0bln income in 2006: Oltchim, the railfreight company Marfă, further energy companies and the remaining government holdings in Romtelecom and also Postelecom (80% of which is owned by the Post Office) and the National Radio Communications Company (SNR) which is the main provider of radio communications and also a player in the fixed telephony market since the start of 2004. Meanwhile Post Office privatisation is to take place over four years.

At the other extreme the 'top ten' companies in terms of profitability now comprise a diverse group including four oil giants (Petrom, Rompetrol's Petromidia, Petrotel, and Lukoil); three companies in telecoms (Romtelecom, Orange and Vodafone); two other industries (Mittal Steel Galaţi and Dacia) and one of the store companies (Metro). Meanwhile SMEs continue to attract priority although the National Agency secured only 1.0tln.lei for assistance in 2005 compared with the 4.0tln sought. With the help of British experts, the EU and the Romanian government are arranging a €3.0mln project to help SMEs wishing to supply multinational companies (2005); while $50mln of new finance for SMEs is being provided by Magnus Holding (USA) with a minimum loan of $100,000 against guarantees. Also in 2005 the Centre for Electronics (Bucharest) has launched a Technological & Business Incubator – financed by €2.0bln from the Ministry of Education and Research and €1.0bln from the Centre's own funds – enabling students and others to develop up to 10 new businesses with state of the art IT and specialist advice, with options for paying rent or sharing profits in partnership. And Global Finance (Greece) has launched a €300mln fund to help Romanian companies go into Europe. Currently only giants like Flamingo, Petrom and Rompetrol are active, with Mobexpert (furniture) and Altex destined to follow.

Conclusion

Despite international pressures, Romania's transition has elements of its own distinct 'Sonderweg'. There have been peaceful transfers of power, at national and local level, although election participation levels are not encouraging and democratisation process has not been decentralised to all levels of government. After deposing the 'sultan' in 1989 both centre-left and centre-right have worked through a democratic system and a capitalist economy. Yet some believe in a more developed civil society while others seem comfortable with a more authoritarian outlook. For the country remains divided with too many transition winners repeating their earlier successes under communism; thereby reinforcing the distance between the elites and the masses. Hence "there is still no 'collective memory' on which to build Romania's identity as a truly democratic nation nor any motivation for collective action to realise it" (Carey & Eisterhold 2004, p.7): the lack of a shared past retards progress to a democratic future. Yet while leadership falls to a closed political society "comprised of the same elites as produced by the communist hierarchy" (Carey 2004b, p.605), it would be wrong to see all parties in the same light. Gallagher (2005, p.10) is scathing in his criticism of PSD, shaped by Iliescu into "legitimising the creation of a new oligarchy" – and business class – on the shoulders of a submissive population that that has enjoyed a token share of the spoils through share vouchers and privatised apartments. Other parties have absorbed opportunists from the former communist elite – a prisoner to the mindset that cannot equate transparency with effective leadership – and so there is no simple black and white distinction between the parties. But the centre-left may take its constituency for granted and rule as an oligarchy while the disparate opposition forces of the centre-right struggle to combine effectively with party leaderships manoeuvring for advantage in order to maintain and enhance their personal followings. Hence there is a certain polarisation between the neo-communists and reluctant democrats of the PSD – heirs to Ceauşescu's régime of highly personalised power whereby "the state was looked upon as a source of political power and enrichment" (Craiutu 2004, p. 5) – and a radical but fragmented opposition that sought a break with the past but inherited no significant reformist inspiration from the old communist party and "lacked the resources to challenge the ruling post-communist coalition" (Gallagher 2005, p. 5) where endemic corruption connected political strength with fixing a tribe of dependents

But the opposition succeeded during 1997–2000 and again in 2005 although there is evidence that 'resources' in social capital are insufficient to accomplish a radical shift in the short term. Strong leadership can hardly rest on the shifting sands of unstable coalitions serving a constellation of interests and networks. Of course the inheritance is a formidable one considering that during 1990-6 patronage networks were dominated by former state managers and resources were allocated disproportionately to largely obsolete SOEs; while during 2001-4 every effort was made to restore and reinforce PSD client networks. It is hardly a disaster that elites are in permanent disagreement to the extent that government and opposition cannot even agree over procedural matters, let alone matters of foreign policy or fundamental domestic issues such as restitution. Poverty reinforces a culture of dependence on strong leaders whereby those in power may choose to assist specific clients and win their allegiance rather than advance the public good where the beneficiaries are less visible. Democratic institutions may get in the way of direct (and corrupt) actions at problem-solving that also serve to reinforce political networks and enhance stability. And it was inconceivable that, given the unstoppable progress on the European agenda, that traditional values would somehow be eradicated by 2007. By the standards of Western Europe – and indeed its northern neighbours in ECE – Romania may remain a semi-democracy for the foreseeable future. For if the theory of dependency is appropriate then wealthy Westerners will be welcomed as buyers of land (hopefully for the same price as in London or Paris!), builders of villas and entrepreneurs who will clean wells, lakes, rivers – and even toilets.

Chapter Six

Problems of Industrial Restructuring and Environment Illustrated with Reference to the Chemical Industry

Introduction

Industry lies at the core of the restructuring problem: how to convert a state-owned enterprise geared to self-sufficiency regulated by the central planning process, technologically-backward with much over-manning, into a complex of private companies geared to competition in the global economy? In the early years a conservative administration grossly underestimated the task facing any government seeking to retain a substantial state sector; given the heavy financial losses sustained and the demands for investment capital to modernise (combined with union resistance to job losses). Privatisation that was seen initially as a means of engaging the population as a whole, through voucher systems, and rewarding elements of the former nomenclature through attractive EMBO deals has gradually gathered momentum driven by the demands of a functioning market economy (FME) and the onerous financial responsibility of SOEs that remain unprofitable after a more than a decade of downsizing. In the space of a decade President Iliescu swung from a promise that the country would not be sold to a willingness to accept a token Euro for an enterprise that a foreign capitalist was prepared to invest in. Although modern technology would accelerate redundancies the hopelessness of the status quo was appreciated by the mid-1990s when there was virtually no FDI going into heavy industry, yet EU negotiations were providing a period of grace only to 2000 as regards opening the Romanian market to competition. Thus the inherited technology of the 1980s had somehow to be aligned with European norms.

The dominance of industry under communism was still apparent in the late 1980s with 37.1 per cent of the occupied population in 1985 rising to 38.1 per cent in 1989 (46.8 to 47.5 for salaries) despite a slight fall in the contribution to national income from 59.0 to 58.1 per cent. The subsequent decline of industry's relative position has been substantial: 44.1 per cent of value added in 1990 falling to 30.9 in 2003, with a slight revival in 1994 (not sustained) but stability since 1998. The share of salaries has fallen from 47.2 per cent in 1990 to 40.9 in 2003 but with stability since 2000 while the occupied population share – falling from 36.9 per cent in 1990 to 24.8 per cent in 2003 has shown stability since 1999. In the process industry was overtaken by services for both occupied population and value added in 1992 (also agriculture for the former) and by salaries in 1993. There is now a hope that the bottom has been reached and a massively restructured sector now has potential for steady growth, indicated by an average of 5.3 per cent during 2001–2005. There have also been substantial gains by industrial shares on the Bucharest Stock Exchange, notably in 2004 with some of the greatest successes in favoured sectors of communism: for example, Turbomecanica (a leading weapons' manufacturer) up 177 per cent; while Antibiotice, Oltchim, Petrom and Rulmenţul Braşov all gained over 100 per cent. Some investment companies also did extremely well, such as Tidal Wave Trading, with stakes in Braiconf Brăila and Socep. But it remains to be seen to what extent employment levels can recover in absolute terms given the over-manning and low productivity under communism: hence the relentless decline in salaried employment in industry from 3.85mln in 1989 to 1.85mln in 2003, with decline arrested only briefly between 2000 and 2001 (Table 6.1) means that industry accounts for 57.0 per cent of the overall decline in salaries (8.16 to 4.59mln) and is all the more significant because losses in most other sectors like agriculture and hotels and restaurants arise largely from a switch to self-employment. The decline was extremely painful and was socially sustainable thanks to a gradualist approach by successive governments, an expanding social programme and opportunities for work in labour-intensive subsistence agriculture (gradually transferring underemployment from the factory to the field) and the black economy. There has been a turnaround in clothing (since 1999) with signs of stability in metals and machinery, electrical engineering, wood processing, cellulose and paper, furniture, leather and food.

A New Culture for Industry: Globalisation

Industrial development has been a cumulative process in which a growing number of centres have emerged, often with quite highly specialised functions (recalling Figure 3.1) with comparatively little in rural areas (Popescu 1995). The project for a diverse range of industrial systems with complementary location patterns researched by Groza (1993, 1998, 1999) and Popescu (1994b) was heavily based on a protected home market and reached an extreme position under communism – with its central planning and artificial pricing – that reinforced the inherited complexes and created many more on the basis of self-sufficiency (which explains why the Romania was so strongly opposed to Khrushchev's plan for Comecon specialisation). It transferred the population from farms to factories in a way that the visionaries of the previous generation could only dream about, but at enormous cost in terms of surpluses extracted from agriculture by coercion, the social burdens of commuting and subsidised exports of manufactures which in some cases did not repay the costs of imported raw materials. The collapse of the system in 1989 and the weakness of the home market meant a rapid and disastrous opening-up to the world economy with material and quality requirements that do not match the inherited structure with relatively low technology and high labour inputs. There has been a massive change even though the state has injected cash to sustain state industries that in many cases became "veritables gouffres financiers" (Groza 1999a, p. 189). The restructuring process has scaled down the state's responsibilities in favour of investment and management geared to effective market penetration while many new ventures have appeared.

Table 6.1: Employment in industry 1990–2005 (thousands)

Year	A	B	C	D	E	F	G	H	I	J	K	L	M	N	O	P
1990	3846	267	137	173	792	347	221	302	94	43	204	176	414	258	127	265
1991	3643	278	162	175	768	263	184	268	87	38	183	190	394	244	125	262
1992	3245	271	171	175	625	232	161	258	89	36	161	154	328	206	105	249
1993	3017	263	172	164	544	219	139	241	80	32	163	138	273	200	96	261
1994	2856	260	177	165	498	191	128	233	83	28	150	136	221	208	98	252
1995	2615	253	177	147	446	180	116	211	77	27	141	123	185	189	83	238
1996	2586	251	194	149	403	190	109	209	66	28	148	119	189	203	83	224
1997	2443	225	201	146	363	181	106	217	69	27	129	118	159	180	83	218
1998	2272	181	194	129	316	162	91	160	81	22	124	104	128	245	83	220
1999	1991	154	183	107	269	146	74	142	76	18	102	92	102	239	76	191
2000	1873	140	181	95	218	132	78	128	70	17	95	85	95	261	85	173
2001	1901	141	178	95	217	126	80	122	70	16	99	84	98	290	98	165
2002	1891	136	169	85	217	127	79	117	76	17	99	77	91	302	101	167
2003	1848	128	149	76	224	119	87	110	78	16	106	72	84	303	102	166
2004	1741	118	143	63	204	114	89	103	75	15	103	63	78	281	100	163
2005	1672	114	143	57	189	113	98	100	72	12	89	60	67	259	93	168

A Total; B Extractive industries; C Electricity gas water and recycling; D Metallurgy; E Metals and machinery; F Transport equipment; G Electrical engineering; precision optics, radio and television; H Oil, chemicals and rubber; I Wood processing; J Cellulose and paper; K Furniture and others; L Building materials and non-metallic mineral products; M Textiles; N Clothing; O Leather and footwear; P Food, drink and tobacco

Source: Statistical Yearbooks: Table 3.13

Indicators of Change

Changes in industry's position in the national economy are mirrored by the sectoral breakdown. Value added by sector shows a growth for food and tobacco averaging 17.0 per cent in 1990–92 and 25.4 per cent 2000–2002 with smaller gains for wood (including furniture and paper) from 6.5 to 9.0, for electricity, gas and water (7.5–11.2 per cent) and publishing (0.6–1.7 per cent). Meanwhile engineering was the big loser declining from 26.1 to 17.5 per cent, followed by textiles, clothing and leather (13.1–9.9 per cent) and building materials (5.4–4.0 per cent), with smaller losses by chemicals (10.4–9.6 per cent), extractive industries (8.2–7.5 per cent) and chemicals (10.4–9.6 per cent). Taking more specialised categories over the decade 1990–2000 there were major absolute declines with indices for 1990 (relative to 100 in 2000) of 410.2 for rubber and plastics, 313.9 for metal construction and products, 308.3 for chemicals, 285.8 for textiles, 276.7 for machinery and equipment (excluding electrical), 219.1 for building materials, 209.6 for metallurgy, 202.2 for wood processing (excluding furniture, cellulose and paper), 190.6 for food and drink, 183.3 for oil processing and 177.1 for cellulose and paper. The better performances did not necessarily indicate superior strength, for restructuring was sometimes delayed for strategic reasons: hence mining (153.6) did better than manufacturing (172.9). Meanwhile the best performances in the 1990s came from furniture and others rising to 100 from 70.9, clothing (72.7) and electrical goods (82.9). Relative to indices of 100 in 2000, the only sectors currently declining are mining and quarrying 99.2; chemicals 99.0; metal construction and products 97.1; electricity, gas and water 95.4; and wood processing (excluding furniture, cellulose and paper) 85.1; but once again these are mostly sub-sections of the broader categories initially referred to. In terms of current prices (Table 6.2) the picture is dominated by the relatively rapid rise for electricity and water (5.5 per cent in 1990 rising to 10.4 per cent in 1995–96 and 17.9 per cent in 2003). By comparison most other sectors have declined but oil processing has grown while food has remained stable along with metallurgy, wood products and furniture, while the big losers have been extractive industries and metals and machinery

Privatisation
Privatisation has made great progress because although there are some difficult cases facing the Authority for Recouping State Assets (ARSA) the proportion of private industrial businesses rose from 96.1 per cent in 1997 to 99.2 in 2005 (Table 6.3): the number of private companies rose by 67 per cent from 35.0th to 58.6th, while SOEs declined by 64 per cent from 1.4th to 0.5. Although the latter are relatively large in terms of value-added, the private sector share in this respect has nevertheless risen from 42.5 per cent in 1998 to 81.7 per cent in 2003. Foreign industrial companies have played an important role in recent trends with a growth from 500 in 1997 to 1,575 in 2000 and 3,112 in 2005. Finally, statistics have been published since 1996 to show the number of enterprises and their average employment in different sectors. They show that the huge industrial bastions of the communist era have been heavily cut down to size. In 1996 32,525 enterprises employed 2.72mln: an average of 84 per enterprise. But during 1996–2003 enterprise numbers went up 60.9 per cent to

Table 6.2: Structure of industrial production (per cent) according to current prices 1990–2005

Year	A	B	C	D	E	F	G	H	I	J	K	L	M	N
1990	8.9	5.5	8.5	13.4	10.9	6.9	9.9	2.8	2.2	3.5	5.7	6.5	14.9	0.3
1991	8.8	7.7	9.6	11.1	9.7	6.5	10.4	3.3	2.3	3.6	5.7	5.7	15.3	0.3
1992	7.6	11.0	10.6	10.5	9.0	6.7	11.0	3.4	2.2	3.9	4.2	4.5	15.1	0.3
1993	6.8	8.9	8.8	8.7	10.5	8.6	9.7	2.8	2.2	2.9	3.7	4.9	20.0	1.5
1994	7.1	13.6	9.5	9.8	9.7	7.7	9.1	2.7	2.8	3.7	2.9	3.9	16.4	1.1
1995	6.9	12.9	10.4	8.6	8.0	7.7	10.8	3.1	2.6	3.8	3.2	4.1	16.8	1.1
1996	6.7	11.7	10.4	8.6	10.4	6.4	9.9	3.1	2.7	3.9	2.8	4.3	17.8	1.3
1997	7.8	13.4	11.6	7.1	8.9	8.3	8.9	2.8	2.4	4.2	2.6	3.6	17.2	1.1
1998	6.8	14.7	9.7	7.5	10.0	6.3	7.5	3.0	2.5	3.8	2.4	4.6	19.7	1.5
1999	5.3	20.7	9.0	6.5	9.2	7.9	7.6	3.7	2.4	3.5	2.2	4.8	15.7	1.5
2000	5.6	15.6	11.4	6.1	7.6	10.1	8.7	3.7	2.3	3.3	2.1	4.6	17.6	1.3
2001	5.7	15.1	13.2	6.2	7.6	10.8	8.0	3.5	2.3	3.3	2.1	5.0	15.9	1.3
2002	5.3	17.5	11.8	6.2	7.9	11.1	7.3	3.7	2.6	3.1	2.0	5.9	14.3	1.4
2003	4.9	17.9	10.9	6.5	8.4	10.1	7.7	3.8	2.6	3.1	2.2	5.9	14.6	1.4
2004	4.6	17.4	10.0	6.6	8.8	9.3	8.4	4.0	2.8	3.4	2.3	5.8	15.2	1.4
2005	4.7	15.8	9.3	6.4	10.5	12.0	7.2	4.9	2.5	3.2	2.1	4.8	15.3	1.4

A Extractive industries; B Electricity water and waste recovery; C Metallurgy; D Metal products, machinery and equipment; E Electrical precision and transport equipment; F Oil processing, coking and nuclear fuel; G Chemicals and rubber; H Wood products; I Furniture and other branches; J Building materials; K Textiles; L Clothing and footwear; M Food drink and tobacco; N Printing and publishing

Source: Statistical Yearbooks: Table 16.1

Table 6.3: Enterprises in industry, commerce and other services by ownership 1997–2005

Year	Total Number (inc.FC) thousands				Percent Private				Foreign Companies (FC)			
	All	Ind	Com	OS	All	Ind	Com	OS	All	Ind	Com	OS
1997	316.8	36.4	226.1	54.2	98.9	96.1	99.7	97.4	6102	500	5060	542
1998	318.4	39.3	222.0	57.1	99.1	96.8	99.8	97.8	8018	790	6415	813
1999	318.7	41.5	217.4	59.8	99.1	97.1	99.8	98.0	9285	932	7287	1066
2000	308.1	42.2	202.8	63.1	99.4	98.1	99.9	98.7	9629	1575	6648	1406
2001	311.3	43.5	192.6	75.2	99.4	98.3	99.9	98.9	8942	1655	5820	1467
2002	315.1	47.3	177.7	90.1	99.6	98.8	99.9	99.4	9371	1721	5777	1673
2003	349.1	51.8	179.3	118.0	99.7	98.8	99.9	99.5	9778	2128	5797	1853
2004	394.5	56.4	191.2	146.9	99.7	99.1	99.9	99.6	11311	2485	5228	3598
2005	433.0	59.1	200.4	173.5	99.8	99.2	99.9	99.7	14532	3112	5978	5442

Sectors are for Industry (Ind), Commerce (Com) and Other Services (OS)

Source: Statistical Yearbooks: Tables 15.2 and 15.7

Table 6.4: Enterprises and labour in industry 1996–2005

Sector	Enterprises			Employment th			Employment/Enterprise		
	1996	2003	2005	1996	2003	2005	1996	2003	2005
Extractive Industries	168	502	676	266.5	158.0	134.2	1586.3	314.7	198.5
Electricity Gas & Water	558	1411	1706	240.2	169.1	161.3	430.5	119.8	94.5
Metallurgy	322	481	438	163.8	79.7	66.8	508.6	165.7	152.5
Engineering	4544	8918	11045	698.7	446.8	441.8	153.8	50.1	40.0
Chemicals	2029	3222	3669	211.6	112.3	105.1	104.3	34.8	28.6
Wood Processing	8232	14821	17607	270.4	250.7	247.1	32.8	16.9	14.0
Building Materials	959	2048	2650	124.3	73.9	64.9	129.6	36.1	24.5
Textiles & Clothing	7075	9684	10428	465.5	537.1	465.3	65.8	55.5	44.6
Food Drink & Tobacco	8638	10731	10841	281.8	200.3	204.6	32.6	18.7	18.9
Industry: Total	32525	51818	59060	2722.8	2027.9	1891.1	83.7	39.1	32.0
Services	276338	297243	373970	1848.2	1866.0	2182.7	6.7	6.3	5.8
Total	308863	349061	433030	4571.0	3893.9	4073.8	14.8	11.2	9.4

Source: Statistical Yearbooks Table 15.5

52,344 while employment declined by 25.5 per cent to 2.03mln and the average employment per enterprise fell by 53.6 per cent to just 39 (Table 6.4). To be sure variations between sectors were considerable with averages of 315 for extractive industries and 17 for wood processing in 2003, but the former figure was down 80.1 per cent from 1996 compared with 51.5 per cent for the latter. And in the case of coal mining (one of sub-categories into which the extractive industries can be broken down) the average came down by 85.7 per cent from 14,127 to 2,016.

Redirection of Trade
Redirection of trade has been particularly successful for clothing and footwear that made up almost half Romania's exports to the EU at the end of the 1990s, thanks to a potent combination of labour cost and productivity advantages, although this may not be sustained indefinitely as wage levels creep upwards. Metals and machinery have potential advantages as trade barriers are removed; also timber products but not necessarily furniture where higher productivity is an issue – combined with good design and short delivery times – despite Romania's advantages through long experience, ample capacity, skilled labour and access to raw materials The producers of electrical equipment also increased their exports (both relatively and absolutely) while steel, oil and chemicals continued to lose ground. It seems that where investment has facilitated a quality of production up to international standards Romanian goods compete effectively (though some involved only limited value-added). And with poverty limiting the home market, the importance of export growth – backed by FDI – helped to sideline the strategic arguments entrenched in the early 1990s, all the more in view of the EU's FME agenda. However there was a boost through growth from 2000 with even faster growth in 2001, especially where exports were prominent: machinery and equipment (+14.8 per cent) and clothing (+15.1 per cent) as well as publishing (+34.1 per cent); rubber and plastics (+26.3 per cent); tobacco processing (+11.3 per cent); and electrical machinery (+10.7).

Spatial Effects of Restructuring
These vary according to the locations of the industries suffering the greatest contraction and their correlation with the geography of new enterprises that, despite some stimulation by regional policy, is heavily biased in favour of Bucharest and the western counties. Spatial systems have been examined al length (Groza 1993, 1998, 1999; Popescu 1994b) with the 'utopia of a judicious distribution' replaced by a 'répartition naturelle' (Groza 1999a, p. 194). A switch to a greater emphasis on consumption boosted food industries in Călăraşi, Ialomiţa and Tulcea counties (fishing in the latter), while durables and equipment did relatively well in Argeş, Braşov, Bucharest, Constanţa, Dâmboviţa, Gorj – also Alba, Cluj, Sibiu and Timişoara. On the other hand, the chemical 'bastions' of Bacău, Brăila, Giurgiu, Mehedinţi, Mureş, Neamţ and Vâlcea were hard hit – as were some vehicle producers that lost their automatic monopoly over the home market. And although the mining areas were specially treated at first (especially Alba, Gorj, Hunedoara and Maramureş), the financial crisis of 1998-9 forced the painful restructuring – defying the final phase of 'mineriada' – of a sector that reflected the logic of communist self-sufficiency in its most extreme, so much so that foreign investment is virtually impossible to secure.

An interesting exercise performed by Young (2001) attempted to highlight the 'local' component in changes in employment in industry during 1990–95 when the average decline of 13.7 per cent was multiplied up to four times in extreme cases. Table 6.5 summarises the picture which shows some quite extreme positive and negative values that invite scrutiny. Thus for example two adjacent counties well-known for their mining and metallurgical industries have very different profiles with +19 for Hunedoara and -27 for Caraş-Severin. The mining industry as a whole was protected from heavy redundancy until 1998 but particularly so in Hunedoara where the coal miners from the Jiu Valley were patronised the government and used on several occasions as an unofficial militia to intimidate liberals on the centre-right of Romanian politics. On the other hand Caraş-Severin's Reşiţa steelworks was particularly vulnerable because virtually all its ore and coking coal was imported. Market pricing for minerals and transport resulted in almost immediate shutdown of the blast furnaces and reduction in steel making to the level sustainable from scrap. Hence the 'local' factors produced very different outcomes in the two counties. Popescu (1998) extends the review of the local to a range of criteria – privatisation, unemployment and occupation structures – to highlight the diversification process that was bringing an upsurge to the centre and western areas of the country by the end of the 1990s, assisted by foreign investment and the growth of SMEs to complement the larger installations within specific industrial districts (Groza 1999c). The approach was then extended through the Phare programme for 'industrial restructuring areas' launched in 2001 and referred to further in Chapter 10. However, locations per se do not appear to be part of the problem since the communist régime was always careful to balance its rhetoric in favour of backward areas with an underlying demand for efficiency in the interest of high growth rates nationally. Ceauşescu's aberrations did not tend to distort routine locational decision-making given the desire to maximise the national growth rate.

Externalising Decision Making
This is the inevitable result of a globalising approach heavily reliant on FDI. As the 1990s revealed massive problems over competitiveness the government pushed for more R&D to prevent the country becoming 'technological colony', although this is largely unavoidable and may be seen as a proverbial 'blessing in disguise' since it improves the penetration of Romania's exports and reduces energy intensity. It also means more efficient use of raw materials (especially in the case of imports) and an improvement in flexibility and productivity (through appropriate work practices) to make more competitive use of labour and management skills as well as programmes of education and training. Romanian industry has a diverse structure and enjoys several advantages that foreign investors find attractive. However, there is some concern over FDI in the sense that while new technologies may generate competitive exports there is a danger in 'lohn operations', seen as a form of industrial colonialism where the foreign partner supplies both the equipment/technology and raw materials. 'Lohn' has helped relieve unemployment in depressed mono-industrial areas, but there is a high level of dependence and a danger of relocation further east (Ukraine, Pakistan or China) with any adverse change in wage competitiveness.

Table 6.5: The local component of shift-share analysis for industrial employment change 1990–95

Values	Counties
Over +12.5	Argeş (28), Bacău (15), Braşov (16), Bucharest (45), Galaţi (14), Gorj (22),
+7.5 to +12.5	Hunedoara (19), Prahova (27),
+2.5 to +7.5	Alba, Cluj, Dâmboviţa, Vaslui
+2.5 to -2.5	Bihor*, Brăila, Constanţa, Covasna, Harghita, Iaşi, Maramureş*, Neamţ*, Teleorman*
	Bistriţa-Năsăud* Botoşani*, Dolj*, Ialomiţa*, Mehedinţi*, Olt*, Sălaj*, Vrancea*
-2.5 to -7.5	Arad#, Buzău*, Giurgiu#, Mureş*, Satu Mare*, Suceava*, Timiş*, Tulcea#,
-7.5 to -12.5	Vâlcea#
Over -12.5	Sibiu#
	Călăraşi (-29)@, Caraş-Severin (-27)[]

* Industrial employment change above the national average of -13.7% for 1990-5; # ditto: more than three times the national average; @ ditto: more than twice the national average; [] ditto: more than four times the national average
Note: values in the first column comprise only relative indicators of positive or negative effects of local factors with the scale extending between +45 and -29 Values for individual counties are quoted only for the highest and lowest groups.

Source: Young (2001) p.238

SOEs in Less-Dynamic Sectors show different responses to the autonomy they now enjoy. While the Bucharest bus manufacturer Rocar remained relatively uncompetitive and heavily dependent on government orders, with a reputation for militancy discouraging international cooperation, the mining companies in Baia Mare and Deva each set up a j.v. to use modern technology to maximise gold production (albeit with controversial environmental implications). In the chemical industry, Azomureş (Târgu Mureş) offer high quality and punctual delivery for exports of fertilisers, melamine, photographic paper and other chemical products around the world. And Oltchim (Râmnicu Vâlcea) has gained additional know-how through its own resources and j.v. projects – with the energy company SIF Energies (energy), Messer Group (gas distribution) and Pozzi (polymethane synthesis) – to combine new technology with the Romanian company's land, infrastructure and workforce (the latter retrained for a quality culture rejecting the 'this will do' mentality). As a result Oltchim was able to offer quality products and services at competitive prices in the PVC and petrochemical market in 2001. It is impossible to review all sectors and the aim here is to provide a discourse on a selected number in order to show through examples the issues and problems that are being taken tackled. What emerges is the essential need for new investment to modernise both to comply with environmental standards but also to enhance quality and efficiency for export penetration. Staying with old technology to protect jobs is not a viable long-term option because quite apart from quality considerations energy costs remain high.

Environment: Industrial Pollution and Prevention

Under communism industry was a major source of pollution. Ninety per cent of air samples for zinc pollution in the Baia Mare area in the early post-communist years were above 300ppm (the Romanian Environmental Protection Agency monitoring threshold for sensitive areas) and 70 per cent over 500ppm (the threshold for less-sensitive areas): unpolluted areas would score just 100ppm against the highest recorded value of 23,330! All samples for lead were above 100ppm whereas an unpolluted area would score 20 (compared with 50 and 250 which mark the thresholds for monitoring less-sensitive and sensitive areas respectively) and 75 per cent were over 500ppm ('environmentally hazardous' in the USA) and 60 per cent were over 1,000ppm ('environmentally hazardous' in Romania), with 8,720 the maximum recorded, with some aggravation from motor vehicles (Pălăseanu 2000, pp. 53–4). In the case of copper the highest reading was 7,040ppm (against 50 for unpolluted soils) with the complication of temperature inversions in mountain depressions leading to massive concentrations of pollutants in areas such as Petroşani. A quarter of Romania's rivers became too polluted for water to be usable for fisheries or irrigation. Monitoring during the early post-communist years revealed that the Săsar was polluted with lead by the Romplumb smelter and Herja mine to the extent of 4.4 times the legally-permitted maximum; while ammonia levels in the lower Mureş were 2.4 times the maximum due to the Azomureş factory and Cristeşti sewage works. Coalmining at Petroşani and the synthetic fibre industry at Săvineşti polluted the Jiu and Bistriţa respectively. Problems still arise through periodic ammoniac releases beyond legally admissible levels from chemical factories (such as the Amurco complex in Bacău) and toxic gases emitted by electric arc steel furnaces threaten to halt production at the Oţelu Roşu plant near Caransebeş. Polluted water remains a hazard with 500,000cu.m of petroleum waste water released accidently from a lagoon at Arpechim refinery in 2007 to threaten the Teleorman stream.

The Impact of Pollution

The impact of pollution was all too evident in terms of human health; as in Baia Mare where the pollution caused by copper and lead smelting was aggravated by inadequate protein and vitamins in the food eaten by most children (Ipatiov 1996). More than a tenth of Romania's territory has been exposed to excessively high levels of pollution over recent decades and some eight million people were living in environmentally unsafe conditions at the start of the transition (of whom two million were already suffering chronic disease – and lower scholarly proficiency in some cases): an important part of the wider problem of degrading human resources, not to mention the additional burden of unattractiveness for new development. Heavy concentrations of dust, sulphur dioxide and heavy metals have damaged soils and forests, while some livestock deaths have arisen through pollution, for instance horses in Sibiu county whose deaths are linked with cadmium and lead poisoning. There is a great risk of damage to drinking water and fish stocks from tips of 'steril' associated with lignite quarries and underground mines. Tipping of waste and overburden sterilised substantial areas and constituted a nuisance in terms of dust and water pollution; also quarries for lignite, bauxite, stone and refractory sand; sometimes damaging scenic areas and causing unnecessary resource depletion when minerals were not fully processed due to backward technology. Environmental damage also arose through some industrial processes, for example timber harvesting with obsolete equipment, poor technique and inadequate law enforcement resulted in considerable environmental damage, notably through the long skidding distances involved in dragging tree stems to the nearest road. Hence the importance of SAPARD funding to extend forest roads beyond the present effective density of 5.3m/ha (partly by repairing the 7,000kms that are presently inoperative through heavy rain damage).

The Baia Mare Accident

The Baia Mare accident of 2000 was particularly serious; arising as a leak of 50–100t of cyanide at Bozânta near Baia Mare at the Aurul plant of the Australian-Romanian gold mining company. Exceptionally heavy rain in January, 2000 meant that a reservoir containing heavily-polluted water overflowed and affected the Lăpuş river and then the Someş which in turn fed into one of the Danube's major tributaries: the Tisa/Tisza. it was three days before matters were brought under control by which time 100,000cu.m of cyanide-polluted water had been released. Levels of up to 12.40mg/l of cyanide were recorded (with 0.1 the maximum permitted) ranging initially across Hungary from 3.7 in the upper reaches to 2.8 in the Szolnok area and 1.0 on the Serbian border. 30–50 per cent of fish were killed and fishermen's livelihoods were threatened, while water supplies for Szolnok were disrupted when abstraction had to stop and left 80,000 people without a supply. Aurul lost $350,000/week until production resumed in June. Hungary filed a compensation claim and during a subsequent lawsuit in 2005 seeking $146mln damages the company (now Transgold, including a 17.2 per cent stake by the UK company Oxus Gold with interests in Central Asia) blamed the damage on the overdosing of antidote in Hungary. The processing of 2.0mln.t of material annually by cyanide leaching is still permitted but huge improvements have been made in Baia Mare and it seems unlikely that such an accident could be repeated. However the plant was reported working at only 15 per cent capacity after a legal battle in Hungary in 2005, with further problems in 2006 due to disruption through freezing and bank restrictions on credit leading to lay-offs for two-thirds of the 100 workers remaining.

Cost Calculations Zinnes (2004, p. 445) assessed environmental damages at a minimum $480mln for the environmental degradation of agriculture and fisheries; $600mln plus for acidic emissions affecting buildings, equipment and vehicles; $370mln for the deterioration of human and animal health; $200mln plus for water pollution; $160mln (each) for the loss of wood in 400,000ha of damaged forests and the waste of raw materials through inefficient use (including pipeline losses): cumulatively adding up to almost a tenth of GDP. The response was initially inadequate. Under communism a National Waters Council and National Council for Environmental Protection had responsibilities under the Environmental Protection Law of 1973 but this was "a legal curiosity [and] never seriously implemented" (Ibid, p. 447). Since 1989 the key institution has been the Ministry of Waters Forests and Environmental Protection (MWFEP) that received a lot of help (for example, through Phare) yet "slowly but continuously disintegrated into a moribund and dysfunctional (dis)organisation" (Ibid). Change occurred from c.1998 with ministry reorganisation based on the recommendations of international experts. The EU Country Report of 1998 thought that the strengthening of enforcement capacity was very necessary since the monitoring of air and water pollution was far behind EU requirements. But in a further Report (1999, p.7) the ministry was still found to lack sufficient capacity to fulfil its role as the main instrument to implement the environment 'acquis', partly because several sectoral ministries had major responsibilities while MWFEP had only a consultative role, effectively reducing environmental considerations to a secondary role.

Responses to Environmental Problems

Romania was the first candidate country to participate in the EU Life programme whereby industrial sectors were assisted in preventing pollution and adopting cleaner technologies and communities helped over water quality, air pollution, refuse and traffic: any individual or organisation may apply for funding (half from the EU and half from the Romanian government) if they show they have the expertise. Legislation was enacted through the environmental framework law 1995, seeking to comply with EU standards, including mandatory compliance schedules and – after much foreign assistance – provided for regulation through a system of permits that have to be based (theoretically) on EIA or an environmental audit (Zinnes 2004, p. 449).

Much responsibility for monitoring and enforcement regarding air/water pollution and solid/hazardous waste rests with the county EPAs (and the eight subsequently given regional responsibilities) although water quality regulation was passed back to the public utilities considered to have greater experience. Enforcement was initially weak due to inadequate training and budget funding, although a 1999 amendment to the 1995 law allowed them to charge – and retain – fees for permits. But an Environmental Fund (EF) for clean-up projects gained parliamentary approval in 2001 – though it needs to be increased since many rivers remain degraded – with some payments generated from a 3.0 per cent levy on sales of ferrous and non-ferrous waste and the packaging involved in production and importing of goods. The PPP is now in force and privatisation must take environmental liability into account. But there is an obvious incentive for the individual company because "firms that survive will be those that have modernised because modern equipment better protects the environment" (Ibid, p. 446). There is clear motivation over waste reduction, while automatically "as the industrial sector modernises it will invest in newer technologies which are actually far more environmentally friendly" (Ibid, p. 455). Meanwhile the cultural attitudes of communism are changing with the younger political class evidently more inclined to take initiatives.

There was also recognition of trans-frontier and climate change issues, although (anomalously) legislation over atmospheric protection (e.g. from waste and hazardous substances) and environmental liability was delayed, while despite scope for economic instruments to be used in environmental protection (under the 1995 law), there was no environmental fund until the first (somewhat disappointing) version was adopted in 1999 (having been part of the government's election platform in 1997): the environment guard consists of EPA enforcement staff without augmentation or additional budgetary funding. Critics also point to the limited capacity of MWFEP and lack of effective lobbying of the legislature by ENGOs that need to be much more active. Zinnes is certainly right to insist that environmental protection is not a luxury that can wait, while Welch (1997) emphasises the challenge facing the entire region in taking on board EU environmental imperatives in the context of the socialist legacy. The ECECs must resist pressure to 'sell their environment' simply to attract any economic developments (with priority attaching to relief of unemployment following de-industrialisation, as well as the development of independent local government). But Zinnes' argument does not allow for spatial variations for there are extensive areas with pristine environment highly suitable for conservation projects and rural tourism.

Harmonisation 2000–2004
Romania signed the Kyoto Protocol while, in connection with a national medium-term development strategy for the economy, environmental policy for 2000–2004 was to focus on harmonisation with EU directives, including: financial instruments to embrace the environmental 'acquis', especially for water exploitation, environmental protection in industry and agriculture, protection of soil and damaged land. There is also provision for consolidation of institutional capacities to stimulate dialogue between the authorities and civil society on programmes for the environment and socio-economic development with respect to damaged areas, protected areas and

forested regions, waste management and water resources. Moreover, a policy shift from recovery to prevention was intended through an integrated system of monitoring; environmentally-friendly products (including promotion of ISO14,001 and other standards to achieve environmentally-friendly processes); decentralisation for administrative autonomy and the PPP, with action to establish environmental protection competences among local communities and achieve more environmental protection by companies to cut public spending; and economic instruments of environmental policy rather than 'command and control', including reduced budget subsidies for activities with a negative impact on environment and support for activities to reduce polluting gas emissions and contribute to ecological restoration. The cost of adaptation is €30–40mln and new projects (from 2003) must conform at the outset, but 1999–2002 projects by 2006 and pre-1999 projects by 2014.

Good progress has been recorded in key areas like metallurgy by reducing noxious emissions through upgraded equipment (such as modernising aluminium electrolysis at Alro-Slatina) while filters have been installed at the Ductil metal dust factory (Buzău) and the Baia Mare smelters for lead (Romplumb) and copper (Pheonix). Some installations have to be closed like the Famos synthetic fibre factory in the heart of Suceava, now reprofiled for less hazardous processes (polyethylene and aluminium pipes). Oil products have been recovered from the phreatic water table and in the worst cases of land pollution soil has been removed by the efficient but expensive method of cut and fill. Special funding and technology has been harnessed for land restoration around uranium mines (like those of Ciudanoviţa and Lisava in Banat) to remove the danger of radioactive contamination of groundwater and ultimately the Caraş river – with international implications since this river flows into Serbia. Where pollution is not a major problem derelict mines with their quarries or shafts, decantation ponds and waste tips constitute both eyesores and safety hazards. Several such installations in the Anina coalfield have been cleared away as at Uteris on the hillside above Steierdorf where a level terrace – suitable for a sports field – has now been provided. Wastewater treatment has been improved e.g. at the Doljchim (Craiova) and Nitramonia (Făgăraş) chemical plants – also the lead-zinc factories at Baia Mare (Romplumb), Copşa Mică (Sometra) and Zlatna (Ampellum) – while a plant for the recovery of useful substances has been installed at Petrobrazi (Ploieşti).

The cement industry has been active in cutting emissions, for example. Heidelberg have fitted electric filters and obtained ISO14001 environmental certification for its factories at Bicaz (Moldocim) and Deva (Casial) acquired in 1998 and 2000 respectively. The industry is also attempting to use power station slag and ash for special cement types; also tyres and oil waste as fuel. Meanwhile, a waste heap of phosphor plaster at the Fertilchim chemical plant in Bacău (50ha and 50m high) was reclaimed in 2003 by covering it with soil to make it an artificial feature for a park; with the impervious shield technique to protect the water table (as at the Bicapa plant in Târnaveni). A significant success has arisen over the recycling of batteries in the Bucharest area where new technology appears to have eliminated the local 'lead mafia' previously responsible for pollution arising from the seepage of sulphuric acid and emissions of noxious dust through processing residual material after the parts with the highest lead content were taken over by the Neferal company. The national network of some 750 antiquated and clandestine smelters included scores of such furnaces operated by the Roma communities in the Jihlava-Sinteşti area of south Bucharest, with no provision for environmental protection. 2001 saw the launch of a scheme by Dacia to encourage the trading-in of old cars in return for new ones at lower cost and, where finance can be found, government has been extending this initiative to all cars over 12 years old in a bid to remove a significant source of pollution (while also setting standards for imported second-hand vehicles).

Environmental Education
The culture is gradually changing as ENGOs, like the groups forming the Environmental Partnership for Central Europe (EPCE), expand environmental education, for example to recognise symptoms of pollution (such as heavy metal poisoning) and recruit assistance for monitoring and clean-ups: A French project in Galaţi is disseminating the concept of eco-business through green business parks with lichens as bio-indicators to measure pollution. USAID has been encouraging dialogue in several towns (Alexandria, Braşov, Miercurea Ciuc and Slobozia) to identify common actions for community development, for instance an Agenda 21 local coordinating committee in Miercurea Ciuc with working groups for environmental protection and decentralisation and human organisation. Living Heritage, which includes the Romanian Carpathian Foundation and Belgium's King Baudouin Foundation, is also supporting pilot projects in sustainable development and local capacity through actions among NGOs and local governments in Bihor, Braşov, Harghita, Maramureş, Sibiu and Suceava. Yet serious incidents still arise. The hazard of toxic waste import is demonstrated by the recent case of a shipment of 100t sent from France to an Arad firm concealed as raw materials and there are still stores of dangerous waste within the country as well as hazards arising from wartime ammunition dumps: one was found near Secu resort (Reşiţa) in 2001 when police noticed that ordnance were being sold as scrap.

The Chemical Industry

This industry is selected for case study at this stage because it introduces the environmental dimension as one of several themes relevant to post-communist industrial restructuring. Despite its well-trained and motivated staff, this industry was (like mining) a big loser in the westward redirection of trade, with a steep downward trend in competitiveness that called for radical restructuring with labour flexibility and hard budget constraints (while retaining some advantage with the rest of the world) (Table 6.6). However, while chemicals are seen as one of the transition 'losers' the industry's share of the total value-added shows a relatively modest decline from 10.4 per cent in 1990–92 to 9.6 per cent in 2001–2003 (albeit with a rise to 12.2 per cent in 1993–95), thanks to the 'cushion' of oil refining: raising its share from 26.0 to 36.9 per cent while plastics and rubber have declined slightly (24.5–21.2 per cent) – with new investment, for example by Brandt rubber and plastic in Sibiu – and other branches more steeply (49.5–41.9 per cent). The employment size of the average unit is highest in oil refining (406 in 2003 after 2,089 in 1996) while units in the rubber and plastic business are much smaller (21, down from 40) and other sectors 51 (down from 165). The problem – least threatening for plastics and rubber, as well as paper, glass and ceramics – is exacerbated by the growth of the industry well beyond its domestic raw material base and the problems of financing petrochemistry feedstocks highlighted overcapacity. Much of the technology was obsolete and so, despite weak markets and low profitability, there was a great need for upgrading to raise quality and energy efficiency to EU standards as well for environmental reasons. Priority was given to the key oil refineries of Arpechim (Piteşti) and Petrobrazi (Ploieşti) in 1996 through foreign credits with government guarantees, while the Oneşti (Bacău) refinery was assisted by Columna Bank and Euro Trading and the Danubiana and Policolor factories benefited from early privatisation. The PVC chain was broadly competitive but lower fixed costs were offset by the costs of older technology, with the cost of feedstocks again a constraint.

Chlorine-Sodium Products

Govora (Vâlcea) exported 80 per cent of its production under communism and was fully exposed to reduced demand after 1989 (600 to 60t/day); also falling prices for sodium products while raw material prices and rail transport costs increased. With rising coke and natural gas costs in 1999 the heavy soda producer Upsom (Ocna Mureş) faced competition from Belgium, Poland and USA in ECE and Middle East markets for calcinated soda and other products. However, it held on to its home market especially in Transylvania-Maramureş and part of the Banat and Moldavia market (also more widely as the sole domestic supplier of some products) through good relations with the chemical, glass and non-ferrous metals industries; albeit with some competition from Chimcomplex Borzeşti (near Bacău) and Govora near Râmnicu Vâlcea. Based on brine from the local saltfield of Târgu Ocna, as well as inputs from the methane gas pipeline system and major oil refineries, the former specialises in sodium and chlorosodium products as well as polyethylene, organic solvents, pesticides and dyestuffs. Once considered for privatisation by Borsodchem (Hungary) in 1999, enterprise has been shown by construction of a private power station (to reduce energy costs) and also a $42mln investment for chlorinated solvents and anhydride including commissioning in 1996 of a 100,000t/yr NaOH plant under German licence (with electricity consumption reduced by 30 per cent), followed by a new detergent factory in 1998. Typical of the close linkages between factories, Chimcomplex gets some products from Govora and Nitramonia Făgăraş while also supplying some of its own output to Nitramonia and the Oltchim complex at Râmnicu Vâlcea, despite competing with the latter (and the Turda factory) over chlorosodium products. Indeed Chimcomplex is not untypical of the Romanian chemical industry as a whole in developing through stages of increasing complexity from caustic soda (sodium hydroxide) and sodium chloride in 1954 as the chlorine supply triggered extensions into acetylene and PVC in the 1960s, chlorinated paraffins in the 1970s and ammonium chloride and sulphurised isobuthylene in the 1980s to extend the profile to organic solvents, inorganic chlorides, synthesis intermediates and pesticides. Joining with the adjacent Oneşti complex of oil refining, petrochemicals and rubber in 1969 (before separating in 1990), it was fortunate that under state ownership is was possible to install a modern chloro-alkali complex (for caustic soda, hydrochloric acid and chlorine)

Table 6.6: Production in the chemical industry (th.t unless stated otherwise) 1985–2005

Year	A	B	C	D	E	F	G	H	I	J	K	L	M	N	O	P
1985	1835	447	836	814	3497	187	3097	628	204	156	1245	184	14	7.2	16.0	n.a.
1986	1971	466	895	846	3692	217	3278	664	210	173	1298	196	15	7.5	16.0	n.a.
1987	1693	450	894	817	3385	202	2897	638	208	152	1428	178	14	6.5	14.0	n.a.
1988	1825	473	918	821	3409	209	2995	653	217	161	1500	175	14	6.9	18.0	n.a.
1989	1687	453	889	763	3337	180	2805	640	204	149	1494	168	15	6.9	13.0	n.a.
1990	1111	332	632	552	2178	129	1744	474	155	102	893	135	13	5.1	11.0	494
1991	745	291	471	461	1375	94	1090	350	113	55	540	95	10	4.4	7.0	454
1992	572	223	452	372	1733	87	1398	272	91	36	398	58	6	3.2	5.0	351
1993	527	182	371	324	1620	82	1317	256	97	30	349	56	8	3.8	2.0	477
1994	491	186	449	291	1443	67	1163	304	138	27	386	46	5	3.2	2.0	590
1995	477	179	504	372	1809	90	1449	331	131	41	465	49	7	3.5	1.2	755
1996	422	172	536	321	1841	106	1464	322	123	37	390	44	6	3.7	1.1	803
1997	329	182	547	323	951	91	850	339	132	29	368	38	4	3.1	0.7	463
1998	229	178	462	310	468	73	451	320	123	23	344	35	6	3.0	0.7	283
1999	234	170	415	297	834	54	763	298	130	16	327	34	7	2.8	0.5	194
2000	181	147	391	343	1255	55	1054	331	132	20	342	36	11	3.2	0.3	162
2001	59	145	448	346	1155	53	940	366	136	23	373	60	47	3.9	n.a.	431
2002	58	132	454	353	1137	53	920	479	163	15	447	72	128	7.3	n.a.	537
2003	65	160	406	382	1445	45	1348	566	185	12	394	80	133	11.2	n.a.	512
2004	28	149	398	414	1422	63	1222	694	234	12	479	100	162	12.4	n.a.	389
2005	11	162	346	443	1611	34	1682	774	241	12	546	87	155	14.2	n.a.	273

A Sulphuric acid; B Hydrochloric acid; C Soda ash; D Caustic soda; E Synthetic ammonia; F Carbide; G Chemical fertilisers; H Basic macromolecular/plastic products (polyethylene, polystyrene and resins); I PVC;J Synthetic rubber; K Major petrochemical intermediates (ethylene, propylene, benzene, toluene, xylene. octanol and phenol); L Paints and varnishes; M Detergent; N Tyres (mln); O Dyes and pigments; P Antibiotics (t)

Source: Statistical Yearbooks Table 16.3

given the pressure for environmental improvements in 1990s; opening the way for privatisation by Romanian Commercial Services in 2003, at which time there were still 1,000 employees.

Ammonia and Fertiliser

This is another section hit hard by falling demand combined more expensive hydrocarbon inputs and consequent pressures to reduce costs for export. While some capacities have closed, several ammonia plants have been upgraded with new reactors to save around 5.0 per cent on raw material and energy costs, plus recovery of the hydrogen formerly burnt off. But there seem to have been wide variations in business success, with the superior efficiency of some companies evident immediately after the revolution. One success story concerns Amonil (Slobozia), established in 1969 (and privatised by Columna Bank, Eurotrading Chemicals and Romferchim), producing urea, ammonium nitrate and liquid urea fertiliser. Renovation has extended to the Kellogg ammonia plant to recover the residual heat that is now supplied to the town – as well as the ammonia synthesis and urea synthesis reactors that are now cost effective (having secured greater efficiency and quality with lower energy consumption and environmental risk). It was reportedly doing well in 1999 with home market sales to large farms, in competition with Doljchim (Craiova), and some exports to Europe as well as Asia (India, Philippines and Vietnam) and Latin America (Brazil and Ecuador). Another competitor of Amonil is the Romanian-UK company InterAgro established in 1993 and controlled by Romanian businessman Ioan Nicule. It's main business is fertiliser with several factories acquired typically as rescue operations beginning with Romania's first nitrogen fertiliser factory – Azochim Săvinești – established in 1956 and upgraded with German (Salzgitter) plant in the early 1970s. With a capacity of 300,000t of ammonia and urea, it was modernised in 1994 but work had to stop for lack of funds. It was acquired by InterAgro in 1997–98 and recommissioned in 1999 and the high-tech plant is profitable once again. Meanwhile the Sofert plant at Bacău dates to 1975 using a Kellogg (USA) ammonia plant and Stamicarbon (Netherlands) technology for urea 80 per cent of which is sold abroad thanks to environmental upgrades and ISO9002 quality certification in 2000. It also supplies some 100,000t of complex fertilisers (NPK) from its modernised plant – based on Iprochim (Romania) and Kaltenbach Turing (France) technology – to the home market. After reducing its workforce from 3,000 to 600 fall in demand in 2003 led to further lay-offs and a conservation régime before a return to profitability and acquisition by InterAgro in 2005.

Azomureș and Nitramonia

The group has also taken over other problem factories. Another rescue occurred at Azomureș (Târgu Mureș) which exported fertiliser, melamine, photographic paper and other chemical products worldwide thanks to a reputation for punctual delivery and high quality (assisted by purchase of patents from Kony Siroku – presently Konica – in 1981). It also modified its product range after 1989 to secure profitability by the mid-1990s and attracted a majority shareholding by Transworld Fertilisers in 1998. But like other producers it faced a crisis through rising gas prices in 2005-6 when layoffs occurred. InterAgro also moved to restart production at Nitrofertilizer (Făgăraș): a section ('Grup Azot') of a complex that started in 1922 as the country's first major producer of explosives (situated well clear of the town!). It diversified first into the intermediate ammonium nitrate (in 1936, when the name Nitramonia was adopted) and then under communism into fertilisers, resins and plastics. Markets were lost initially after 1989, but after the national defence work was hived-off (as Rompiro), the rest – once again named Nitramonia – was successfully privatised in favour of the Fletcher Group (USA) – renamed S&T Oil Equipment – in 2003 after modernisation had proceeded on the basis of 12 'centres' identified in 1998 (among which formaldehydic resins – sold to various industries including metallurgy – along with ammonium nitrate and mine explosives offered the best prospects for profitability). The main foreign links were with Bulgaria, Greece and Turkey – also Lebanon and Mauritania. However the privatisation contract was not correctly discharged and the assets were placed under ARSA in 2004 whereupon the business was divided into five units, one of which was the fertiliser business acquired by InterAgro in 2005 (other parts of the old complex have since been liquidated since Nitroexplosives collapsed in 2006 and is now up for sale by ARSA; so only 550 now work in a complex that supported 10,000 under communism). Nitramonia (a name that is reportedly up for sale) had close links with the nearby factory Viromet (Victoria) – originally conceived as a strategically-placed producer of war materials for the Axis during World War Two – which was acquired by InterAgro through privatisation in 2002 and now employs environmentally-friendly technology to produce formaldehyde derivatives (methanol), synthetic resins and plastics.

Donawchem (Turnu Măgurele)

This factory was also taken over in 2004 with the attraction of export by river. Like Sofert it comprises a Kellogg ammonia factory and Stamicarbon urea plant with ammonium nitrate by Kaltenbach (France) and complex (NPK/UAN) fertiliser units based on Norsk-Hidro technology (900,000t in total). The factory is well located to engage in foreign trade with regard to both inputs (phosphate and catalysts) and finished products. Moreover, a water supply is immediately available (by contrast the Amonil plant needs a 40km pipeline) while river and air currents dissipate pollution. But a failure to modernise during the 1980s and the decline in demand for fertiliser after 1989 made for low productivity compounded by poor labour discipline (including theft) and breakdowns in electricity and gas supplies with consequent heavy losses: 2.0mln.cu.m of gas in each case due the thermal inertia of the technological process geared to continuous production. Prices were in any case too low to cover costs, but after being reduced to bartering urea for gas to keep production going, a link with Columna Bank generated the cash to pay-off debts, secure raw material and catalysts and raise output to achieve near-maximum efficiency and start upgrading to eliminate sulphur dioxide pollution. At the same time Euro Trading Chemicals were able to find new markets. Worker morale improved through the negotiation of salary increases and housing/welfare benefits: several residential blocks at various stages of completion were taken over by the combine, finished to Western standards and allocated to employees. There was also help with special needs (handicapped children), retired persons and local services (through church repair).

Other Problem Cases

Fertilchim (Năvodari) had to reduce production by 95 per cent given the drop in demand from agriculture and reorganisation by breaking down into sections was complicated by the integrated nature of a complex technological process. The liquidator sold the works quickly to a Romanian-Italian j.v. Marway Commercial prepared to invest $450,000 to overhaul the plant and restart production (apart from closure of the sulphuric acid and phosphoric acid plants due to environmental problems). It was expected that 250 jobs would become available in 2000 (and more through other ventures in the area). Great problems also arose at Archim, the fertiliser factory in the Tudor Vladimirescu area of Arad, where Moldavian workers operated sophisticated western equipment. It was forced to close in 1990 but restarted in 1996 and was sold the following year to GTI Gaz of Bucharest, in collaboration with Universal Process Equipment of New Jersey (USA). The $100mln for purchase and modernisation was meant to secure 1,100 jobs producing, once again, the entire range of chemical fertilisers under good environmental concerns with no danger of soil contamination. But the deal fell through and liquidation was put n hand in 1998 with production reduced to a very low level, while some additional income was secured by selling assets and renting space. Romfosforchim (the largest sulphuric acid producer in the region) was another candidate for liquidation by the centre-right government after closure in 1997 for environment reasons, with SOF tackling the disposal of land, buildings and equipment. On the other hand at the historic Ampellum (Zlatna) factory sulphuric acid production restarted in 1996 after four years of technical improvements to bring emissions within admissible limits.

Petrochemicals: The Oltchim Complex

Established in 1966 with its first unit commissioned in 1968, the works is located on the Olt river south of Râmnicu Vâlcea for the convenience of links with the local saltfield (Ocnele Mari) and the Govora soda factory (a supplier of carbon dioxide). There was also the prospect of a lignite coal supply from Berbeşti to Govora power station but most crucial were the 60km ethylene and propylene pipelines from Arpechim oil refinery (Piteşti). Oltchim has an integrated profile based on salt and petrochemical intermediates: initially an electrolysis plant for chlorine and caustic soda and a PVC stream (1966-70) followed by plants for pesticides and organic intermediates in the 1980s. The company maintained its own R&D and used efficient processes based on licences from BASF and Krupp-Kautex (Germany); Mitsuitoatsu (Japan) and Union Carbide (USA). It is the sole producer of raw materials for PVC but is also responsible for two-thirds of Romania's chloro-sodium products as well as 60 per cent for pesticides and 80 per cent for oxo-alcohols. An effective management team under Constantin Roibu prevented a 'black hole' syndrome in the early transition years and in 1997 Oltchim was able to launch a $350mln four-year investment programme to upgrade the PVC chain with foreign credits (backed by government guarantee) for the hydrolysis plant. Both the chlor-alkali and petrochemical divisions have developed since 1990 through copolymers and plastifiers: note the 'Panpast' plant for ecological windows and doors – from PVC profiles without lead and tin – for a European market, while the 'Oltpan' facility for 'sandwich' polyurethane foam insulating panels has also developed an export business.

Further modernisation in 2004 was linked with extended vinyl chloride and PVC production. In a situation where hazardous products raised environmental costs, the pollution record has been vastly improved and ISO14001 certification for international environmental management standards reflects improvements in the filtering of waste water during 1997–99 to reduce residues by 50.0mg/l from the 1974 level to 18.9mg/l now (below the maximum limits for chlorine and solid residues flowing into the Olt). Pollutants like ethyl chloride and chlorinate residues are now burnt according to European standards. Links with agriculture developed in 1999 in a bid to overcome financial blockage when Oltchim took over local poultry and pig breeding farms – also a combined fodder factory and a food canning factory – so that payment for the factory's pesticides was secured in kind through cereals, vegetables and fruit. Cereals were processed at the fodder plant (supplying the livestock units) while vegetables and fruit went to the canning factory; and finally animal products and canned goods were sold in local shops. However, despite receiving a Juran award in the large enterprise category – reflecting Oltchim's quality culture – the privatisation essential for further investment has proved elusive, partly because of a desire to retain the combine as a single unit. A deal was reached with Exall in 2001 involving a $10mln purchase plus an investment of $150mln over three years to increase efficiency, pay-off debts and cease dependence on state-guaranteed credits. But Exall failed to pay up on time; since when there has been some interest from Grivco (Romania's largest fertiliser maker) and from Austrian and Israeli companies. Elsewhere the oil refineries are struggling to invest in new plant to reduce the cost of producing petrochemical feedstocks. Rompetrol's Petromidia refinery has been importing from TGR Hungary and Lukoil's subsidiary in Bulgaria but will now be assisted in modernising old plant (based on 1980s technology and last used in 1996) by Dow Chemicals' know-how. Dow will also deliver ethylene that will be repaid by Rompetrol's polymers when they resume production. A final effort is being made in 2007 to privatize the 95 per cent state holding including a debt for shares conversion.

Plastics

Downstream activities show some close linkages with the petrochemical complexes and the modernisation of Oltchim (already discussed) is reflected in the extension of government guarantee for foreign credits for Oltplast (Drăgaşani). Varied activities are now distributed around the country e.g. Platex (Tulcea) started to make plastic packaging in 2001 – with an extra 80 jobs in the polypropylene film facility – helping Romanian food, clothing and paper-board industries to enter foreign markets (in the former case by reducing spoilage levels which were high even by ECE standards). Foreign involvement is a common feature, notably the Italian connection. Latina Plastics is a Romanian-Italian j.v. created in 1993 to produce plastic sheets for food packaging and for medical industries; Metal-Star (Timişoara) is another Italian-Romanian j.v. set up 1994 with capital contributed by Sigma Group Engineering with the aim of producing PVC windows and doors: subsidiaries were expected in major cities with substantial exports to Russia. Then in 1999 Italian entrepreneurs entered into discussion with Galaţi CCI and the Baloga Group over j.v. production of PVC sewerage pipes and associated waste recycling (also use of slag waste from the local steel industry for road work) although high levels of taxation were seen as a disincentive. Again, the Hungarian company TVK has bought a majority stake in Plastico (Covasna), producing well below capacity at the time (1997) because of difficulties over the supply of raw materials. Another notable case concerns the French company Plastique Val de Loire with the Elbromplast factory in Timişoara for plastic injection moulded products.

Pharmaceuticals

Traditionally the industry has been dominated by low-volume domestic producers supplying the cheaper end of the market, with more sophisticated goods imported where finance was available. Exports have gone mostly to the CIS pending conformity with Good Manufacturing Practice (GMP), compulsory for drug producers in the EU. The market for medicines grew by 28 per cent to €1.0mln in 2004 and continued to rise in 2005 with consumption still low compared with the west – and only half the p.c. level in the Czech Republic, Hungary and Poland. But company shares are strong, despite delayed payments and blockages reflected in friction between private companies and the state health care budget. Over the longer term the industrty should grow by 8–10 per cent annually to reach a production value of $1.2bln in 2010 with further privatisation and upgrading by domestic firms (as well as some closure of loss-making facilities) and more capacity by foreign manufacturers. Currently Romanian companies – with Antibiotice, Sicomed and Terapia in the lead – dominate on volume (reflecting investment in new production technology and introduction of new products) and all have significant exports.

Antibiotice
This company started in 1955–56 as the first SEE producer of penicillin, extending into ointments and creams with the consolidation of pharmaceutical industry in Iaşi. Under communism the enterprise was a major partner in a national drug production system: concentrating on penicillin and derivatives, while supplying active substances to other SOEs: Biofarm and Sicomed in Bucharest and Terapia in Cluj-Napoca. But since 1990 the business has developed independently with its own nationwide distribution network starting during 1993–96 with depots in Bucharest, Cluj, Craiova, Constanţa and Satu Mare. It has developed new medicines for cardiovascular and digestive afflictions, including Nystatin and VitaminB12 in 1997–98 – registered for export to Canada and the USA in 2002 so that they now account for a quarter of total turnover and 80 per cent of the total value of exports. A $21mln investment plan in 1999 for re-equipment (30 per cent from own funds) secured GMP for all five production lines and boosted profits in 2000 through enhanced competitiveness in foreign markets. The company is now a leader in anti-infectious drugs, with plans for new medicines for blood pressure in collaboration with the Turkish company Eczacibasi; there was also collaboration with India in 2004 over penicillin and the French Aventis Group for tuberculostatic drugs. Current policy is to expand exports particularly in Africa, Asia and Moldova; while a new logo plus rebranding and new packaging to mark the company's first 50 years (also a planned research centre) all suggests an interest for active partners. As a 'strategic producer' the Romanian Ministry of Health is the majority shareholder in Antibiotice (53.0 per cent)

responsible for privatisation in favour of an appropriate buyer (after transfer organised on the same principle used when APMSH handed over tourism assets to the Tourism Ministry). Broadhurst Investment Fund (USA) and Romanian Investments Company (Cyprus) each held 6 per cent of the shares in 2001, though the former now has 7.7 per cent (after interest was shown in 1998 by the American company ICN Pharmaceuticals, with investments in Hungary, Poland, Russia and Serbia). The company is profitable but has debts arising from $10mln owed in 2003 by the healthcare system. Nevertheless 15 companies are reported to be interested in acquiring the company.

Sicomed

This is another large player: a producer of medicines for human and veterinary use originating as the Bucharest 'Intreprinderia de Medicamente' (but renamed in 1990) and privatised in 1999 with majority ownership by Venoma Holdings (Greece) – the investment vehicle of Galenica North East with minority holdings by EBRD and various investment funds. $40mln is being invested in production technology and human resource development in the interests of GMP. Fined 500mln.lei for breaking competition law by seeking a monopoly over the supply of pain killers containing Piafen, the company's policy is to introduce ten new products each year to strengthen market share and enhance exports currently dominated by the anti-ageing agents Gerovital and Aslavital. A majority stake is now owned by Zentiva (Czech Republic) after a $200mln bid to acquire stock from Venoma and further shares on the stock exchange (although this effort was only partly successful and the total holding is only 75 per cent). However, Zentiva want to build up a regional growth platform from Sicomed's vast distribution network in Romania with 20 new branded drugs anticipated over the next three years.

Other Domestic Companies

Biofarm (Bucharest) was privatised in 1997 as a producer of drugs from animal and vegetable raw materials; borrowing to upgrade to meet EU and national drug standards. The company was very profitable in 2004, producing syrups and solutions with exports to Belarus, Moldova and Russia, and attracted heavy share buying from the Banat and Oltenia holding companies; reducing Robert Ferran's stake from 49.9 to 17.5 per cent, while a 24.3 per cent interest is held by Igohealthy (USA). Finally Terapia was set up in Cluj in 1921 and featured in the mass privatisation of 1996. Taken over by the financial fund Advent International in 2003, it now concentrates on cardiovascular products, with a network of warehouses in Braşov, Bucharest, Cluj, Constanţa, Craiova, Galaţi, Iaşi and Timişoara and an expanding business with Poland, Russia and Ukraine. Terapia was then acquired by Ranbaxy (India) in 2006 for $324mln (for 96.7 per cent stake) as a strategic purchase offering access to the European market. $20mln was invested during 2006–07 in upgrading production, packaging and warehousing, while the company now has clearance to test and distribute drugs coming in from outside EU. There is now the prospect of a powerful base in Cluj to launch European expansion, although Ranbaxy have also acquired factories in Belgium, Italy and Spain. Reference should also be made to the success of Sidan (Bucharest), the restructured (1991) laboratory at the Oncological Institute producing anti-cancer medicines since 1962 and now with export growth e.g. USA.

Interest has been reported by Ranbaxy, as well as another Indian company Lupin. Also, a joint Romanian-Chinese medicine company Sinorompharma was reported in 1998: mainly for export of basic drugs using Chinese technology and equipment.

Foreign Companies (Excluding Recent Acquisitions)
Dominate on value through imports while FDI modernisation of the pharmaceutical industry is in its early stages. However, a big change occurred when GSK (GlaxoSmithKline), opened their Braşov factory to meet GMP and export to ECE and the EU. They gained first place in the market wirh 10.8 per cent of production (by value) after a strategic partnership was established in 1998 when the company's predecessor (SmithKlineBeecham, that later merged with GlaxoWellcome) paid $30mln for 65 per cent of Europharm – the leading Romanian pharmaceutical company in the research, production and distribution of pharmaceuticals and cosmetics – and then bought the remaining 35 per cent in 2003. A new $13mln factory was opened in Braşov in 2002 (dedicated to solid oral dosage medicines: antibiotics, vitamins and medicines for cardiovascular, digestive and neurological diseases) and $2.5mln was invested in 2003 in new production lines and offices. New products include pharmaceuticals produced in cooperation with CIBA GEIGY and Bayer. The company also helps in the community through the 'Partners for Life' foundation: working with WHO, World Bank and UNICEF on the national HIV/ AIDS programme (as well as a care and prevention model for HIV/AIDS in Giurgiu county). It also maintains a hospice ('Casa Speranţei') in Braşov and launched a vaccination programme in 2000 by donating 60mln.lei to help children in two isolated areas of Prahova County (Aricești Zeletin and Şotrile). Meanwhile other foreign companies active on the Romanian market supply from abroad. Novartis Pharm Romania scored a compounded annual growth of 50.9 per cent in 2001–2004, as the second company in the Romanian pharmaceutical industry. Others are Hoffman-La Roche (with Pharmacia), Pfizer and Schering. The Romanian-Slovenian Montero Group was set up in 1993 by three entrepreneurs as an importer and distributor of pharmaceuticals, with a good distribution network to private drugstores where 90 per cent of its products are sold. It had distribution centres in ten Romanian cities in 2001. Finally, Ipsen (France) is prominent as a pharmaceutical supplier while Canada's Technophar Equipment invested $5.0mln in 2001 to build a gelatine capsule factory (needed in the pharmaceutical industry) at Cornu in Prahova, following an earlier investment producing parts for the industry. Sanofi-Aventis are also a leading player on the pharmaceutical market.

Other Products

Henkel Romania started in 1994 as a subsidiary of Henkel Austria (Henkel Central Eastern Europe in 1998) and has made good progress in cosmetics (especially 'Taft' soap), adhesives and above all 'Rex' detergent: the latter in collaboration with Apollo (Galaţi), with the aim of acquiring a majority of shares. Apollo believed in the 1990s that only a quarter of detergents used in Romania were produced domestically and hence Romanian factories worked well below capacity. Unilever competes with its Bona brand after a $190mln purchase and development of the Dero factory in

Ploieşti in 1995, and European Drinks are now investing €10mln in a new factory in Bihor that will also produce plastic materials, car windscreen wash and distilled water. The privatised company Carom (Oneşti) is the only major synthetic rubber producer in Romania – with interest in privatisation at one stage by Macrochem (Lublin) a subsidiary of Itera, part of Gazprom. But Du Pont's Aectra Group is marketing its technology in Romania so that Rolast (Piteşti), Artego (Târgu Jiu) and Arteca (Jihlava) hope to manufacture high quality rubber products under licence for use by Daewoo in Craiova and also for export markets. Technology is available through barter systems and through credits, with eventual payment through the sale of products. Du Pont has also been interested in supplying insecticides suitable for use on small farms and is cooperating with Romanian companies in the field of packaging materials since 1995-6. The dye industry has contracted heavily with Colorom (Codlea) trying to stabilise at 10 per cent capacity after heavy redundancy among the workforce of 2,400 in 1989 and liquidation of 20bln.lei of debts through the sale of assets like the canteen, club, creche, farm and tailor's shop in 1998. Policolor of Bucharest is the largest lacquers, dyestuffs and industrial coating manufacturer in Romania and a majority interest was acquired by Whitebeams Holdings (USA) along with an association through majority stake with Orgachim (Ruse) – the largest equivalent company in Bulgaria – with a view to joint marketing and a unitary sales network in the paint sector with consolidation to extend from an enhanced domestic wholesaling network in the late 1990s to enhance Balkan exports linked with a Marshall (USA) licence. Salt (as opposed to brine) is still produced at Slănic-Prahova, Târgu Ocna and Ocna Dej, while a new $22mln recrystallised salt factory was reported at Ocna Mureş by Evaterm (Switzerland).

Chapter Seven

Building Materials and Textiles Clothing & Leather: Contrasts in the Nature of Foreign Penetration

Introduction

The examination of Romanian industry continues in this chapter with two further sectors. The stories are interesting in themselves. Building materials have been of great importance throughout Romania's modernisation given the need for an urban scale of construction and the availability of suitable raw materials. But the share of value-added has been sliding from a high of 5.9 per cent in 1992 to 4.1 per cent in 2004, though more moderately for production value (Table 6.2) from 3.5 to 3.2 per cent. The textiles, clothing and leather (TCL) industry is also traditional: Romania's oldest fur factory has been functioning in Oradea for 80 years. And there was a great expansion under communism during a period when home production of clothing largely died out, even in the rural areas. The sector has also been sliding down from the high level of 13.1 per cent of value-added in 1990–92 to 10.3 in 2004 (12.2 to 6.9 per cent for production value), although it regained the 1992 level of 10.0 per cent (or slightly better) on five occasions, including 2001–2004. Both sectors register a sharp decline in the average size of firm as a result of the increase in their number during 1996–2003: in the case of building materials from 959 to 2,650 (2.8 times) with average employment falling from 130 and 24 respectively and for TCL a growth in firms of just 35 per cent while average employment has fallen moderately from 66 to 45 (much more in textiles – 76 to 31 – than in clothing – 62 to 49 – and leather 59 to 49). However there are two significant differences. In the case of building materials employment of 190,000 in 1991 has fallen relentlessly to 72,000 in 2003 and 60,000 in 2005 although the current building boom may help to stabilise the situation. By contrast, although there is also a decline in TCL from 471,000 to 419,000 there was an increase to 2003 (489,000) when it was the only industrial sector to show a growth in employment over 1989. This was due to a big growth in clothing from 203,000 to 303,000, though the figure fell back to 259,000 in 2005 (from 42.7–61.8 per cent of the total for the sector during 1996-2005). The initial gain more than compensated for the losses in textiles from 185,000 to 84,000 in 2003 but note the further decline to 67,000 in 2005 (declining overall from 39.8 per cent of the sector total to 16.0 per cent). Meanwhile leather and footwear registered a significant gain from 17.5–22.2 per cent of the sector (83,000 to 93,000 with a peak of 102,000 in 2003). The second difference arises in the level of foreign penetration. The building materials sector is headed by the production of cement and concrete where three foreign companies – Heidelberg, Holderbank and Lafarge – have a dominant role and have achieved a substantial technological improvement. TCL is not without its foreign investment but the dynamic clothing sector is mostly in Romanian hands because foreign interests exploit low cost labour and can operate on a lohn basis without the need for major technological change.

Cement, Concrete and Other Building Materials

The sector is dominated by cement production that expanded massively under communism to provide capacities in all major regions. The new factory at Bârseşti near Târgu Jiu in Oltenia opened in 1965, followed by three others by 1967 (Câmpulung, Deva and Hoghiz) using the new dry system which subsequently displaced the older wet method at earlier communist projects at Bicaz and Medgidia and even older factories at Aghireş, Fieni and Turda. Capacity now exceeds 10mln.t but production has fallen from 12.2mln.t in 1985 to 9.5 in 1990 to 6.0 in 2003 (while averaging 6.2mln.t during 1994-2003) (Table 7.1). Domestic demand fell after 1989 while production costs (reflecting high energy consumption) and transport costs made export generally uneconomic. There were also pollution problems although these were eased to some extent by the installation of more filters. However cement has been one of the success stories for privatisation because the whole sector was restructured during 1995–99 and this led to investment of some $400mln (including $120mln for environmental protection). The industry is profitable and overwhelmingly in the hands of international companies. In 1997 Cimus (Câmpulung) and Temelia (Braşov) – the latter a producer of lime and plaster as well as white cement – were privatised by EMBO but control subsequently passed to Holcim and Heidelberg respectively. Other disposals in 1997 were: Cimentul (Turda) to Holderbank Financière Giaris of Switzerland (Holcim) – the first involvement of a large cement company; followed by Casial (Deva) – producing cement, gypsum and lime products – to Lasselsberger (Austria). Also in the same year SOF shares in the Romcim group with 9.5mln. t capacity in cement works at Hoghiz, Medgidia and Târgu Jiu (plus a concrete business, an asbestos factory and the Aghireş plasterworks) were sold directly to the French company Lafarge (which was also acquiring interests in Czech Republic, Poland and Russia at the time). Then Moldocim (Bicaz) was sold to Heidelberg in 1998 and Romcif (Fieni) was privatised by EMBO in the same year (although Holcim bought a substantial interest in 1999); while Alchim (Aleşd) went to Holcim in 2000.

The Cement Market

The cement market is small but expanding, given the building boom (180kg/cap in 2000 requires 4.5mln.t compared with a capacity of 12.0mln) while the international market is highly competitive in view of the prominence of Mediterranean and Southeast Asia producers. Consumption is now rising and stands at 334kg/pc (538 in EU) and this trend should continue through new property (also thermal insulation) as well as demand for motorways, other roads and port/airport developments.

Table 7.1: Industrial production: building materials, textiles and footwear 1985–2005

Year	Building Materials								Textiles Clothing & Footwear								
	A	B	C	D	E	F	G	H	I	J	K	L	M	N	O	P	Q
1985	12.2	11.2	1038	na	387	1466	5708	n.a.	280	1098	695	279	74	74	185	47.0	112
1986	14.2	13.0	1026	na	398	1604	5991	n.a.	295	1151	727	285	74	71	201	50.4	116
1987	13.6	12.4	870	na	374	1680	6199	n.a.	283	1132	705	274	75	68	184	50.3	113
1988	14.4	13.1	817	na	377	1870	6479	n.a.	277	1102	689	258	74	56	189	47.2	109
1989	13.3	12.2	836	na	374	2013	6277	n.a.	261	1109	709	261	74	65	170	45.7	111
1990	9.5	3.0	691	17	57	307	3451	6.8	189	845	536	202	58	53	149	38.5	88
1991	6.7	2.3	633	16	46	250	1585	6.6	141	711	437	174	45	46	106	68.3	68
1992	6.3	1.9	512	15	44	206	946	6.7	105	481	289	103	29	41	87	0.1	44
1993	6.2	1.7	618	18	46	165	466	7.2	115	438	271	102	25	48	86	0.3	45
1994	6.0	1.6	473	19	38	181	419	7.7	89	445	293	114	32	59	72	0.7	49
1995	6.8	1.8	499	19	42	203	424	8.9	82	395	190	44	21	74	81	3.0	52
1996	7.0	1.7	626	21	41	216	395	9.6	84	302	187	44	20	67	67	4.5	37
1997	6.5	1.7	493	22	30	185	335	9.5	76	276	173	46	24	79	67	9.0	36
1998	6.6	1.8	410	24	31	160	154	10.9	61	240	170	33	20	70	42	14.4	31
1999	5.6	1.6	447	26	27	95	166	11.4	49	200	143	36	24	81	28	19.4	31
2000	6.1	1.7	362	32	30	129	139	11.7	50	194	145	38	24	83	30	31.7	38
2001	5.7	1.8	n.a.	33	32	137	194	12.4	47	213	159	48	25	82	30	80.3	67
2002	5.7	1.9	n.a.	41	42	137	154	13.4	57	219	170	59	29	86	26	100.6	74
2003	6.0	1.9	n.a.	42	35	265	122	13.9	57	228	177	53	29	82	22	138.2	80
2004	6.2	2.0	n.a.	39	32	152	134	14.2	60	246	201	52	29	83	21	154.0	75
2005	7.0	1.8	n.a.	41	22	133	182	14.2	52	151	112	47	25	85	16	144.2	72

A: Cement mln.t; B: Lime mln.t; C: Bricks and blocks (mln); D: Porcelaine sanitary items th.t; E: Glass th.sq.m; F: Glassware th.t; G: Reinforced concrete fabrications th.cu.m; H: Finishing materials for walls/ceramic floors mln.sq.m; I: Cotton wool flax and hemp yarns th.t; J: *Fabric mln.cu.m; K: *Ditto cotton only; L: *Ditto wool only; M: *Knitwear mln.pieces; N: Acrilonitrile th.t; O: Synthetic fibres and yarns th.t; P: Clothing tln.lei (mln.lei 1985-1991); Q: Footwear mln.pairs. * indicates a change in the basis of collecting figures in 1995 which destroys comparability with earlier years.

Source: Statistical Yearbooks Table 16.3

All-round profitability underlines the success of privatisation that leaves Lafarge with 32 per cent, Holcim 30 per cent, Heidelberg 22 per cent and Tagrimex Romcif 16 per cent but companies have had to increase productivity through redundancy and there has also been a trend towards outsourcing for security, cleaning and maintenance that began with Heidelberg and Lafarge and was then copied by Holcim in 2003. Prices on the home market have been kept fairly high: arousing government suspicion of price-fixing in 2003 when home market prices reached $80/t, compared with $50 in Poland, $55 in the Czech Republic and $60 in Hungary – and much higher than export prices, especially in the case of dumping at $24/t. This reflects the observation by Dăianu (2004, p.404) that "post-privatisation competition in the cement industry proved limited as a former oligopoly industry has changed to a sum of regional monopolies". A new factor in the situation is the plan by Sabanci Holdings (Turkey) for a $150mln greenfield cement factory with 1.0mln.t/yr capacity, although further detail is lacking.

Lafarge
Lafarge, with almost a third of the market in 2002 and a production of some 3.9mln. t, joined the Romanian cement market 1997 with a $250mln investment (extending to 2002) made primarily in upgrading cement plants – 50 years old in the case of the Medgidia plant with 3.50mln.t capacity. Obsolete equipment has been dismantled, including the first three production lines at Târgu Jiu commissioned in 1963–64 and derelict since 1992 leaving 3.00mln.t of capacity. Indeed lines 4–6 could also be disposed of because the remaining lines (7–9, attracting $1.0mln investment for environmental protection in 2000) have 1.0mln.t/yr capacity that is far in excess of the 350,000t actually produced. 100 per cent waste recycling has also been introduced. Finding that the cost of labour was 10 per cent higher in Romania than the average for the group, the company announced in 1999 that the workforce of 2,500 at Medgidia would be reduced gradually to 500–600 with redundant workers offered indemnities or re-entry courses. But in response to lay-offs at Medgidia the company set up a business incubator that has had some success in stimulating around a dozen SMEs. Meanwhile at Hoghiz, with 1.60mln.t capacity, help over redundancies in 2000 was focused more on agriculture. However, total employment was still 4,000 in 2001. Innovations elsewhere include a 'multibat' masonry cement (saving time and energy) developed by the company a decade ago and now available in Romania. Also investment was made in new technology in 2001 to increase exports and facilitate delivery of special cement for road projects in Romania. About half the production is exported in order to boost output at the plant close to the Black Sea coast. Indeed Medgidia is now mainly an export factory – located within a short rail haul of Constanța and despatching to Spain and Portugal as well as several African countries including Cameroon, Egypt and Nigeria. However the export price of $25/t was much lower that the home market price of $40/t in 2001. Meanwhile the company is expanding in plaster, aggregates and concrete (including prefabrication). The concrete and aggregate units at Bucharest, Buzău and Ploieşti have been amalgamated into one business and the merger extended to new acquisitions in Transylvania at Miercurea Ciuc and Năsăud in 2002. Other acquisitions include the quarry aggregate unit Romet (Baia Sprie) in 1999 and the concrete unit SUT (Iaşi)

that can produce 105cu.m/h using ballast loaded at Boureni pit at Paşcani. Lafarge-Romcim also has an association accord with the large Romanian building company Arcom in respect of plasterboard: the new unit Lafarge Arcom Gips produces cardboard plaster plates, along with concrete, quarry/river aggregates, lime, plaster and gypsum.

Holcim Romania

Holcim Romania involves the Swiss Holderbank interest with 28 per cent market share in 2002, arising from the acquisition of the white cement producer Cimentul (Turda) in 1997 with 1.36mln.t capacity, followed by the grey cement factories Cimus (Câmpulung) in 1999 and Alchim (Aleşd) in 2000, with capacities of 2.20 and 3.50mln.t/yr respectively. The company has invested €280mln in a programme extending to 2005. The Turda works, founded before the First World War, is the sole Romanian producer of white cement – but also produces regular cement (0.45mln. t/yr) as well as lime, plaster and refractory bricks – and is the only one still using the wet process: raw materials are transported 2-15kms by narrow gauge railway, and the availability of over 50 years supply will help to keep costs low. With labour cut from 1,800 to 600 in 2000, the works operates efficiently using natural gas and pollution is no longer a problem since the newest furnace (number seven) incorporates the latest European standards and conforms with current environmental legislation. However, the company first spent €70mln to modernise Aleşd to serve the northwest – and to complement its Hungarian plants at Eger and Miskolc in supplying a broad border zone that has been quite dynamic in recent years. It also operates the largest grey cement production kiln in Romania – 4,000t capacity at Câmpulung; which is well-located to supply the dynamic Bucharest market with which there is a direct railway connection. Indeed the Câmpulung factory is now completely automated to ensure consistent quality and reduced energy consumption (including the use of alternative fuels). There is also a pre-blending bed for raw materials. Holcim are now investing €160mln over three years in modernisation and environmental work including €100mln at Câmpulung. This is on top of previous investments of €334mln, with a particular focus on co-processing to burn a wide range of waste materials: petroleum, plastic, paper, textile, leather, rubber, wood and chemical compounds (which can also be used at Aleşd). Holcim have also improved efficiency over the delivery of stone obtained by conveyor from a quarry at 1,000m on Dl. Hulei. A huge Caterpillar excavator can now take 12t 'bites' delivered to the conveyor system by five 37t/55t lorries from Belaz of Belarus.

Aggregate (sand and gravel) plants are operated by Holcim in the Piteşti area at Piscani, Râncăciov and Zărneşti. It also has a network of 14 ready-mix concrete stations (11 greenfield) including three in Bucharest – Chitila, Pipera and Progresul with the latter including the Bucharest Despatch Centre. The company has been spending €80mln over 4-5 years in modernising these installations and improving the environment. Part of this programme includes automatic 120cu.m/hr environmentally-friendly concrete plants (EFCPs), avoiding dust and noise: the first was opened by modernisation at Piteşti, followed by new facilities at Cluj, Craiova, Oradea and Ploieşti (all in 2002), followed by Arad, Braşov (by modernisation), Bucharest (Chitila), Sibiu, Timişoara and Târgu Mureş by 2005, when total investment by the company reached €300mln. Italian, Spanish and Swiss automated technology secures 120cu.m concrete/hour, with reduced noise and dust emissions while facilitating recycling. The company is also proud of its new service in 2005 for unloading palette cement bags by tail forklift. Meanwhile non-modernised plants remain in Bucharest (Pipera and Progresul) and in Satu Mare while an old plant at Curtea de Argeş not longer operates.

Heidelberg

Heidelberg, trading as Carpatcement, hold 22 per cent of market share after securing a majority holding in Moldocim (Bicaz) in 1998 with 3.10mln.t capacity (followed by a $15mln investment to 2003) and likewise in Casial (Deva) in 2000. The latter had already absorbed $35mln of investment under Lasselsberger, including electric filters to obtain ISO14001 environmental certification (subsequently sought by Heidelberg for all its factories in the region). However the company has now gained strength in the Bucharest area by purchasing a majority interest in Tagrimex-Romcif (Fieni) in 2002, partly by taking over Holcim's interest, which makes it the leading player in the Romanian cement industry. With 1.60mln.t capacity, Fieni is a dry cement producer with an advantageous location. An employee association bought 30 per cent of shares in 1995 and then increased the holding to 40 per cent in 1998 before selling half as an investment vehicle for Holderbank in 1999. However Tagrimex of Bucharest became the majority shareholder at the time in a business that holds 18 per cent of market share. Indeed, Fieni is the single most important cement plant and – with early investment to reduce power consumption – is a profitable unit exporting 30 per cent of its production. Six old furnaces using the wet system have been given up in favour of a new line using the dry method (turning out 3,000t/day) with a total capacity of 1.60mln.t. There was also investment in 1999 to reduce pollution by electrostatic filter equipment and the company is building up to 100 homes for employees. Heidelberg then acquired the Temelia (Braşov) limeworks in 1999 followed by a $6.2mln investment during 1999-2000 to update production, including the introduction of environmental lime used in thermal power stations to clean water, soil and woodland; in line with its philosophy of 'permanent interaction with the market, clients and the environment'. Finally there are 12 concrete plants, managed by Carpat Beton, in Bucharest (three) and Arad, Bacău, Braşov, Craiova, Iaşi, Piteşti, Ploieşti, Suceava and Timişoara; and seven aggregate plants, run as Carpat Agregate, at Buriaş and Cornetu (Ilfov), Doaga (Vrancea), Ghioroc (Arad), Feldioara (Braşov), Milcoiu (Mehedinţi) and Slătioara (Olt) – and seven quarries at Aciuţa (Arad), Brănişca (Hunedoara), Iglicioara (Tulcea), Maidan (Caraş-Severin), Malnaş (Covasna), Porceni (Gorj) and Şoimoş (Arad). There are too many other aggregate producers to give a complete picture but Strabag (Austria) have a 21bln.lei investment at Jena (Timiş) for the automated production of 80t/hr of ballast; operated by just three employees with its own electrical power set. Production is geared to the rehabilitation of national roads (especially Timişoara-Caransebeş) and local roads.

Glass and Ceramics

Float glass manufacture involves number of long-established enterprises. Geromed (Mediaş), established in 1919, is one of Romania's four large glass manufacturers producing flat, tempered and laminated glass. It is intended that obsolete equipment over 20 years old will be replaced through a $150mln investment for a float glass line to compete in an environment of highly volatile prices. 60 per cent of capacity was used in 1998, mostly for export to Europe and the Middle East. Meanwhile the Bucharest glass producer Stirom was acquired by the Greek Yioula company in 2003 and has been enlarged through a €25mln investment (including a €20mln EBRD loan) in new technology, including furnace refurbishment, and an extended distribution system to produce glass for packaging currently imported from Bulgaria. Furthermore a local consortium is buying the float glass producer GES at Boldeşti-Scăeni (Prahova) and although Guardian International's proposed $100mln investment in a new plant did not succeed, Saint Gobain (France), who already have a glass fibre plant at Piteşti, have invested a similar amount to develop a site at Călăraşi during 2004–2006 (with an €10mln industrial gas factory by Air Liquide alongside). With a piped gas supply laid on specially, the company will produce 600t/glass daily for industrial use: half for the home market and half for export to Bulgaria, Greece, Poland and Serbia. With efficient furnaces opened in 2006 producing 600t/day, the company dominates the Romanian market along with Yioula. 215 workers are employed plus 1,000 indirectly through subcontracting.

Specialised Production

This concerns the German Gerofast company producing termoplan glass at Tunari; also plastic doors and windows from 1996, while Gerom (Buzău) is Romania's largest glass-making company, producing windows for all models of cars made in Romania as well as eco-friendly glass bottles to replace plastic goods in 2002; while Sticla (Turda), whose 75th anniversary year fell in 1996, installed new technology in the mid-1990s and doubled its exports of household and laboratory/thermal resistance glass. After experiencing low demand for its basic products in the mid-1990s Gegsat (Târnăveni) introduced new technology for thermo-insulating glass as well as aluminium and PVC fittings. Particularly good results were obtained for aluminium mirrors in West European and US markets during 1995-7. Vitrometan Mediaş dates to 1922 and is now part of Deru Glaswarenvertrieb of Bamberg – producing clear/coloured glass items and lead crystal. Finally a small project for decorative glass was launched in 2001 in a workshop on the Murano model by a former mayor at Găgeni (Prahova) for export to USA/Canada, Japan and Western Europe – beginning with Galle-type vases for Germany. There is a tradition of glass jar making but the entrepreneur brought in glass blowers from Mediaş and Turda and now has workers who were formerly working at Plopeni armaments factory. Glass globes have been supplied for park lighting at Anvers and an interest in coloured glass windows is now developing. And Forever Pipe have set up the 'Mill Cell' venture with Concordia of Câmpina in respect of glass products for the construction industry; with factories at both Câmpina and Lugoj. However parts of the industry are under threat because of old technology (small furnaces of 150t/day over 50 years old that are expensive to operate in the context of rising gas prices and cannot compete on world markets).

Ceramics and Porcelain

Apullum (Alba Iulia) and Arpo (Curtea de Argeş) have joined KPCL of Germany in a j.v. for ceramic and porcelain production involving German know-how and Romanian raw materials, production and management. Apullum invested $50,000 in 2000 for plates and dishes for export to Western Europe. Profits in the first quarter of 2001 amounted to $0.16mln on turnover of $3.50mln. At Arpo, privatised by EMBO in the early 1990s, a modern German kiln was installed to cut the baking cycle from 48 to 6-8 hours: enabling increased production and massive reduction in gas consumption per production cycle, opening the way for export growth up to three quarters of the production. Another modern kiln was installed during 1997. Indeed the enterprise, which dates to 1974, is doing particularly well at home and abroad while former competitors in Cluj and Dorohoi have closed (and even Apullum have had to close a section). 550 workers produce vases and figurines, but Chinese goods are only a third of the price. Meanwhile Mondial of Lugoj, owned by Villeroy & Boch (Germany), specialise in bathroom suites sold through the shops of their partners in Bucharest (five), Braşov (three) and Constanţa (two) plus single shops in 11 other towns: Arad, Bacău, Cluj, Craiova, Galaţi, Oradea, Satu Mare, Sf.Gheorghe, Sibiu, Sinaia, Timişoara – also Ciumani (Harghita) near Gheorgheni.

Other Products

There is still a substantial output of sun-dried bricks produced on the edge of villages by teams of Roma. But a commercial scale has also operated using kilns (like the long-established tile works at Jimbolia in Banat) while the communist era saw the manufacture of building blocks using diatomite as at Pătârlagele (Buzău). Some of these units have been privatised by EMBO e.g. in 2000 an employee association bought a majority holding in Refractara (Baru Mare) making fireclay bricks and thermo-isolating plates. There has been some modernisation e.g. by Ceramica (Iaşi) with installation of a fully-automated tunnel oven (the most advanced in the country) in 2001 in collaboration with an Italian company to reduce fuel costs by 60 per cent and rejects from 10 per cent to less than four. The oven works efficiently even a low gas pressures, experienced at Iaşi, lying at the end of the pipeline. And while Stimet (Sighişoara) closed in 2005 after a bank credit was refused, the new Siceram company is completing a €20mln investment modernising brick ('Termobloc'), tile and roof tile production. Foreign interests developed when Wienerberger (Austria) opened a depot in 1998 to sell 'porotherm' bricks made in Hungary. 40mln bricks were sold during 2000; some to companies building for the National Dwellings Agency. In 2002 the company made an €18mln investment creating 80 jobs to produce 130mln bricks/yr at Gura Ocniţei (Dâmboviţa) where good quality clay is available: this is the first entirely new installation in the sector post-1989. Wienerberger have also received an EBRD loan of €4.0mln to acquire a brickworks in Sibiu in 2004. Meanwhile the Austrian interest in producing quality building materials in Romania (rather than cheap aerated autoclaved concrete blocks) was extended when Lasselsberger took over Sanex (Cluj) and Cesarom (Bucharest) – the latter from Zalakeramia (Hungary). Then Tondach went into roof tiles in 2004 by taking over Cama (Sibiu) and – evidently impressed by the local clay – followed this up with a greenfield development in the town. In 2004

Tondach were joined by Bramac (Austria) who produce cement blocks. There are now enough Austrians in Sibiu wanting to get home for the weekend for flights to Vienna to be laid by a partnership involving Austrian Airlines and Tarom. Hamer (Luxembourg) have acquired Macon (Deva) a producer of building blocks of other materials including terracotta; while reference should also be made to the regional concrete fabricators that have been privatized and now compete within the home market. Elpreco (Craiova), who started in 1963 and went into autoclaved aerated concrete in 1965 – switching from Polish to German (Hebel) technology in 1970 – are now part of the Broadhurst portfolio and after €30mln of investments over 10 years they are successfully marketing concrete, paving and tiles nationwide. Other units from the communist period include Valmet (Hunedoara) currently experiencing a boom in concrete and steel products. Wood products lie outside the scope of this chapter but it is relevant to mention the progress made by foreign investors in improving the quality of beams for structural use as well as boards, window and doors with the latter a speciality of the Nusco Grup's 'Pinum Producţie' factory in the former state complex at Pipera in northern Bucharest (producing 10,000/month, with a good export business). Beyler produce metal/PVC doors in Bârlad and have an export business in addition to a chain of shops in Romania; while a string of companies have started turning out special products for the building industry including Baumit Wopfinger who started at Teiuş but now have a €30mln programme covering units in Bucharest as well as Banat and Moldovia. Other companies include Coilprofil (Belgium) along with Isopan (Italy) for insulation panels and Xella for autoclaved cellular concrete.

Wallboard and Plasterboard
Traditionally Romania has also made use of ferro-concrete, concrete sheets or ceramic tiles with asphalted cardboard, bitumen or mineral wool for insulation but without protection against water infiltration and large heat loss. Although obsolete technologies and materials are still used, change is now occurring and higher quality materials, including fine ceramics and tiles are now profitable since the additional investments are recovered in five to seven years with the help of export demand. The Arcom Group – one of the most important building and assembly holdings in Romania (set up in 1969 as the Romanian Building & Assembly Enterprise and reorganised as Arcom in 1991; turnover €41mln 2006) – inaugurated the first wallboard plant in the country near Bucharest (3.2mln.sq.m/yr) in 1999 with $10mln-worth of US equipment and design from a subsidiary of the Babcock Corporation. The company did not initially appreciate the possibilities for wallboard, but with privatisation and much experience in North Africa, Middle East, Central Asia and India, they now expect to use a lot in their own activities. Meanwhile, starting in 1994 – and acquiring Gypsum Turda in 1999 – Rigips Romania leads in plasterboard and ecological paints. Their new factory offers a 'Casoprano' range of decorative ceilings. The plasterboard market totalled 9.0mln.sq.m in 2001 with average annual growth expected at 20–25 per cent. A Romanian subsidiary of the Swedish Lindab Building Corporation was founded in 1994 to manufacture construction profiles and ventilation systems in Bucharest with a $2.0mln investment completed at the end of 2001. The company holds 65 per cent of the Romanian market for metal

roof tiles and part of the production was exported to Bulgaria in 2002. And as part of the company's expansion in the region, Henkel Bautechnik Romania opened a DM6.0mln factory near Bucharest in 2000 producing 'Ceresit' building adhesives previously imported. Meanwhile, Umwelttechnik (Austria) have made a €2.0mln investment at Orțișoara near Timișoara to produce sewerage cannulars and Hirsch Parozek (Austria) have invested €5.2mln 2006-7 in polystyrene sheet production at Rascruci (Cluj) for the building industry.

Textiles, Clothing and Leather

Difficult conditions since 1989 reflect the underlying problems of unstable fiscality, an initially weak banking system and a depressed domestic market, combined with trade dependence for the quality market catered for through franchises for Benetton, Lacoste, Marks & Spencer and Steilmann. But clothing producers were able to take advantage of low labour costs to develop their export business as access to the EU improved during the 1990s with the removal of duties and quantitative limitations on many textiles (and footwear). Romania moved into first place for the export of ready-mades to the EU: worth €2.4bln in 1999 (47 per cent of all Romanian exports) compared with sixth place (worth DM448mln) in 1993 when Poland led with 1.3bln. In the meantime some Polish companies withdrew while Romania progressed thanks to low salaries (although wages cannot remain so low and the advantage will be eroded without gains in productivity). The main markets in 2001 were Italy (25.0 per cent), Germany (15.7), France (8.0), UK (5.2), Turkey (4.1) and The Netherlands (3.4); while annual growth has exceeded 10 per cent in recent years as regards output and employment. However 85 per cent of textile exports are generated by outsourcing or outward processing trade (OPT), sometimes known as the 'lohn system'. Indeed 90 per cent of clothing companies are forward processors but the system is likely to contract – by as much as 50 per cent – with EU accession and consequent migration to the CIS and Asia in search of cheaper labour. Romania is already competing with Moldova and Ukraine as well as Bangladesh and China. Chinese competition is exacerbated (a) by the end of quotas on OECD countries for imports from low wage economies and (b) US subsidies for Texas cotton growers who export to China. In 2003, trade minister E.Dijmarescu advocated alternative markets in Latin America and Middle East, but another solution is greater export to Europe under domestic trademarks; calling for development programmes to improve international marketing activity extending back to the spinning and weaving mills. And it is also significant at a time of rising incomes at home that the clothing industry can secure only some 15 per cent of the domestic market.

Romanian Clothing Collections

Romanian clothing collections with original design are highly desirable but extremely challenging to realise when the market is suffocated by cheap/low quality goods. The German GTZ programme seeks to boost Romanian exports to Germany – partly through the supply of business catalogues – by encouraging firms to develop their own collections by way of modern marketing, like the Moda Tim ready-to-wear factory in Timişoara which succeeded in creating its own designs and concluding sales contracts with major stores in Germany. Then 2005 saw great problems in the industry with 85 per cent of the 8,900 clothing companies tied to the lohn system – facing problems of an appreciating leu, higher electricity charges and high interest for Eximbank loans. Only 300 companies are 'large' with capacity to survive. Among Romanian private companies, Someşul Tricotaje and Flacara (both from Cluj) have launched their own ready-made brands – following Jolidon that has always sold its own brand and does not accept lohn work. Flacara has gone from bankruptcy to export success with privatisation and a 40bln.lei investment, plus recruitment of 18-20 year olds. Some work exclusively for the Romanian market with their own brand names (like Chic&Cher, Dinasty and Jolidon) while others do both. Siret (Paşcani) – formerly the Paşcani Knitwear & Curtains Enterprise founded in 1972 and concentrating on curtains, lingerie and sportswear – is a flexible, competitive private company employing 1,500 and exporting 70 per cent of its production to the EU (especially Germany, France and The Netherlands) and also to the USA and Canada, thanks to high quality production and investment in modern technology.

Siret also runs its own shops in Romania. Its former branch factories at Dorohoi, Frasin and Hălăuceşti – transferred to the Târgu Frumos knitwear enterprise in 1983 – but only Hălăuceşti remains after Dorohoi and Frasin closed in 1990. It has consolidated its Paşcani operations and has sold a 5,000sq.m four-storey building. Another Paşcani clothing firm, Integrata, signed contracts with several Italian companies in 2001, while Tricotton (Panciu) installed high performance equipment during 1993-6 and regained traditional links with Germany, Italy, Sweden and the USA; paving the way for further modernisation. Among the enterprising smaller companies is Textila (Sibiu) one of four companies emerging from the break-up in 1991 of a larger entity established in 1949. Concentrating on fashion, it was revamped in 1995 with new machinery and increased capacity from 2,000 to 10,000 knitwear pieces/month needed for it own collection (sold in part through it own 'Flore' shop in Sibiu) and lohn work for France, Germany and Italy by companies such as Lacoste, Max-Mara and Pelo. Mondial (Satu Mare) – starting as a tailoring cooperative in 1935 – was privatised in 1995 and now concentrates on women's wear entirely for export for Steilmann (Germany) and UK firms Next, Trump and Kapelle. It opened a new factory at Vadu Crişului (Bihor) in 2002. Indeed several new businesses are opening in western Romania where labour is available in small towns (e.g. Intertextiles at Aleşd in 2000) or former heavy industrial centres (Meropa Knitwear in Hunedoara).

Developing Links with Western Firms

Four Romanian-Italian j.v. ready-made clothing enterprises in Râmnicu Sărat – Lazar Impex, Via Vinezia, Gardenia and Prestige – merged into a holding company (Lazar Group, with a total employment of 650) and successfully competed with other firms (including the loss-making military clothing factory) to obtain orders from NATO for uniforms for the East European military. The Group also succeeded in exporting ladies' underwear through collaboration with an Italian partner with each year's production contracted for in advance. Alt Group (Germany) invested

DM1.0mln with Pantex (a Braşov company – successor to the former Fabrica de Postav şi Tesătura de Moda Wilhelm Scherg – producing elastic tape and ribbon) to rehabilitate and re-equip space in Târgu Secuiesc in 1997 for the production of sports clothing (with a soft texture through chemical washing) for sale in Romania and also France, Germany and Italy. Amatex at Sânleani near Arad is another Romanian-German clothing factory dating to 1997: it produces 1.25mln pieces/yr of children's clothing for Textilwerk Gebrüder Ammann in Germany and maintains its own 'Tiffany Kids' shops in Arad and Timişoara (the latter known as 'Terra Complex'). Moldova Tricotaje (Iaşi) is selling its cotton and cotton-type products in Austria, Germany and USA due to partnerships with C&A, Neckermann and Quelle (Austria and Germany) and Walmart (USA). 13 Decembrie (Timişoara) was privatised by EMBO to produce the Pasmatex company specialising in fancy ribbons and bands. Labour was cut from 870 in 1990 to 260 in1997, but exports increased and cooperation with Triumph International (Austria) started a knitted underwear section in 1998 employing 120 and brought new technology to other branches. Tricotaje (Ineu) was started in 1974 by the Tricoul Roşu (Arad) knitwear enterprise, but it is now an independent company with 100 per cent Romanian capital making lingerie, trousers, shirts and sportswear. Partnerships were forged with French companies in 1990 and employment has risen from 800 to 1,400 in 2001. Meanwhile the Ikos Conf ready-made clothing factory at Odorheiu Secuiesc was able to update itself through a Romanian-Canadian j.v.: high performance machines raised productivity and paved the way for exports to the west in 1997. And Moda (Arad), with a €4.2mln turnover in 2006, export women's readymades to Germany, The Netherlands, Spain and UK (in addition to their domestic business through Metro and Selgros stores).

More Direct Interventions by Foreign Firms
These have been widened (particularly since 2000) through German capital provided for the ready-made clothing factory at Sântana de Mureş: 363 employees in 2002 rising to an expected 800 in 2003; while SEE's biggest trouser factory was opened in Sf. Gheorghe by the German Leineweber group (also with factories in Portugal) with a €10mln investment employing 400 cheap skilled workers in 2002. Cantex (France) opened clothing factories in north Moldavia, first at the Formen factory in Botoşani and subsequently at the C-Smart factory in Darabani with 300 workers expanding to 500 in 2003. The Dutch fashion house Stadel Maier (traditionally involved with embroideries and tapestries) set up a subsidiary in Satu Mare in 2002 in the form of the j.v. Astarom. An Italian link is exemplified by the bankrupt SOE Camping Urziceni (producing tents, sleeping bags and travel bags) which was purchased by Stecolflex of Italy and over a four year period become a major sportswear producer exporting 95 per cent of production to important companies and fashion houses in Europe, after a $1.1mln upgrade involving state-of-the-art sewing, stitching, button-holing and padding equipment; while the employment of 280 increased by 200 with the expansion into sportswear (also tents and sleeping bags for the army). Further expansion arose through a bankrupt factory in Feteşti where employment doubled from 250 to 500 after a $1.6mln investment with meal tickets and bonus systems to retain staff. Availability of premises in areas with fiscal incentives can be an important incentive. In the coal mining town of Anina

(Caraş-Severin) Vartex Textil, a Romanian-Italian enterprise involving Bellandi of Florence, produces woollen goods from pieces through a finishing and parcelling operation employing 100 people (and possibly doubling) in a former state warehouse adjacent to the railway station. The Italian knitwear firm Ame Damasa has also set up in a former restaurant. Meanwhile worldwide restructuring of the Chicago, USA firm Sarah Lee led to the transfer of production by a subsidiary company to Romania where it is represented by the Rosko Textil lingerie factory in premises acquired at Curtici in 2000 with an investment of €5.5mln by the end of 2002. And Korean Garments bought space in Orşova for a textile/readymade factory to offset rising transport cost by serving European markets through use of low cost labour within the region. It collaborated with the Cazanele enterprise (producing cotton and polyester fabrics) – available for privatisation – because of empty space where Korean Garments could generate 200 new jobs and help relieve the town's 25 per cent unemployment in 1999.

New Purpose-Built Premises   Alison Hayes (UK) started on women's ready-mades in Urziceni in 1994; followed in 2000 by a €5.0mln investment in Buzău employing 700 at a new factory – opened in 2003 on a formerly derelict site – using the latest machinery with training on site. The German company Steilmann – with its network of shops through franchising – bought the Sighet clothing factory in 1997 and now employs 1,500 there; subsequently 4,000 in Craiova, 2,000 in Sibiu and 500 in Mangalia. It went on to plan a $20mln greenfield fabric plant in Sibiu in 2002 in the hope of collaborating with foreign clothing firms as well as local companies producing coat hangers (Mainetti) and special cloth treatments (VKS). Finally, UCO Textiles (Belgium) opened a €15mln factory employing 200 on the Giurgiu industrial park producing denim material. There is of course a danger in the current pattern of rising wages and industrial growth since workers are looking for jobs that pay better in other industries, while clothing is hard-pressed in view of keen global competition. Sonoma (Bacău) and Textila Oltului (Sfântu Gheorghe) would like to employ Chinese workers at 4.0mln lei monthly (below the industry average of 5–6mln) but risk contravening EU rules that require average wages to be paid to foreign workers.

Upstream Activities: Spinning and Weaving
Excess capacity resulted in some cases of liquidation like Carpidarfil (Darabani) which was part of Uzinele Textile Moldova (Iaşi) before 1989. There was no interest in purchase until 2000 when it had accumulated debts of 5.0bln.lei against share capital 7.0bln.lei. In other cases bankrupt factories were reported 'stolen' piece by piece. Some privatised factories failed like UTA (Arad) and others such as Zimbrul (Suceava) which could not attract orders and Universal (Zalău) which could not attract workers for average wages of 2.5mln lei (even though there were 14,500 unemployed in the town, including 4,300 women, and working conditions were considered good). Much of the industry was technologically outmoded and struggled to compete with Asian countries for access to West European markets. However in 1998 the spinning sector was also hit by high import duties on imported cotton, wool, flax and hemp that attracted worker demonstrations outside the Finance

Ministry. However Dorobanțul (Ploiești) did well: privatised in 1997 followed by a $10mln investment and retaining a workforce of 2,500 despite low monthly salaries of only 1.5mln.lei. Some foreign investment occurred: Coates (UK) started producing sewing thread in Odorheiu Secuiesc where a new factory in 2002 replaced the old premises used initially. Spinning by Textila (Calafat) made big efficiency gains (with three shift working) thanks to restructuring, modernisation and input from Turkish partners (1995–96); while Phare regional development funding has brought 'Sintelectro' dyeing technology to Târgu Mureș. In weaving Eltex (Prejmer) specialises in woollen fabrics supplied to Romanian companies (for example, SNCFR and the justice and national defence ministries) and exported to Japan, Sweden and the USA. In 2000 it was able to invest from its own funds to install Italian weaving machines for blankets as well as fabric to supply its own projected ready-made clothing factory (it also planned retooling of the finishing line and upgrading of the carding shop).

Moldavian Factories   The link from textiles to clothing is also evident in the case of Iașitex, originating in the Leo Geller workshop – started in Iași in 1903 with Italian support – which became Tesătura in 1910, by which time Geller had 400 looms as well as bleaching/dyeing facilities. Acquired by the Romanian Commercial Services portfolio in 2003, the factory is now a major exporter of clothing and interior decorations, while retaining domestic sales of cotton/polyester yarns and fabric to other Romanian factories. Moldosin (Vaslui) uses its own polyester thread for ready-mades and plans to open its own shops. However the great problem is that the emphasis on lohn operations for clothing has broken many of the traditional links with Romanian cloth production. Buhuși has been hit hard with cloth production down 12.0–5.5mln.sq.m with 4,000 lay-offs during 1990–96: half the 1989 workforce. Lack of orders from the clothing industry has exposed the drawback of out-of-date machinery, but other problems have been closures among fibre producers e.g. Dunacor (Brăila) and a section of polyester production in Iași (see below). The wool supply from state farms dwindled to1.4th.t in 2000 compared with 4.0-5.0th in the 1980s. Some new clothing businesses have started in the town – e.g. the Romanian-Italian 'Fashion House' venture – but they offer little compensation especially since they are not integrated with the local cloth factory (Popescu 2000–2001).

Synthetic Fibres

This section highlights the serious problems faced by the textile sector when chemical yarns were badly hit by falling demand and competing imports at a time of rising raw material and energy prices. A major crisis arose at Dunacor (Brăila), the country's largest and most complex unit for the production of artificial fibres and cellulose by-products – conveniently situated in the local free zone in an unpolluted area close to transport services – but struggling to maintain continuous operation (with the threat of frost damage) and forced to reduce employment from 8,211 in 1989 to 2,458 at the end of 1996 to become one of 20 heavy loss-making companies linked with the Phare crisis programme in 1997. Terom (Iași) survives after upgrading as a producer of polyester threads to supply a range of textile and clothing factories:

ATA (Odorhei), Siretul (Paşcani), Rotrico (Roşiorii de Vede), Textila Teleorman and Trimond (Bucharest) as well as sales in Europe, the Middle East and North Africa. Its suppliers are oil refineries and some foreign companies like Moghilev (Belarus) and Hoechst (Germany). A major foreign interest arises in the case of Fibrex Nylon (Săvineşti) – an integrated producer turning out polyamide yarns and the nylon intermediate caprolactam – affected by problems faced by Radici Nylon Bergamo (RNB): the parent company (specialising in textiles, chemicals and plastics) that started with Pietro Radici's factory for household materials in 1946 and now operates in 15 countries. An Italian investment was made at Săvineşti in 1973 but attempts to update the technology before 1989 failed. RNB acquired a majority holding in 2000 and installed new machines for yarn and tyre cord (to improve quality) while new boilers reduced energy consumption for steam generation and pollution from the power plant was eliminaterd by new ecological equipment; meanwhile a gradual reduction in the workforce from 3,970 to 1,500 was envisaged in 2000.

Fibrex is thus a complementary unit alongside Italian plants at Casnigo, Novarra, Pistoia and Villa d'Ogna. It needed investment in new technology to reduce power consumption massively at a time when the caprolactam price fell from $1,350/t at the factory at the beginning of 2000 (against production costs $1,250) to the point where it could be brought to the factory for less than $1,000 (compared with current production costs at Săvineşti of $1,350 based on rising raw material and energy costs from $1,025 to $1,275). Thus the margin changed from $+100 to more than $-275 due to the rising price of phenol and ammonia (aggravated by the US energy crisis in February 2001) and recession in the nylon market which finally brought caprolactam production at Săvineşti to a halt (having previously continued for some time at a loss). Petrom took over a parcel of shares in 2001 in respect of debts arising from supplies from Arpechim refinery and there was hope for an improved situation in late 2002, although nylon is not in fashion. However, despite carefully selected market niches Fibrex has become merely a producer a polyamide yarn and tyrecord using imported caprolactam (indeed all raw materials are now obtained internally through the Radici Group) and the company was renamed Yarnea in 2004. It is disappointing that the company is celebrating its fifth year in Romania with the sale of all its surplus space: the only business left to the Fibrex company. Meanwhile RNB has invested in Moldofil (Câmpulung Moldovenesc) in the Bucovina LFA in a j.v. combining investment in the technological updating of fibre production with Moldofil's contribution of land and buildings. As in the case of Yarnea, improved quality has opened the way to global markets either directly to Hungary and Italy or indirectly through Romanian clothing producers whose quality products can now be sent abroad, like Ardeleana (Satu Mare), Croitex (Oradea), 1 Iunie (Timişoara) and Tricotton (Panciu); though the workforce has declined from 800 to 350.

Flax and Hemp

Romania produces long fibre hemp sought after for the ecological clothing currently fashionable in Western Europe. Until the revolution flax and hemp each occupied 80,000ha and there were 17 factories for hemp and 18 for flax. But the business contracted to just 1,000ha of hemp and 500ha for flax supported by just three processing units; while the Central Union for the Flax & Hemp Industry had just 30 members in 2001. But Germans think that flax/hemp cultivation should be boosted and have even suggested that investment could create over 80,000 jobs. In 1998 Treu Hanf of Berlin (an investment fund specialising in the hemp industry) bought a 96 per cent stake in the Carin (Iratoşu) hemp factory near Arad. 80 per cent of production is now exported and Carin has a research partnership with BMW (for motorcar interior tapestry) with experimental cultivation at Lovrin. A Romanian-German company Cerce Prod Invest (for research, production and investment in flax and hemp) has been set up in Constanţa by a group of German investors who have also bought the Galir (Mangalia) flax processor with the help of IBD, an organisation set up by the German government to provide consultancy services for Germans willing to invest in Romania. The new owners also have a flax retting installation in Oradea and intend to buy a spinning mill in Suceava. Meanwhile Mangalia already had two factories for textile ready-mades belonging to German companies in 1999: Steilmann (already referred to) and Murk. Finally, Fältin (Fălticeni) is a producer of linen, hemp and mixed threads and fibres for the footwear and foodstuffs industries, acquired by the Belgian company Uniwear in 1999.

Footwear

The industry contracted initially from 111mln pairs in 1989 to 31mln in 1997–98 (of which about a quarter were exported) but there was a revival to 80mln in 2003 before a renewed slump to 72mln in 2005. Meanwhile 56mln pairs are now imported for domestic consumers who now prefer leather with a soft touch and specific aesthetic qualities that require special processing. This reflects a big technology gap for leather footwear with much of the Romanian equipment obsolete. Fewer skins are being processed: sheep skins declined from 2.14mln.sq.m in 1989 to 0.99 in 1998 – cattle from 15.77 to 5.81 and pig from 5.00 to 0.69 – reflecting reduced livestock numbers as well as obsolete technology in the tanning yards where privatisation was delayed (likewise in the spinning and weaving mills) compared with footwear, knitwear and ready-mades where there was early pressure for restructuring. The Banatul (Timişoara) leather footwear factory was founded in 1963 and privatised in 1991 as Banatim, with a $1.0mln re-engineering investment linked with a sports footwear contract (4,000 pairs daily) with Adidas-Solomon for export to France, Germany and Italy (2002). Export performance has been good with 90 per cent output organised through the lohn system in 2003. Meanwhile the Clujana (Cluj) footwear factory had to close in 1999 with 3,000 employees before restarting in 2004 with lohn work on a vastly smaller scale: just 100-150 workers plus the hope of reaching 500 in 2005 with a switch back to its own production (but still with enough surplus space to attract a cluster of light industrial firms). Meanwhile new factories are appearing through foreign investment. Salaska Prod (Italy) planned a $2.0mln investment at Teliu (Braşov) using high performance machines and a workforce rising from 150 to 500 – in two shifts – by the end of 1998 producing women's shoes (with a second factory for men's shoes for follow in 1999 and provide a further 1,000 jobs by 2002). This did not materialise but a new Italian shoe factory – the largest in Romania – was built in Timişoara (Calea Şagului) with an $8.0mln investment in 2000 to employ 1,500. Lloyds Shoes of Germany – part of the multinational Ara Shufabriken enterprise – are relocating production from Gozo (Malta) to Romania to increase profits, while Reroman (Italy) opened a footwear factory in Oradea in 1998. But reference should also be made to the many small concerns established by foreign investors, especially Italians. Typically employing 10–20 workers, there are thought to be hundreds in the Timişoara area, spreading to a number of the smaller towns of the West Region.

Chapter Eight

Agriculture: Overcoming the Subsistence Rationale

Introduction

The dual role played by Romanian agriculture intensified after the revolution through the strains of transition. Under communism much progress was made in raising productivity and transferring surplus workers to other occupations. Yet the cooperative farms ensured that agriculture would remain the employer of 'last resort' with obligations (combined with security) for people who failed to find an alternative role in the economy. But the subsistence function increased after 1989 with the rapid decline of industrial production and the marginalisation of rural workers for whom smallholdings could be regarded as social security (quite apart from the equity argument of overcoming the abusive nature of communist collectivisation). Meanwhile the shift to free trade meant that the urban consumer was hardly dependent on local farmers since imports from the EU could be readily sucked in. often with advantages in terms of both price and quality, given the lack of investment in improving the efficiency of Romanian private farms. In this chapter the return to 'minifundia' will be examined along with government measures to achieve greater diversification by regional policies. A second section will review agricultural production and the prospects for a competitive industry. Unfortunately space does not permit complementary study of restitution procedures, government agricultural policy and infrastructure (mechanisation, irrigation, fertilisation, marketing and rural credit).

A Subsistence Logic for Peasant Agriculture

Despite the economic merits of large farms the political imperative of land restitution, combined with a sharp reduction in salaries throughout the economy, ensured a return to 'minifundia' validated by the land law of 1991, albeit with scope for association wherever this was desired. The 'Individual Farming Index' constructed by Swinnen & Mathijs (1997) compares the total area of individual farms in 1995 with the situation in 1989. For example if there was a change from 25 per cent in 1989 to 75 per cent in 1995 then the index would be 75–25 divided by 100–25 i.e. 50 divided by 75 and then multiplied by 100 which is 66.7. Despite a high index of 55.2, Romania is well behind Albania (94.2) but ahead of all the other collectivised ECECs: Bulgaria (45.4), Czech Republic (22.1), Hungary (17.3) and Slovakia (3.1). There seems to a be a close *inverse* relationship with cooperative farm productivity but also a positive relationship with agricultural employment i.e. small semi-subsistence farms are more acceptable (indeed essential) when non-agricultural employment is limited and farming becomes once again the employer of last resort, accounting for 28.2 per cent of total employment in Romania in 1990 (3.06mln out of 10.84) rising to 40.8 per cent in 2000 (3.52mln out of 8.63), with a relatively small contribution to GDP of just 11–12 per cent. With agriculture fundamental to the lives of Romanians who depend very heavily on home-produced food, almost all rural people (as well as many urban dwellers) undertake agricultural work at some time during the year in vegetable gardens if not in the fields. 51.3 per cent of those working in agriculture are occupied on their own small farms while another 42.0 per cent are unpaid family members; leaving 0.5 per cent as cooperative workers and just 6.2 per cent (0.22mln) as employers or employees on larger holdings. But few people see farming as a route to prosperity and even under conditions of poverty there are limits to the intensification that smallholdings can sustain. Because of restitution those occupied in agriculture tend to be elderly with a higher share for the over-55s (33.7 per cent) than the under 35s (28.6 per cent).

Restitution Scenarios

The situation is obviously far from ideal. Modernisers widely believed that land restitution would be advantageous in strengthening the work ethic, while competition would increase efficiency and the quality of production. Market demand would stimulate development through improvements on individual farms and the provision of better advice and trading facilities, including processing capacity in local centres – and of course a strong market economy across the country as a whole (Heller 2000). Diversification was also anticipated through adaptable SMEs to generate a wider range of products at a time when eastern markets were contracting and FDI stimulation of the non-agricultural economy was very limited overall and spatially polarised in a few urban centres. The best potential was seen in wood processing and tourism (particularly relevant to rural areas and the alpine model of pluriactivity) as well as services for the automotive industry and car owners; complemented by a range of 'niche markets' to encourage enterprise, boosted by counselling centres and Phare projects to create regional 'clusters' of specialised production (especially where there was little immediate prospect of FDI). The optimist, looking for rapid transition to West European conditions through a restructuring of rural settlement through demographic and economic change, might also have anticipated the privatisation of non-agricultural enterprises and a considerable growth of new business underpinned by émigré capital and return migration of Romanian workers from the towns. In other words, private enterprise might blossom and help build prosperity after decades of under-investment in the rural areas.

The Worst-Case Scenario
The worst-case scenario emphasised the relative backwardness of rural conditions reinforced by capital shortage, delayed privatisation and stagnant commercial activity. In addition, the peasantry might be radicalised by inadequate land restitution and an ultra-conservative attitude among the rural elites. Any newly-created SMEs might be

constrained by the low technological level in agriculture: hence they might struggle to achieve economies of scale and face the threat of bankruptcy, with the likelihood of only limited assistance from Romanian banks heavily committed over 'soft' loans to SOEs. There were other complications, involving idealists anticipating a return to the rural conditions of the pre-communist period with a high level of rural self-sufficiency; for the villages were now satellites of an urban-industrial system from which country people were debarred by limited cash resources: they could not take any real advantage from the market economy. While many older people appreciated their independence (despite the great effort required to run a mixed farm at a low technical level), life on a small farm was no longer inevitable for the young in the way it had often been a generation earlier. As a result of rural-urban migration, the family unit was no longer so cohesive, with aggravation of the generation gap between the elderly farmers who were now the owners of the restituted farms and the young people who had received a good education before migrating to the towns and were now, in many cases, returning to the villages disillusioned by redundancy. Young people finishing school in the villages in the early 1990s naturally saw agriculture as offering only limited opportunities compared with various forms of government service. The situation was not helped by the lack of a clear vision for the future: instead there was prolonged hesitation by the neo-communist government over the necessity and urgency for market reforms as coercive agricultural organisations collapsed and pluralism was enhanced by the restoration of the political parties and the Uniate church. With a pervasive sense of stagnation and financial 'blockage', Romanian society seemed to degenerate "into a political apathy" (Shafir & Ionescu 1994, p.126). The sense of malaise found some outlet in nationalism, with negative implications for inter-ethnic relations in Transylvania where rising unemployment among Romanian migrants from Moldavia was aggravated by some sense of discrimination by Hungarians successfully reclaimed historic vested interests. Social scientists began to extend the geographers' notions of instability and risk (conventionally related to earthquakes, floods and landslides) to the socio-economic plane (Bălteanu 1992).

Farm Structure

It should not be supposed that agriculture involved only small peasant farms. New associations were encouraged and (despite the lack of a formal land market) the more active farmers could enlarge their own restitution holdings through unofficial sharecropping arrangements. State farms continued until the centre-right government of 1997–2000 privatised (or closed) intensive pig and poultry farms while arable land not used for restitution was leased out for commercial farming by 2003. However in 1998 3.23mln farms of 5.0ha or less occupied 3.99mln.ha: 81.9 per cent of holdings occupied 37.9 per cent of the land; while 0.71mln 5-50ha farms (18.0 per cent) occupied 5.19mln.ha (49.3 per cent). There were only 503 larger private holdings (less than 0.1 per cent) but they occupied 12.8 per cent of the land (1.34mln.ha) (Table 8.1) (Râmniceanu 2004). However, minifundia became the dominant feature of life in most rural areas outside the main lowland zones; accentuated by fragmentation since many small farms were divided into several small plots dispersed over a wide area (Figure 8.1) Meanwhile the contraction of industry and the decline in spending power restricted the expansion of the tertiary sector. Hence the role of agriculture as 'employer of last resort' was increased on a truly grotesque scale so that between the census years 1992 and 2002 agriculture (with forestry and fishing) increased its share of rural employment from 50.2 to 58.2 per cent while industry declined from 27.8 to 16.9 per cent. Throughout agriculture productivity was low so that household incomes for farmers in 2001 averaged just 4.33mln.lei. And 57.5 per cent of this represented the equivalent value (e.v.) of agricultural products consumed by the household. Even so the total sum was well below the level for employees (7.29mln with 13.1 per cent e.v.) and only slightly better than pensioners (4.19mln with 32.0 per cent e.v.) and the unemployed (3.85 and 27.8 per cent). Low values for size, efficiency, yield and capital stock were complemented by high levels of labour input and technological obsolescence, not to mention inflation which in the context of a 'price scissors' – with equipment and fertiliser prices rising nearly three times faster that those for agricultural commodities – reduced investment to a trickle (Davis & Gaburci 1999). Access to credit was poor but it was in any case too expensive – and risky if commitments were taken on board in advance of unpredictable market realisations.

Table 8.1: Farm structure 1998

Farms	Size Group	Percent	Area ha	Percent
3233,361	5.0ha or less	81.9	3992,641	37.9
424.033	5.1-10.0ha	10.7	2175.058	20.7
288,753	10.1-50.0ha	7.3	3015,407	28.6
503	50.1ha or more	*	1341,967	12.8
3946.630	All	100.0	10525,073	100.0

Source: Râmniceanu 2004

The Logic of Semi-Subsistence
Although it was easy enough to get clearance to go to market – for farmers needed only a 'certificat de producător' to differentiate them as agricultural producers (not liable to taxation on agricultural income) from other traders operating under the commercial code – the open market functioned imperfectly by western standards with inadequate transport and poor intelligence resulting in substantial variations in prices through time and space. Contract growing (with all the complications of transport and quality control) was hardly feasible for smallholders in an inflationary situation while a proliferation of middlemen handling small surpluses was seen as recipe for driving farmers into deeper poverty. Hence the logic of concentrating on subsistence – with a high level of non-marketed agricultural production and minimal investment; concentrating surplus production into enterprises linked with acceptable markets. Carpathian farmers tended to restrict their dealings with the market primarily to the sale of livestock – in line with local fodder potential – for which a state marketing system (sometimes stimulated by competition by local food processors) was relatively dependable (also milk where local collection operated) complemented by subsistence arable farming restricted to maize, potatoes and vegetables. A series

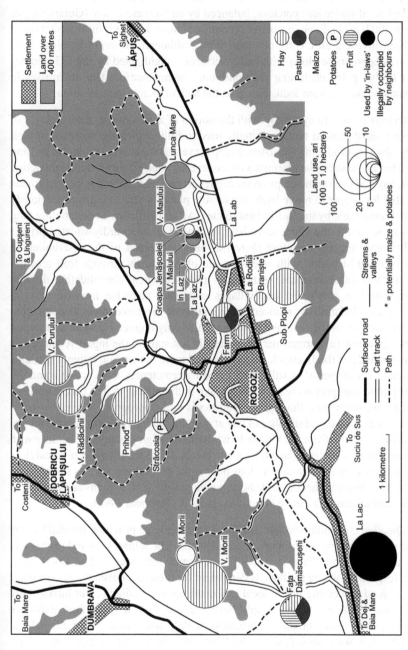

Figure 8.1 A fragmented holding in Rogoz, Maramureş

of land use surveys made in the commune of Corbu (Harghita) between the 1930s and 1990s show that rye, oats, hemp and lucerne – prominent in 1933 – had all disappeared by 1977, while the addition of the 1994 picture underlined the long-term decline of maize and potatoes, balanced by an increase in hay (Guran-Nica & Turnock 2002, p.28). Even in a better economic climate it is doubtful if capital could have been invested efficiently on small farms, although for larger holdings rural credit was appropriate along with better services – highlighted by the EU Country Report (2000, p.46) criticising the continuing dominance of state enterprises in upstream and downstream industries, plus the lack of export specialisation.

Low Intensification   In sympathy with the notion of agriculture as the employer of last resort, most peasant farmers initially tried to fully exploit the potential of their smallholding by producing subsistence crops (even on the more outlying strips) and making full use of subsidiary farmsteads ('conace' or 'sălaşe') with modest production of fruit, hay and even some crops on the higher ground. Indeed land reform has made it possible for people to move back into remote places where living was previously rendered impossible by the loss of land to the CAP and difficulty of commuting long distances on foot to the cooperative base or to tend an awkwardly-situated private plot. In some respects therefore there has been a reversal of the discrimination of the communist period with intensive use of core areas through fruit-growing and viticulture (also vegetable growing) – plus settlement consolidation through 'sistematizare' to emphasise key villages and other selective improvements in infrastructure – balanced by reduced grazing pressure in remoter areas, depopulation and some conversion of farmland to forest. This is highlighted by some destruction of orchards where (a) current market prices did not support the inputs required and (b) the demands of the livestock sector required more maize cultivation. Of course the scale of the dispersal is still conditioned by remoteness from schools and the lack of public transport on roads that can take nothing more than a cart. Clearance of weeds and scrub from the higher meadows is only appropriate where the soil is not too thin and increased supplies of hay at outlying stations will support the annual movements of cattle from the village in winter to the high grazings in summer with spring and autumn spells at the intermediate levels. There are always ecological risks with intensification in mountain regions but simple precautions such as surrounding small arable plots with hedges and checking the proliferation of paths and cart tracks (which channel run-off) can be effective (Muică & Zăvoianu 1996).

Diversification   is quite possible and some families have provided for children by extending their business into tourism, small shops, hair salons, bars and restaurants where the capital and labour is available: even small industries such as sawmilling, baking (especially where a village is dependent for bread on a distant town) or other forms of food processing where local raw materials are available. But increasingly through the 1990s the young people have escaped from a small farm existence by finding their way abroad – especially to Italy and Spain (often illegally at first until visas were abolished for the Schengen zone) – where they have found a more rewarding role although not one that is conducive to family stability and contentment. Moreover, Heller (1999) found rural-based organisations were relatively disillusioned over development prospects given the falling incomes of the late 1990s and the prominence of barter in preference to cash transactions underpinned a serious shortage of capital for investment and a lack of profitable local markets. Market opportunities for non-agricultural village goods, like textiles from Sândominic (Harghita) and furs from the Gilău (Cluj) mink farms have declined since 1989. But some villages cater for urban demand in ecofarming and tourism and a number of 'offshore' foreign contacts have emerged, notably in clothing through cooperation with existing workshops, as at Gilău, or the creation of new small factories (often using former cooperative farm premises) as at Estelnic near Târgu Secuiesc. Thus while some communities have access to a choice of employments such as Sânmartin in Harghita where the land is farmed by associations, most are in the position of Plăieşii de Jos commune and have to fall back on their own fragmented holdings.

A Carpathian Survey

This reveals variations among the peasantry even within particular environments. Using data from the commune 'fişe', compiled annually by the National Commission for Statistics, a survey was conducted during the 1990s in the Nehoiu-Berca area of the Buzău Subcarpathians and in four other rural mountain regions: the Arieş valley in the Apuseni Mountains (Alba), Maramureş in the north, Vâlcea in the south and Harghita in eastern Transylvania (including the Corbu area already referred to). These regions had a population of 471.5 thousand in 1986 including 137.9 in a total of 12 small market towns (Turnock 2006). Two other areas were included from the west with strong urban-industrial cores complemented by a modest rural population in the surrounding areas: Reşiţa and Retezat with a population of 393.0 thousand of which 319.9 was urban (primarily through Petroşani and Reşiţa but with nine other towns as well). The survey concentrated on livestock, reduced to standard units on the basis of a conversion system reflecting the average meat yield from each cow, pig, sheep or head of poultry. These units were then related to the land available (again with different land types – arable, hayfields and rough pasture – combined through a conversion system) and also to the number of rural households (Figure 8.2). Taking all the seven areas, with a total of 115 communes the results were: 2.07 animal units per land unit/household combined in 1986 (representing the end of the communist period) and 1.28 as the average for 1998–2000. But there were also interesting variations between the regions and generalising for the two periods Apuseni emerged with 2.11 animal units per household/land unit combined, compared with 0.92 for Retezat at the opposite extreme. In the Apuseni there is relatively little land (1.12 units per household) but stocking is intensive with 2.23 animal units per household and 2.00 per land unit in 1998-2000 (although down from 2.21 and 3.21 respectively in 1986). Of course fodder is the key and the decline since communism arises in part through the loss of deliveries that were made by the state in the context of production plans.

Labour Strategies

Now the communities are self-sufficient and they have to balance the labour of mowing the meadows and managing stock on unenclosed grazings against the market prices for livestock. Retezat boasts 3.27 land units per household, reflecting

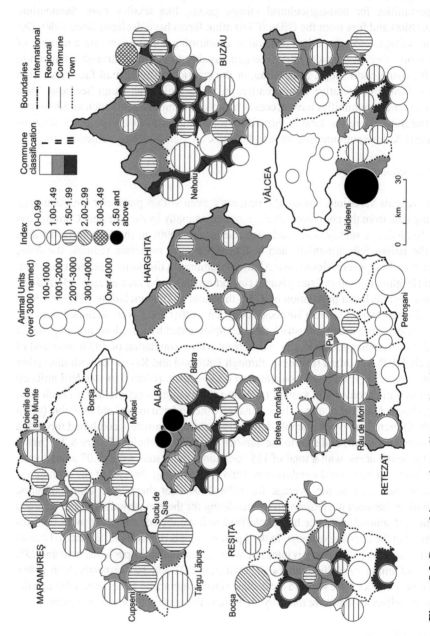

Figure 8.2 Carpathian regions: livestock units

a good local fodder supply that attracts a high stocking rate of 2.36 animal units per household but without a high level of intensification: only 0.72 per land unit (down sharply from 5.12 and 1.57 respectively in 1986). Reşiţa (with a combined index of 1.03) is similar with 4.91 land units per household sustaining 2.36 stock units per household but only 0.47 per land unit (down from 3.59 and 0.73 respectively in 1986). Significantly Reşiţa and Retezat are the highly urbanised areas while Apuseni is heavily rural with many small isolated communities. The largely Hungarian population of Harghita (combined index 1.06) comes close to the Retezat-Reşiţa model with a particularly sharp decline in activity with stocking levels that were above the average (per household and per land unit) in 1986 but below it in 1998–2000, while Maramureş (1.44) and Vâlcea (1.50) incline towards the Apuseni model with land per household that is below the average – 1.39 and 1.41 units respectively – but intensively used, although the stocking levels per household are no better than average. Finally Buzău is not well-endowed with land (1.33 units per household) but it is stocked at a level only slightly above the average which means that the activity per household is low. Of course not all relevant factors can be taken into account such as the accessibility of some of the land (difficult in much of Retezat where national park restrictions are also in force) and the problems of labour for haymaking in elderly households.

Regional Variations These clearly apply, with some areas clearly demonstrating a greater interest in making the fullest use of the fodder and grazing potential. It could be argued that such commitment will depend on the level of dependence on agriculture. So analysis sought to relate stocking levels to households using the three salary groups: 21 communes were placed in Group I with more than 0.33 salaries per household; while 27 were in Group II with 0.33-0.10 salaries/household with 67 in Group III with fewer than 0.10 (i.e. less that one household in 10 had salary income) (Table 8.2). Although stock units predictably declined less in Group III communes that elsewhere, the exercise reveals that fewer salaries do not always result in more animals being reared. Group III households averaged 1.72 animal units during 1998–2000 and while this was higher than the 1.44 for Group I it was lower than the 1.92 for Group II; although when allowance is made for the land resources there is greater intensification in Group III with 1.10 animal units per land unit compared with 1.01 for Group II and 0.87 for Group III (Table 8.2). Individual areas produce more variation although the scope for analysis is limited by the lack of any Group III communes in Harghita, Maramureş and Reşiţa. In these areas there is slightly heavier stocking in Group II communes in Harghita but no significant difference with Group I in Retezat while the better performance in Class I in Maramureş reflects the tradition of seasonal migration by people without regular work at home when the wives are left to look after the farming.

In areas with all three groups represented, progressively higher stocking rates per land unit emerge in Reşiţa. (0.39 for Group I, 0.47 for Group II and 0.64 for Group III) but not in Apuseni where the lack of salaries results in high migration (while in Buzău and Vâlcea Group III values are higher than Group I but lower than Group II). When households are considered there is a neat gradient in Buzău with 1.02 stock units per household for Group I, 1.57 for Group and 1.64 for Group III whereas for

Table 8.2: Levels of intensification in stock-rearing in Carpathian survey areas 1998–2000

Area/Group	A	B	C	D	E	F	G	H	I	J	K
Group I	21	37.6	25.4	15.39	22.7	51.1	32.6	-36.3	1.44	0.87	0.68
Apuseni	2	1.8	0.6	1.82	2.6	6.9	4.3	-38.5	1.66	2.14	0.71
Buzău	2	5.9	5.1	4.96	6.1	8.0	6.2	-21.6	1.02	1.05	0.82
Harghita	1	0.9	0.4	1.01	0.8	1.0	0.5	-47.8	0.66	0.60	1.22
Maramureș	6	6.3	2.9	3.31	6.5	12.8	9.7	-24.1	1.51	1.55	0.51
Reșița	4	13.9	12.7	1.20	2.2	10.7	5.4	-49.4	2.44	0.39	0.54
Retezat	3	4.5	2.4	1.54	2.0	5.8	3.3	-42.6	1.66	0.74	0.77
Vâlcea	3	4.3	1.3	1.54	2.5	5.7	3.1	-46.6	1.24	0.72	0.62
Group II	67	137.3	80.7	14.24	72.6	224.7	139.0	-38.1	1.92	1.01	0.20
Apuseni	8	5.2	2.6	0.68	4.6	19.5	11.9	-39.9	2.57	2.31	0.15
Buzău	13	23.1	16.9	3.05	17.2	37.1	27.0	-27.3	1.57	1.16	0.18
Harghita	8	15.4	8.0	1.79	9.3	24.7	13.4	-45.5	1.45	0.87	0.19
Maramureș	15	33.4	10.3	4.79	22.1	54.2	39.3	-27.6	1.78	1.18	0.22
Reșița	7	20.3	16.4	0.59	4.0	14.4	9.5	-33.9	2.40	0.47	0.15
Retezat	10	30.0	20.7	2.06	8.6	48.4	21.7	-55.2	2.53	0.72	0.24
Vâlcea	6	9.9	5.9	1.28	6.9	26.5	16.2	-38.9	2.34	1.63	0.18
Group III*	27	36.6	27.2	1.77	23.5	60.7	40.4	-33.5	1.72	1.10	0.07
Apuseni	5	5.4	3.2	0.33	4.0	13.7	8.9	-35.6	2.22	1.64	0.08
Buzău	12	16.2	11.5	0.74	10.6	29.9	17.4	-41.7	1.64	1.07	0.07
Reșița	4	6.3	4.9	0.13	2.1	4.5	4.0	-11.1	1.95	0.64	0.06
Vâlcea	6	8.8	7.5	0.57	6.8	12.6	10.1	-20.0	1.48	1.15	0.08
Total	115	211.5	133.3	31.40	118.7	336.5	212.0	-37.0	1.79	1.00	0.07
Apuseni	15	12.3	6.3	2.83	8.5	40.1	25.0	-37.7	2.95	2.03	0.26
Buzău	27	45.1	33.4	8.75	33.8	74.9	50.6	-32.5	1.50	1.12	0.33
Harghita	9	16.3	8.5	2.80	10.1	25.7	14.0	-45.6	1.39	0.86	0.26
Maramureș	21	39.7	13.1	8.10	28.5	67.0	49.0	-26.9	1.72	1.24	0.28
Reșița	15	40.5	34.0	1.92	8.2	29.6	18.9	-36.1	2.30	0.47	0.23
Retezat	13	34.6	23.1	3.61	10.6	54.2	25.0	-53.7	2.36	0.72	0.34
Vâlcea	15	23.0	14.8	3.39	16.3	44.9	29.4	-34.6	1.81	1.28	0.21

A Number of communes; B Land units (total) th; C :Land Units (arable) th; D Salaries1998-2000 th; E Households th; F Stock units 1986 th; G Stock units 1998-2000 th; H Percentage decline in stock units 1986/1998-2000; I Stock units per household 1998-2000; J Stock units per land unit 1998-2000; K Salaries per household 1998 * There are no Group III communes in Harghita, Maramureș and Retezat.

Source: Commune files compiled by the National Institute for Statistics

Apuseni and Vâlcea Group I again has the lowest values but Group II scores better than Group III. So it seems clear that while agriculture has a fundamental importance for family subsistence and the provision of small amounts of cash through livestock sales (along with some casual marketing of manufactured products like plum brandy) it is not a serious contender for intensification even when labour is available because migration to other parts of Romania (and increasing abroad) gives a much higher return. And when income is secured through migrant labour it is rarely invested in farm development. Dumitru et al. (2004) suggest that people who earn money abroad invest in housing and consumer durables rather than local agriculture or business in general. This reinforces the notion of agricultural work as an employment of last resort, although traditions vary and there appears to be a greater readiness to migrate in Banat and Transylvania than in the southern and eastern regions that could be reflected in the greater agricultural activity among the poorer groups in Buzău and Vâlcea.

A National Agency for the Mountainous Zones

Government aid for agriculture was initially restricted to the state sector and although the centre-right administration gave modest assistance to all farms this approach has since been modified to favour only commercial holdings. The future for small farms therefore lies in amalgamation to form viable units with the surplus population redeployed in other occupations. This is clearly a long-term process but diversification has been on the agenda from the start through a curious experiment in special support for the mountain regions. At a time when the government was short of ideas – and finance – a Commission (later Agency) for the Mountainous Regions was commended by R. Rey (1979; 1985), a veterinary specialist from Suceava county who had strong enough political connections to argue (openly but unsuccessfully) for micro-cooperatives in the 1980s as an alternative to the more uncompromising consolidation envisaged under the 'sistematizare' policy being adopted at the time. The advocacy of more informal 'micro-cooperatives' in areas of dispersed mountain settlement (like Vrancea) was ignored in the 1980s, but Rey used his influence over the the NSF government in 1990 to get a Commission for the Mountain Zones set up with 28 county commissions. Rey was also 'networked' into European mountainology structures, on which his advice was doubtless based in the first place, and so the Commission joined Euromontana in 1991 before its transformation into a National Agency for the Mountain Zones – NAMZ ('Agenţia Naţională a Zonei Montane') in 1994, within the agriculture ministry. Seeking to reverse the downward spiral of agricultural activity, brought about by low prices that could not stimulate higher inputs, the agency quickly assimilated elements the European mountain agenda including (by 1995) the idea of a 'mountain charter' incorporating principles of sustainability and a development strategy addressing the needs and potentials of each mountain area. The aim was official recognition of naturally- and socio-economically-disadvantaged areas, requiring an inter-disciplinary approach to secure adequate environmental protection and alleviate poverty arising from low technical endowment of farms through stimulative prices and technical assistance. However before any legislation was passed the initiative was downgraded by the new government in 1997 – appreciating that rural poverty was not simply a mountain phenomenon – although

Rey was able to head a Mountains & Underprivileged Regions Department within the ministry. He was able to set up a National Association for Mountain Rural Development ('Asociaţia Naţională pentru Dezvoltare Rurală-Montană: Romontana') to represent mountain dwellers in partnership with government and participate in conferences in Romania and Europe. When a further change of government restored the NAMZ and its county offices in 2001, it became possible to create an inter-ministerial National Mountain Council ('Consiliul Naţional al Muntelui') in Bucharest (with 28 county fora) starting in 2003 and convening annually to debate mountain policy. Rey's vision included networks that would connect individual communes with higher order centres (Rey & Gîţan 2002 pp.146-7) and a mountain commission within the Academy of Agricultural & Forest Sciences.

Legislation

Legislation was also achieved after a mountain law on the French-Italian model, prepared pre-1997, with criteria for delimiting the mountain area, was accepted by government in 2002 (significantly the International Year of the Mountains). The criteria involved an altitude of 600m (hence climatic limitations and a short growing season) and slopes of 20 per cent (i.e. too steep for the use of normal agricultural equipment) – also a combination of the two 'where each factor taken separately is less acute but the combination results in an equivalent disadvantage'. The mountain area now officially comprises 703 communes (109 partially) – some 3,960 villages – and 90 towns (18 partially). There are some 975.4th households with a total population of 4.0mln of which exactly a half are based in agriculture. The mountain area comprises 7.69mln.ha (31.9 per cent of the national total of 23.84mln.ha); of which 3.27 is in agriculture (22.0 per cent of the national total of 14.85mln.ha): 0.79 in arable (8.4 per cent – 9.4mln.ha), 0.01 vineyards (3.7 per cent – 0.27), orchards 0.07 (28.8 per cent – 0.25 per cent) but grazings 2.30 (46.7 per cent – 4.93), hayfields 1.33 (38.9 per cent – 3.42) and non-agricultural land 4.43, of which forest comprises 3.90 (49.3 per cent – 8.99). Perhaps surprisingly the share of livestock is below the share of total area, such is the scale of the lowland industry: 30.0 per cent for sheep, 28.9 per cent for cows, 26.1 per cent for goats and 19.5 per cent for beehives. In 2003 Ordinance 318 provided for an inter-ministerial committee within the agriculture ministry to represent a wide range of interests including public administration and finance, economy, health, education and social security, culture and environment, public works transport and housing. There was also to be a working party ('colectivul de lucru') coordinated by the NAMZ, while committees for the mountain area would represent similar interests at the county level.

The 'Mountain Law' 2004
Law 347 sought sustainable development by safeguarding protected areas and avoiding soil damage through erosion and compaction; while stabilising the population – with attention to the development of services, agriculture, industry and crafts, agro-tourism, professional support and education – through an integrated approach taken by the ministry and the NAMZ. In 1996 it had been agreed in principle that that rights should be restored to people in the Apuseni and elsewhere who had

traditionally enjoyed privileged access to wood in connection with local manufacture and trade. This was approved in 2000 (Law 144) when woodworkers who were not woodland owners gained the right to 10cu.m wood/year (maximum 15cu.m/family); also a 50 per cent reduction in rail transport costs – or free use of roadside common pasture (for one day in each case) providing local regulations were respected. Simple documentation is required when selling planks ('scânduri'), beams, barrels, tubs and cart shafts, with declaration of the timber source (validated by the 'Ocol Silvic' for special types of wood). Young people up to 35 years can receive 25cu.m of wood for building a house, while both categories can also buy wood for processing, building and repairs at half price. Other measures provided agricultural support e.g. higher milk subventions in the mountains – 1,800lei/l at the time compared with 1,400 – and heifer grants: 1.35mln compared with 1.00. In addition, two laws passed in 2002 had particular relevance: state support for young people in rural areas and regulation of animal breeding and welfare (including grazing and fodder).

The Farming Profile

The farming profile is one of small units, averaging 3.0ha: 348.8th (36.9 per cent) below 1.0ha; 318.4th (33.7 per cent) of 1-3ha; 157.8th (16.7 per cent) of 3.1-5.0ha; 76.0th (8.0 per cent) of 5.1-8.0ha; 31.4th (3.3 per cent) of 8.1-12.0ha; 10.3th (1.1 per cent) of 12.1-25.0ha and 1.3th (0.1 per cent) over 25.0ha. The average hay harvest is 2-3,000kg/ha with a second of 0.5-1.0t/ha, but harvesting, drying and transfer to storage are slow processes and hence there is a loss of nutritional value. Potatoes (yielding 10-15t/ha) are generally sold, while maize (3-4t/ha), rye (2.5t), barley (2.5t), oats (1.5t) – and occasionally wheat (2.5t) – are reserved for farm use. Cattle numbering some 0.79mln are mainly Brown, Romanian Spotted (a Simmental variant) and Pinzgau, with some local varieties like the Dorna; while Turcana sheep (Ţigaie where the climate is relatively milder) number 2.7mln and are kept mainly for milk. Other animals include horses (increasing since 1990 for use in transport work and agro-tourism), pigs and poultry, and 'Mioritic' and 'Carpatin' sheepdogs (also some small efficient 'Pucleu' dogs). Declining employment in mining makes for particularly heavy dependence on agriculture by a demographically-ageing population. Farmers need to become more highly mechanised through milking machines and mowers for more intensive cattle rearing and dairying; and assisted to realise the full potential for cereals, potatoes and fruit as ecological products. But there are further difficulties through the lack of food processing facilities so that some milk is still fed to pigs. Better environmental protection (for example, against floods through repair of retaining walls) is also a priority. In some communities settlement is highly dispersed (especially where secondary farmsteads are used) and this complicates the provision of a modern infrastructure (Buga 1996).

Institutions

A Mountain R&D Institute was opened at Cristian-Sibiu in 1991 for research into farm viability (including an interest in mountain sociology in connection with business plans for small industries, handicrafts and agro-tourism). It was closed during 1997–2000 but was re-established as a Research & Development Institute for Mountain Issues with a World Bank-financed programme for 2002–2004 on sustainable agricultural technologies for mountain farm development. A Federation for Mountain & Rural Development was founded in 1991 as a non-profitmaking NGO to mobilise farmers, specialists and agencies for both economic and social-cultural development. It provides technical assistance for farm development; complementary activities (exploiting local resources including small-scale food processing and agro-tourism) and helps in obtaining farm inputs and in marketing. It continued to be supported by the 1997–2000 government. A Foundation for Agriculture & Food Economics was founded at Reghin (Mureş) in 1992 with Swiss finance. Concerned with the development of mountain farming, it helped to set up milk production associations at Lunca Mureşului (Aluniş commune) and at Breaza and Idicel-Pădure in Brâncoveneşti commune. It also administered a credit scheme through a team of four rural development specialists. Recognising the tremendous effort needed in education to develop both awareness and skills among the mass of the peasantry, close links between the Agency and the equivalent organisation in France led to a Training & Innovation Centre for Development in the Carpathians (TICDC) in Vatra Dornei in 1994 to provide education and training for the development of mountain villages through courses and workshops. It became a Euromontana member in 1996 and trained some 750 mountain farmers during 2002–2004 alone with World Bank assistance. A Dorna Mountain Farmers' Association was started at Vatra Dornei in 1994 – with 2,700 members – helped during 1994–2000 by a German firm concerned with advice for agriculture and the food industry. Linked with NAAC, TICDC and the veterinary service, the Association has helped in many ways including marketing and warehousing, loans and feasibility studies, handicrafts and agricultural shows (from 1995), as well as education and training.

The Meadow Research Institute was started at Braşov in 2002 with an FAO-supported programme for 2002–2003.Through a study of the altitudinal zonation of grazing – taking the three bands of 600–1,200m, 1,200–1,800m and 1,800–2,400m – experiments at 600m at Măgurele and Vlădeni (Braşov); 1,200m at Dealul Sasului (Argeş) and 1,800m at Maliţa in the Făgăraş and Blana in the Bucegi have shown that the grazing season declines by 7.5 days per 100m of altitude while the consumption of fodder required to gain weight by 1.0kg increases by 1.5kg of grass mass per 100m. The altitudinal limit for forest is 1,600–1,800m with 2.0deg.C average temperature (-7.5deg. in January and 10deg. July) with maximum productivity at 1,000–1,200m with a density of 490cu.m/ha at 100 years; while natural grassland produces over 9.0t/ha of grass mass (decreasing upwards through cooler temperature and downwards through lower rainfall). This has implications for subventions that should increase by 10 per cent for each 100m of altitude above the 0-600m band (Maruşca 2002, p.83) when milk production in Câmpia Crişurilor is compared with the situation at 1,500m in the Apuseni. It is also relevant to mention that Bistriţa-Năsăud is a source of ecological fruits based on a long tradition of research started by the pharmacist Albert Wachsmann of Prundul Bârgăului who combined his interest in fruit trees with European connections to create an orchard of remarkable variety. The need for development after World War Two led to the creation of a research station for fruit trees in Bistriţa.

Diversification Plans

Diversification plans were circulated across all mountain areas during 1991–94 through the newspaper 'Viaţa Munţilor' with a print-run of 10,000 copies (developing into a magazine during 1994–96) as well as a TV programme on mountain civilisation. In 1991 Phare supported the piloting of initiatives in farming, agro-tourism and small industries: 55 projects on multi-sectoral sustainable development were financed in the key counties of Alba, Bistriţa-Năsăud, Harghita and Suceava; with additional support from France and Germany. Education made significant progress through 80 high school mountainology classes plus vocational schools with a focus on mountain agriculture in Alba, Braşov, Prahova (two) and Suceava. The proposal for a mountain university at Vatra Dornei was not implemented but a number of primary schools threatened with closure due to falling numbers were kept open. The economic press made much of the potential for rural community tourism based on the charm of mountain villages. Various localities were identified with particular attention to several localities in the Eastern Carpathians. Model farm buildings were designed in the light of architectural studies in several areas to see how modern buildings could harmonise with traditional styles (Mitrache et al. 1996). Rural tourism developed quite strongly through the activities of the NGO Naret and the fiscal incentives granted in 1994, with considerable foreign support as well from the Brussels-based 'Opération Villages Roumains' (OVR) set up in 1989 to oppose Ceauşescu's 'sistematizare'. OVR also helped to create a Romanian Rural Foundation for local projects through liaison with Timişoara University of Agricultural Sciences, Fédération Nationale des Foyers Ruraux (France), Fondation Rurale de Wallonie (Belgium) and the 'Institut Européen d'Écologie (based at Metz in France), with further help from Phare, the French Ministry of Foreign Affairs and Belgium's Wallonie Region. It is clearly very necessary to improve agricultural practices by fertilising pastures to correct soil acidity, by planting fruit trees and by improved animal breeding. There is also an emphasis on machinery suitable for small mountain farms at local agricultural shows such as various tractors and accessories in the 18–45hp range and very small 8–12hp machines for 'motorcultoare' are also available. The Agency is also concerned with the improvement of rural services, including the extension of electricity supplies. Road maintenance is a key concern; not only the national roads providing the principal transit links, such as Braşov-Ploieşti, Cluj-Oradea and Târgu Mureş-Bacău/Suceava, but new projects of which Petroşani-Băile Herculane is the most ambitious (apart from new highways for the Eurocorridors) and the numerous local roads that need to be better maintained for all-year availability.

Area Projects Including The Apuseni Mountains
Government contacts by Euromontana quickly extended to Austria, Germany, Italy and Switzerland with good results over the improvement of the Pinzgau herd. The village of Morăreni in the Ruşii Munţi commune of Mureş county was paired with St Legier (Switzerland), leading to NAMZ support for an experiment in technology transfer to intensify agriculture and improve incomes. Activity extended into stock-breeding and home industries with the marketing association 'Promorăreni' a particularly

interesting development. In Valea Doftanei (Prahova) the Agency became involved in a pilot project for integrated local development covering local industry (including food processing), improved fodder supply and educational/technical back-up. Several county plans were founded on 'baseline' surveys and included proposals to revive traditional crafts, improve farm roads and encourage agricultural societies. However, the Agency has taken a particularly deep interest in the Apuseni where there is still a large but dispersed population on the high surfaces. The need to repair flood damage was taken on board as the basis for a special development programme for this area in 1996 (Abrudan & Turnock 1999) including better road access between the six constituent counties – Alba, Arad, Bihor, Cluj, Hunedoara and Sălaj (Josan 1997) – and to coordinate activity in other ways (Pogan 2002). The OVR initiative was successful is establishing a 'reţea turistică' in the villages of the upper Arieş valley where the major development of winter sports is now likely at Arieşeni. Furthermore, during 1995–97 Phare contributed €0.95mln for mountain agriculture and integrated development, followed by a programme by the International Fund for Agriculture Development (IFAD) in 1998 (Ianoş 1999); while a meeting in Alba Iulia in 1999 by the UNESCO national commission and the Alba prefecture and CC prompted a wide-ranging Apuseni-Tirol comparison (although discussion covered all Romanian mountains). Measures were taken to stimulate settlement by young families and revive traditional privileges for craftsmen, while the Alba area of the Apuseni also had the benefit of encouragement for teachers to move into remote areas through bonuses worth up 80 per cent of their normal salary. As applied across the county in response to a law of 1997, 13 categories of difficulty were recognised and simplified into three groups in Table 8.3, set alongside the majority of the towns (Zone 1) that did not qualify. The special problems of the Apuseni are evident in the case of the more difficult areas (Zone 3 and Zone 4) with 81 schools (nine in commune centres) compared with only 14 (including one commune centre) in other parts of the county. Although the bonuses were payable only to qualified teachers who agreed to live in the villages concerned (commuters were not eligible) the complex scheme is an

Table 8.3: Salary bonuses payable to qualified teachers in deprived areas

Alba	Zone 1			Zone 2			Zone 3			Zone 4			Total		
Section	a	b	c	a	b	c	a	b	c	a	b	c	a	b	c
Apuseni	0	0	2	71	24	3	19	7	0	53	2	0	143	33	5
Other Areas	0	0	5	93	33	1	4	1	0	9	0	0	106	34	6
Total	0	0	7	164	57	4	23	8	0	62	2	0	249	67	11

Zone 1: very good services (towns of Aiud, Alba Iulia, Blaj, Câmpeni, Ocna Mureş, Sebeş and Teiuş): no bonus payable; Zone 2: some limitations (including the towns of Abrud, Baia de Arieş, Cugir and Zlatna): bonus up to 18% payable; Zone 3: poor services and road access but within 20kms of a town : bonus of 20-50% payable; Zone 4: virtually no services and low accessibility (more than 20kms from a town) and severe winter conditions: 60-80% bonus payable. a. villages; b commune centres; c towns.

Source: Ministry of Education, Alba Inspectorate.

interesting example of thinking at an early stage in the development of regional policy when several ad hoc initiatives were being taken.

Other Modernisation Strategies While the traditional mixed farm of the Carpathians is certainly capable of offering modest rewards, it does not offer an attractive prospect to school leavers who show a strong preference for work in industry and the tertiary sector (especially government service in one form or another). The mountain farms therefore need to be modernised to achieve greater efficiency for both meat and dairy produce. A big improvement in distribution is needed, including better links with the food processors and an improved technical base for an ecologically sustainable agriculture. In such regions there is tacit support for the 'Bavarian approach' of family farming linked with pluriactivity. For, even though occupational specialisation may seem the ultimate ideal, it is clear that there are economic and cultural reasons why this may not be attainable in the short term. In the Carpathians, the small farm base is socially fundamental; so diversification may offer a way forward in Romania and in other mountain regions. Yet a rural social policy is needed to safeguard the infrastructure: improve housing standards, extend electricity supplies and extend motor vehicle access to the small villages. A better agricultural advisory service is also required along with measures to encourage small businesses in rural areas. But the urban network remains deficient in many areas because some historic 'lands' still lack an urban centre. County plans reflect these needs, with additional local centres (currently villages) proposed for Bihor at Popeşti, Sâmbăta, Tinca and Vadu Crişului to strengthen the base of urban hierarchy. However, while the planning profession in Bucharest was looking into the needs of rural areas underpinned by agricultural development, expansion of the market system, improved land management (including measures to control erosion) and pluriactivity, the pace of change was restricted by the low level of investment. Ecological production should be a viable option as regions are declared free of genetically-modified organisms (beginning in 2006 with 16 settlements in the northeastern part of Bistriţa-Năsăud county, thanks to the efforts of the National Federation for Ecological Agriculture). Individual counties are also being classified as 'ecological' for certain products including Suceava for cattle (and Galaţi for vineyards). However it is doubtful whether small farms will be able to cope with the administrative procedures.

Other Regional Programmes

Although the mountain initiative (including the specific focus on the Apuseni) has been an enduring regional initiative, it was joined by others in 1996 for electoral reasons. The Danube Delta was also seen as suffering from complex problems, while rural poverty was also recognised in Giurgiu county (south of Bucharest) and also in Botoşani and Vaslui counties in Moldavia. The aim was to improve infrastructure (including salary premiums to retain professional staff), accelerate agricultural development and secure job creation through SMEs and fiscal concessions. Limited investment programmes were drawn up. However, as the new government moved closer to the EU and the accession process began, many other special cases were noted when Guvernul României şi Comisia Europeană (1997, p.39) referred to rural areas with complex problems: the whole of the Moldavian Plateau and the Romanian Plain for rural poverty, along with the Sălaj-Bistriţa area of Transylvania; while a set of regions were being undermined by rapidly-declining industries, particularly Banat and Hunedoara for mining-metallurgy, Braşov and Piteşti-Ploieşti with large concentrations of chemical and engineering industries and the Jiu Valley and Oltenia for coal mining. There were also several severely-polluted areas (Baia Mare, Copşa Mică and Zlatna) and problems of land degradation in the Curvature Carpathians. Rather that extend the list of *ad hoc* regional plans the government (as already noted) set up a nationwide regional development organisation to work with the relevant agencies. Research moved to identify 'less-favoured' rural areas and considerable progress was made on the basis of both infrastructure (Nadejde 1999; Nica 1999) and non-agricultural employment opportunities (F.Bordânc pers.com) (Figure 8.3). There has been no official response, although the concept was applied to mine restructuring in 1998 and some aspects of regional survey (ANDR 2000a).

Agricultural Production

Instead of the present emphasis on subsistence, Romanian agriculture now requires a stronger market-orientation and more value-added through a food processing industry burdened in transition by obsolete technology and surplus capacity. As already discussed, higher farm productivity depends on reduced fragmentation with stronger associations and marketing systems and improved agricultural extension; not to mention a better environment for land transactions and the enforcement of business contracts (Mete et al. 2003, p. v) which can all make for a more efficient business. This is being demonstrated in lowland areas through foreign investment by European agribusiness backed by modern refrigerated transport. For some years it has been possible for foreigners to acquire land in Romania provided a company is set up within the country and there has been much activity by Italians in Banat (exceeding 150,000ha in Arad, Caraş-Severin and Timiş counties during 1998-2004) and by Greeks and Turks (as well as Italians) in the SouthEast including 15,000 in Constanţa county. Yet despite low labour costs, only parts of the agricultural sector are competitive – wheat and sunflowers, wine and cheese (accredited ecoproducts made from buffalo, goat or sheep milk, particularly after accession) and possibly maize and pork – in contrast to beef, chicken, milk products and sugar beet that have encountered greater import competition. With domestic food consumption below the regional average (with a relatively high consumption of bread and cereal-based products in relation to the 25 per cent of total calory intake that is of animal origin – boosted even so by high self-consumption of milk and dairy products), exports provide the best scope for expansion of output. The agriculture ministry has helped through its 'Fondul de Garantare şi Creditului Rural', while producers have sought more competitive prices – for example, for cereals, live animals, vegetable oils and wines – plus better quality and packaging, along with farm consolidation and integration of the food chain. However results have been very mixed since net exporting of agricultural products ceased dramatically in 1990 and a trade surplus in agricultural products was achieved only briefly in 1999. From virtually nothing in 1990, agriculture was responsible for 6–7 per cent of total

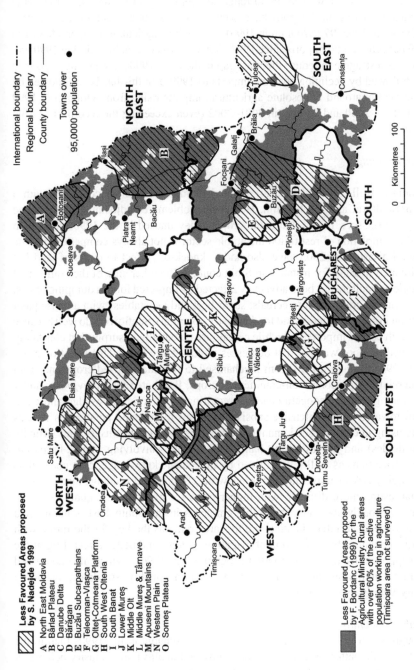

Figure 8.3 Less favoured agricultural areas

exports during 1991–95, rising to 9 per cent in 1996 before falling to 3–4 per cent in 2000–2002. The downward trend reflected overall export growth, for in absolute terms annual agricultural exports have been stable at $250–450mln apart from three good years in 1995–97 ($700mln in 1996). Meanwhile, agricultural imports have run at 6–9 per cent of total imports since 1994 after a 13–16 per cent high during 1990–94. There was a struggle to reduce the trade gap in the early 1990s, with rising exports to 1996 followed by declining absolute imports to 1999. But this has been followed by a dramatic turnaround in absolute agricultural imports rising from $400mln in 1999 to $1.0bln in 2000 and $1.2bln in 2001–2002 (even exceeding the record of $1.1bln in 1990).

Arable Farming

Romania is well-endowed with arable land: 9.4mln.ha in 2003 compared with a total agricultural area of 14.7mln. However, problems of adjustment, aggravated by a price scissors, meant that some cropland lay unused in the 1990s (and even with the completion of restitution the arable sector is not always competitive) while the flood disasters of 2005 have also had a 'knock-on' effect in terms of land left uncultivated in 2006 for instance in Sibiu county. The other side of the coin is that domestic agriculture has been adversely affected by imported food at dumping prices, depressing the areas sown to cereals, sugar beet and vegetables (with a consequent reduction in seed production and food industry potential). Sunflowers do well because of the high cost of imported oil while cereals are potentially in surplus but constantly threatened by poor weather that depresses yields (Table 8.4). This situation arose in the 1990s through a shift from mechanised to non-mechanised crops and from commercial to traditional non-commercial crops. It affected land previously under cash crops grown by cooperatives and requiring agronomic knowledge and cash. A shift towards labour-intensive subsistence crops highlighted potatoes as well as maize: using uncertified seed, manure rather than chemical fertilisers (and virtually no pesticides) and harvesting by hand. This action – involving family farms but some associations as well – was driven by inadequate knowledge, cash constraints and a highly risk-aversive attitude. Meanwhile, fragmented holdings made sowing and harvesting more difficult, with higher costs for transport and quality control. However, broadly speaking, the arable emphasis in the South East is maintained in spite of reduced intensification and this area remains the key for the future with potential enhanced by restoration of irrigation systems and better forecasting of the kind supported by the EU-supported programme in 1996-7 which also addressed constraints inhibiting agricultural exports such as quality standards, including sanitary-veterinary conditions.

Cereals (Especially Wheat)
Although wheat prices were generally higher in Romania in the 1990s than in the EU (despite the latter's higher and more consistent quality), the industry believes it can compete internationally given time for private sector investment to address the problem of high production costs: $115/t on the market in 1998 compared with world price of 90. Fortunes have fluctuated due to unpredictable weather and marketing

Table 8.4: Production of major crops 1985–2005

Year	Wheat/Rye			Maize			Sunflowers			Sugar Beet			Potatoes		
	Area	Yield	Prodn	Area	Yield	Prodn	Area	Yield	Prodn	Area	Yield	Prodn	Area	Yield	Prodn
1985	2396	2337	5599	3090	3846	11903	466	1494	696	275	22.3	6145	321	20.4	6631
1986	2544	2497	6354	2856	3811	10901	461	1872	863	268	20.1	5397	329	15.6	5187
1987	2399	2798	6713	2787	2699	7527	474	1573	747	260	20.1	5217	317	13.0	4141
1988	2415	3575	8632	2579	2781	7182	466	1513	705	248	19.6	4869	326	11.0	3621
1989	2359	3364	7935	2733	2472	6762	434	1512	656	256	26.5	6771	351	12.4	4420
1990	2298	3212	7379	2467	2756	6810	395	1409	556	163	20.1	3278	290	11.0	3186
1991	2217	2507	5559	2575	4072	10497	477	1281	612	202	23.3	4703	234	7.9	1873
1992	1475	2188	3228	3336	2046	6828	615	1257	774	180	16.1	2897	219	11.3	2602
1993	2307	2321	5354	3066	2605	7987	588	1180	696	97	18.3	1776	249	14.8	3709
1994	2441	2535	6186	2983	3131	9343	582	1309	764	130	21.3	2764	249	11.8	2947
1995	2501	3082	7709	3109	3184	9923	714	1304	933	133	19.9	2655	244	12.3	3020
1996	1798	1760	3164	3277	2926	9608	917	1193	1096	136	21.0	2848	257	13.9	3591
1997	2424	2964	7186	3038	4171	12687	781	1095	858	129	21.2	2725	255	12.5	3206
1998	2033	2561	5208	3129	2756	8623	962	1115	1073	118	20.0	2361	261	12.6	3319
1999	1687	2776	4682	3013	3627	10935	1033	1243	1301	65	21.6	1415	274	14.4	3957
2000	1954	2280	4456	3049	1603	4898	877	821	721	48	13.8	667	283	12.2	3470
2001	2559	3034	7764	2974	3066	9119	800	1029	823	39	22.4	876	277	14.4	3997
2002	2310	1924	4441	2894	2902	8400	906	1105	1003	42	22.9	955	283	14.4	4078
2003	1748	1429	2496	3200	2993	9577	1188	1268	1506	45	16.9	764	282	14.0	3947
2004	2318	3403	7867	3274	4441	14542	977	1595	1558	21	32.3	673	266	15.9	4230
2005	2497	2965	7390	3269	3952	10388	971	1381	1341	25	28.9	730	285	15.9	3739

Area: th.ha; Yield:kg/ha (th.kg for sugar beet and potatoes); Production:th.t

Source: Statistical Yearbooks: Tables 14.7, 14.8 and 14.9

conditions but government desires an adequate production for self-sufficiency, while seeking to enhance efficiency on large farms to secure exports. The 1997 harvest was depressed through lack of nitrogen and phosphorous after thin snow cover in the southeast made it difficult to fertilise the crop with tractors (since the tyres caused damage) while aviation methods were not financially viable. Although heavy summer rain affected parts of Banat, Moldavia, Oltenia and northern Transylvania in 1997 Romania had a 2.5mln.t wheat surplus undercut by Hungarian and Turkish cereal and flour imports amidst calls for tariffs to protect Romanian millers (and a ceiling on duty free imports). There were also cases of border picketing by the Agrostar union claiming that tariff increases against Hungarian wheat were not being implemented. Farmers were therefore discouraged from sowing winter wheat in the autumn of 1997 and the decline continued in 1998 in the aftermath of flood and landslide damage in the early summer (destroying 40 per cent of production over 0.41mln.ha in Moldavia and Transylvania) after late frost damage in Dobrogea, southern Moldavia and eastern Wallachia.

Fluctuating Harvests Continue   A new crisis was reported at the end of 1999 regarding stocks of cereals for bread – after a poor harvest from a sown area of 1.3–1.4mln.ha that was depressed to the critical limit for self-sufficiency and from which less than 5.0mln.t were harvested (including only limited quantities of poor quality seed). But as a spur to enhance competitiveness the government nevertheless granted export licences in 1999 and bought wheat from farmers only at low prices which depressed sowings for 2000: down again to below 1.4mln.ha. Production then fell from an estimated 7.0mln.t to 4.5mln.t in 2000 (including rye) after the worst drought in 50 years; but at least the target of 3.5–4.0mln.t needed for the bread supply was exceeded. Good weather in 2001 produced a wheat harvest of 7.8mln.t, but after severe drought in 2002 the 2003 harvest fell to 2.5mln.t – well below the 4.0mln.t required for bread and seed (after a forecast of 7.1!) through high temperature, lack of rain and pest attacks. With 0.24mln.ha frost-damaged and a further 0.18mln.ha drought-damaged to an extent of 50–100 per cent, yields of 2,200–3,000kg/ha in western Transylvania and Banat fell to 850 in Dobrogea, Moldavia and Muntenia. Production of barley and rye – for beer and animal feed – was also insufficient; giving rise to customs-free imports in autumn 2003 of 100,000t barley, 12,000 rye and 500,000t maize for fodder. Meanwhile wheat was imported earlier in the year, with some consolation for consumers because import prices were no higher than those for home production.

Export Potential   Lower wheat sowings were expected in 2003 (1.8mln.ha) but the 2004 yield reached an average of 3.8t/ha, the highest in history and there was further good news – through forecasts by both the EU and the US Agriculture Department – of Romanian exports of some 2.65mln.t of wheat and 2.0-2.7mln.t of maize by 2005 (on a similar scale to Hungary with some 2.55 and 2.45 respectively and well ahead of Bulgaria with 1.60 and 0.38) with sunflower seed exports as well. The 2005 wheat harvest was estimated at 7.3mln.t with only 5.0 needed for bread and other forms of home consumption. The expectation is that wheat production should stabilise at around 7.0mln.t – of baking quality (24–25 per cent gluten) and conforming to phyto-sanitary requirements – from 2.15mln.ha, with a growth in surplus to allow export of some 1.7mln.t. Subsidies for wheat were phased out in 2005 except for less-favoured areas that received assistance at double the old rate. At the same time it was decided that 124,000t of wheat may be imported without customs – and more where the price is competitive with home production; thus providing an outlet for a bumper crop in Hungary such as was realised in 2004. Meanwhile maize production could stabilise at 11.5mln.t – a yield of 3,400kg from 3.4mln.ha (2000); slightly up on 1996 when the harvest of 10.4mln.t was equivalent to 3,150kg from each of 3.3mln.ha. It is significant that since 1998 Romania has enjoyed the service provided by the Constanţa cereal terminal which also handles Hungarian wheat and maize exports (with likely custom in future from Bulgaria, Serbia and Ukraine using the Danube-Black Sea Canal).

Oats and Rice Difficult marketing conditions for oats may restrict the cultivated area to 600–650,000ha for a production of 2.0mln.t production, mainly for animal feed. And rice production suffered a major collapse with a desperate situation in 1997 through lack of capital, rising costs and expensive loans. There were 70,000ha in rice plantations by the end of the 1980s, but despite some export potential the business of companies like Oltriz (Olteniţa) and Stănriz (Stăncuţa, Brăila) was neglected in the face of imports of inferior quality rice. Pedo-climatic conditions in the southeast are good for rice (by European standards) and Chinese help was reported in 1998 over 40,000ha of plantations in Brăila, Călăraşi, Constanţa and Ialomiţa counties. The turnaround is being continued by Riso Scotti (Italy) who have made a €30mln investment in the Giurgeni-Vlădeni area of Ialomiţa county involving land and state-of-the-art processing. A further investment of €25mln – enlarging their landholdings (in Brăila, Olt and Dolj counties as well as Ialomiţa) from 4,000 to 10,000ha – will make Romania the largest rice growing area in Europe and third in the world. Over 400 jobs will be secured for growing and processing, particularly in the Giurgeni-Vlădeni area of Ialomiţa with a factory at Giurgeni with the most advanced equipment for processing and wrapping; though there is also a strorage at Drăgăneşti-Olt. The company have also indicated an intention to launch new foods (e.g. rice cakes) at affordable prices. Meanwhile, soya has experienced marketing difficulty but growth is expected due to protein needs for animal feed: 119,000t from 85,000ha (1,400kg/ha) in 1996 rising to 340,000t from 200,000ha (1,700kg/ha) in 2000.

Technical Crops
Sunflowers (for example in Ialomiţa) have also enjoyed comparative stability because they are typically grown more exclusively on large holdings (associations and state farms) and require high inputs of labour, machinery, seed, fertiliser and irrigation water. The sown area should stabilise at around 715,000ha with a slight increase in output through improved technology (0.93mln.t 1996 to 1.10mln in 2000) to meet all the country's edible oil requirements. But interest has been boosted by the need for biodiesel production, starting with two projects in the Bărăgan (by Belgian and Portuguese investors) and smaller ones by Constanţa and Vaslui by Romanian companies Argus and Racova. Meanwhile the low market price of sugar is removing the incentive for many peasant farmers to produce sugar beet; effectively

perpetuating earlier price controls for sugar (imposed in the interest of consumers) that set beet acquisition prices at the sugar factories below many farmers' production costs. While the EU forecast a self-sufficiency gain in cereals of 110 per cent during 1997–2003 and 105 per cent in oilseed the level for sugar beet was limited to 61 per cent (though higher than the dismal 43 per cent level scored in 1997). The area under sugar beet fell sharply from 201.0th.ha in 1991 to 45.2 in 2003: only 73.0th. t of sugar were produced (with 85 per cent of sugar needs imported) compared with 0.40mln.t in the early 1990s. Despite subsidies only five of the 12 factories took out contracts with domestic beet producers (linked with upgrading of technology for more efficient processing) because it was often cheaper to process imported crude sugar. There have been calls for reduced VAT on sugar, but beet-growing interests also want higher taxes on both crude and refined sugar imports to match the price for sugar from domestically-grown beet. After EU accession Romania will need to negotiate a quota in order to retain some domestic sugar production – most optimistically for 175,000t compared with annual consumption of 500,000t. There was criticism of the Năstase government for negotiating unrealistically high quotas: with 30,000t of sugar produced in 2004 there is little chance of hitting the quota of 110,000t which is the threshold for subsidies.

Flax, Hemp and Tobacco
These are also problematic crops. Up to 1989 some 80,000ha was used for each crop, with processing through a network of 35 factories (18 for flax and 17 for hemp). But during the 1990s the area collapsed to 1,000ha for hemp and 500ha for flax to supply the 30 members of the Central Union for the Flax & Hemp Industry. However Romania produces the long-fibre hemp needed for ecological clothing which is highly fashionable in Western Europe and good prospects for growth are emerging through collaboration with Germans who think that Banat has the best climate and soil for hemp and would like to see a profitable processing industry supporting thousands of hectares of cultivation. Using appropriate technology the industry could supply the motor industry with material for vehicle interiors and provide a basis for the privatisation of the retting industry by securing up to 300 jobs in bankruptcy-threatened factories in towns like Sânnicolau Mare. The Carin factory at Iratoşu (Arad) was acquired in 1998 by Treu Hanf of Berlin – an investment fund specialising in hemp production. 80 per cent of production is now exported and Carin has a research partnership with BMW (for motorcar interior tapestry) with experimental cultivation at Lovrin (Timiş). Finally, in 2002 tobacco planters were granted state subsidies of 21,000lei/kg (for raw tobacco delivered for processing) as part of a project to restore the viability of Romania's National Tobacco Corporation (NTC), along with help to install modern fermentation plants to improve tobacco quality. The agriculture ministry is supporting production of inexpensive cigarettes for low-income smokers but employment at NTC was cut from 3,700 to 2,800 in 2002. There was a prospect of bonuses for tobacco growers in 2005 to boost output that is less than half the quota negotiated with the EU.

Vegetables and Fruit

There is large sale of fresh vegetables in the shops and also a substantial canning industry involving some 37 companies in the production of 280,000t of fruit and vegetables in 1997 with a 75 per cent increase expected to 2000. Serious marketing problems initially arose for producers as state warehouses disappeared without private wholesalers to take over the handling of onions, garlic, root vegetables, cabbage, potatoes, apples, pears and grapes; so urban markets depended mainly on imports. A continuing problem was the 'double gear market' that sees registered tax-paying producers unable to operate (through wholesale markets) because small producers can sell free of tax and VAT. Moreover, the benefits of alignment with the EU are constantly being undermined by the black trade of the 'market mafia' (including alcohol and wine). Some large farms have failed to prosper as private operations with rising energy costs for glasshouses a serious challenge. The Potato Cultivators Federation revealed that the area of potatoes grown from superior quality seed declined from 15,000ha to 2,300 during the 1990s (following the demise of the cooperatives) because of the failure of individual farmers to purchase seed potatoes from reputable sources. At the same time, virus-infected surfaces doubled from 14 to 30 per cent. It was therefore suggested in 1998 that subsidies should cover the price differential between seed and consumption potatoes. Meanwhile, some vegetables have done well, notably water melons, with a production of 215,000t in 1989 (15th in the world) rising to 940,000t in 2001–2002 (then sixth largest in the world after China with 8.5mln/t, Turkey with 1.9mln, USA with 1.2mln and two others). In 2003 there was also a special programme financed by \$15–20mln of credits to support efficient greenhouses with irrigation and heating to reduce the cost of food imports. This initiative was followed up during the 2004–2005 winter with subsidies for vegetable producers who received 5,000lei/kg (up from 3,000/kg) for market sales with documentation showing that thermal power was used during October 2004–May 2005. Another growing interest is the relaunch of horticulture with the aim of developing flower exports: damaged after 1989 through excessive imports from tropical countries but especially from The Netherlands. Apiculture can also be profitable when handled by experts abreast of modern technology. Romanian honey is sought for mixing by companies who may combine 15 different types (using a secret recipe); though some Romanian honey – such as acacia honey – is sold abroad without mixing. Romanian exporters include Băneasa Apiculture Complex, exporting to Western Europe, USA, Israel and South Africa in 2002.

Rebuilding the Market System
More could be done to supply the domestic market with fresh fruit and also to make fruit juices and quality brandies. In general fruit production has declined due to deterioration of orchards, partly through limited use of pest and disease control substances. This is unfortunate in view of the history of research on fruit growing dating to the nineteenth century and extended through the Bistrița station after World War Two which created new plum varieties used for 'compot', preserves and brandy. In the hilly regions it was unfortunate that many new owners chose to cut down orchards in order to obtain more land for maize, although the lack

of a distribution system for the fruit makes animal fodder a more appropriate use (especially in a situation where orchards were established on an intensive scale on unstable hill slopes). The situation over plums is particularly problematic after they accounted for two-thirds of all fruit produced in 1938 when they were processed in drying kilns and 'marmelada' factories as well as small brandy distilleries. They still account for half the fruit produced but there was much neglect in the communist period through a preference for apples and pears. In 2002 Romania was the world's third plum producer with 0.50mln.t (after China with 4.2mln and the USA with 0.58). There is certainly scope for rebuilding the orchards and commercialising the plum brandy industry that is traditionally an informal rural business. Reference should also be made to domestic cherries that amounted to 85,000t in 2002 when Romania was tenth world producer. Picking and marketing is a seasonal activity of great importance in the Oaş region of Satu Mare. Forest fruits are also important: Constanța forestry directorate was selling hawthorn and roseberries to the medecine firm Bayer (Germany) in 2003. Meanwhile imports of exotic fruits have soared, for example bananas from Ecuador and Honduras; coconuts from Ivory Coast, dates, figs and nuts from Iran; lemons, oranges and tangerines from Greece and Turkey; and passion fruit from South Africa. Some imported fruits could be grown in Romania and in 2001 a privatised state farm at Ostrov (Constanța) started the experimental harvesting of kiwi fruit previously imported from Greece. Dobrogea soil is suitable and two hectares have now been planted, but the trees need protection against cold air currents, while drought depresses the yield. A major issue for fruit is always the variable quality of production from private farms: flood damage in 2005 damaged a canning industry ever fearful of becoming dependent on small peasant farms (with Chinese imports likely as a result).

Viticulture
The wine industry has experienced difficulty through restitution and under-investment while fortunes have fluctuated through good vintages in 1994 and 1995 contrasting with the ravaging of grape production in 1998 by pests, disease and drought. Romanian wine is expected to do well with an EU self-sufficiency level projected to rise during 1997–2003 to 110 per cent. However, Romanian vineyards are relatively unproductive: 4,900kg/ha grapes in Romania compared with 6,850 in EU and a profit of only €1,200/ha in Romania compared with €8,000 in EU in 2003, while domestic wine consumption has been depressed by the popularity of beer. Hence, despite wine exports of 500,000hl in 2002, Romania could eventually become a net wine importer. Wine producers claim excessive fiscal burdens (1,600–1,800 lei/bottle plus 700 for the fiscal stamp) that should be gradually reduced – with wine treated as a food rather than an alcoholic beverage – to provide funds for new vine plantations. In 1998 maintenance costs were reckoned at 4.6–7.8mln.lei/ha while new plantations cost 22.0–27.8mln.lei/ha. The matter was crucial in the run-up to EU accession since hybrid vines are banned: yet they account for 243,700ha in Romania – half the vineyard area – and expanded during the 1990s through cultivation by peasants over areas of less than a hectare (with small planting distances and vine prop support). These small areas – lacking modern technology – are inadequate for profitable farming and in any case climate and soil are unfavourable. This follows

mistakes made earlier when cooperatives established vineyards on poor soils on sloping land where other crops were not profitable. Establishing new vineyards with young noble strains costs €10,000/ha with no yield for three years. Such plantings declined sharply from 21,300ha in 1990 to 4,600 in 1996. Only 300ha/yr were planted during 1999–2002 when the minimum needed to maintain the noble vineyard area was 5,500ha: hence the ageing of noble vineyards and falling demand for viticultural planting material.

Investment and Research   The Association of Wine Producers thinks that $350mln investments are needed over eight years to boost sales by expanding the area of noble vineyards by 13,000ha. Contributions are made by Romanian research – such as Pietroasele (Buzău) viticultural research station established in 1893 – while the French Institute for Cooperation with East European Countries and Hérault Department provided assistance to the value of some €20,000 in 1998 for vineyards in Constanța. The German Agency for Technical Cooperation is working with Odobești Vine Growers Association (Vrancea) in 2003 to launch several of their wines on the European market: an area of 256ha of noble vines was identified for special attention and financial assistance provided for a headquartering establishment using German pressing machines and filters. The German GTZ programme also seeks to boost Romanian bottled wine exports to Germany. State support has been given to the extent of 75 per cent of the interest on credits (with a grace period of one year) granted to producers creating or restoring plantations on compact surfaces of at least 1.0ha. However with 100,000 families involved with small vineyards in 2000, there are also proposals to create stronger producer associations to negotiate contracts with the viticulture companies. And wine exporters were looking for a higher export bonus in 2005 to cope with high bottling, labelling and promotion costs. The key point is that less than a tenth of the 6.00mln.hl (that make Romania the sixth world producer) is quality wine and hence production is poorly represented in Europe. Hence much better use must be made of the country's 240,000ha of 'negotiated surface'; following the example of UK expatriate companies Halewood (1997) and Recaș (1998) which are now exporting much of their output.

Livestock Farming

Livestock numbers declined sharply after 1989 with no respite until the lowest recorded level was reached in 2002 when a national recovery programme produced two consecutive years of improvement (despite high feed prices resulting from drought in 2003) (Table 8.5). Particularly serious problems arose in the case of intensive rearing units that emerged as independent commercial businesses, following the break-up of large trusts of the AEI (Asociația Economică Intercooperatistă) type established under communism. Indeed during the 1990s decline was most evident in the state sector: 26 of the state's 109 pig and poultry farms were liquidated in 1997, in addition to 20 privatised (while arable farms remained intact until the concession programme of 2003). Particularly poor results obtained in the livestock sector that could no longer be sustained when the centre-right government came under pressure to repay foreign loans in 1998-9. Falling domestic demand hit the meat producers and low prices (controlled until 1997) reflected the threat from competitive imports. Gifts of food from abroad helped to depress market prices; while drought (e.g. in the southwest in 1993), created a further complication with reduced availability of fodder prompting heavy sales of livestock at low prices in the worst-affected areas; given the lack of special assistance to farmers experiencing natural disasters and the high cost of insurance. But a progressive reduction in the number of animals was to be expected at a time of rapid inflation, aggravated by a price 'scissors'. Units without their own supply could not normally secure enough fodder to maintain numbers when dependent on the proceeds of a previous sale of finished animals, especially when under pressure to sell (whereas peasants were in a better position to hold out in the hope of getting better prices: although they too would not want too many unsold animals with winter approaching and would have to take advantage of the few opportunities for local sale available to them, especially with few private buyers to compete with the state procurement system). On the other hand the case of Aylex Trading of Bucharest, a combined fodder producer with a majority interest in the poultry farms of Avicola (Buzău), underpinned the logic of close business links between fodder production and livestock rearing farms.

Restructuring Large Farms
The situation in poultry units became particularly serious because of pricing anomalies in 1996 when 43 state poultry farms were in difficulty through rising costs for feed, including cereals (especially barley) and protein supplements; while 12 were bankrupt by the autumn and were placed in conservation. Only a third of total annual capacity was then operating: 0.30mln.t of chicken and 3.0bln eggs. With feed prices reflecting levels of 450lei/kg for wheat and 500lei/kg for barley while the price for chicken was fixed at 375lei/kg, the farms could hardly break even. Thus without price liberalisation or higher subsidies the farms were bound to collapse eventually and early in 1997 poultry (and pork) units needed government support to finance their animal feed until the new harvest. Small wonder therefore that the government took drastic action including the removal of price controls and some financial support for new technology in privatised pig and poultry complexes through $100mln of World Bank credits in 1998. Meanwhile cattle farms were also in a poor situation. At the Agricola farm at Ciulnița (Călărași) 36 of the 40 sheds were empty in 1997 when the farm had only 100 cattle for fattening in 1997 plus 200 milk cows and 100 young cattle; whereas in 1992 there were 6,000 cattle being fattened. The problem was again one of high production costs in relation to controlled market prices: one kilo of meat cost almost 4,900lei to produce but sold for only 2,200lei. Stock levels were spiralling downwards as each sale could only sustain a reduced number of animals through the following cycle. Where bank loans were obtained to overcome financial blockages high interest payments became a major burden; absorbing a fifth of income from meat sales by one Ialomița complex (while salaries were a mere 2.5 per cent). Livestock farmers in general were also looking for customs exemptions for imports of fodder and technological equipment for stock breeding as well as stimulating subventions for exports of meat and meat products. This reflects concern over unfair competition from EU countries where direct and indirect subsidies enable meat to sell in Romania at 40 per cent of the normal production value in the EU. The situation was not helped by a Romanian Intelligence Service report on

Table 8.5: Livestock and basic food products 1985–2006

Year	A	B	C	D	E	F	G	H	I	J	K	L	M
1985	7.04	14.78	19.39	114.0	2397	52.5	1.95	40.7	7.24	1958	824	12.1	73.5
1986	6.69	13.65	18.17	121.4	2486	50.7	1.90	39.9	7.85	944	1667	14.2	81.7
1987	6.70	14.09	18.12	125.3	2453	50/1	1.91	38.9	7.32	1480	969	15.3	80.2
1988	6.56	14.33	17.83	127.3	2297	52.3	2.07	37.9	8.07	1508	1196	15.8	92.0
1989	6.42	14.35	17.29	127.6	1911	45.3	1.89	35.4	7.04	1580	914	12.1	78.5
1990	6.29	11.67	16.10	114.0	2232	44.2	2.06	38.2	8.08	1453	954	10.6	63.5
1991	5.38	12.00	14.73	121.4	2023	46.1	2.20	32.5	7.18	1165	848	8.3	52.0
1992	4.35	10.95	14.63	106.0	1895	44.9	2.30	28.0	6.14	1167	905	10.4	37.8
1993	3.68	9.85	12.80	87.7	1935	47.3	2.44	26.0	5.63	2182	1339	9.9	26.4
1994	3.60	9.26	12.25	76.5	1852	53.6	2.79	25.1	5.41	980	1033	9.8	28.6
1995	3.48	7.76	11.68	70.2	1846	56.8	2.95	24.3	5.57	917	1314	10.4	25.4
1996	3.50	7.96	11.19	80.5	1868	57.2	3.02	23.2	5.78	1632	1431	11.2	23.9
1997	3.43	8.23	10.48	78.5	1705	56.2	3.06	22.1	5.27	1416	1179	10.5	19.4
1998	3.23	7.10	9.76	66.6	1672	54.3	3.00	20.3	5.33	1036	874	10.2	17.0
1999	3.14	7.19	9.25	69.5	1521	52.6	2.99	18.8	5.67	936	1107	11.2	13.5
2000	3.05	5.85	8.98	69.1	1414	51.6	2.87	18.2	5.71	1301	1295	11.7	17.1
2001	2.87	4.79	8.52	70.1	1415	53.2	2.96	17.6	6.00	1353	1122	12.6	13.4
2002	2.80	4.45	8.11	71.4	1604	55.1	3.08	16.7	6.43	952	1077	13.4	16.2
2003	2.88	5.06	8.19	77.4	1699	57.7	3.20	16.9	6.64	2088	1078	17.4	10.0
2004	2.90	5.14	8.34	76.6	n.a.	59.8	n.a.	17.5	7.38	1744	1230	19.1	13.1
2005	2.81	6.49	8.08	87.0	n.a.	60.6	n.a.	18.4	7.31	1647	506	17.7	13.4
2006	2.86	6.62	8.30	86.6	n.a.	n.a.	n.a.	n.a.	n.a.	n.a.	n.a.	n.a.	n.a.

A Cattle (mln); B Pigs (mln); C Sheep and goats (mln); D Poultry (mln); E Meat (th.t); F Milk (mln.t); G Milk: average output per cow (th.l); H Wool (th.t); I Eggs (bln); J Fruit (th.t); K Grapes (th.t); L Honey (th.t); M Fish (th.t)

Source: Statistical Yearbooks: Tables 14.10, 14.11, 14.12 and 14.14

agriculture at the end of 1995 highlighting the degradation of national wealth in animal breeding: compared with 250 animal and poultry breeding farms operating to capacity at the start of the 1990s only 20 were still working efficiently while the rest were using only 15–40 per cent of their production capacities (and some were liquidated). Breeding centres for Maramureş Brown and Holstein cattle (within the research and production units of Sighetul Marmaţiei) were close to extinction, while the sheep breeding units for Merino (Constanţa) and Karakul (Botoşani) were threatened with closure. However there are now signs of reconstruction, assisted by SAPARD funding for large farms like Mihai Popescu's automated pig-rearing unit at Coamele Capra (Iaşi) and the Agricola International egg incubator near Bacău. With 11 farms in Buzău and Galaţi counties, Aylex Group are investing €26mln in a large new farm to treble dead meat production to 30,000t.

Mountain Regions
Mountain regions also experienced a sharp decline even though peasant farmers used natural fodder at virtually no financial cost. Some relaxation occurred after the excesses of the former régime's strict checks on sales and registration of newly-born animals. There was more on-farm consumption of meat (including informal sales) but also lower stocking levels. This was partly due to the lack of imported fodder previously supplied in connection with communist production plans. But there was also the reality of falling demand and transitional problems linked with termination of cooperatives specialised in livestock production – with inappropriate buildings and technical equipment for small-scale farming; inefficiency by processors passing high production costs on to producers farmers or consumers; inadaptability of marketing systems for small-scale farming (with the lack of local abattoirs or regular local livestock markets); and higher relative input prices (energy, fodder and fuel) inaccessible for small-scale producers. Hence small producers adjusted livestock numbers to their family needs and limited local selling opportunities. Only rarely do family farms buy young animals; reproduction is seasonal; stock graze in the open (stabled or enclosed at night) with some use of green fodder: only large private farms use concentrated feed and modern stabling like the former state farms. While farmers appreciate that outputs depend on inputs, most lack the financial means to supplement the fodder that their own holdings can generate. Reduced use of veterinary services is also understandable but counter-productive. Another factor concerns the low productivity of grazings and hay meadows. Many areas were overgrazed with the result that erosion increased and some pastures were invaded by poor herbaceous plant associations and bushes (indeed stock kept by the former cooperatives was often of poor quality and unsuitable for breeding). Furthermore the downward spiral was maintained as young people found work abroad and farming was left increasingly to the older generation.

Sheep Rearing   Sheep rearing was adversely affected through opening up to world markets and the impact has been felt not only for mutton and dairy products (since there is a significant milk production) but also wool which enjoyed the strong support of a protected home market. While sheep were kept wherever grazing was available some Carpathian villages specialised in the management of large flocks based on transhumance – for both wool and mutton – combined with the privatisation of agriculture and lack of subsidy. The shepherds of Jina near Sibiu, maintained very large flocks under communism by combining summer grazing in the Carpathians with winter grazing on the plains (where local CAP officials were often satisfied with token payments). Prices were such that "each sheep paid for its entire annual cost with a single kilo of washed wool" (Stewart 1997, p.70) and people visiting Jina would jokingly remark that they were 'going to America'. After 1989 free trade eroded the profits previously available on a protected wool market, while tougher negotiating with private farmers created complications on the transhumance routes (especially the slow spring return with new-born lambs). Hence flocks have been reduced and capital has been placed in new businesses: the embargo trade with Serbia, wool dealing with Turkish lorry drivers and speculations in the Caritas pyramid investment fund to finance new filling stations on the trunk roads of Transylvania. Thus, "using their extended kin networks [the Jinars] expanded their activities from the mountains into the plains, using their home base as a sort of bank, secure from the depredations of the state and outsiders" (Ibid, p. 72). Since 1989 some 200 families have moved from Jina into lowland villages around Sibiu, acquiring houses from departing Saxons (and often taking their jobs as well). There is a clear need for higher productivity on mountain grazings where summer seasons at the 'stâna' are becoming less acceptable. Better defence against wild animals explains why shepherds in the Apuseni are training dogs to guard sheep from cages placed in trees so that they can detect the presence of wolves without endangering themselves. In addition, EU regulations require that the pasture stations use stainless steel utensils (rather than the traditional wooden equipment) and organise on the basis of family associations or companies in order to sell milk and cheese: hence the seven 'stâne' in the Brusturoasa area of Bacău county's Trotuş valley have formed 'Asociaţia crescătorilor de animale din zona montană'. Private slaughter of animals for the Easter festival (the main opportunity for selling mutton and lamb) has also been stopped although special authorised centres are allowed to operate at this time of year.

Dairying

Substantial improvements in the dairying industry should be noted following the increase in the milk price in 1997 (to 1,000lei/liter) and the final removal of price controls to allow producers to cover costs. And while the fresh market is the main attraction, Romanian dairy products – especially cheeses – are finding export opportunities. A modern complex for dairy cow breeding has opened at Beştepe (Tulcea) using cows from local farms (Corbeanca and Nazarcea) plus high performance cows from Denmark. A major drive has been made in the Bucharest area thanks to a $40,000 three-year World Bank project (with the help of the Research Institute for Cattle Rearing at Baloteşti) to improve management on small private family dairy farms destined to supply local processors. This follows earlier Dutch assistance during 1995–6 to develop milk production associations in the Bucharest area. Foreign capital in involved in a project at Bocsig near Ineu (Arad) where the commune sold 816ha to Fertila (Italy) in 2005 for an €5.0mln investment in a dairy farm and milk factory to produce 18–20,000l milk daily (50,000l eventually) using milk from the company's own farm and from 500 cows on other farms in the area. Furthermore during 2005–2006 there has been substantial SAPARD assistance for dairy farms across the country. The business has also been extended through the import of stock such as the 500 Holstein cattle brought into the Bozovici area of Almăj: farmers should recoup on the outlay through higher milk sales over a two year period and this will also enable the creamery in Bozovici to work at its full capacity of 25,000l/day (8,000 at the time), with further outlets secured in Drobeta-Turnu Severin in 1998. However Romanian breeding has produced fine brown ('Bruna-Schwyz') cattle in Maramureş: animals in six localities (Berbeşti, Rona de Sus, Sighet, Şieu, Săpânţa and Onceşti) are producing over 6,500kg milk each. This reflects the work of experts at Animal Breeding and Research Station at Sighetul Marmaţiei over three decades in supplying animals with high biological potential. Finally it was reported in 2001 that the attraction of the village name of Cocorăştii Colt in Prahova county encouraged a Chinese entrepreneur – advised by a Chinese trading company – to buy the residue of the local cooperative (20ha of arable) with the intention of starting a dairy farm. Overall quality remains a problem: despite a subsidy of 3,000lei/l barely a third of milk production was fully compliant with EU regulations on the eve of accession.

General Trends
The market situation is quite finely balanced with regard to milk, pigmeat and poultry. Privatised poultry farms are now viable, for instance Agricola Bacău, specialising in poultry meat and eggs, invested in state-of-the-art production facilities to achieve quality production of 27,000t of chicken in 2004. Self-sufficiency remains below par for beef despite exports to the former CEFTA: this is due to low competitiveness with regard to the slaughter weight for young cattle (as well as the milk yield for dairy cows). Exports of live animals include some buffalo cows and 'brown' Maramureş cattle to the UK. A problem arose in the run-up to EU accession through failure to meet the end-of-2004 deadline over introducing a cattle 'passport' scheme through ear-tagging which meant a year's delay before the country could be declared brucelosis-free (though subsidies for cattle in 2005 depended on compliance with the earmark passport to put an end to unidentified beef). Horses have been exported in significant numbers – mainly to Italy – earning €40mln annually, but the trade has been compromised due to animals arriving in poor condition. The largest number of horses is found in Maramureş for traditional reasons, although many are required for forestry work as well as agriculture. Meanwhile sheep can still be profitable given the demand on world markets especially the Middle East involving some 70,000 animals in 2004–2005, with opportunities for the Moldavian sheep mafia ('mafia oierilor') to organise large consignments at grazing stations in the Vaslui area (reasonably close to the ports) and evade taxation on transactions reputed to be worth some 75bln.lei. All livestock categories increased during 2002–6 but cattle (2.1 per cent) and sheep/goats (2.3 per cent) only marginally compared with poultry (21.3 per cent) and pigs (49.0 per cent). Moreover, interest in ostrich breeding has been reported since 2000. The birds put on a lot of weight between one and six years and profit comes from meat with low cholesterol content recommended for people with heart disease ($30/kg) – an alternative to beef – and skin for 'de luxe' leather articles (also eggs and feathers). Good feeding and accommodation is important. Romanian breeders claim an income of $1,000 per ostrich with sale of

meat, chicks and eggs – seen as a 'get rich overnight' option at a time of concern over beef in western markets in 2001. Breeders are reported in the Sibiu area (where two engineers claim to have paid $20,000 for 15 ostriches from Belgium through an Internet contact) with others from Piatra Neamţ, Simeria and Tulcea. There is a need for marketing centres: two were in prospect including one in Bucharest in 2001. Frogs are harvested in Danube Delta for live export to Austria, France and Italy to provide delicacies. The nature reserve authorities were allowing 300,000 to be collected annually in 2003. However the search for new enterprises has to combine with the radical overhaul of the system of marketing and processing which is only gradually emerging in the form of new private commercial organisation. In the process many of vertically-organised state farm complexes have withered, like the former establishment at the village of 30 Decembrie (renamed 1 Decembrie) in the Bucharest suburban fringe where over 2,000 people used to be employed not only in farming (with a focus on livestock and fruit) but also in an abattoir, processing units and a network of 25 shops in the Bucharest-Giurgiu area.

Chapter Nine

Transport: Seeking Capital to Reconnect with the West

Introduction

Romania's position on the edge of Europe in close touch with the Middle East can exploited through ease of navigation involving the Black Sea and eastern Mediterranean. However, in the nineteenth century the first concern lay in overcoming Ottoman political impediments on trade with Western Europe and developing the ports of Brăila and Galați (followed by Constanța) for trade via the western Mediterranean; also improvements on the Danube (such as the Iron Gates) to develop trade with Central Europe. At the same time, the railways overcame many of the deficiencies of the rudimentary road system and also forged new international connections, while pipelines became crucial for the oil industry. In the inter-war years the roads were selectively upgraded and air services started in competition with the railways. Communism continued the momentum although not on a level commensurate with European standards that are now becoming the norm on the international routes. Moreover with road/rail disrepair an obstacle to economic development, upgrading requires private capital and international funding: €630mln annually from the EU as part of a total spending on infrastructure that should total €1.0bln in 2006 from state and private funds as part of the 2006–2008 programme covering all economic sectors. At the same time privatisation in the transport field is increasing although the picture is very varied. Air passenger transport was Tarom-dominated with 98 per cent in 1994 and 96 per cent 2003 (falling further with new low-cost airlines) while the freight level for the state fell to 30 per cent in 2000 and 9.0 per cent in 2003. Privatisation of rail passenger transport was nil until the limited leasing of 2005 while 93 per cent railfreight was still in state hands in 2003 and pipelines remain a state interest absolutely. However for road passenger transport the state's 97 per cent share in 1995 was cut to 9.0 per cent in 2003 and roadfreight has also seen rapid privatisation with the state's role cut to 25 per cent in 2000 and 5.0 per cent in 2003 (Table 9.1).

Rail and Road Transport

Historically the railways were given priority (as noted in the early chapters) and this policy was reinforced under communism given the strategic importance accorded to railways by the FSU. But now a more balanced approach is needed because while transport is fundmental for modernisation, ANDR (2000a, p. 47) refers to "an extensive and diversified transport system [that is] insufficiently developed and

Table 9.1: State and private activity in transport 1995–2005

Year	State majority interest*						Private majority interest*					
	Rail	Road	River	Sea	Air	Pipeline	Rail	Road	River	Sea	Air	Pipeline
Passenger Transport (mln.passenger/kms)												
1995	18879	12026	23	n.ap.	3215	n.ap.	0	317	1	n.ap.	200	n.ap.
1996	18356	10144	15	n.ap.	2222	n.ap.	0	2698	2	n.ap.	106	n.ap.
1997	15795	9103	14	n.ap.	1774	n.ap.	0	4428	2	n.ap.	82	n.ap.
1998	13422	5467	12	n.ap.	1776	n.ap.	0	3485	1	n.ap.	51	n.ap.
1999	12304	4390	5	n.ap.	1837	n.ap.	0	3933	6	n.ap.	50	n.ap.
2000	11632	4084	8	n.ap.	2161	n.ap.	0	3616	7	n.ap.	51	n.ap.
2001	10996	3662	9	n.ap.	1972	n.ap.	0	3411	10	n.ap.	48	n.ap.
2002	8502	1134	11	n.ap.	1778	n.ap.	0	4148	7	n.ap.	67	n.ap.
2003	8529	858	8	n.ap.	1690	n.ap.	0	8597	8	n.ap.	70	n.ap.
2004	8633	593	10	n.ap.	1437	n.ap.	5	8845	9	n.ap.	176	n.ap.
2005	7960	334	0	n.ap.	1562	n.ap.	25	11477	24	n.ap.	531	n.ap.
Freight Transport (mln.t/kms)												
2000	17982	3597	407	2151	17	1392	-	10691	2227	3666	2	0
2001	15899	2835	318	43	11	1770	203	15709	2428	1430	1	0
2002	14867	1707	574	212	10	1780	351	23643	3067	1121	1	0
2003	14647	1512	357	0	8	1590	392	29342	3164	611	1	0
2004	14262	1330	154	0	0	1898	2760	35890	4136	412	7	0
2005	12926	866	17	0	6	2211	3656	50665	5130	140	1	0

A Rail; B Road; C River; D Sea; E Air; F Pipeline

* Prior to 2000 figures were given for state, mixed and private companies. The 'mixed' category was very small and in this table has been combined with the state figures.

Source: Statistical Yearbooks: Tables 17.2 and 17.11

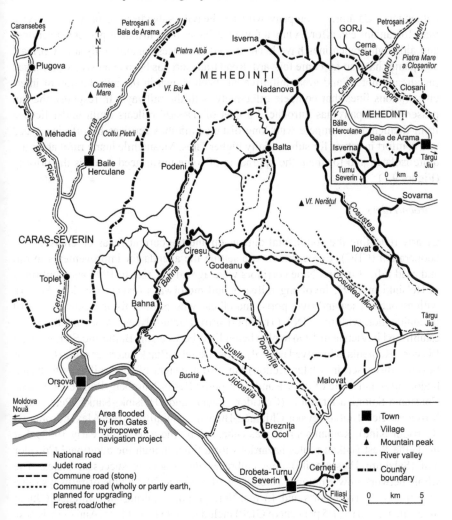

Figure 9.1 Rural road modernisation in the Mehedinţi Plateau

of poor quality" requiring substantial development to improve access to European
corridors and make the most of Romania's strategic location in Europe connected with
the Danube and the Black Sea. The railway expansion of the 1980s has not continued
(apart from the approach to Calafat bridge) partly because of a sharp decline in
traffic since 1989 but also because of the claims of the road network. Labour has
been reduced considerably and reorganisation has taken place to increase efficiency
and moderate subsidies which are still very large in the passenger domain. Since the
division of the industry into an infrastructure company and separate businesses for
freight and passengers a major contrast has emerged between the freight company –
'Marfa' – which is profitable and can cope with competition from private companies
(indeed it is in line for privatisation to secure capital for new locomotives needed
when EU state railway systems are opened to foreign competition) and the

passenger – Călători – company which is heavily subsidised to provide a service that Romanians can afford. Only a few lines have so far lost their passenger services and although branchlines have been offered to concessionaires only a few private companies have so far come forward. Road transport has been extensively privatised (as already noted) and great initiative has been shown in the introduction of inter-city minibus lines that compete effectively with the railways. In response the rail passenger company has introduced a fleet of 'Desiro' railcars (built under licence from Siemens) to compete with long-distance minibus services by offering speed and comfort in return for substantially higher fares. Meanwhile many rural areas are quite isolated and for them the upgrading of some unsurfaced roads is the priority (Figure 9.1).

Eurocorridors

Clearly reflecting the continental dimension and the current focus on cross-border cooperation (CBC), Eurocorridors are setting the agenda for improvements in rail and road infrastructure. Nine corridors were agreed at Crete in 1994 and confirmed at Helsinki in 1997; involving railways and motorways (except Corridor Seven), with associated sea and river ports, and all carrying priority for upgrading by 2010 in conjunction with the TINA (Transport Infrastructure Needs Assessment) Group established in Vienna in 1996 to plan better links between the Baltic and ECE with the EU core. Romania is involved not only in the Danube-Black Sea river route (Corridor Seven – discussed in a later section) but also a system of road-rail axes featuring major cities and some of the sea and river ports: Berlin/Nürnberg-Prague-Budapest-Constanţa-Salonika-Istanbul (Corridor Four) and Helsinki-Sankt Petersburg-Moscow-Kiev-Liubashevska-Chişinău-Bucharest-Dimitrovgrad-Alexandroupolis (Corridor Nine). Romania's role was enhanced by the wars in the early 1990s that made the West Balkan routes hazardous for a time; though the additional Corridor Ten (Salzburg-Thessaloniki) now embraces the Yugoslav successor states. The whole network now embraces 18,030kms of road and 20,290kms of railways (also 38 airports, 49 river ports and 13 maritime ports); requiring an estimated €90bln investment to 2015 (1.5 per cent of GDP) including help from Phare. And there is now a trend for renewed integration through space development policies in the Central European, Danubian and Adriatic areas – including transport and urban infrastructure – to safeguard the natural/cultural heritage and reduce regional differences.

The Caucasus and Central Asia
The scope of international planning has also been extended to integrate with the maritime basins of the Adriatic Sea, the Barents-Arctic, the Black Sea and the Mediterranean. In Romania's case the Black Sea traffic to the Caucasus, Central Asia and the Middle East is handled by the ferry services to such ports at Batumi, Izmir, Poti and Samsun; taking account of independence for the former Soviet states of the Caucasus and Central Asia and the consequent extension of the European system by the 'Transport Corridor Europe-Caucasus-Central Asia' (TRACECA) which embraces the Black Sea routes (e.g. Constanţa to Poti), as well as the 'Logistic Express Railway' between the Black and Caspian seas (operational in 1997):

the Baku-Turkmenbashi (Turkmenistan), the ferry across the Caspian and the land routes to Uzbekistan and Kazakhstan. In the late 1990s President Constantinescu strongly supported this revival of the 'Silk Road' given the potential for trade in hydrocarbons, oil equipment, grain and other foodstuffs, with Romania well-placed through Constanţa port and free zone (chosen as the terminus for Corridors Four and Seven) as well as combined transport services and a long-established oil industry (Celac 1998). Although it is at present inconceivable that the EU will expand far into this region – apart from endeavours to support democracy in Georgia and Ukraine – and that Russian influence will be eclipsed, there is nevertheless a logic behind Black Sea integration that could lead to an energy ring (involving Romania's Cernavodă nuclear power station) – linked with the trans-European energy network – and an optical fibre line connecting Istanbul, Varna, Constanţa and Chişinău, as well as better links between the major Black Sea cities in which the private airlines could find a role. Economic support is available through the Black Sea Trade & Development Bank created 1996 by the 11 member states as a regional development finance institution, backed up by promised financial reforms in 2000 to achieve convertibility and repatriation of profits. This all gives Romania a potentially strong regional role on the basis of its own experience in rehabilitating public services, developing the labour market through training and retraining, improving the tourism and business infrastructures, investing in R&D, technology transfer, higher education units, and the ITC and multimedia infrastructure.

A Balanced Investment Programme
This is now essential in the light of Romania's strategic location in Europe (connected with the Danube and the Black Sea) and to provide reasonable equality in terms of accessibility to national and international networks for all cities and regions, since poor roads are often cited as a main reason why investors are discouraged. Although statistics point to an extensive network with a high level of modernisation (Table 9.2) this does not adequately meet the needs of the current transition. The task is essentially one of upgrading existing facilities. However, the new Calafat-Vidin bridge over the Danube will provide another north-south international route of particular importance to the Jiu Valley that will be directly served by one of the main feeder routes (coming from Deva and Târgu Jiu). It is expected that the Calafat bridge will also be the centrepiece of an association for economic, social and cultural CBC projects in the Serbian district of Zaječar as well as the adjacent areas of Bulgaria and Romania. Additional ferries at Călăraşi and Turnu Măgurele will also contribute to CBC , while a further bridge over the Prut at Dărăbani will increase cohesion within the Euroregion covering territories in Romania and Moldova. Furthermore although Corridors Four and Nine will make use of existing roads and railways in crossing Romania upgrading roads to motorway standard will require much new construction on modified alignments and the decision to link the two corridors between Braşov and Focşani involves major reconstruction of a Carpathian road. Transylvanian politics make it inconceivable that Timişoara and Arad should have motorway access to Hungary before Cluj-Napoca and Oradea and so – as in the railway age – the motorway from Bucharest to Braşov, Cluj and Oradea is going ahead simultaneously with the extension of the Bucharest-Piteşti motoway to Sibiu,

Table 9.2: Road transport 1985–2005

Year	A	B	C	D	E	F	G	H	I	J	K	L	M
1985	n.a.	n.a.	n.a.	n.a.	n.a.	n.a.	n.a.	n.a.	n.a.	21.7	38.5	27.9	25.5
1986	n.a.	n.a.	n.a.	n.a.	n.a.	n.a.	n.a.	n.a.	n.a.	22.3	38.4	30.4	25.8
1987	n.a.	n.a.	n.a.	n.a.	n.a.	n.a.	n.a.	n.a.	n.a.	22.4	37.5	29.6	25.3
1988	n.a.	n.a.	n.a.	n.a.	n.a.	n.a.	n.a.	n.a.	n.a.	23.0	37.2	29.8	24.8
1989	n.a.	n.a.	n.a.	n.a.	n.a.	n.a.	n.a.	n.a.	n.a.	23.1	37.0	30.0	24.7
1990	14.7	98.2	58.1	39.1	24.3	4.0	258.7	1.29	311.6	24.0	41.3	29.0	31.0
1991	14.7	98.4	58.1	39.5	25.2	6.0	259.6	1.43	315.5	20.8	42.5	20.7	34.1
1992	14.7	98.4	58.1	39.4	26.8	8.2	275.5	1.59	322.8	25.6	48.7	15.7	35.4
1993	14.7	98.5	58.1	39.7	28.1	9.6	293.8	1.79	326.5	20.5	48.0	15.4	35.2
1994	14.7	98.5	58.1	40.0	28.9	11.2	322.4	2.02	325.7	14.1	39.1	18.3	36.9
1995	14.7	98.5	58.2	40.4	30.4	11.7	343.1	2.20	327.7	12.3	35.6	19.7	40.8
1996	14.7	98.6	58.5	40.7	27.4	12.1	376.8	2.33	256.0	12.8	38.3	19.8	45.1
1997	14.7	98.7	58.5	41.2	27.4	12.5	390.2	2.45	250.5	13.5	43.4	21.7	39.0
1998	14.7	98.7	58.6	41.6	27.4	13.0	405.7	2.59	245.7	9.0	37.0	15.8*	43.0
1999	14.7	98.7	58.7	41.6	27.3	13.3	417.8	2.70	242.6	8.3	36.9	13.5*	40.6
2000	14.8	98.5	63.7	39.0	27.2	13.5	427.2	2.78	239.2	7.7	35.9	14.3*	41.3
2001	14.8	98.5	63.7	39.3	27.0	13.8	438.0	2.88	237.9	7.1	35.2	18.5*	41.2
2002	14.8	98.7	64.1	39.5	26.7	14.1	447.3	2.97	238.5	7.0	40.3	25.3*	47.3
2003	15.1	98.5	63.9	39.5	25.8	16.1	463.1	3.09	235.9	9.4	47.8	30.9*	55.1
2004	15.7	98.3	63.7	40.2	25.4	17.8	482.4	3.23	234.7	9.4	47.9	37.2*	61.6
2005	15.9	98.1	64.0	41.3	22.0	17.3	493.8	2.36	197.4	11.8	53.9	51.5*	68.3

A National roads (th.km); B Ditto: percentage modernised including a light asphalt surface; C County and commune roads (th.km); D Ditto: percentage modernised including a light asphalt surface; E Number of buses (th); F Number of minibuses (th); G Number of trucks (th); H Number of cars (mln); I Number of motorcycles/bicycles (th); J Passenger-kms.(bln); K Ditto: percentage of all passenger transport; L Road freight (bln.t/kms): * denotes a new methodology preventing comparability with earlier figures ; M Ditto: percentage of all freight transport (excluding sea transport).

Source: Statistical Yearbooks: Tables 17.1, 17.12 and 17.13

Deva, Timişoara, Arad and Nădlac. For the railway the need for double track will create problems between Orşova and Drobeta-Turnu Severin where the foundations of the stilts and viaducts supporting the realigned single track railway were flooded by the rising river level (following implementation of the Iron Gates hydropower project) and another line may have to negotiate the mountains to the north. It is also possible that the Vâlcele-Râmnicu Vâlcea project (almost completed under communism) could be required to carry freight traffic so as to reserve the Predeal route for high-speed running. The total investment required is ernormous and a start is being made with the help of the banks (including JBIC) and EU ISPA funding. At the same time connecting roads and railways need attention as finance allows but Romania does have the support of a World Bank Transport Restructuring Project (2000–2009) concerned with the effectiveness of the National Motorway & National Roads Organisation; also the commercialisation of railways and completion of an integrated railway information system (IRIS).

Progress in Highway Construction By the end of 2007 there should be 298kms of motorways on the the the routes Bucharest-Piteşti, Bucharest-Cernavodă and from Adunaţii-Copăceni to Giurgiu. This network should increase to 1,800kms in 2013 including the 42km Bucharest-Ploieşti highway started in 2007 at Moara Vlasiei by a Romanian consortium involving UMB Spedition, Pa&CoInternational and Eurotrading Construct. This will divide at Ploieşti with one route to Moldavia and another – the Transilvania Motorway – to the frontier at Borş near Oradea (526kms). In view of the difficult section in the upper Prahova valley between Comarnic and Predeal (costing €1.3bln alone) – and the level of progress currently being made by the Bechtel company in Cluj county at the time of writing – completion in 2013 seems uncertain. The route across Transylvania will be relatively direct running from Braşov close to Făgăraş, Sighişoara, Târgu Mureş, Câmpia Turzii, Cluj, Zalău and Oradea. The extension of the existing Cernavodă and Piteşti motoways to Constanţa and Nădlac respectively will create another 224kms of new road with the Nădlac-Arad section scheduled for 2010. The Piteşti-Sibiu route is problematic because the EU is not happy about funding a motorway on this section and a concession arrangement may be necessary. Meanwhile the Moldavian road to the Moldovan frontier at Albiţa may be not be built to full motoway standard beyond Focşani initially given the current traffic. The final element in the picture is a link between Târgu Mureş, Piatra Neamţ and Roman (230kms). Motorway taxes will be imposed at a rate of some five new lei/ 100kms (below the general level of seven to eight in the West). The new roads are very necessary in view of the delays for transit traffic in negotiating town centres. Truck companies in Timişoara say the cost of getting across the city is equivalent to 40kms of normal driving. However the shortage of construction workers is limiting progress with Bechtel 1,500 workers short of the 3,400 they require (with particular problems over the skilled/key workers and local managers). The search is on in the surrounding counties of Alba, Bihor, Cluj and Sălaj as well as other parts of Romania – and even among some unemployed in Hungary. The problem is a source of some irritation in government when annual allocations are not fully taken up (only €50mln of €78mln allocated in 2006) and regrets the lack of penalty clauses for late completion.

Cost is also an issue which prevented faster progress in the past. €12.8bln is needed for the present seven-year programme of 1,800kms to be shared equally between the national budget and other sources (EU funds, banks and concessionaires). However there is no doubt that business will be transformed through a new generation of commercial complexes. ProLogis of Denver (USA) – the world's largest owner and developer of distribution facilities – are starting with the 8.0mln.sq.m ProLogis Park for distribution firms operating on the Piteşti motorway (14kms from the centre of Bucharest): two tenants are already taking up space including 10,700sq.m by Kuehne & Nagel for local and regional distribution. Under a longer-plan which may take half a century to complete a more northerly west-east route is planned from Petea through Satu Mare, Baia Mare, Dej, Bistriţa and Vatra Dornei to Suceava besides the roads between Braşov, Târgu Secuiesc and Focşani and from Târgu Mureş to Roman; also the further ramifications connected with Corridor Four: Arad-Deva (direct); Arad-Oradea; Cluj-Sebeş and Făgăraş-Sibiu. Meanwhile many existing roads need overhaul including the Transfăgăraş road from Curtea de Argeş to the Făgăraş and Sibiu areas: liable to lengthy closures due to snow and also dangerous due to a cratered surface and the risk of roof falls in the summit tunnel. A new Carpathian road is being built to connect Băile Herculane with Petroşani as part of a programme of regional development measures to boost the depressed Jiu valley coal mining region around Petroşani. Conflict with wild animal movements in the southern part of the Retezat National Park will be solved by means of a viaduct, following pressure from Greenpeace.

Ports and Shipping

Traditional export staples boosted the importance of the leading ports through the last century, but the renewed growth under communism has hinged on the diversification of exports and the growth of imports to sustain the industrialisation programme. Capacities increased and integrated river-ocean shipping became available not only through the Danube delta but the Danube-Black Sea Canal (DBSC) as well. There was a sharp decline in the 1990s first through a highly-controversial privatisation of the merchant fleet involving sales abroad. Corona Shipping International negotiated prices from the SOF for four ore carriers in addition to settling Petromin's bank debts that had caused the ships to be tied up as security. There was a desire in 1998 to set up a new national shipping company, involving operational vessels drawn from the present shipping companies – mainly Navrom and Romline – all in a precarious economic situation. With a total marchant fleet of 163 vessels in 1998 (1.45mln.dwt), separate sectors for trade, containers and passenger transport were considered. The fishing fleet also experienced problems with 51 per cent of Ocean Fisheries acquired by Greek investors in 1997 and saved from bankruptcy. Vessels laid up in the Danube and also at Midia were scrapped but others were repaired and put back into service with those still working. However, the main focus in this section is on the ports: both the seaports – dominated by Constanţa but complemented by two others on the Black Sea coast (Mangalia and Sulina) as well as Tulcea, Galaţi and Brăila on the lower reaches of the Danube – and the numerous Danube river ports. During the recession years it was not without significance that the separate counties of Brăila, Constanţa, Galaţi and Tulcea were all supporting the ports in their respective county towns which all acquired free zones, along with the small port of Sulina in the Danube delta and the river port of Giurgiu, located south of Bucharest. Meanwhile all the maritime and river ports have needed repair and modernisation.

Constanţa

Constanţa has been prominent ever since the Bucharest railway link was completed in 1895 followed by the Istanbul cable in 1905 amd the opening of the northern harbour, designed (like the Danube railway bridge) by A.Saligny. Further enlargement followed the plan of 1934 and went a stage further under communism. Rail routes multiplied although the primacy of the Bucharest link – now widened to two tracks and electrified – was maintained in view of the failure to complete the line through the Buzău valley to Braşov. Meanwhile road links have improved through the bridging of the Danube at Giurgeni-Vadu Oii in 1970 and then the duplication of the railway bridge in 1987 to provide the basis for the present motorway route. However, port traffic slumped with the economic decline of the 1990s while the Danube waterway was closed for a time by the NATO bombing campaign (linked with the Kosovo War) when fallen bridges blocked the river at Novi Sad and limited traffic to 23–24mln.t/yr (50 per cent transit traffic) during 1996–2001. But recovery is now underway in what is one of the largest Black Sea ports with an area of 3,626ha and an annual capacity of 85mln.t. Firmly linked with Central/Eastern European trade with Asia, it is also a key port in the context of the combined transport TRACECA corridor given the ferry link with Georgia. The route should see a great increase in hydrocarbon movements from the Caspian (delivering an anticipated 100mln.t of oil to Europe by 2010) on top of the trade in grain, cotton and oilfield equipment – not to mention trade with China by an alternative overland route to the Trans-Siberian. American businessmen are in Constanţa, responding to Romanian proposals for a Constanţa-Trieste pipeline via Serbia, Croatia and Slovenia which will now go ahead after agreement was signed in 2006 (despite US preference for a route through southern Hungary to Croatia at the time of the Kosovo War). Constanţa already has pipelines to oil refineries with 32mln.t capacity.

Development at Constanţa began with Saligny's northern port: originally a quay with landing depth of 8.28m. Traffic of 1.4mln.t in 1911–12 rose to 6.4mln in 1934 and 8.9mln in 1966. Expansion turned southwards in 1962. The old port covered 722ha and 84 docks, with an annual operating capacity of 78mln.t (40 per cent for oil and by-products). Vessels of 200,000dwt can be accommodated in the sea sector compared with only 5,000dwt in the river sector. There are specialised zones for oil and petrochemicals, cereals, minerals, steel, fertilisers and general merchandise; also a 110,000sq.m container terminal with annual traffic of 66,000t and Ro-Ro equipment. Further port development occurred at South Constanţa, from 1976 for ships of up to 250,000dwt – extended to Agigea in connection with the new DBSC. The total port area is 2,460ha with 42,880sq.m of covered space, 84,085sq.m of uncovered space and 120,000sq.m. of docks, with 14.5–19.0m depth at the quays (the greatest available on the Black Sea). Midia, with its own DBSC link, comprises 370ha of land and a basin of 290ha enclosed by two breakwaters (total length 6,800m). 1,415m of quays provide seven berths with 8.0–9.0m depth. There is rail and road access; also a shipyard – with floating docks, quays and cranes – for repairs to vessels of up to 5.5m draught and 65,000dwt. Midia's 2.0mln. t capacity is closely related to the local petrochemical complex and Fertilchim chemical fertiliser complex at Năvodari, based on phosphorous, sulphur, ashes and fluor (though it needs new technology and is looking for a foreign partner).

Rehabilitation
The operating company was privatised in 1997 and rehabilitation is proceeding with seawall extensions (5,900m in the north and 5,560m in south) to reduce the effect of waves within the port, though the project was interrupted in 1989 through lack of funds. Repairs have been needed following the collision that led to the sinking of 'Xou-Xiu' and 'Paris' early in 1995. In that year there were calls by 4,261 ships: 2,250 cargo ships, 724 bulk carriers (solid), 472 bulk carriers (liquid), 244 Ro-Ro vessels and 571 port containers. Constanţa had the lowest charges among Black Sea ports in 2003, though piloting and tugging costs are relatively high. A passenger terminal feasability study has been carried out, given the Istanbul service and the possibility of attracting cruise ships. The Neptun IT system at Constanţa port – considered one of the most complex in Romania – deals with shipping movements in the port. There is also a feasibility study for 26.7MW of wind-powered generating capacity in 2002. Japan is participating heavily in the port's modernisation: a Japanese expert drew up the master plan and $200mln has been promised by the JBIC: 75 per cent for the container base (with confinancing by EIB and Phare) costing a total of $154mln in 1997; also for a 1.0km breakwater extension and terminals for cereals and LPG (both by the Romanian-Austrian Company ARTS).

Specialised Facilities
Hydrocarbons are catered for by an oil terminal handling crude oil, black fuel (for power stations) petroleum and petochemicals; serving the users of imported crude oil, foreign oil companies and exporters like Lukoil (who intend to export half the production of their Petrotel refinery) and the Oltchim petrochemical complex. The oil terminal storage is 1,740cu.m, divided between the north (with a depth of 11.5-13.5m for ships up to 80,000dwt) and the south (19.9m for vessels of up to 150,000) and annual capacity is 30.0mln.t. There is also an LPG terminal of 850,000t built at Midia by Sumitomo (Japan) leading an international consortium: gas can be transferred from ships to the pipeline system. For agricultural products there is the largest storage facility for cotton in Europe. And a modern cereal terminal with a capacity of 3.9mln.t – one of the largest on the Black Sea – has been opened at a cost of €80-100mln. Grain is expected to comprise a fifth of port traffic in future with an expansion of exports from Hungary and Serbia as well as Romania (though it could also serve Bulgaria and Ukraine). South Constanţa container terminal has been constructed by Mitsubishi and local partners for the start of operations in 2004. It comprises 11.4ha with a capacity of 337,000 containers growing to 1.0mln (greatly extending the capacity of some 50,000 containers provided by two older facilities operated by Socep and Umex).

The auction for operational control realised bids of \$2.2–5.8mln/yr with Japanese and South Korean companies overtaken by Spain's Gruppo Dragados. Container ships of up to 25,000dwt can be accommodated and services include the Constanţa-China container line by 'Ukraine' (Levant Maritime Services). Maersk Logistics Romania (part of Denmark's Moller Group) started container transport operations for CEE in 2002. Containers are a major factor in the upward growth of port traffic with a seven-fold increase predicted for 2001-14 on the basis of services for Bulgaria and Serbia as well as Romania. Finally, Romtrans have a large facility for transfers from sea-going ships to canal, road or rail transport at the mouth of the DBSC. Reference should be made to the local free trade zone (Constanţa/Basarabi) encouraging investment through fiscal advantages. Industrial activities include the Dutch Van Gulik company's project to assemble engine components brought from The Netherlands that started in 2001. The latest plans envisage a 100ha artificial island at the southern edge of the port for more commercial space; also redevelopment of old silos and warehouses for new business including hotels, restaurants and shops.

Other Black Sea Ports (including the Danube Delta)

Mangalia is a specialised port for general goods covering 170ha of which 120ha comprises the harbour basin enclosed by 3,000m of breakwaters. There are 400m of quays with a depth of 9.0m and maximum capacity is 10,000dwt. It has rail and road access; also two dry docks (624x58m) for building ships of up to 55,000dwt and repairs of up to 150,000dwt (there is a also a 360x60m dry dock for repairs of ships to 300,000dwt). The annual operating capacity of 400,000t can be extended to 1.0mln. Additional rail capacity could be provided by the projected doubling of the Constanţa electrified railway. In the case of Tulcea and Sulina the county authorities sought backing for their ports from Ceauşescu in the communist era. A free port was established at Sulina in 1978 comprising a small basin with 7.0m depth separate from the small riverside facility for passengers and general cargo. Tulcea presided over a massive programme for agriculture and forestry in the delta, coupled with sand quarrying at Caraorman and the regularisation of the sinuously-winding Sfântu Gheorghe channel. However, it is difficult to see great potential for Sulina because, although trans-shipment to river barges can be accomplished, the town is small and isolated with problems regarding limited draught. The 100ha free zone provides for shipping and storage with a basin for sea-going and river ships (maximum depth 7.0m) as well as 5,000sq.m of warehousing, although it would be beneficial if the zone included the cannery (arousing investor interest) where a section was modernised to meet export demand in 1996. At Tulcea the industrial port has 230m of quays embracing a river component where a depth of 3.0m and capacity of 3.0mln.t contrasts with 7.5m for the maritime section needed for ores such as bauxite – brought in carriers of up to 25,000dwt – where annual capacity is 1.04mln.t. There is also a commercial river port with 3.0-3.5m depth and capacity of 0.85mln.t and an ocean fishing base for vessls of up to 8,000dwt with 360m of quayage, a depth of 5.5m and annual capacity of 0.2mln.t A ferry service from Reni (Ukraine) began operating to Istanbul via Tulcea in 2003.

Galaţi and Brăila

Galaţi and Brăila are both river and seaports with transfer facilities and developed in close proximity to serve the principalities of Moldavia and Wallachia respectively, with particular dynamism after 1829 when the Ottoman trade monopoly was broken. At the time Dobrogea remained an integral Ottoman province and the only direct contact with the Black Sea was through the Danube. Both ports grew rapidly after the railway arrived in 1872 but limits were imposed by the draught of only 10m downstream. They enjoyed free port status until 1883: Brăila from 1836 and Galaţi from 1837; while Galaţi also headquartered the European Danube Commission during 1856-1945 (and currently the the the port administration for the martime Danube – Hârşova to Crişan – set up as a national company in 1998 and restructured in 2003). With a special function for timber exports, the main development occurred at Galaţi during 1877-91 under A.Saligny's plan for a basin with quays, docks, stores and silos. Presently there are 6.3kms of quays in a basin of more than 100ha where activity grew substantially with the opening of the metallurgical complex. Brăila port, specialising historically in cereals (with a commodity exchange for cereals opened in 1882) is somewhat smaller but can accommodate ships of 6,000dwt. Modernisation took a similar path to Galaţi but started rather later in 1886 according to a plan by Gh.Duca. A small industrial port was built at Chişcani to the south in the communist period mainly to serve a cellulose factory and power station. Galaţi is also an important ship-builder (including ore carriers of up to 55,000dwt) while Brăila has a ship repair yard. Both ports have become free zones.

The Current Situation

Today's Galaţi port comprises first the old quays and basin (presently berths 17–32) with a depth of 7.3m and 1,150m of quayage, used for passengers and general cargo. Second there is a new basin used for timber and some metallurgical products with 1,010m of quays, a depth of 7.3m and a capacity (including the older facilities) of 2.4mln.t. To this may be added a downsteam section (berths 36–53) with 840m of quayage, a depth of 7.5m and a capacity of 3.7mln.t. Finally the mineral port (berths 1–16) built by Romportmet started with 100m of quays in 1975: it handles ore and coke for the metallurgical works, with which it is linked by conveyor belt. Now there are 920m of quays, a depth of 7.3m and accommodation for 25,000dwt vessels with 2.2mln.t capacity, although a navigable channel from the Danube to Sidex was opened in 1996. Galaţi also has its shipyard building vessels of up to 65,000dwt. Meanwhile Brăila port consists of the historic quays and basin with 4,225m of quays, a depth of 6.3–7.5m and 2.8mln.t capacity, while the industrial port offers 350m of quays and a depth of 6.3m. Berth capacity is 190,000t for general goods or 350,000 for bulk cargoes. Total traffic (including Tulcea and small ports like Chilia, Măcin and Sfântu Gheorghe) is estimated at 15.70mln.t for 2005 of which 14.30 is river traffic and only 1.40 maritime (Galaţi should account for 10.20mln.t – 9.60 river traffic and 0.60 maritime). The two ports can be used for trans-shipment from sea-going ships to river barges and they have good rail facilities with an electrified link to the Constanţa system at Făurei. There are plans for a container terminal at Brăila while Galaţi is refurbishing berths (18–21 in the older part and 35–44 in the newer part) using the 'vertical quay solution' to increase operating capacity and shorten turnaround time, with the intention of concentrating more on cereals in future (according to the National Infrastructure Development Programme – NIDP – of 1999). There is also silt to be cleared; while a particular problem at Galaţi is the instability of some of the old quays, dating back to 1889, and two sunken vessels – the 'Transilvania' and 'Slatina' – that must be removed from the older and newer ports respectively. Environmental concerns are now receiving greater attention thanks to the Galaţi anti-pollution vessel 'Eco 2000'. Urbanproiect has been working on a development plan for the Galaţi-Brăila-Tulcea area including bridges over both the Danube (in the Brăila-Galaţi area) and the Prut (Giurgiuleşti); also ports on the Prut at Oancea and Falciu, an airport for the Brăila-Galaţi-Tuluceşti area and upgrading of the Bucharest-Făurei-Galaţi railway for high-speed running.

The Danube

Navigation from the Danube to the Black Sea was secured by the Sulina Canal in the nineteenth century and the current navigation depth of 24ft/7.3m follows the standard set at that time. But there is a current priority to strengthen the river banks against erosion and recondition the beacons (while preserving the delta's ecosystem) and increase the depth to 27ft/8.0m – using a dredger purchased in The Netherlands in 2001 – in the interest of large ships that cannot enter the DBSC. 32kms were initially improved under a €60mln programme (partly financed by an EIB credit of €38mln, with some investment from Japan) and rehabilitation has now proceeded (2001-5) on the remaining 19kms of the 51km canal. The salvage of the wreck of the 'Rostock' is also required in this section of the river. Meanwhile the extension of the dykes on either side of the navigation channel at Sulina has advanced further into the Black Sea in order to protect the dredged channel from the southward drift of sediment from the Stambul Veche section of the Chilia delta. The dykes now extend for some 10kms into the sea and are extended by some 200m each year. Dredging involves the removal of 0.6-0.8mln.t of material annually in order to maintain the movement of some 85mln.t of shipping significant for bauxite processing at Tulcea and the Galaţi metallurgical industry. However the importance of the Sulina Canal has been reduced slightly by the Romanian project during 1980s to cut through the meanders on the Sfântu Gheorghe channel to shorten the distance to the sea (although the capacity is small compared with the Sulina facility).

The Chilia Channel

The Chilia Channel was used by Ukrainian shipping until 1997, when the Prorva Canal became impassable. The Ukrainians then had to start paying some $1.0mln/yr to use the Sulina route until 2004 when a new canal opened on the Bystroye/ Bastroe arm: initially 5.8m deep for vessels of 3,500dwt, increased to 7.2m for ships of 6,200dwt in 2005. Acting in defiance of international agreements over the conservation of the Danube delta, the controversial new canal was started in May 2004 and the first part was opened after three months although work is set to continue until 2008. The work will damage a UNESCO World Heritage Area that Ukraine sanctioned only in 1998. Involving the removal of 1.5mln.cu.m of sand and mud, it is seen as the most ecologically damaging of three options to restore the link between the Chilia arm and the Black Sea without the need to use Romanian waters (the alternatives were the old navigation along the Ochakivsky Rukav and a sluiced canal further north – suggested early in the twentieth century – linking Solomonov Rukav to Zhebryanskaya Bay on the Black Sea). Ukraine now hopes to divert over half the 2,000 vessels currently using the Sulina route through lower fees of just half the 75c/cu.m of displacement levied at Sulina. When building started in 2004 (and in response to international concerns over environmental damage in the fragile delta region) the UN requested in 2006 that Ukraine should start consultations with Romania as an interested neighbour but the matter has not been considered and Ukraine's unilateral seems set to continue.

The Danube-Black Sea Canal

This canal now provides a further access to the Black Sea via the Cernavodă-Constanța route much discussed in history and achieved initially as a portage railway in 1860 (the basis for for the Bucharest-Constanța line of 1895) before a major effort to dig a canal after 1950. However the country's technical capacities were grossly overestimated and the project was abandoned after Stalin's death in 1953 under the 'new course' when Romania became solely responsible for the Sulina navigation channel through the delta (thus removing one of the major irritants which had probably triggered the scheme in the first place). However Ceaușescu decided to try again in the context of the enlarged perspectives offered by Germany's Rhine-Main-Danube Canal (finished in 1992) and the 'Europa' concept of a North Sea-Black Sea link revealed to him on visits to Western Europe. The main canal was built during 1976–84 – 70-90m wide and 7.0m deep – and involved 294mln.cu.m of excavations, mainly across the watershed (with reduced width); while the 30km branch from Poarta Albă to Midia and Luminița (L.Tașaul) followed during 1984–93 with a width of 50m and a depth of 5.5m. The canal can accommodate individual vessels of 5,000dwt (only 2,000t to Midia), length 16.8m, draught 5.5m; also lines of six 3,000t river vessels (total 18,000dwt) with a pusher of 2,400-3,200hp (but only one 3,000t barge and pusher on the branch). Ports at Basarabi (27ha for land surface and basin), Cernavodă (19ha) and Medgidia (39ha) all cater for passengers as well as grain and general cargo; also oil products at Basarabi and Cernavodă and cement and limestone at Medgidia. The canal appears to be operating profitably in the hands of a national company although traffic is reportedly constrained by high tolls: hence other means of transport may be competitive, or else the longer shipping route through delta may be taken. Annual canal capacity is 60-70mln.t but barely 10mln was being used in the mid-1990s and the present level is only some 15 per cent.

Further Improvements

These have been made to the river upstream through the hydropower and navigation schemes at Iron Gates I (above Drobeta-Turnu Severin) and Iron Gates II (Ostrov Mare), while further deepening is now needed between Brăila and Călărași (following a low river level during the 2003 drought). But navigation suffered a setback through closure in 1999 when NATO bombing of Novi Sad during the Kosovo War destroyed bridges and blocked the river. Eventually a pontoon barge bridge was lifted fortnightly – and then weekly – before the EU agreed to rebuild three bridges in 2001, with clearance of the river by four domestic enterprises and a Hungarian-Danish holding company, with transit taxes reduced from DM3/t.cap. to DM1. Reopening was then celebrated by a 'Cruises of the Danube' programme operating from May 2002, with the aim of making Romanian ports more attractive not only for Romanian cruiseships but others organised by Hapag LLoyd, Peter Deilman, Pheonix Reisen and Scylla Tours and TUI. Bolstered by the Europe-Central Asia concept, the intention of the riparian states (acting closely in concert) is to make maximum use of the Constanța-Rotterdam corridor through muilti-modal centres at the European ports, including Constanța which is one of the regional centres for the distribution of ores, coal, grain and containers. Computer-aided navigation safety systems are now available (compatible with European norms), with improved customs procedures and regulations harmonised between countries. As already noted free zones have been created to stimulate trade. Romania's river fleet has seen some modernisation. Petromin operates on the Danube with a new pusher ('Mercur') built at Oltenița according to the specification of the German authorities operating both the upper Danube and the Danube-Main-Rhine Canal. Finally it should be emphaised that Danube navigation should harmonise with the environmental concept a green corridor and most especially the protected area in the delta.

Other Developments   A canal link with Bucharest was discussed in 1880 and subsequent study in 1927 gave rise to parliamentary approval by an enabling law in 1929 but momentum was lost in the depression. There are options involving both the Dâmbovița with a port at Glina and the Argeş where the logical base would be at 1 Decembrie (formerly 30 Decembrie) just outside the railway ring in both cases. The latter option was favoured by a new study in 1982 which aimed at an integrated development of the Argeş valley for irrigation, hydropower and flood control as well as navigation. Work started in 1986 but was halted by the revolution (when 70 per cent complete) and eventually placed under a conservation régime in 1994. In 2003 there was a reference to a €450mln investment that might hopefully be completed by 2008 with the help of a Swiss consortium working with several Romanian companies. Then in 2006 the project was revived with the aim of completion in 2011 with €1.0bln of investment through a PPP in the canal and its 'noduri hidrotechnice' at Oltenița, Budeşti, Gastinari, Copăceni and Mihăileşti-Cornetu as conceived by Constantin Avadanei who was also responsible for the Danube-Black Sea Canal. It is possible that there could be more ferry traffic across the Danube in line with CBC projects, including a Lom-Rastu ferry which could attract EU support for a new port that could have a function on a north-south route between northern Europe and the Balkans. And some the Danube tributaries (in addition to the Prut) could be improved for navigation in the context of transit routes through Hungary.

Romania's River Ports
Romania's river ports vary in capacity from 1.34mln.t at Giurgiu, to 1.20 at Orşova, 0.80 at Turnu Măgurele, 0.72 at Zimnicea, 0.60 at Drobeta-Turnu Severin, 0.45 at Călăraşi and Oltenița, 0.35 at Moldova Nouă, 0.27 at Calafat and 0.10 at Drencova. The maximum size of barge than can be accommodated grades downwards from 3,000t at Turnu Severin and Orşova (with depths of 4.5m and 4.2m respectively)

to 1,500-2,000t at the others given the shallower depths of 3.5m at Giurgiu, 3.0 at Calafat, Drencova, Moldova Nouă, Olteniţa and Zimnicea and 2.8 at Călăraşi and Turnu Măgurele. The length of operating quays varies from 610m at Turnu Măgurele to 500m at Orşova, 440m at Zimnicea, 350 at Calafat and Călăraşi, 300 at Turnu Severin, Moldova Nouă and Olteniţa, 250 at Giurgiu and 190 at Drencova. Cargoes are quite diverse but timber is prominent at Drencova (traditionally raw timber from the Berzasca area) as well as Giurgiu and Turnu Măgurele, while Zimnicea handles steel and Călăraşi grain. The large metallurgical and fertiliser industries of Călăraşi and Turnu Măgurele respectively affect the traffic profiles considerably. An important development is the $75mln Giurgiu container terminal (2002) which could be implemented through partnership between the Romanian state and foreign investors during 2002–28. Moldova Nouă also has a free port project based on the berths of the copper mining enterprise: this is a local authority initiative that was supported by Germany's Nordrhein-Westfalen province in 1997. The project includes a ferry service to Serbia (complementing the link between Turnu Severin and Kladovo and the Turnu Măgurele-Nikopol ferry project of 2002 due to open in 2005). Meanwhile the Mureş could be developed through ports at Alba Iulia and Deva, while the Someş could be used by traffic heading for Dej, Jibou and Satu Mare. Most likely however is the rehabilitation of the Bega Canal originally scheduled for completion in 2005 to reconnect Timişoara directly with the Tisa and Danube. But despite engineering feasibility studies possible canal extensions along Romania's western frontier are unlikely to be realised.

Air Transport

Romania is integrated into the intricate web of European air services with a modest long-haul component and also a domestic network. In this review the emphasis is placed on Romanian airlines but it is worth summarising the situation over flights between London and Romanian airports to illustrate the extent to which the provinces are now involved. There are direct flights from London to Bucharest by British Airways and Tarom but it is also possible to travel via Amsterdam (KLM), Budapest (Malev), Munich (Lufthansa), Paris (Air France) and Vienna (Austrian Airlines). Apart from journies via Bucharest, provincial airports can be reached from London in the cases of Cluj (with British Airways and Malev via Budapest), Iaşi and Sibiu (with Austrian Airlines via Vienna) and Timişoara (with Alitalia via Milan, Austrian Airlines via Vienna, British Airways direct and Malev via Budapest). For foreign airlines there is growth, albeit in the context of a poor country with only 4.2mln tax payers in 2003. Flights are increasing and larger aircraft are being used e.g. BA is now flying an Airbus daily to Bucharest. Provincial airports are entering the picture at both ends e.g from 2005 Lufthansa offered direct flights from Bucharest to Düsseldorf as well as Frankfurt. Low cost airlines are making an appearance: Italian Volare flies to Venice six times/week from Bucharest and four from Timişoara. As regards Romanian aviation several new domestic operators have appeared, while the state company Romavia is different from Tarom in being subordinate to the defence ministry with the task of organising flights for government, the presidency and parliament. In addition to passenger services (commercial and otherwise) there is a small but dynamic air freight buisness. A new generation of dirigible airships has been developed to fly in Romania in 2004 using the UK Advanced Technologies Group 'SkyCat' design for freight transport. The Romanian partner Romaero (Ghimbav) was working in 2001 with a total of ten British and US companies and was itself responsible for design of the cargo module. Military aircraft include refurbished MiGs and Puma helicopters, while training aircraft include the GAT-II general aviation trainer sold by Enviromental Tectonics Corporation to Romtehnica (the weapons and ammunition dealer) for pilot 'spatial disorientation' training to international and NATO standards. Finally, Utility Aviation have over a hundred planes and helicopters for agricultural and tourist purposes, though demand has fallen through land restitution.

The National 'Flag-Carrying' Airline (Tarom)

Tarom was established in 1955 and in 1990 was typical of state airlines in transition states through its ageing fleet of Soviet aircraft, a proportion of non-viable 'political' destinations in its timetable and the challenge of restructuring operations on the basis of profitability. Tarom was slightly different however in already finding a significant part of its business in Western Europe and North America. Moreover it had good links with UK planemakers and included BAC 1-11 aircraft in its fleet. Nevertheless the transition required substantial adjustment and – without a development fund to restructure its fleet – the speed of renewal would have been very slow if new plane acquisitions had depended solely on the company's own revenues. Tarom therefore found itself heavily dependent on government support to cope with tough competition from western airlines enjoying significant state assistance. Further pressures arose over amortisation (which the government seeks over a relatively short period) and unfavourable exchange rates for the purchase of planes. So the airline has at times been on the verge of financial collapse; not to mention the embarrassment of stowaway passengers, luggage thefts and flying accidents – the latter including the loss of one its three Airbuses that crashed on take-off from Otopeni. Yet Tarom earns profits abroad (despite losses at home through taxation and rising fuel prices) and assistance over fleet modernisation has attracted offset agreements: up to a quarter of the value of contracts for new planes comes back to Romania as technology transfer for branches that can assimilate it and create new jobs.

Seeking Viability for Privatisation

Tarom has been forced to reduce its programme and concentrate on the most profitable routes. Long-haul flights have largely ceased in favour of a predominantly regional role. Lufthansa Consulting wanted all long-haul flights stopped in order to eliminate high stop-over/refuelling costs at Shannon on North American routes and Tashkent for Beijing. Instead virtually two-thirds of the business is based on traditional destinations, which show some expansion.The most profitable routes are those to Western Europe (especially since visa formalities have ended); less so those to former socialist countries (notwithstanding an experimental new service to Tallinn). Meanwhile, due to the economic depression domestic flights have attracted fewer passengers, giving rise to some extended flights such as Oradea-Bucharest via Satu Mare and Cluj. The low occupancy on flights from Bucharest to Maramureş and Moldavia meant that barely half the flight expenses were covered, although services to Cluj, Târgu Mureş and Timişoara did well. Withdrawal from domestic flights followed in the late 1990s when Tarom found itself without competitive aircraft. Substantial flight reductions were made during 1996-8 from 5,643 to 4,096 (-27.4 per cent) – and passengers from 738 to 535th (-27.5 per cent) – in order to convert a loss of $20.9mln to a profit of $6.8mln. But the airline is still dependent on state aid for restructuring.

Current Destinations
Initially there were more US destinations in 1998 (previously only Chicago and New York, for which flights were now increased). There were also more flights to Dubai and a weekly airbus flight to Beijing. During 2000 there were new destinations like Parma and Stockholm, although it was mainly a case of strengthening existing routes (Frankfurt, London, Paris and Vienna). Passengers rose by 25 per cent up during the early part of 2000 (over 1999) especially on European and Middle Eastern flights. But this did not secure an improved financial performance and 2001 saw suspensions and cancellations on routes to Abu Dhabi, Barcelona, Florence, Kuwait, Montreal, Stockholm and Tripoli. Also regular flights to Chicago were stopped and those to Beijing, Dublin and Riyadh reduced (London from eight flights weekly to seven). There were also efficiency savings (an on-line booking system in 2005) and deals with other airlines e.g. a Tarom-Malev accord in 2001 to avoid duplication on the Bucharest-Budapest route and shared seats on each flight (marketed in line with the commercial policies of each airline). In 2002 Tarom decided to fly to New York only and use American Airlines for transfers to other destinations including Canada. Beijing continues also as a long-courier destination. According to their map, Tarom currently operate to a range of European and Middle Eastern destinations along with New York/Chicago, Karachi/Calcutta, Dubai/Bangkok and Beijing. However the list of destinations gives only New York apart from the Middle East – Abu Dhabi, Amman, Beirut, Cairo, Damascus, Doha (Qatar), Dubai, Riyadh and Tel Aviv – and Europe: Athens, Brussels, Budapest, Chişinău, Frankfurt, Istanbul, Larnaca, London, Madrid, Milan, Munich, Nicosia, Paris, Prague, Rome, Sofia, Thessaloniki, Vienna, Warsaw and Zurich. There is also an interest in developing charter flights.

Fleet Modernisation
Modernisation was necessary to reduce the role of old aircraft with high maintenance costs and a low rate of flight safety. Three Airbus A310s were acquired in 1992 followed by five Boeing 737s in 1993-4. In 1995 there were 48 aircraft: 34 long haul (11 Boeings – five 737s, three 767s and three cargo-carrying 707s; 10 Ilyushins and Tupolevs; 10 BAC 1-11s and three Airbus A310s) plus 14 short-haul Antonovs. Six years later the fleet was entirely westernised with 16 Boeings (all 737s apart from three 767s) and two Airbus A310s (after one had been lost) with ATRs expected to replace the Antonovs. Meanwhile some old planes were put up for sale with the prospect of scrapping in the event of there being no takers: certainly there is no market for the Russian aircraft that were quickly withdrawn from international

routes, although it was thought that some might find a role in cargo or UN work. Tarom would also like a maintenance j.v. having secured international approvals for repair of all the aircraft types that it operates. As regards the westernising strategy, the Airbus 310 purchases of 1991 were regretted because of high flight costs and low performance, giving rise to the possibility of relinquishment through takeover deals with other builders: Lufthansa Consulting recommended their disposal with the elimination (or leasing) of long courier flights to concentrate on the medium-distance market. However there was interest in the Airbus 330 to replace the 310s in 2000 and four 100-seat Airbus 318s were expected for commissioning in 2004-5 (altering an agreement made in 1995-6 for two 300-seat Airbuses i.e. going for lower capacity planes to overcome losses through low occupancy). These planes are now being delivered (2006–2007) at a cost of $229mln. Meanwhile, the three BAC 1-11s still surviving in 2000 have been sold, while the Boeing fleet continues to expand through additional acquisitions under leasing contracts along with further deliveries of new aircraft after 2000. However flight reductions have reduced the new aircraft required from the eight originally ordered to the four 737-700s purchased in 2001 and 2003 (two in each case) which join the five 737-300s acquired in 1992–93, while the cargo planes were sold in 2001 and the leasing contracts were initially reduced (from five to four) and then terminated.

Domestic Routes Antonov 24s were eliminated by 1998 (withdrawn in favour of Dac Air services) with the prospect of replacement by seven 42-500 planes from ATR (Aero International Regional, acting for British Aerospace, Aerospatiale and Alenia of Italy). It seems that these planes were first sought for deliverery by 2000 for use on regional and domestic routes, following enquiries regarding the Fokker Saab 2000 (carrying 58 passengers at 675km/h) and the Dornier-328. But evidently only two were acquired initially (with their use reported on thrice-weekly services from Cluj to Vienna in 2000), followed by a €40mln financing contract for fleet rehabilitation concluded in 2000 between the government, EIB and Tarom in respect of five ATR 42-500s with Pratt & Whitney engines. With a fleet of seven ATRs, Tarom offered €10 single fares on internal flights during the winter 2004-5 from Bucharest to Arad, Bacău, Baia Mare, Oradea, Satu Mare, Sibiu, Suceava and Târgu Mureş. It is also worth noting that in 1998 10 Boeing-MacDonell Douglas helicopters were ordered to help with accident victims, the monitoring of 'certain perimeters' and to transport anti-terrorist groups.

Privatisation Prospects
Tarom is owned 92.6 per cent by the Ministry of Transport (also Romatsa 5.4 per cent, Muntenia 1.4 per cent and the Civil Aviation Authority 0.5 per cent). The company was first prepared for privatisation in 1997, leading to an updated programme in 1998 with the onset of restructuring to reduce employment, shelve uneconomic routes and rationalise the fleet. This was a time of some optimism with the transport ministry taking over the airline from SOF and offering 66 per cent of shares available for sale with 34 per cent reserved as government's 'golden share'. Tarom then became one of the 64 companies in the PSAL programme negotiated with the World Bank in 2000. A consulting contract for Tarom privatisation was drawn up by ABN AMRO bank and it

was hoped that 25–40 per cent of the stock might be sold in 2000, with optimism linked with a positive balance sheet, high class service and a modern fleet. Documentation referred to the 'spectacular development' of Tarom during 1997–2000 with ABN AMRO Corporate Finance as a strong partner. The sixth ATR 42-500 was expected early in 2000, concluding the first part of the ATR programme; while eight 737s (series 700 and 800) were to enter service later in 2000 and two Airbus 330s were to start operating in 2002, with the rest of fleet of 2000 comprising eight 737s (series 300) and three BAC 1-11s. But the business community was not convinced that the strategy was sustainable; being mindful of the fact that Romania had not yet signed up to the Open Skies Agreement and government bilateral agreements still determined who flew in and out. After drastic pruning of services there was a prospect of profitability in three years on from 2002 – with a $3mln profit expected in 2005 – the first since 1990 – instead of annual losses of $0.6mln annually. Tarom was the most punctual European carrier in 2006 with a particularly high performance for baggage delivery and the airline is responding to low-cost airlines with reductions of their own.

Private Airlines

The break-up of the Tarom monopoly led to new airlines operating with western aircraft in niche markets that included some longer-range flights (for Romanian expatriate communities in South America; also Australia and Canada) compared with Tarom's increasingly short- and medium-range activities. Jaro started in the early 1990s with two BAC 1-11 500s and two Boeing 707s. It was basically a charter airline for Germany, Italy and Scandinavia, but it started some regular flights: twice-weekly from Băneasa to London (Gatwick), offering a £160 'promotional fare', and Băneasa-Timişoara-Düsseldorf. In 1996 services were extended to Catania and Köln; also to Montreal and Toronto. The company poached Tarom crew and technicians by offering better conditions but got into trouble in Canada in 1998-9 over unauthorised flights taking lobsters to Belgium and Spain while licensed as a charter operator between Romania and Canada. Then Dac Air started in 1996 with Bombardier (Canada) De Havilland Dash eight-seaters on domestic flights: initially to Timişoara/ Oradea, then to Cluj, Constanţa and Iaşi and finally to a total of 12 sites: generating competition for Tarom who agreed to transfer to all their rights to domestic and regional routes later in the year. Dac Air also obtained four Canadian Regional Jet Series (CRJ) 200 aircraft from Bombardier – plus an initial order for 16 more planes of both types – for flights to to 20 international destinations including Bologna (from Bucharest), Budapest (from Timişoara), Istanbul (from Bucharest and Constanţa), Munich (from Timişoara) and Venice (from Bucharest and Timişoara); while a feeder service from Cluj to Timişoara gives connections for Budapest, Munich and Venice. Other destinations are Athens, Thessaloniki and the Black Sea coast.

The Romanian-Swiss company Carpatair was started in Bucharest 1999 by a pilot with business and legal backing to exploit a regional niche market, starting with a route to Treviso. But the company moved to Timişoara – selected for its infrastructure and potential as a hub of regional importance – and now there are 12 Saab aircraft (six 340s and six 2000s) operating domestic flights to Bacău, Constanţa, Iaşi, Oradea, Sibiu and Târgu Mureş connecting with international routes to Germany (Düsseldorf, Munich and

Stuttgart), Hungary (Budapest), Italy (charters to Ancona, Bergamo, Bologna, Florence, Naples, Rome, Treviso, Turin and Verona) and Moldova (Chişinău). Passenger numbers are expected to grow to 100,000 2002 and 300,000 in 2007. Its return fare of 701 new lei for Timişoara-Bucharest return was highly competitive compared with Tarom's 810. Carpatair is now experimenting with flights from Craiova where Tarom recently failed to make an impact but it remains to be seen if this will offer any advantage over Timişoara. Angel Airlines started in 2001 and flies ex-British Airways Jetstream planes from Băneasa to a range of domestic airports: initially Baia Mare and Iaşi but now Arad, Constanţa, Oradea, Satu Mare, Suceava and Târgu Mureş as well (some on a codeshare basis with Tarom). There are also international routes from Bucharest to Tirana (to be extended to Bari), Bucharest to Craiova and Rimini (planned) and Constanţa to Istanbul. There are several other companies that require a brief mention: Laro started with a Bucharest-Izmir flight with Ljubljana, Skopje, Tirana and Zagreb as destinations to follow; Acvila Air flies to Ukraine in cooperation with Air Ukraine; while Airom provides tourist charters to the Eastern Mediterranean. Finally, Tiriac Air competes in the charter market averaging one flight daily - usually to Milan, Moscow, Nice, Paris or Vienna with Gulfstream and Boeing planes plus a Bell helicopter.

Low-cost Blue Air started 2004 with two Boeing 737-300 aircraft (with a third in 2005) flying from Băneasa to Barcelona, Lyon, Milan-Bergamo and Timişoara for €19 return. Although the company gained a reputation for delayed flights (especially among 'strawberry pickers' in Barcelona) it has established itself – with flights to Lyon, Maastricht and Rome as well – and was the leading low-cost operator in 2006 with 400,000 passengers. Meanwhile Volare-backed MyAir attracted 220,000 passengers to their low-cost flights from Bucharest to Milan and Venice in 2006 and hope to double the number in 2007 with additional services to France and Spain in competition with Tarom. Other foreign companies are also active with Clickair (Spain), Wizz Air (Hungary) and SkyEurope (Slovakia – based in Bratislava, Budapest, Warsaw and Kraków from 2001) poised to begin operations in Romania in 2006: Wizz Air have started a Târgu Mureş-Budapest service (followed in 2007 with services to Barcelona, Luton and Rome; also from Bucharest Băneasa to these same destinations plus Dortmund, Palma and Valencia) and Sky Europe launched a Bratislava-Bucharest-Sofia service charging €14 for the cheapest tickets (but €50-108 for returns) with a shuttle-bus connection to Vienna. Skye operate a fleet of 737s and hope to make Băneasa its sixth hub (after Prague and the four mentioned above) offering new servivces to Budapest and Rome while other destinations (Dublin, London, Manchester, Milan and Paris) and under study. But it was reported at the end of 2006 that the authorities had withdrawn the flight rights of Spain's Air Madrid (Bucharest-Barcelona) and Italy's Club Air connecting Bucharest, Bacău, Timişoara and Cluj with Ancona, Bari, Bologna, Florence and Verona. With the 'Open Skies' régime now operating – enabling any operator will be able to fly to Romania – Germanwings (the low cost division of Lufthansa) – is flying to Romania and Easyjet plan a Băneasa-Milan route. Moreover, Romania has reached an FAB (functional airspace block) agreement with Bulgaria based on the complementarity of the facilities in Bucharest and Sofia; enhancing safety (for Sofia has installed the SATCAS air control system by Alenia Marconi of Italy) while making more effective use of infrastructure in line with the EU 'Single European Sky' concept. It is hoped that other SEECs will join.

Airports

Improvements are a priority at the three 'international' airports in Bucharest, Constanţa and Timişoara controlled by the Ministry of Transport and 13 domestic airports (plus four new projects: Alba Iulia, Bistriţa, Braşov and Galaţi) with administration transferred from an independent corporation for regional airports to county councils in 1998. The latter now have the potential to operate as regional airports, enjoying funding under regional development programmes. At the same time it was suggested in 2000 (by the transport minister, perhaps as a regional development initiative) that Bacău, Iaşi and Suceava should become international airports and Iaşi at least appears to be rising to the challenge.

Bucharest: Otopeni and Băneasa
Named after Romania's most famous aviator Henri Coanda, Otopeni airport was opened under communism to allow the older congested facilities at Băneasa to be geared to domestic traffic, with large aircraft also kept well away from the city centre. The original terminal building has been upgraded, with €280mln invested during 1994–2000 in expansion including a new departure terminal and a second runway to strengthen its role as as a transit hub for Asia-Europe links with some 3.0mln passengers annually. The British Airport Group – representing firms active in airport development – is hoping to share in the work connected with a further €650mln programme for growth extending to 2020 over 600ha including four new modules (for a total of 80 gates). For long constrained by the power of taxi drivers, the airport has now improved its public transport provision (with the prospect since 2000 of a Japanese-financed Otopeni-Băneasa roadside monorail) and road-rail information, while local commercial growth includes a four star transit hotel. However a mainline rail connection is now expected as well as a metro service that will be accommodated at a new multi-level facility. It has also started to handle some internal flights due to sound pollution problems at Băneasa in 2000 and a modern air freight centre has been built by Bucharest International Cargo Centre: a multi-modal cargo platform with an annual capacity of 30,000t and new road connections in 2001. Delamode (UK) are operating a 3,000sq.m airfreight platform integrated with their seafreight and European road services. The MacDonnell Douglas MD11 Combi seems the most likely cargo transport plane but a high level of efficiency will be needed to cope with stiff competition from KLM and Lufthansa. The fuel situation is being improved by Romanian Fuelling Service – a Romanian-British j.v. involving BP that will also operate at Băneasa, Constanţa and Timişoara – involving new equipment by BP to reduce costs and refuelling time: the monopoly of Romarc Fuel will be broken and Tarom's heavy fuel costs (40 per cent of the company's total expenses) will be reduced by a quarter. Shell have invested in a 14,000sq.m aviation fuel depot (14,000sq.m facility) while also funding an upgrade at Petrobrazi refinery. The airport will remain under state control although 15 per cent of the shares are to be sold. Meanwhile Băneasa became known as an international airport in 1998, with passenger and freight facilities and daily charter flights to Trieste. However a foreign investor was needed to supplement modest improvements such as traffic surfaces and the rehabilitation of beacons with new terminals and hangars, cargo handling and runway extensions. Given the rapid growth of the area Băneasa has

limited potential and the planning process is aiming at a new airport on the south side of the city (possibly near the motorway intersection at Adunaţii-Copăceni).

Provincial Airports: Constanţa and Timişoara
Constanţa (Mihail Kogălniceanu) airport is under the transport ministry and is being upgraded after many years of heavy use as an important destination for tourist charters. Likewise Timişoara's Traian Vuia airport has grown very rapidly since 1989 in sympathy with the city's business fortunes. A modernisation for 2002–2015 is being financed by the ministry, along with Timiş CC and the Italian company Sane that operates four airports in Italy and will finance 60 per cent of the programme, including the aircraft maintenance facility, a business terminal and commercial centre and access roads. Annual usage by 250,000 passengers is set to increase to 1.0mln as an airport of international standards. Currently there are 92 flights weekly with Austrian Airlines and Carpatair operating as well as Tarom, not to mention the tourist helicopter link with Băile Herculane started in 2001. Some Tarom international flights call at Timişoara, such as the Florence service with connections from Satu Mare (also the New York and Chicago flights in the past). Since resuming services to Romania in 1994, British Airways has been considering passenger, cargo and mail services to Timişoara. Arad is supporting Timişoara as the key international airport for a trans-frontier region and there are proposals for a road-rail-air intermodal transport nearby a Giarmata.

Other Upgrades
Upgrades are taking place at Baia Mare, Caransebeş, Craiova, Deva, Iaşi, Oradea, Satu Mare, Târgu Mureş and Tulcea, including runway extensions to attract international links. Arad is developing its airport with a 120ha commercial area as part of the Curtici-Arad free zone with a cargo terminal (including storage and distribution) backed by €2.0mln of Phare assistance in the context of CBC and the DCMT Euroegion in particular. Arad has combined transport facilities, including a container warehouse and rail access, and there could be further assistance – expected since 2002 – from investors (including companies from Hong Kong, Malaysia, Germany and USA) interested in the development of Corridor Four. Bacău's upgrade, with a 2,500x80m runway, has secured flights to Bologna, Rome, Trieste and Verona by Carpatair from 2002 and a back-up function for Chişinău (with Iaşi and Suceava both smaller at the time 1800x40m). Italian businessmen involved in environmental protection and town planning have provided a helicopter for emergency medical cases. Meanwhile at Iaşi the CC have invested on the strength of an agreement with Angel Airlines over Bucharest flights, but with international flights to Germany, Greece, Italy and Turkey as priorities, as well as connections through Budapest including Australia. Iaşi has now secured a Vienna service run by Austrian Airlines four times weekly. Suceava benefits from calls by Bucharest-Cernăuţi flights reflecting stronger economic relations across the old province of Bucovina. Both the General Consulting Company (representing an international operator) and Carpatair are interested in leasing the airport with enlargement and upgrading to international standards. Thus there is a three-way competition in Moldavia and it is interesting to recall the suggestion of the transport minister in 2000 (perhaps as a regional development initiative) that these three airports should develop to international status.

In Transylvania there has been much expansion at Cluj where runway extension from 1,850 to 2,500m required deviation of the Someş river in 2001. There are now international connections with Austria and Germany, including the Tarom Bucharest-Munich service. Braşov CC have concluded a protocol with Gunay (Turkey) for an international airport at Ghimbav to be included in the ring road programme. Gunay will finance the building and will operate the airport for a period before it becomes the council's propety. And Sibiu has found German investors (including companies administering Frankfurt, Munich and Stuttgart airports) willing to get involved in the upgrade, especially members of the business club Ost-West Wirtschaftsclub Bayern with interests in airport administration. €50mln is now being spent on modernisation (22mln from government and the rest from the city and county using their own funds and an EIB loan) with work by the German Lindner company as well as a local company (Con-A) and Dafora from Mediaş. There are now enough Austrians based in the city to justify weekend flights to Vienna. A further dimension arises from the projected €40mln investment at Simeria to provide an effective airport for the Deva-Hunedoara area where the combination of these towns, with Simeria, could create a new metropole for the province. However an alternative idea is to build at Vinţ closer to Alba Iulia and Sebeş. Finally, Bistriţa is keen to see an airport for northeastern Transylvania while the Italian company Imprenditoriale Sincogero Spa will build a new airport between Brăila and Galaţi as part of a portfolio of projects that may include housing and road building.

Chapter Ten

Settlement Patterns: Urban Planning and Development

Introduction

As the discourse turns to spatial arrangements within Romania it is appropriate first to recall previous comments on the regional system that places groups of counties into eight large regions appropriate for EU accession (Table 10.1). While the counties still comprise the highest level of local government, the regions now enjoy a degree of autonomy in planning their respective areas despite the importance of finance and direction from the centre combined with the influence of the relevant CCs and municipalities. Hence the individual regional plans have their distinct characteristics apart from their harmonisation with the various 'axes' of the national plan (concerned with job creation, regional development, agriculture, transport and environment quality) that tackle the twin challenges of growth and poverty alleviation. Thus the plan for the relatively poor North East region drew attention to the many aspects of deprivation that the planners needed to address (ANDR 2000a) while its success over SAPARD funding – €1.63bln in 2006: three times the regional average – suggests there is no shortage of enterprise. At the same time the prime importance of the county unit tends to weaken regional development and there is some criticism over lack of cohesion which inhibits a regional centre like Timişoara in the West Region from acting as a conduit passing growth projects down the hierarchy to areas of high unemployment like the Jiu Valley coalfield and the industrial towns of Caraş-Severin (the county centre of Reşiţa and smaller towns like Anina, Bocşa and Moldova Nouă). But various national strategies have been launched from the centre; beginning during the 1990–96 period with ad hoc regional programmes: first for the Carpathians as a whole and later for a specific mountain region (the Apuseni) and lowland areas including the Danube delta and parts of Moldavia. There were also incentives for 'free zones' involving ports and other places important for transit. Then the centre-right government of 1997–2000 introduced the regions and accelerated restructuring through 'less-favoured areas' for the mining zones (from 1998) (Borcoş & Vîrdol 2001) and 'industrial restructuring areas': groups of industrial centres supported by Phare finance for innovatory SMEs in a bid to complement the RICOP programme for the down-sizing and privatisation of 'problem' companies (Figure 10.1) (Popescu et al. 2003). There was also legislation encouraging local initiative (through fiscal incentives for local authorities or private companies) in setting up industrial parks: a significant decentralising measure. Finally the frontier regions can take advantage of Phare finance for cross-border cooperation (CBC) especially where 'Euroregions'

Table 10.1: Regional profiles

Criterion	Romania	Bucharest	Cen	NE	NW	S	SE	SW	W
Population 1992 (mln)	22.81	2.35	2.70	3.75	2.91	3.56	2.96	2.46	2.11
Population 2003(mln)	21.73	2.21	2.54	3.74	2.74	3.36	2.86	2.33	1.95
Popn. Trend 1992=100	95	94	94	100	94	94	96	95	92
Urban pop'n (percent)#	53.4	88.8	59.2	40.8	51.2	40.7	55.2	45.3	61.7
Fertility#	378	288	383	460	385	378	375	365	339
Natural increase (th)#	-2.5	-3.1	-1.1	0.0	-2.4	-4.2	-2.0	-4.2	-4.0
Infant mortality#	16.7	10.4	15.1	20.1	14.2	19.3	18.2	15.1	15.6
Life expectancy (years)*	70.5	72.2	70.8	70.8	69.5	70.6	70.3	70.6	69.9
Employment (th.pop)*	385	368	403	366	412	372	370	396	406
Empl: agriculture(p'cent)*	41.4	6.6	34.0	51.2	45.9	48.6	44.7	51.2	35.9
Empl: industry (percent)*	23.2	27.3	30.7	19.1	22.2	22.8	20.6	19.3	26.7
Empl: services (percent)*	35.4	66.1	35.3	29.7	31.9	28.6	34.7	29.5	37.4
Unemployment rate @	8.8	4.7	8.5	11.8	7.8	8.2	9.9	9.1	8.2
SME's (th.popn)*	17.5	34.4	17.5	12.0	18.7	13.5	17.8	15.9	15.2
GNP p.c. (mln.lei)+	39.7	79.5	42.4	28.7	37.2	32.1	35.1	33.2	42.4
FDI ($p.c.) 1990-2000	127	604	91	17	82	54	35	83	114
Ditto growth 1998-2002	4.2x	5.4x	4.3x	3.7x	4.1x	3.9x	3.6x	3.7x	4.5x
Industrial wages (mln.lei)#	4.87	5.17	4.45	4.27	4.34	5.02	5.21	5.81	5.17
Monthly spending (ditto)#	2.79	3.50	2.90	2.56	2.97	2.53	2.75	2.56	2.81
Living space (sq.m)#	14.1	15.7	14.7	12.5	14.5	13.7	13.6	14.0	15.0
H'hold water supp.(cu.m)#	32.8	54.9	33.1	24.1	32.1	24.3	33.2	34.2	37.4
Piped water*	54.9	52.5	52.9	47.7	69.1	48.3	74.0	38.2	61.4
Sewage network*	21.7	47.5	25.5	25.1	23.5	17.2	21.4	13.1	25.1
Hospital beds (th.popn)#	6.5	10.5	7.1	5.7	7.2	4.8	5.5	5.8	7.3
Criminal convictions[]	383	281	342	425	393	331	428	462	381
Rural poverty (percent)◇	n.a.	33.0	37.3	43.6	33.0	33.4	41.9	35.2	34.8

* 1995-7 av; ◇ 2000; # 2003; + 1998-2002 av; [] 1998-2003 av; @1991-2003 av.

Fertility: live births/th.women; Infant mortality: deaths under one year/th. live births; FDI: cumulative figure for large investments (exceeding $1.0mln) only; Monthly spending: household average; Piped water and sewage: percentage of localities served; Criminality: convictions/100,000 people; Rural poverty: households

Source: Statistical Yearbooks

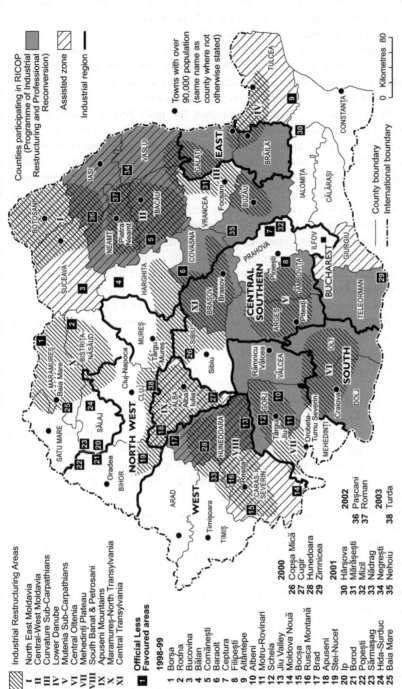

Counties participating in RICOP (Programme of Industrial Restructuring and Professional Reconversion)

Assisted zone

Industrial region

● Towns with over 90,000 population (same name as county where not otherwise stated)

County boundary

International boundary

0 Kilometres 80

Industrial Restructuring Areas

I   North East Moldavia
II Central-West Moldavia
III Curvature Sub-Carpathians
IV Lower Danube
V   Mutenia Sub-Carpathians
VI Central Oltenia
VII Mehedinţi Plateau
VIII South Banat & Petrosani
IX Apuseni Mountains
X   Maramureş-North Transylvania
XI Central Transylvania

Official Less Favoured areas

1998-99

1 Borşa
2 Rodna
3 Bucovina
4 Bălan
5 Comăneşti
6 Baraolt
7 Ceptura
8 Filipeşti
9 Altântepe
10 Albeni
11 Motru-Rovinari
12 Schela
13 Jiu Valley
14 Moldova Nouă
15 Bocşa
16 Rusca Montană
17 Brad
18 Apuseni
19 Stei-Nucet
20 Ip
21 Borod
22 Popeşti
23 Sărmăşag
24 Hida-Surduc
25 Baia Mare

2000

26 Copşa Mică
27 Cugir
28 Hunedoara
29 Zimnicea

2001

30 Hârşova
31 Mărăşeşti
32 Mizil
33 Nădrag
34 Negreşti
35 Nehoiu

2002

36 Paşcani
37 Roman

2003

38 Turda

Figure 10.1 Aspects of regional development

provide some institutional frameworks. These initiatives are more fully discussed elsewhere (Crețan et al. 2005) and are merely noted here as important structures and opportunities for local authorities to exploit.

This chapter concentrates on the changing urban landscape with respect to building and environment as well as transport and other services. Communism facilitated a massive transfer of population from rural to urban areas but with excessive use of apartment blocks, very limited provision for private cars and commerce and priorities in public transport for links between residential and industrial areas. Apartment blocks are still being built but their average size is now much smaller and there is also provision for villas sometimes in groups within closed compounds. Indeed the 'socialist cities' inherited from communism are now being thoroughly westernised with an accelerating pace of change. The 'learning curve' confronting local authorities is daunting and effective leadership is certainly being shown although it is unfortunate that more research is not being done to highlight variations in performance that will be all-important if the large provincial cities are to realise their potential as metropoles. In this chapter some general themes on urban development are followed up with a review of the capital city that deals with the inner and outer zones as well as the long-neglected topic of cohesion across the rural hinterland. For provincial towns there is a review of salient development trends followed by an examination of central place characteristics for six groups of towns (differentiated by population size, occupational change and service profile) and the rural zone.

Urban Development

The transition has brought deindustrialisation but a greatly-increased private sphere in business generally and more choice in housing (at least for the better-off); all of which makes for new priorities in public transport. Town centres are now showing many similarities to the West European CBD with a rapid expansion of shopping (initially with an emphasis on kiosks) along with offices, hotels and entertainment. Car parking space is now at a premium in large cities as vehicles compete with pedestrians on the wider pavements and with recreational space on the housing estates. Some cities (e.g. Bacău) are reportedly grid-locked while green space is constantly under pressure with photogrammetry revealing a shrinkage from 11.0–4.7sq.m per inhabitant during 1989–96 (when 16–20sq.m are needed to absorb carbon dioxide). Not surprisingly urban fringe zones are highly dynamic commercial areas for light industry and warehousing as well as shopping and entertainment. Local authorities initially struggled to keep pace, with small towns particularly short of money for the maintenance of utilities and public buildings; though there is much assistance from Western Europe e.g. 2,000 chairs from London's old Wembley Stadium were given to Târgu Mureș (with free delivery) to assist their summer theatre project. Accommodations with private enterprise are leading to novel solutions, as in Iași in 2000 where streets were leased for token rentals to entrepreneurs who handled the cleaning and festive lighting in return for advertising opportunities throughout the year. On the other hand in Constanța the Greek Prodeftiki company has been carrying out a four-year rehabilitation programme (2002-6) for 410kms of city streets with national and local finance.

Illegal Constructions

Constructions without a 'certificat de urbanism' posed a stiff challenge to the local authorities during the early transition years when new legislation was awaited and local authorities lacked the experience and resolve to take effective control. Thus the growth of kiosks was not properly regulated and Roma families built 'palaces' without proper approval, for example in Timişoara. Luxury dwellings were built illegally at the lakeside at Surduc (Timiş) in a protected zone important for the rehabilitation of the lake for tourism, while many second homes appeared without authorisation in small resorts like Rânca on the slopes of the Parâng above Novaci. Even prestigious commercial buildings appeared without planning consent. Meanwhile on the housing estates many new garages were hidden behind blocks of flats; reducing the open space and creating pollution hazards for children playing on land degraded by litter and discarded vehicle parts as well as oil and petrol spills. There was also some development of unauthorised 'pubs' in working class residential districts: small windowless boxes selling alcoholic drinks while lacking sanitation and liable to attract criminal elements preying on local residents. There were also cases of unauthorised demolition, for instance Constanţa's Continental Hotel in the city's historic centre, the historic monument Cerchez House in Botoşani and further abuses in Sibiu's historic 'Golden Barrel' area.

The Planning Process

The planning process itself was sometimes improperly organised. The system involves an urban plan to show development at three levels – all subsidiary to the national plan ('plan de amenajare a teritoriului') and county plans deriving from it: GUP for the general level comprising each administrative unit (including tourist stations); ZUP for the zonal level, such as central areas of towns and villages (and for protected areas); and DUP for further detail as appropriate. However some detailed plans were adopted prematurely (to expedite construction permits) without the general plans and zonal plans to provide an essential context, while the control system tended to be an excessively bureaucratic maze, involving a string of approvals that encouraged people to take direct action while the authorities were constrained by a lack of trained staff and computer-based information. However, by the late 1990s the MHPPW was achieving the necessary discipline in construction, with an adequate cadastral law, more accessible procedures and stiffer penalties. There was more thorough police investigation of irregularities and better cooperation with the justice ministry (following an embarrassing incident in Roşiorii de Vede in 1997 when an authorised 60sq.m development was expanded to 100sq.m without permission). And much closer local authority supervision makes it possible to establish the exact timing of infringements.

The Romanian Capital: Bucharest

With a population of almost two million – some six times greater than the largest provincial city – Bucharest has enjoyed a surge in foreign investment which is noted in Table 10.2. During 1997–2005 some $3.4bln has flowed in (not counting privatisation revenues or projects involving less than $1.0mln). From 78 projects during 1997–2000 with an average value of $5.6mln the pace accelerated to 250 projects with an average value of $12.0mln during 2001–2005. Bucharest is very much a boom city, although it is not fundamentally different from other urban areas as regards the problems of transition (Mehedinţi 2000) (Figure 10.2). However in view of its size and the scale of housing development under communism the city is highly differentiated in economic, social and political terms (Popescu 1999, 2000). It is also divided into six units (sectors) for local government although there is also a central administration, headed by the general mayor, to maintain an overall view. Social tensions generated by transition were exacerbated by housing shortage (and soaring real estate values) while areas with a large Roma population – like Ferentari – were perceived unfairly as prone to high criminality. The problem of illegal buildings was manifested by the 'overnight' construction of the wholesale-commercial 'Puzdrea Complex' behind the Free Press House in contradiction of the approved urban development concept; while the Columna Bank proceeded with an ultra-modern headquarters building in a select residential area of the city. The authorities eventually took action through a special department in 1997 to remove illegal constructions; with attention also to unauthorised changes in use (for example, dwelling accommodation used as warehousing space) and buildings on municipal land that were not paying rent.

Much industry remains in the inner city but with heavy lay-offs and technological updating to improve productivity and efficiency and increase competitiveness. However the larger enterprises are to be relocated during the first three years of EU accession and should make for cleaner air while also providing large areas for redevelopment. Meanwhile commerce was privatised quickly and many new businesses appeared although the early emphasis on kiosks has been modified by the rapid expansion of supermarkets and shopping malls since the late 1990s. The key locations are shown on Figure 10.2 along with the main concentrations at the district level which often correlate with the stations on the metro system which has been evolving since the 1980s. Some extensions are underway while the early idea of a southern loop through the industrial suburbs has been abandoned and the some important links have been provided on the surface by fast trams. The metro has helped to limit pollution (along with the exclusion zones for heavy lorries) but private cars have increased greatly. To ease congestion trams do not enter the central area beyond the four termini shown on the map, although there have been some extensions in the suburbs. Meanwhile transformation is occurring to the built form through the central area conservation project between Ceauşescu's 'Casa Poporului' to the south and quality shopping areas to the north. And there has also been a rapid growth of office space through purpose-built business centres with an early concentration at Calea/Pţa.Victoriei complemented by an explosion of other groupings mainly to the north with a particular emphasis on the Colentina river axis which is also attracting much quality housing. Park and playground facilities have improved, along with services in the outer suburbs, but a unitary concept for the wider city region is still lacking. Some integration may be possible as a result of the Metropolitan Transport Authority, inaugurated in 2006 to coordinate the Bucharest Transport Company (running the buses and trams), the metro (Metrorex) and other operaters over an extended area. However, a regional transport system needs to reduce concentration on Bucharest itself, partly by rethinking the role of the city's seven radial railways (and the 'centura') for a more coordinated network for whole area, including satellite neighbourhoods and other 'new entries'.

Table 10.2: Foreign Direct Investment in Bucharest 1997–2005

Period	Sectors													Total	
	1		2		3		4		5		6				
	a	b	a	b	a	b	a	b	a	b	a	b		a	b
1997-2000	1	1.1	18	80.9	7	29.3	25	89.6	4	102.5	23	136.0		78	439.4
2001-2005	3	57.3	70	710.1	29	337.2	67	657.6	56	1111.1	25	121.3		250	2994.6
Total	4	58.4	88	791.0	36	366.5	92	747.2	60	1213.6	48	257.3		328	3434.0

1 Agriculture; 2 Industry; 3 Construction & Property; 4 Commerce; 5 Telecommunications, Transport & Logistics; 6 Finance, Hotels, Medical and Other Services. a: projects; b: investment $mln (converted where other currencies were involved)

Sources: Guran-Nica 2002 and Regional Development Agency

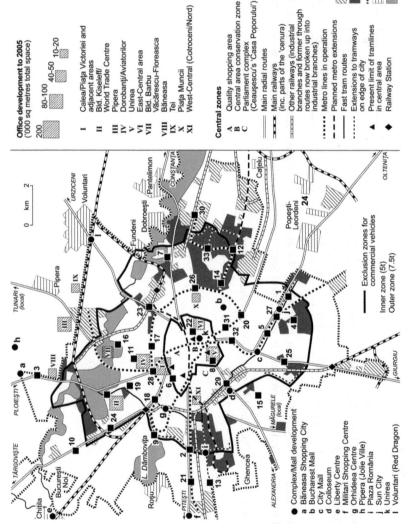

Office development to 2005 ('000 sq metres total space)
200 | 80-100 | 40-50 | 10-20

■ Main commercial areas, many with traditional open markets

- I Calea/Piața Victoriei and adjacent areas
- II Bld. Kiseleff/World Trade Centre
- III Pipera
- IV Dorobanți/Aviatorilor
- V Unirea
- VI East-Central area
- VII Bld. Barbu Văcărescu-Floreasca
- VIII Băneasa
- IX Tei
- X Piața Muncii
- XI West-Central (Cotroceni/Nord)

1 Apărătorii Patriei
2 Armata Poporului
3 Băneasa
4 Berceni
5 Brâncoveanu
6 Buzești
7 Chișinău
8 Coșbuc
9 Crângași
10 Dămăroaia/16 Februarie
11 Dorobanți
12 Dristor
13 Drumul Taberei
14 Dudești/Grigorescu
15 Ferentari
16 Floreasca
17 Galați
18 Gara de Nord
19 I Mai/Domeniilor
20 Mihai Bravu
21 Militari (Complex Apusului)
22 Moșilor (Halele Obor)
23 Obor/Colentina
24 Pajura
25 Progresu
26 Piața Muncii
27 Ptă. Sudului
28 Ptă. Victoriei
29 Rahova
30 Republica
31 Timpuri Noi
32 Tineretului
33 Titan

Industrial areas
Main apartment complexes of communist period
Edge of built-up area of city
Villages beyond city boundary
Colentina river & park belt

Central zones

A Quality shopping area
B Central area conservation zone
C Parliament complex (Ceaușescu's 'Casa Poporului')

Main radial routes
Main railways (inc. parts of the 'cenura')
Other railways (industrial branches and former through routes now broken up into industrial branches)
Metro lines in operation
Planned metro extensions
Fast tram routes
Extensions to tramways on edge of city
Present limit of tramlines in central area
▲ Railway Station

● Complex/Mall development
a Băneasa Shopping City
b Bucharest Mall
c City Mall
d Colloseum
e Liberty Centre
f Militari Shopping Centre
g Orhideea Centre
h Pipera (Jolie Ville)
i Plaza România
j Sun City
k Unirea
l Voluntari (Red Dragon)

Exclusion zones for commercial vehicles
Inner zone (5t)
Outer zone (7.5t)

Figure 10.2 Transport and commerce in Bucharest

Provincial Towns and Cities

Local government has gained a new lease of life through democratically elected councils at both the town/commune and county levels. The inherited two-tier administrative hierarchy has been preserved in its entirety, although 53 additional towns have appeared (the total reached 313 in 2005); and the number of communes is 2,850 (162 more than in 1989, before allowing for the increase in the number of towns). The fragmentation reflects wider aspirations for independent status among localities which were absorbed into larger units through the communist reorganisation of 1968 and now see autonomy important for their future development (Greif 1999). In some cases the motive arises through ethnicity – where a village feels alienated from the rest of the commune – but generally there is a desire to have a budget which is not centralised in the key village of a larger commune. Meanwhile, the counties remain unchanged at 41 (including Ilfov: the immediate rural hinterland of Bucharest) despite a flurry of interest in resurrecting some of the old counties of the inter-war period – thereby restoring the former administrative status of towns like Lugoj and Mediaş (along with some advocacy of an intermediate tier between county and municipality) (Săgeată 1999, 2001).

Local administration has gradually become more proactive with dissemination of 'good practice' for effective local government and a return to traditional entrepreneurial values. A \$2.3mln USAID project in 2002 through RTI International helped the administration in a range of large towns: Baia Mare, Braşov, Focşani, Mangalia, Oradea, Piteşti, Ploieşti, Târgu Mureş. Leading towns are enhancing cohesion across their counties using computers: by the end of 2001 all the the mayors' offices in Braşov county were connected by a computer network. At Bistriţa architecture students were invited to a summer camp in 2006 to discuss ideas for the rehabilitation of this historic Saxon town. And with the boom in real estate the Euriska property management company began to promote real estate development among local authorities in 1997 and launched dialogue on the theme of 'urban concept' in such places as Bacău, Cluj, Focşani, Iaşi, Oradea, Piteşti, Târgovişte and Târgu Mureş – some of the stronger county towns. As a result more local initiatives have been taken and modern technology is being assimilated: with foreign assistance Oradea's chief architect has used GIS to produce a set of city maps including functional areas and fiscal zones. Since 2000 it has become common for town councils to raise capital through bonds with interest rates set between the bank borrowing and lending rates: Romania's improved credit rating mean that state guarantee is not needed. The leaders were Braşov, Deva, Ploieşti, Timişoara and Zalău, along with Mangalia and Predeal seeking finance for sport and recreation (for example, seafront improvement and an Olympic-standard sports hall at Mangalia and a new piste at Predeal); Bacău and Piatra Neamţ for cultural interests; Constanţa, Oradea and Târgu Mureş for street improvements; and Alba Iulia and Sebeş for water, sewage and infrastructure (schools and housing as well at Medgidia). Some local businesses have come up with important innovations: e.g. entrepreneurial training by Lafarge-Romcim at Medgidia through a business incubator (with nine cells over its 700sq.m of floorspace) placed under the management of 'The Foundation for the Assistance of the Underprivileged Social Categories' for a five year period with the possibility of extension. The Foundation will set up new firms and develop projects already in existence.

Entrepreneurial Local Government

Proactive councils are now operating effectively after the communist era of passive response to central planners, highlighted by 'city manager' appointments as at Reşiţa and Slatina. Oradea is not alone in coping simultaneously with industrial change, improved water supply and waste treatment, dstrict heating and ecological landfill, a ring road, green space ('Oradea Verde') and pedestrianisation and cultural heritage especially connected with the fortress ('Cetatea Oradea'). Councils are handling substantial local budgets that are not now totally determined centrally but follow from the yield of local taxation and the council's business as an entrepreneur e.g. selling land or negotiating loans. They are also getting used to consulting their citizens when formulating plans for business, retail, leisure and housing. The large towns are booming even through many appear to be declining in population though emigration (Timişoara from 333.4th 1992 to 303.6 in 2005 – and despite 5,000 new homes built during the 1990s). Some are also becoming highly entrepreneurial in their approach and have attracted a disproportionate share of foreign investment. Timişoara is the best-known example but Cluj-Napoca is catching up after the early years were somewhat clouded by controversy surrounding a former mayor (the nationalist G.Funar) leader of the erstwhile Party of Romanian National Unity. As an attractive university city (with a sistership agreement with Sowon in South Korea), it has a strong IT company profile arising from a €80mln investment by Ruwel (Germany) for integrated circuits; the Romanian Brinel company which has foreign cooperation with Microsoft, Compaq, IBM and Intel; and the Romanian-German company Sistec producing applications and especially games for mobile phones with sales in USA, Hong Kong, India and China. Meanwhile, Alfa Global Solutions has been operating in the European and American IT market as a supplier of complete solutions since 1997. Cluj stands to make further progress thanks to the Bucharest-Oradea motorway and Jucu industrial park. Meanwhile Italian investors have their sights on Baia Mare as a base for wood processing and furniture. Constanţa seeks a 100ha artificial island at the southern end of the port to provide more commercial space while redeveloping old silos and warehouses for hotels, restaurants and shops. And Ploieşti is starting its intended transition to metropole status by 2025 with a €450mln. programme to focus of health and education along with infrastructure and the reclamation of polluted land.

Smaller towns are also making rapid progress. Under a popular mayor Zamfir Iorguş the council at Mangalia on the Black Sea coast has achieved the ISO9002 standard for service quality (clean, rehabilitated streets; good security; cultural programmes and intense civic activity including help for the poor, the homeless and HIV-AIDS sufferers). Foreign investors have consolidated the industrial base through Daewoo Mangalia Heavy Industries and German capital in ready-mades, while the town offers the Black Sea Business Centre, a hotel/conference complex and tourist companies for the surrounding resorts of Jupiter, Neptun-Olimp, Saturn and Venus as well as Mangalia itself. Paşcani, west of Iaşi, has emerged well from industrial restructuring (Groza 1991–92, 1994) with surplus space made available for SMEs; while Rădăuţi (northwest of Suceava) has been proactive in providing facilities for foreign investors in manufacturing and services thanks to a package put together by the town council, Suceava CCI and the National Council of SMEs. Plots can be leased for 49 years minimum, without paying local taxes during the investment period (up to four years) and with a two-year transition thereafter to work up to the full rate. Space is also available in council-owned buildings rent-free for three years (with exemption from taxes on local communal utilities). Companies who invest a minimum of DM0.1mln and employ at least 40 persons will get a 50 per cent discount on local taxes on buildings for five years.

Accessing European Funding

Accessing European funding is a major indicator of urban enterprise and Timişoara is an outstanding example (Popa & Junie 2000). As the economic core of West Region the city made early use of the INFOREG project to disseminate European information (followed by the other county centres of the region). Since 1997 Timiş county has received c.€60.5mln relating to 31 programmes and 128 projects highlighting production, human capital and infrastructure. The first category includes a regional centre for the promotion of economic activities by the local CCIA as well as a large industrial park in Timişoara; assistance for SMEs over the rehabilitatiom of buildings and access to the European market; innovative production; a handicraft centre; marketing and export activities; and rehabilitation of declining industrial zones. Human capital covers management training through 'Centrul Judeţean de Asistenţa şi Formare Managerială Timiş' (also education, innovation, university-business links and labour market inclusivity) while infrastructure covers waste water treatment; regeneration of rundown urban areas; and the development of services in priority zones. Road modernisation has made good progress through widening of the Arad-Timişoara road and the direct route to the Hungarian frontier at Cenad; with the Bucharest-Piteşti-Nădlac highway to follow.

Other programmes have also assisted in the development of the international airport and the installation of electronic control at the railway station. Meanwhile the Timişoara 'primaria' (city hall) has obtained some €37mln for an ecological rubbish dump for the area and a wholesale market for farm produce (including rehabilitation of the Iosefin retail market). Initiative has also been shown in forging a trilateral collaboration Pančevo-Timişoara-Cincinnati for know-how in local economic development, linked with the attractaction of foreign firms in the IT domain with a view to technology-transfer to local universities and businesses. Reference should be made to the early collaboration between Timiş county and its Hungarian neighbour Csóngrad which formed the basis of a wider cross-border programme for the Danube-Criş-Mureş-Tisa Euroregion – contributing to the development of the automotive industry in the border town of Sânnicolau Mare. The Timiş-Csóngrad informational system is encouraging cooperation among the local authorities for economic development and cultural exchanges in the border zone, including tourism coordination and development of managerial capacities in the frontier zone. In particular the project 'Centrul agro-industrial româno-maghiar de informare şi incubare' is helping with production, sorting, marketing and processing, including the creation of the Dumbrăviţa and Csóngrad 'camera agricolă'.

Larger Urban Regions

A major concern is the need to plan for an urban zone that extends way beyond the administrative area of a single town or city. The restrictive limits of Piteşti are forcing the takeover of flats for offices and small shops while people who accept €80,000 for a two-room apartment can use the money to acquire a large plot in a commune like Bradu on the edge of the city where new housing complexes are emerging at Gavana and Tudor Vladimirescu. The property developer Imotrust has a €4.2mln/3,300sq.m residential project in Arad which is dwarfed by a €50mln scheme for housing, commerce and industry in the wider area. Indeed some neighbouring communes are experiencing substantial population growth, like Holboca (five kilometres east of Iaşi) with a population exceeding 12,000. Others are attracting business to the point where local taxes sustain large budgets for the local authorities e.g. Giroc (9.6mln.lei) and others that form a constellation around Timişoara: Dumbrăviţa, Moşniţa Nouă, Săcălaz, and Sânandrei. But some suburban growth is not adequately regulated and despite an unsurfaced road leading froim Zorilor on the edge of Cluj in the direction of Făgetul Ierii the new villa suburb of Europa is developing 'ad hoc' with no local plan (PUZ) and no services. So while the city councils have many problems arising within their own territories – the marginal areas of Ploieşti (Bariera Unirii, Bereasa and Mimiu) are effectively rural areas generally lacking surfaced roads and sewerage systems; while Timişoara's Iosefin suburb complains about its poor amenities and services –there is a strong case for developing links between cities and their surrounding suburban communes with regard to planning and services and the development of some formal associations. In 2005, 'Zona Metropolitană Oradea' brought together eight communes although progress in the integrated developmenrt for roads/transport and water/sewage has been slow; while Cluj aims to associate initially with seven communes (Apahida, Baciu, Chinteni, Ciurila, Feleacu, Floreşti and Gilău) and later with 14 others to extend the metropolitan zone to 400,000 people and 188,000ha. Meanwhile a Târgu Mureş metropolitan zone was agreed by the CC in 2006 to include 14 surrounding municipalities one of which (Ungheni) is now a town in its own right. This is a natural process although formal links are not, of course, a precondition for collaboration. There are also some links emerging among neighbouring towns that can sometimes help in updating infrastructure, for example Brăila and Galaţi have a joint interest in housing and airport development through a project affecting a 15km section extending each side of the county boundary including provision for a new bridge over the Danube. Arad and Timişoara are further apart but together they constitute the dynamic core of West Region, while their origins are not dissimilar given Arad's bastion fortress (now to be refurbished) and Timişoara's associations with the historic 'cetate' of which only fragments remain. Given the development pressures, Timişoara has done well in selling off land for commercial development as well as buildings that new private owners wish to refurbish. But this has made if difficult for West Region to find all the administrative accommodation it needs (with the renting of private accommodation as a solution) and given rise to speculation that the 'capital' should be transferred to Arad. Meanwhile there is no doubt that Timişoara's international airport is a great asset to the region and also for cross-border relations and Arad's support in this regard is therefore appreciated.

Braşov has also teamed up with the nearby towns of Codlea, Predeal and Săcele (as well as the communes of Cristian, Ghimbav, Prejmer and Tărlungeni) to create an Association for Sustainable Development for coordinated actions over the wider area. And in Alba county the towns of Alba Iulia, Sebeş and Teiuş are combining with the communes of Ciugud, Cricău, Galda de Jos, Ighiu, Sântimbru and Vinţ to create a 'microregiunea de dezvoltare' with a population of 100,000 to boost prospects of EU funding, while the county council's 'plan urbanistic' for the whole area will help Alba Iulia to solve its problem of land shortage. But a higher level of integration is evident in the grouping of the towns of Deva, Hunedoara and Simeria as a new 'metropole' with a combined population of some 170,000 located roughly half-way between Cluj and Timişoara. Deva (the centre of Hunedoara county) is a modern and progressive city with a booming property market in the expanding southern suburb of Dealul Păiului – with 12ha sold to an Italian builder; also an attractive central area by virtue of the castle hill, though sadly the Romanian Academy's control system for protected conservation areas is blocking both surfaced road and gondola options for improved access to the substantial castle ruins. There has also been some disappointment over the conception (originating in 1991) of an administrative palace for the prefecture as well as the town and county councils: this proved far too expensive and the 15,000sq.m of space on 14 floors was destined for sale to private business – hopefully for €4.0mln – with continuing outlays for conservation in the meantime.

Meanwhile, Simeria – lying on the main Mureş corridor – naturally likes the union proposal and will play a major role through a €40mln airport project (involving the Luxembourg company Fibelfin) for the suburb of Şăuleşti; while Hunedoara (a depressed metallurgical bastion – albeit with 140ha for redevelopment – lying aside from the through routes) has taken a more sceptical view. A joint plan issued in 2007 envisages that Deva will spread southwards into a new suburb (Archia) and also northwards towards the Mureş (while avoiding marshy land); while Hunedoara grows eastwards to Valea Seacă and also westwards to the former metallurgical plant. Simeria's growth has been conceived in relation to the local airport and a central shopping mall (Santuhalm) but there is an alternative concept involving an airport further east at Vinţ that would serve the Alba Iulia and Sebeş areas as well. Other key details include a container terminal on the railway and a river port on Mureş at Şoimuş; while the proposal for a single 'primar' for 'Hunedoara Mare' in 2008 may be premature.

Aspects of Urban Planning
Some authorities face horrendous problems such as air and water pollution in Baia Mare where the cleaning of the Săsar has been a great improvement. But Ocnele Mari (Vâlcea) is in danger of disappearing because of subsidence arising from brine pumping: the priority is now to rebuild the town in such a way as to retain the identity of the constituent communities. Three other small towns in Vâlcea also face landslide threats: moderate in Băile Olăneşti and Govora but severe in Călimăneşti were two hectares are affected. Sinaia is under threat through the instability of deforested slopes. And following an accident at the colliery that has led to complete closure the local authority in Anina (Caraş-Severin) is struggling to expand the economic base and stave off terminal decline.

Industry and Business Centres   The larger towns are seeking to revive their industrial areas. Those in the west especially are seeking to provide extra space: thanks to its agricultural areas to the northwest Oradea has created 70ha of industrial parks with 20 industrial units under construction; while two industrial parks in Satu Mare may extend to 900,000sq.m. Timişoara has laid out a technology park (within the framework of the industrial park legislation) as part of the city's plan for job creation. Slatina once again projects itself as an entrepreneurially-minded county town with 50ha secured for industrial development led by Pirelli Tyre & Cord. Housing can expand on the urban periphery but also on inner-city industrial sites. Much of the industrial expansion in the Cluj area is taking place beyond the city limits e.g. at the Tetrarom technology park at Jucu which has attracted a mobile phone factory for Nokia as well as small relocation projects like the Feleacu sweets factory which will increase production after moving out of the city. Braşov is keen to redevelop the former Lubrifin refinery site and is also proactive (from 2005) over 'Mansard-roofing' of communist-era apartment blocks: adding an extra storey combined with a sloping roof for extra space and aesthetic appeal. House building is being organised in liaison with commercial companies and the NDA, for example in Bistriţa (470 apartments – some by NDA – and 200 houses) as well as Slatina and Târgovişte. The NDA is also prominent in Focşani and Giurgiu while Oradea is providing for its local Social Community Administration and Deva is allocating 300 parcels in Dealul Păiului to young families to complement a fourth block by NDA. New projects can significantly alter the 'cachet' of a particular neighbourhood. In Iasi Păcurari is becoming more attractive thanks to the €14mln Amfiteatru development involving a 70-apartment block and some 50 villas (based on seven models) costing €65,000 (in addition to the land) and commercial spaces; also the €40mln 'Green Park' for small four-level blocks with a dozen apartments. Meanwhile in the surrounding area villas in Valea Lupului (10kms west of the city centre on the Paşcani road) are spreading over land once envisaged as an industrial estate.

Although demand for offices is moderate by comparison with Bucharest, business centres are becoming part of the changing provincial urban landscape, especially since the end of the 1990s when several early plans were realised. Arad International BC (dating back to1997) includes bus and railway terminals plus hall, hotel, business centre, warehouses, hypermarket, industrial services. Timişoara has seven buildings exclusively used for offices in the central area including the Unirii BC: a renovated building of 1850 with banks and company representation on the ground and offices above. In addition to the Maestro and Olimpia BCs, the Romanian-French BC in Cluj secures consulting services for small entrepreneurs in the city and gives opportunities for the French to invest abroad, thanks to the initiative in 1999 by the Owners & Handicrafts Association of Cluj and the Development Agency of Vichy; while in the same year the county CCIA supported Alba BC in Alba Iulia for economic development and European integration. Moldova International BC was built in Iaşi during 1996–99 and has created 200–300 jobs, while in Bacău the 11-floor Blue House (or Glass House) – described as 'architectural gem' – also opened in 1999 as a BC after the original plan for a sport hotel (started in 1991 by the Ministry of Youth & Sport, linked the nearby stadium) was taken over in 1994. The first big trade and entertainment centre on the Black Sea was under construction at Constanţa in 2001: a $10mln mall-type centre owned by Galeria Mall of Turkey with an area of 22,400sq.m: 13,000sq.m on two floors will accommodate 98 shops; also parking for 1,000 cars and a panoramic elevator. There is also a Black Sea Romanian Business Centre at Mangalia. Expansion is now more coordinated with the link between GTC (active in Bucharest over Europe House and America House) and Aura of Israel with respect to over 20 commercial centres of 5–15,000sq.m. Aura will find sites and purchase them while GTC will invest $200mln to build, promote and administer. Thus the BC seems destined to spread down the central place hierarchy (albeit with contrasts in floorspace between the 11,300sq. m available in Cluj, 3,000sq.m planned for Slatina in 2007 and 700sq.m at the design stage in Târgovişte). Although not a formal BC, Grupul Imobiliar Tender plan to invest €350mln in Timişoara's first skyscraper ('zgarie-nori') on the site of a former woollen mill as an office complex (to include the local Euroregion administration) with conference and hotel facilities. With 36 floors it will be 132m high (Romania's tallest building to date: well in excess of Bucharest's International Hotel at 67m) raising questions about the level of local taxation appropriate for such structures and its situation in a residential area. Meanwhile Timişoara successfully completed a new wholesale market 2006 with €1.6mln from the town hall complemented by a €2.6mln loan from the German government.

Transport Planning   Road improvements are underway to cope with growing congestion problems in leading centres like Braşov, Cluj, Constanţa, Craiova, Târgu Mureş and Timişoara (though smaller county towns like Reşiţa and Zalău are not so badly affected). All the large cities are plagued by through traffic for which bypass arrangements are quite inadequate. Forty-five per cent of all traffic in Timişoara is in transit and there will be little relief until the Piteşti-Nădlac motoway is completed with additional bypasses needed on the both the north and south sides to handle the connecting traffic flows to and from the west. Iaşi has been giving much attention to its ring road and underpasses while Satu Mare is planning a northern bypass. In Braşov the Transylvania Motorway (Bucharest-Oradea) will provide a bypass on the southern side of the city but a smaller bypass ('ocolitoarea') is needed to feed through traffic from Bacău and Harghita counties along the northern edge of the city for access to the routes to Câmpulung and Făgăraş as well as the planned Ghimbav airport. A €30mln EBRD loan has been secured for this purpose as well as improved pavements and parking space (much of this planned underneath parks and playing fields). Parking in the cities has been regulated by the Telpark system since 1998 with fee income used to improve facilities (Timişoara has had 12 parks newly-created or taken over, plus over 1,000 individual lots marked out) but high charges are unpopular and there is a big demand for free places. Following UNESCO norms, ticket barriers are being used to control access to historic centres as at Sibiu, currently Romania's first 'City of Culture', while Cluj is experimenting with the Italian system of parking 'pe verticala' involving platforms raised on pillars. While 'facelift' money can be readily spent on roads, pavements, lighting and facades (as at Slatina) there are always counterclaims relating to heating systems, schools and hospitals.

Public Transport   Tramway modernisation is proceding in Ploieşti along with the introduction of a new 5.0km trolley route; likewise in the case of Arad's 220km system – including the former 26km electric railway to Ghioroc – where the work will run in parallel with road improvements in the central area and will feature 34 Tatra trams acquired from Halle. Sibiu has only one tram route – 11kms to Dumbrava and Rășinari – since the line from the railway station to Valea Aurii closed around 1964. But there are plans for five new routes to access the airport as well as the eastern and western industrial areas if money can be found. By contrast Brașov is getting rid of its trams and trolley buses. The latter are regarded as an undesirable 'amprentă' or legacy of the communist east, but the aim is primarily one of easing circulation and removing cables that restrict street development. 190 new 'ecologically-friendly' buses were acquired during 2005-6, assisted by the EBRD loan already referred to; while only minibuses will be allowed in the historic centre and in the suburbs of Prund and Schei. Brașov would also like to tackle another problem of circulation namely the Tâmpa mountain which complicates access between the centre and the Răcădău suburb with some 10,000 apartments. There is a steep, narrow road connection but a 840m tunnel would be a big improvement given the rising number of cars. However although it is included in the PUG the cost of €11mln cannot yet be justified. Meanwhile Timișoara favours rapid rail to connect the main railway station with the airport (and also a link with Arad) while the Bega Canal could be used for both passengers and freight. And 'maxi-taxis' are providing stiff competition in some towns like Zalău where there is pressure for a sharing-out of routes with the official operator 'Transurbis'. To overcome such tensions Slatina is hiring a modern transport fleet of autocars, buses and minibuses – with air conditioning and TV monitoring – through Unicredit Leasing.

Comprehensive Approaches

The leading county towns face massive growth pressures that call for radical thinking over future expansion, given the acute shortage of space in central areas reflected in rapidly rising land prices. €600–700/sq.m is currently realistic in Ploiești while the demand for large office developments (such as for foreign company headquarters) has produced a price tag of €2.0mln for a compact site of 1,000sq.m (i.e. €2,000/ sq.m). Hence the need for imaginative development schemes and the decision by Ploiești to spend €450mln during 2007–25 to emerge as a true European metropole with a revamped infrastructure including better schools and hospitals, business services and amenity enhanced by the reclamation of polluted land. The plan will be formulated by HIS Romania, an enterprise with a Dutch inspiration set up in 1994 to enhance capacity in local government. At the same time, with a population of 375,000 expected by 2025, Cluj faces great pressure on its restricted central area and the PUG forsees ambitious new developments on the southern hills with a mixture of business, commerce and residential areas. According to 'Planwerk Cluj-Napoca' based on work by German and Romanian specialists, pedestrianisation will extend from the initial Bld.Erouilor project and mixed uses will expand along the Someș river (where a beach will emerge from a programme to improve water flow) and the Str. Horea between the main square and the railway station to the north (with industrial restructuring along the railway axis, including the conversion of the former 'Clujana' footwear factory into small units). Given the present intensity of growth involving the Tetararom industrial park at Jucu (already mentioned) as well as two malls – Julius

Mall and Trigranit's larger €140mln Polus City Centre Mall – the city will have to draw in labour from Maramureş and Moldavia. Meanwhile peripheral housing developments are underway: a partnership with Impact Construction (Bucharest) for a €400 5,000 home project on 200ha of municipality land at Dealul Lomb besides another satellite settlement (Tineretului) in the Someş valley involving 1,600 homes by Polus Real Estate.

The Palas project is unfolding on the southern part of the Iaşi historic centre including a City Hall development contract for the 31,000sq.m 'Madison Compound' with Julius Group for 70,000sq.m housing plus 40,000sq.m for commerce, including a hotel and offices (the latter in big demand at monthly rents of €20/sq.m with all the space at the new Technopolis Park now taken up). 94,000sq.m of parking is also envisaged. Another Iaşi project for central area architectural, economic and social rehabilitation involves the Lăpuşneanu Association (representing citizens' interests in Str.Cuza Vodă, Str.Lăpuşneanu and Pţă.Unirii) set to benefit from €100,000 for restoration (half each from USAID and City Hall). In Suceava a former industrial site provides an opportunity being taken up by Imotur for an industrial park and commercial developments; while the Areni Stadium is being relocated in order to make way for the €100mln investment by Adama (Israel) in a 24-floor World Trade Center to provide a business centre for Bucovina with the bottom four floors to serve as a commercial complex. Furthermore in Craiova the Hungarian-Romanian company West Park is responding to a serious housing shortage will provision of four 13-storey blocks to create 308 two/three room luxury flats to sell as €100,000, with a shopping mall and underground parking near the Daewoo factory. Meanwhile in Braşov a civic centre competition has produced a plan to complement four apartment towers with a hotel and a 10-storey office building of 2,000sq.m for the local administration plus retail/cultural facilities and underground parking. And even small towns have gone in for broad-based planning e.g. Cugir in Alba country has produced a strategy for 2006-13 relating to infrastructure and industry; ensuring adequate space for development on the industrial park where there has already been a successful transition in downsizing in engineering and armaments at 'Uzina Mecanică' where 2,500 workers have been much involved since 1996 in work for Daimler-Chrysler and gearboxes for Mercedes. This is complemented by with 10 new enterprises (with a total employment of 1,150) divided between furniture, clothing and meat processing. The plan seeks a business incubator, SMEs, business club and better tourist informationu on the main road at Şibot (complemented by signposted tourist routes, improvements at the Cancul barrage resorts as well as the local forest roads and the agrotouristical 'canton').

Timişoara has been actively planning in several ways. On the economic side there has been a push for more jobs which has been highly successful in view of the foreign investment surge especially from Italy which has resulted in a labour shortage. Dubbed 'mica Italie' after Italian entrepreneurs, in first place, invested $215.8mln in 2,300 companies with mixed/foreign capital, the city has opened an Italian cultural centre (with Italian the preferred foreign language) and Italian restaurants and shops have appeared to serve some 10,000 'descendents of Trajan' who are now busy marrying in the city as well as investing and working. But the city now faces the challenge of further growth as the motorway comes on stream with a saturated labour market that will have to be boosted by in-migration (currently vacancies are advertised only in the adjacent counties of Caraş-Severin and Hunedoara where unemployment rates are high). Green space is also at a premium, especially in Fratelia and Calea Şagului: hence the need to build upwards, with property frequently acquired for redevelopment through several projects (by Nanette Real Estate and other companies) for apartments, shops and offices exceeding €200mln. Tourism has become another priority since central government is concerned with the country's principal interests in the Prahova resorts, Bucovina and the Black Sea coast. With the help of some German money there is more attention to museums and historic building and an extension of the existing 'Tymes Tours' programme; integrating with the county's touring routes and cycleways. In physical terms the city aims to extend the central area ('Cetate') towards the Fabric and Iosefin areas through boulevards and the Cetate ring road. With the help of planners from Padova, the 'Bastion'project for Cetate/ Pţa.Unirii is starting in 2007, although there is a potential conflict arising through the Kaufland supermarkets in the north and south (with Real and Selgros additionally in the north). Meanwhile in the south – across the Bega – the university's popular 'complex studentesc' is a mecca for for night-time entertainment and fast food (traditional and kebab). And redevelopment of the decaying 'Abator' site (dating to 1904-5) for a shopping mall, along with apartments, offices and a hotel, by the Goldale company – combining the interests of Tiriac (Romania) and Riofosa (Spain) – could generate further competition. It is not absolutely clear therefore whether the centralisation model will prevail over the concept of multiple nuclei (maintaining local identity) or conceivably the Bucharest sector model. Meanwhile, although the city has its sights on its 'metropole' function with a possible doubling of population (and trebling of the built-up area) by 2050, the county council would like see some 'spread' of growth away from the city and to this end the villages of Ciacova, Gataia and Recaş have been promoted to urban status, although little new investment has occurred so far apart from interest in the wine industry at Recaş.

Environmental Services

This section covers water and waste management which has seen some responsibility transferred to foreign companies such as Veolia (France) who look after water and sewage in Ploieşti. Romania has substantial water supplies with 25bln.cu.m/yr of usable resources from rivers and lakes (providing the bulk of the supply) and some 6.0bln from underground sources (used only to the extent of 1.3bln.cu.m in 1996 due to recession). However many people in rural areas depend on wells that may fail during dry years (30m wells at Cuzdrioara in Cluj country dried up in 2001) while pollution has been a major problem. Geologists say that 15–20 per cent of ground water resources are polluted with hydrocarbons and other compounds through mining and ore processing as well as the chemical industry (oil/gas pipelines; the Ploieşti refinery complex of Astra, Brazi, Teleajen and Vega; and other refineries at Midia and Oneşti). Some contamination linked with oil dates back to 'oil lakes' created by allied bombing in the Second World War but there have also been recent pollution accidents as well as cases of careless dumping of nitrogenous compounds and untreated human waste near wells. These problems have been addressed and broadly-speaking Grade II rivers (suitable for fishing and recreation) have become

Grade I (suitable for municipal drinking water and food processing) while Grade III (used for irrigation and hydropower but with concerns over public health) have become Grade II (Zinnes 2004, pp. 444–5). On some rivers the improvement has been remarkable e.g. the Săsar at Baia Mare. The record has been patchy however with much assistance for Bacău and Baia Mare (including closure of polluting industries) and also for Tulcea with the Danube delta in mind; while Alexandria, Oradea, Slatina and Suceava suffered some deterioration due to lack of funding. In 2002 there was centralised data on water quality for only 51 per cent of the population and the distribution network was more than 75 years old in places, with problems often acute in small towns, such as in Sulina where the northern part of the town suffered through damage to the pipe crossing the Danube.

Extending Water Supply
Overall 58 per cent of the population have piped water compared with 53 per cent for sewage. There are big differences between urban and rural areas: 95.7 per cent of 4.26mln urban dwellings had a water supply (90.9 per cent through public networks and 4.8 per cent through their own systems – i.e. about a tenth are not served by centralised systems) and 87.9 per cent have sewage (82.5 per cent public); while 42.8 per cent of 3.85mln rural houses have water (14.0 per cent public systems and 28.8 per cent own systems) but only 14.3 per cent have sewage (2.8 per cent by public systems). Improvements are going ahead quite rapidly with EBRD loan capital available for rebuilding large city systems with improved water pressure. The EU is covering 75 per cent of the €98mln project to upgrade the water utility in Constanţa (with a non-reimbursible loan worth €72mln) combining with a €19mln EBRD credit and €7mln from the local authorities. ISPA assistance for water supply is benefiting Constanţa as well as Cluj and Iaşi. Southeast Water (UK) donated an automated chlorination system for Slobozia in 1996, while VEW Energie (Germany) collaborated with Braşov county over water supply and sewerage (through the Apă company) in 1999. The Hungarian subsidiary of Umwelttechnik (Austria) built a drinking water system in the Zalău area in 2004 with €7mln of EU finance (rehabilitating reservoirs and installing pumps and 50kms of pipes). Currently a substantial number of cities are highlighting water supply programmes: the county towns of Bistriţa, Craiova, Giurgiu, Reşiţa, Sf.Gheorghe, Slatina, Slobozia, Târgu Jiu, Tulcea, Turnu Severin, Vaslui and Zalău. Also the towns of Câmpina, Caransebeş, Codlea, Dej, Câmpia Turzii, Făgăraş, Lugoj, Mangalia, Medgidia, Olteniţa, Oneşti, Roman, Roşiorii de Vede, Ţandarei, Tecuci, Turda, Turnu Măgurele and Zimnicea. Meanwhile €380mln of European money is available through Phare to rehabilitate water supplies for 200 small- and medium-sized towns, provided they associate by hydrographic basins and can cope with repayment. All the small towns in Alba, Dâmboviţa and Sibiu counties are now involved, as well Curtici and Nădlac (Arad). Asbestos water pipes in the Capşa, Ciungi and Marceni areas of Bicaz – associated with high cancer rates – need replacement.

A number of new supply sytems are being developed. A dam at Azuga is supplying water to such downstream areas as Buşteni, Sinaia, Comarnic, Breaza and Cornu, with Danish money to upgrade the local water distribution supply at Breaza in 2001 (complemeted by World Bank help sought for gas, housing and social-cultural projects). A similar system is in hand for the Dumbrăveni-Mediaş-

Copşa Mică area of Transylvania; while a new 14mln.cu.m water storage at Zetea (Harghita) is supplying 135kms of pipeline as well as a water treatment facility and a mini-hydropower plant (1.8MW); and water is also being taken from the Someş at Gilău northwards into Sălaj. NIRAS of Denmark are helping with an improved water scheme for Râmnicu Vâlcea and Drăgăşani, based on Bradişor lake and requiring a pumping station in Valea lui Stan and six storage units (financed through a non-reimbursible grant to Râmnicu Vâlcea by Denmark's Environmental Protection Agency in 2000). The rural situation remains unsatisfactory although in addition to the district projects already mentioned there are water and sewage projects for several areas of Arad county (Dezna, Mailet and Pilu), Brăila (the southern part of the county) and Neamţ (Alexander cel Bun, Bistricioara and Durău).

Waste Water Treatment

A properly-costed environmental plan has been slow to emerge but there has been an emphasis on water infrastructure and quality that now needs to backed up with greater attention to waste water treatment (WWT), for there were only 2,770 such units nationwide for industrial and municipal use in 1993 – and furthermore some 30 per cent were defective or out of service. Environmental policy since 2000 has focused on long-term management of water resources in conformity with the Dublin Conference and the Rio Summit (both 1992), assisted by ISPA to the extent of €208–270mln annually during 2000–2006, in respect of drinking water, WWT, solidwaste management and air pollution. But Brussels estimates that $20bln is needed for ecological reconstruction to meet the demanding standards of the European acquis (with 17 directives for water quality standards alone, costing some $18bln.) given the problems documented in many river basins (Bătinaş 2000; Mihăiescu & Haidu 1996). Romania has asked the EU for derogations that will allow up to 15 years for full compliance. In line with European practice the focus of the Water Law of 1996 rested on the environmental management river basins by the NWC through local committees, although the top-heavy administration of 12 basins has been simplified, partly through financial problems aggravated by widespread non-payment of water bills.

At the same time responsibility for water quality has passed to EPAs who need to safeguard both consumers and sub-aquatic fauna. Concern over Black Sea pollution attaches high priority to improved river water quality throughout Romania in view of the impact of the Danube into which virtually all the country's rivers flow. Efforts on the Danube itself include monitoring water management through a pilot centre at Turnu Măgurele: part of the programme for rational cross-border resource management using the expertise of the Rhine administration and the Dutch province of Guelderland. Problems are compounded by inappropriate actions in the past: erosion arising from a reduced alluvium supply (due to damming); salinisation of the meadows through irrigation; and marshiness through massive inflitrations into phreatic level in Olt valley (through dams and dykes). WWT for the whole string of Danube towns from Turnu Severin to Tulcea was highlighted in the mid-1990s – with no cleaning facilities whatsoever at Brăila, Galaţi, Tulcea or Turnu Severin – and JBIC carried out a feasibility study in 2000. Meanwhile the Phare CBC programme for Romania and Bulgaria included 700bln.lei investment to (a) purchase a ship to depollute waters following accidental pollution of the Danube and (b) install monitoring and analytical devices.

Sewage Systems These have still not caught up with supply networks and, even allowing for the clean water lost through damaged pipes, there is still a lot of used water polluting the ground. During 1992–2002 households connected to sewerage increased only slightly from 51–53 per cent. The results can be seen as Răşinari near Sibiu where the mountain stream is choked with sewage (and garbage in the form of tyres, plastic, discarded consumer durables and other waste). A large investment of 12bln.lei was made in Caraş-Severin in 1996 to expand the water purification station in Reşiţa by increasing the decantation apparata from one to four over three years. The cleaned water outflow increased in quality – and also in volume from 313l/sec to 1,059 – so that pollution by household and industrial waste ceased spreading downstream into Serbia. The work has been followed by a €52mln ISPA non-reimbursible funding for 98kms of new water pipes and 30kms of sewerage piping; while sewerage has also been installed in the smaller towns Bocşa, Moldova Nouă and Oraviţa, as well as the villages of Goruia, Lupac, Mehadia, Văliug (while roads were also upgraded as part of a wider scheme). Expansion of WWT in Cluj reduced river pollution in 1996, while European banks financed ecological treatment in Piteşti in 2000 on a 2.5ha site with recycled material packed for sale. Since 2000, €4.2mln of EU finance has restored the Jiu valley's sewerage networks focusing on the Danitoni station. Since the winning Romanian consortium took care of the collector sewers of Aninoasa, Lupeni, Petrila, Petroşani, Uricani and Vulcan, direct discharge of untreated sewage has ceased while further benefit has followed from the purification of the residual waters as part of a larger programme for environmental improvement. There has been EU help for rehabilitation at Arad, Braşov, Craiova and Iaşi: also the Black Sea coastal towns of Constanţa and Mangalia, assisted by Denmark's Environmental Protection Agency. And in 2004 Bacău received a loan of €13mln under the Municipal Environmental Loan Facility (set up in 2000 specifically for ISPA cofinancing) to supplement the initial grant of €39mln for WWT. Meanwhile Sebeş has used a bond issue to deal with its water and sewerage rehabilitation in 2002, while Timişoara collaborated with Umwelttechnik (Austria) over a €2.0mln factory for sewage systems at Ortişoara.

Flood Control

There is a vast amount of work to be done to protect hydrographic basins from pollution and flood. Romanian-French hydrographic cooperation is improving knowledge of the régime of the Argeş-Dâmboviţa-Ialomiţa basins (through information systems and water prognosis) with a particular focus on organic pollution at Curtea de Argeş that impacts on the storage lakes providing water for Bucharest and Piteşti. Through the Siret pilot the same partnership helped to establish independent management bodies for river basins in 2000 and establish tariffs for water supply and sewage systems and well as staff training and IT equipment. Meanwhile JBIC worked with NWC on control of river pollution in Prahova as well as the residual waters discharged from seven Danube towns in 1999, while Dutch organisations have helped over monitoring and ecological reconstruction in the Mureş, Prut and Siret basins. Under the LIFE environmental programme the EC has been helping to improve air quality in Oradea and habitat conservation in the Iron Gates Natural Park (protecting 16 rare species of bats living in mountain caves in 2001). And the US Trade & Development Agency contributed to a feasibility study on the management of hydrographic basins in 2003, integrated into local administrative networks: Burgess & Niple (Cleveland) have been involved in pilot water management while Lockheed Martin (Bethesda, Maryland) contributed forecasting prediction technology through a $46mln system of automatic recording stations to help to minimise flood damage in 2004. NWC can now envisage an integrated computerised system for monitoring 'hydro-meteorological events' as well as water quality. There is also much ENGO activity: the Tisa programme – involving organisations from Hungary, Romania and Serbia coordinated by EPCE – including such work as the Ecotur (Sibiu) educational project for the Târnave basin; while 'Pro Europa Liga' (Târgu Mureş) is concerned with a five-country monitoring network; and the Transylvanian Carpathian Society (Satu Mare) is researching on endangered species in the Ilba and Tur valleys near Baia Mare.

Disasters in 2005 – a terrible year for flooding in Romania with a serial crisis affecting Banat, Transylvania and southern Moldavia. Heavy rain in the Eastern Carpathians (which may combine with snow melt in late winter or spring) can have devastating implications either for the Mureş and Tisa valleys flowing westwards or the Siret on the eastwen side. One such event in September 2005 increased the Siret's discharge from the usual 22cusecs to 2,500, with serious damage to villages in the lower valley (Măicăneşti, Nămoloasa, Năneşti, Tudor Vladimirescu and Vadu Roşca) and the railway link with Moldavia was cut between Adjud and Pufeşti. The Buzău was also affected and while the Siriu barrage safeguarded the main valley, the Calvini bridge over the Bâsca Chiojdului tributary was damaged; gaving some opportunity for local Roma to profit by ferrying stranded travellers with their horses! Difficulties continued into 2006 with a rapid spring snowmelt causing the Danube to flood the Bistreţ area of Dolj (including Dunăreni, Măcesu de Jos and Plosca) .Investment is now needed to rebuild the villages affected and improve defences for the future with World Bank finance. In the process the failings of NLIP were revealed and the Aquaproiect company was accused of misappropriating funds obtained without tender for the construction of embankment defences in Banat. In 2007 it will be compulsory for owners to insure their property while the authorities are now making inventories of houses at risk through siting on floodplains (3,500 in Bacău county alone). River regulation is far from complete: in Vrancea (where 16 people died in floods in 2005): the Râmna has been dealt with but 31 projects are outstanding involving the Putna, Milcov and Râmnicu Sărat.

Waste Management and Recycling
This is another major element of pre-accession environmental policy (Thomas 1999), highlighted by events during the early transition years when Romania was used as a dumping ground for toxic waste that would have been expensive to dispose of in Western Europe. A national strategy for waste management in 2003 required a radical change in mentality with a focus on recycling to deal with half the plastic waste (a substantial quantity given that 70,000t of raw material are imported annually for packaging). PET (polyethylene terephthalate) bottles are a particular concern with European Drinks using 2,000t of polyester each month in 2003, followed by

Coca Cola (using up to 1,000t) and the mineral water companies. Meanwhile in 2002, JBIC financed $2.0mln of research on hazardous waste produced by 500 Romanian factories, with 30 per cent recycling agreed with the EU by 2005. The first ecological tip – complying with EU norms – opened at Constanţa in 1995 with the help of the French Sater-Parachini Group and is operated by the Tracon company. Arad negotiated with Schonmarkes (Germany) over waste recycling in 1996 and the following year Braşov contracted with the authority in Umbria (Italy) for a new garbage platform near Râşnov meeting international standards. Then Spain's Economics Ministry contributed €250,000 for a waste collection facility for Galaţi and Brăila in 2002, while Tracon opened an ecological household waste dump and sewage installation at Muchea (Brăila) in the same year (as at Constanţa). And Prahova have commissioned three eco-friendly landfills since 2000 – with another planned for Vălenii de Munte – to stop ground and water pollution.

With SAPARD finance Iaşi has created a centralised waste treatment/sewage system at Hălăuceşti (a suburban community benefiting from the extension of water and methane gas supplies); while ISPA help is being provided for solid waste management at Piatra Neamţ; and the Dej-Gherla and Turda-Câmpia Turzii waste platforms are being rehabilitated. Integrated waste mangement schemes are reported for Argeş, Buzău and Teleorman counties as well as the Baia Mare area of Maramureş. Following the $11mln regional ecological dump at Reghin (Mureş), an extended network is now developing at Alba Iulia, Bacău, Bihor (Oradea), Bistriţa, Botoşani, Constanţa, Giurgiu, Gorj (Târgu Jiu) and Suceava. Meanwhile rural waste schemes are relatively unusual but Neamţ has projects for Bistriţa, Scăricica and Viişoara. Given that the average age of cars in Romania at the turn of the century was 13.5 years, attention has been given to the disposal of vehicles over 12 years old through a scheme in 2001 for Dacias (with 10mln.lei discount for new cars against Remat certificates for old cars correctly disposed of) which government extended to all types through larger subsidies of 30mln.lei for the purchase of new cars from validated sources and wider provision of recycling centres (although the subsidies were stopped by the new goverment in 2005). Spending on waste management is still quite modest – a €1.0mln project for 2002-4 continued an earlier €600,000 project realised in partnership with Germany – whereas Romania will need to spend €6.0bln over the first ten years after accession in order to implement Brussels legislation.

Conclusion: A Synthesis based on 'Quality Of Life' Indicators

Towns vary considerably and there are many criteria available. An interesting survey was undertaken in 2006 by 'Capital' magazine surveying 'quality of life' among the 50 largest towns according to 24 criteria which included economic structure and countryside access as well as levels of modernisation. Table 10.3 gives the results. These bring out regional variations with the seven North West towns gaining the highest average score of 5.64 followed closely by 5.60 for Central region's six towns and then fairly even gaps down to West (5.37 – seven towns); South East (5.03 – seven); South (4.83 – seven); South West (4.59 – five); and North East (4.23 – ten). The larger towns generally have better ratings: thus the top ten average 394.8 thousand population; the second quintile 170.2 and the next three 97.3, 88.3 and 72.4. Again

Table 10.3: Quality of life survey of Romania's 50 largest towns 2006

Position	Town Name	Index	Popn.	Change	Region	Position	Town Name	Index	Popn.	Change	Region
1	Bucharest	7.60	1925.0	+0.9	B-I	26	Giurgiu	4.83	69.8	-3.4	S
2	Timişoara	7.25	303.6	-8.9	W	27	Slatina	4.80	80.3	-7.0	SW
3	Constanţa	7.10	306.3	-3.0	SE	28	Târgovişte	4.78	90.6	-9.8	S
4	Sibiu	6.65	154.2	-16.2	Cen	29	Brăila	4.77	218.7	-9.8	SE
5	Braşov	6.58	282.5	-19.9	Cen	30	Baia Mare	4.75	140.9	-6.3	NW
6	Oradea	6.50	206.2	-8.5	NW	31	Botoşani	4.60	117.3	-1.9	NE
7	Arad	6.25	168.6	-11.9	W		Sfântu Gheorghe	4.60	62.1	-13.8	Cen
	Cluj-Napoca	6.25	310.2	-2.4	NW	33	Tulcea	4.57	92.9	-2.2	SE
9	Turda	6.05	57.7	-10.3	NW	34	Hunedoara	4.48	72.4	-18.3	W
10	Ploieşti	6.03	233.7	-5.6	S		Roman	4.48	71.3	-7.4	NE
11	Piteşti	5.95	171.1	+5.3	S	36	Buzău	4.47	136.6	-6.1	SE
12	Lugoj	5.87	45.6	-16.0	W	37	Deva	4.45	68.8	-11.0	W
13	Târgu Mureş	5.80	147.1	-10.7	Cen		Piatra Neamţ	4.45	109.7	-5.2	NE
14	Satu Mare	5.59	115.2	-15.8	NW		Suceava	4.45	106.7	+0.8	NE
15	Bistriţa	5.43	82.1	+3.2	NW	40	Petroşani	4.42	45.1	-15.5	W
16	Galaţi	5.28	298.4	-2.9	SE	41	Alexandria	4.35	51.7	-11.4	S
17	Iaşi	5.25	307.4	-6.9	NE	42	Turnu Severin	4.12	109.4	+1.9	SW
18	Craiova	5.10	300.2	+0.1	SW	43	Călăraşi	4.10	73.9	-3.1	S
19	Mediaş	5.08	54.6	-27.7	Cen		Tecuci	4.10	43.3	-7.3	SE
20	Bacău	5.00	180.5	-6.6	NE	45	Târgu Jiu	4.05	96.3	+3.3	SW
21	Medgidia	4.95	44.5	-9.1	SE	46	Focşani	3.90	101.0	-0.8	NE
22	Zalău	4.92	64.1	-1.7	NW	47	Slobozia	3.80	52.6	+3.2	S
23	Râmnicu Vâlcea	4.88	111.7	+3.4	SW	48	Oneşti	3.75	52.3	-8.4	NE
24	Alba Iulia	4.87	66.4	-8.2	Cen	49	Vaslui	3.25	72.4	-1.8	NE
25	Reşiţa	4.85	86.3	-21.8	W	50	Bârlad	3.15	71.4	-5.8	NE

Population given in thousands for 2005 with overall change since 1990.

Source: Capital magazine 'quality of life' survey (2006) according to 24 criteria

while the eight cities over 250,000 average 6.30, the 17 others above 100,000 average 5.19 with the other 25 (falling to 44.5 for Medgidia) on 4.72. However the lowest-placed city over 250,000 (Craiova) is in 18th position and the lowest-placed city over 100,000 population (Focşani) is placed at 46 while the highest in the lowest group is Turda in ninth position. It is also clear that there is no correlation between the scores and population growth since 1990. The growing towns are scattered across the table from Pitesti (+5.3 percent) in 11th place, followed by Bistriţa (+3.2) at 15, Craiova (+0.1) at 18, Râmnicu Vâlcea (+2.3) at 23, Suceava (+0.8) at 37=, Turnu Severin (+1.9) at 42, Târgu Jiu (+3.3) at 45 and Slobozia (+3.2) at 47. While quality of life is not irrelevant the key considerations here are the extent of redundancy among migrants post-1989, subsequent FDI, natural population increase and the propensity for migration abroad.

Towns as Service Centres

Introduction and Methodology

This section attempts a review of the provincial towns as service centres. The study is based on two main sources. First the census data for 1992 and 2002 shows changes in population and also in employment: both the total activity and work in industry (including extractive industries and energy). Typically there has been an overall decline during the decade with a sharp fall in industrial employment balanced by growth in services. The second source concerns Internet information on the networks of companies involved in banking and insurance as well as shopping (including petrol stations and some aspects of transport). This information obviously does not cover all the chains involved but provides a significant range of examples including some – like RSB and Petrom – that are present in the vast majority of towns, compared with others that only aim to serve the larger cities. It is possible to see differences in the threshold populations, although networks are still developing and there is often a prominent regional bias e.g. BT in Transylvania, while Dasipex (which started in 1998 selling phones for Mobilrom/Orange subscribers) is very strong in Moldavia. Meanwhile for the Vel Pitar bakery – in seven cities including three in the intermediate population range (Giurgiu, Târgu Jiu, and Tecuci) – development is evidently based on appropriate opportunity regarding the acquisition of existing businesses. Discussion cannot generally take account of development programmes and strategies where apparent anomalies arise (unless web information happens to be available) although the origins of the Cosmo empire in Covasna presumably explain why there are three stores in the small town of Târgu Secuiesc where the firm is still partially headquartered.

Population and Employment Trends

Census data is examined with regard to Bucharest and five groups of provincial towns using thresholds of 15, 30, 70 and 150 thousand (Table 10.4). The urban population declined in all categories during 1992–2002 but the rates increased progressively down the hierarchy (from -6.9 per cent for Bucharest to -9.3 per cent for the smallest towns) the only anomaly being the high figure of -9.6 per cent for the

Table 10.4: Classification of towns 1992–2002

Size band and region		No	Total Population 1992	2002	Chge	Occupied/Total 1992	2002	Chge	Occupied/Industry 1992	2002	Chge	Indexes I	II	III
Bucharest	C	1	2067.5	1926.3	-6.8	885.5	820.9	-7.3	481.5	256.7	-46.7	99	97	4b
150-	A	7	1733.4	1604.6	-7.4	812.3	702.1	-13.6	484.3	309.6	-36.1	87	56	3c
350,000	B	8	2196.3	2045.6	-6.9	1008.0	849.0	-15.8	574.3	358.4	-37.6	86	43	3c
	C	15	3929.7	3650.2	-7.1	1820.3	1551.0	-14.8	1058.5	668.0	-36.9	86	47	3c
70-	A	5	547.2	489.6	-10.5	258.4	210.9	-18.4	162.5	108.3	-33.4	75	33	3d
150,000	B	13	1379.3	1272.1	-7.8	659.5	552.6	-16.2	393.8	255.8	-35.1	84	40	3d
	C	18	1926.5	1761.7	-8.6	917.9	763.5	-16.8	557.3	364.1	-34.7	78	35	3d
30-	A	16	840.1	754.8	-10.2	388.1	318.2	-18.0	240.4	155.6	-35.3	80	40	3c
70,000	B	21	998.6	907.8	-9.1	448.3	359.1	-19.9	278.8	169.6	-39.2	87	34	3d
	C	37	1838.7	1662.6	-9.6	836.4	677.3	-19.0	513.2	325.2	-36.6	84	37	3d
30-	D	25	2366.4	2165.1	-8.6	1131.6	946.4	-16.4	666.8	432.9	-35.1	81	41	3c
150,000	E	30	1398.8	1259.2	-10.0	622.7	494.4	-20.6	403.8	256.4	-36.5	85	32	3d
	C	55	3765.2	3422.3	-9.1	1754.3	1440.8	-17.9	1070.6	689.3	-35.7	83	38	3d
15-	A	29	692.0	631.3	-8.9	301.1	242.2	-19.6	198.5	137.2	-30.9	69	17	3e
30,000	B	30	677.1	615.3	-9.1	294.3	227.3	-22.8	176.4	105.5	-40.2	70	18	3d
	C	59	1269.1	1246.6	-9.0	595.4	469.5	-21.2	374.9	242.7	-35.2	64	15	3e
Below	A	64	617.1	559.9	-9.3	255.2	205.6	-19.5	132.3	89.1	-32.6	55	9	3e
15,000	B	71	679.0	641.0	-5.6	282.4	233.2	-17.4	145.2	91.9	-36.8	70	18	3d
	C	135	1296.1	1200.9	-7.3	537.6	438.8	-18.4	277.5	181.0	-34.8	64	15	3e
Total	A	121	4429.8	4040.2	-8.8	2015.1	1679.0	-16.7	1218.0	799.8	-34.3	77	38	3d
Including	B	244	7997.8	7408.1	-7.4	3578.0	3042.1	-15.0	2050.0	1237.9	-39.6	85	36	3d
Bucharest	C	365	12427.6	11448.3	-7.9	5593.1	4721.1	-15.5	3260.0	2037.7	-37.5	81	37	3d

A Towns in Transylvania including Banat and Crişana; B Towns in Moldavia Wallachia and Dobrogea; C Total; D County towns; E Other towns

Indexes I Decline in jobs in industry per thousand people; II Gains in other employment per thousand people; III Code for the balance between the two: 1–5 denote industrial job losses of up to 30, 60, 90, 120 and 150 jobs/thousand – 0 denotes gain; a–f indicates 'compensation' in other sectors greater than the loss in industry (a), or part of the loss (from 75% = b; from 50% = c; from 25% = d and from 0% = e) or negative (f)

Source: Census data.

30-70,000 group. On the other hand there is an inverted progression over the decline of industry because the smallest towns have done best (albeit with a relatively low level of industrialisaton in 1992: 214 jobs/ptp in 1992 compared with 279 for the 30-70,000 group) with -64jobs/ptp ranging upwards to -99 in Bucharest. On the other hand there is, broadly, a progressive reduction down the hierarchy as regards growth of other sectors: from +97jobs/ptp in Bucharest to +15 for the smallest towns, while the 30–70,000 and 70–150,000 categories are exactly the same at +35. Putting the two sets of figures together, activity levels have decreased least in Bucharest (-2/ptp) compared with -58/ptp for the 15–30,000 group, with the smallest towns doing slightly better at -49/ptp. As regards the extent to which employment losses in industry are compensated by growth in other sectors there is a stepwise progression from 98 per cent in Bucharest to 55 per cent in the cities with over 150,000 population, 45 per cent and 44 per cent in the two next lower categories (50 per cent for the county towns and 38 per cent for the others if these two groups are combined) and finally 26 per cent and 23 per cent in the two lowest groups. The two variables of jobs (a) lost in industry and (b) 'regained' through growth elsewhere may be combined into a code where the numbers 1-5 indicate losses of up to 30, 60, 90, 120 and 150 jobs/ptp and the letters a-f indicate compensation through growth in the service sector extending from over 100 per cent of industry's losses (a), to the 76–100 per cent band (b), 51–75 per cent (c), 26–74 per cent (d) and 0–25 per cent (e) plus some rare cases where the other sectors produce losses (f).

Regional Division
Regional division is provided through separate calculations for Transylvania (with Banat and Crişana) as opposed to Moldavia, Wallachia and Dobrogea. This divides Romania into the independent state of pre-1918 (Bucovina excepted) and the other territories then part of the Habsburg Empire and traditionally more developed. It seems that the rate of urban population decline is generally higher for Transylvania (except for the 15–30,000 group) while the decline in activity in less. Taking all categories (apart from Bucharest) the urban decline was 8.5 per cent in Transylvania but 7.4 per cent elsewhere while the industrial decline was less (-77 jobs/ptp compared with -85) and likewise the gain in other sectors (+38 jobs/ptp compared with +36) to give an overall change of -41 compared with -47. This could mean that outside Transylvania relatively more people are claiming some activity in agriculture, while within Transylvania more people have gone abroad in search of work instead of accepting unemployment or under-employment at home; though such a dictinction cannot be proven without more exhaustive investigation. There is in any case an important caveat over these calculations in that significant deindustrialisation occurred before the 1992 census while the 2002 census came too early for the boom in consumer spending evident over the past two years: hence the picture does not fairly represent ther transition period as whole.

Large and Small Towns
Large and small towns also generate a clear and valid contrast. Certainly cities of over 150,000 population have vibrant economies, albeit with significant variations in the cost of food and drink, housing, transport and other services and local taxation.

Figure 10.3 Classification of towns and rural centres

There seem to be particular cost advantages in the west, especially on transport axes, and on the coast so that Craiova and Iaşi do less well – and even Brăila and Galaţi are disadvantaged compared with Constanţa. Second, the county towns have such considerable advantages through their administrative importance and the tendency for commercial firms seeking nationwide coverage to organise their activity on a county basis that it seems appropriate to separate the medium-sized towns on this basis. These towns also have a major industrial role inherited from communism and often reinforced by FDI and the development of SMEs. However the county towns are quite diverse: all the 15 towns in the 150–350,000 bracket are county towns, as are 17 of the 18 towns of 70–150,000 (Hunedoara is the exception) while the remaining eight fall into the group of 37 towns with 35–70,000 population. Hence the alternative calculations that combine the 30–70,000 and 70–150,000 groups and then separate them on the basis of county towns and others. The discussion therefore highlights (a) county towns larger than 150,000 – the emerging 'metropoles', although some towns of 100–150,000 also appear highly attractive for business; (b) the other county towns; and (c) other towns larger than 30,000 (Figure 10.3).

Large Towns (150–350,000 population)

These strong county towns are coded overall at 3c for restructuring with a loss of 86 jobs/ptp in industry but 'compensation' elsewhere of 47 jobs/ptp (i.e. just over 50 per cent). Looking at individual cases, Brăila is in a better situation with a smaller loss – though a smaller compensation (2d), while Iaşi and Târgu Mureş (4c) and Craiova and Galaţi (4d) have a greater loss as well as lower compensation. The others are close to the average but Braşov and Cluj (3b) have achieved better compensation and Oradea (3d) slightly worse. The group generally typically attracts NBR branches – of which there are 19, though several cities of 100–150,000 are also involved. And while the supermarket chains in the early years also tended to look to towns of at least 100,000 they generally overlooked Botoşani, Focşani, Piatra Neamţ, Suceava and Turnu Severin. The large cities are also endorsed by merchant banks that still stop well short of having representation in all county towns: ABN-AMRO, Banca Românească, Banca Turco-Romană, Eurom, ING, Libra, Mindbank, OTP (Robank), Romexterra, RIB, Sanpaolo IMI, Unicredit (including HVB and Tiriac) and Volksbank. Also the many banks with very limited networks (covering no more than 10 provincial centres) cumulatively endorse this group as well: Alphabank (present in only 10 provincial centres), Anglo-Romanian (2), Banca Firenze (8), Citibank (6), Emporiki (3), Eximbank (6), Finansbank (8), Italo Romena – Gruppo Veneto (6), Piraeus (8) and Procredit or Miro (6). The same applies to one of the insurance companies (Interamerican) that serves all cities larger than 100,000, as well as a group of companies – Allianz-Tiriac, Asirom, Ardaf, Omniasig and Unita – that extend their operations thoughout the hierarchy and (cumulatively) a group of companies like Gerroma (4), Global Asigurari (Romanian-Portuguese) (12), Grawe (2) and Garanta (7) with very small networks. It is common to find companies maintaining several branches in the big cities – an average of 10 RSB facilities; but also 6.5 for RDB, 5.5 for RCB and three for Raiffeisen However both Eurom and Piraeus banks overlook Craiova – the fourth largest provincial town – while the

Road Hauliers Federation prefer Târgu Jiu (and they also regard Galați and Brăila as one).

Shopping

The large chains for consumer durables – Altex, Cosmo, Domo, Flanco and Flamingo – naturally cover all the largest cities (with an average of two Domo electrical stores in each city over 150,000) while relatively limited chains such as Alpitex and Mobexpert (furniture) and Steilmann (clothing) are virtally restricted to towns of over 100,000 (though only one of them is represented in Buzău, Botoșani, Suceava and Focșani). The same applies to a group of small companies concerned with home design: Arabesque DIY, Delta Interior Design and Mondial bathroom suites (the latter owned by Villeroy & Boch of Germany who are based in Lugoj); also the home security company UTI. The stronger county towns also have good networks of petrol stations and although Petrom is prominent everywhere this company's strength against the competition (Lukoil, Mol and Rompetrol – usually all three) is quite variable, However, taking all the cities over 150,000 there are 100 Petrom stations and 118 for the competition: hence 15 stations per city on average with Petrom's overall share 46 per cent. But while there is a rough balance in eight cities, Craiova has 14 Petrom stations against six for the competition, with an 11:5 ratio in Iași and 6:4 in Brăila; while Petrom is relatively weak in Cluj (6:13), Constanța (7:17), Galați (2:6) and Ploiești (6:12). Meanwhile all cities enjoy a courier service by Cargus and each has 19 shops (on average) serving Vodafone subscribers.

Medium-Sized Towns (30–150,000 population)

As regards the weaker county towns, the code for restructuring is again 3c with exactly half the industrial loss of 82 jobs/ptp compensated by growth in other sectors. Taking the cities individually Satu Mare and Zalău follow the average, while Sf.Gheorghe and Vaslui have achieved more compensation (3b) as opposed to Alexandria, Baia Mare, Deva, Miercurea Ciuc, Reșița and Turnu Severin with less (3d) – and more so Slobozia and Târgu Jiu (3e). Lower industrial decline applies in Focșani (2a), Alba Iulia and Călărași (2b) and Tulcea (2c); balanced by heavier losses in Botoșani (4c); Buzău, Giurgiu, Râmnicu Vâlcea and Târgoviște (4d); and Suceava (5d). These towns are all well-served by the banks and insurance companies (including the limited-network companies when considered cumulatively) although provision is less generous with an average of 2.5 facilities for RCB and RSB (below the 150,000 threshold) while RDB and Raiffeison provide a second office in only a few cases. The supermarket chains are now moving down the hierarchy – going well below the 100,000 threshold to serve all county towns – but the Transylvanian towns tend to attract most attention: Alba Iulia, Bistrița, Deva, Sf.Gheorghe and Zalău while elsewhere – apart from Suceava – it is the southeast core that is most evident: Alexandria, Focșani, Giurgiu but especially Târgoviște. Alpitex, Mobexpert and Steilmann appear but only two of the three are present in Bistrița, Slatina and Târgoviște; only one (usually Mobexpert) in Alba Iulia, Alexandria, Călărași, Deva and Tulcea – and none in Giurgiu, Miercurea Ciuc, Reșița, Sf.Gheorghe, Slobozia, Târgu Jiu, Vaslui and Zalău. The home design group is also highly selective with

Table 10.5: Petrol stations

Region	County Towns				Other Towns				Rural Areas				Total			
	A	B	C	D	A	B	C	D	A	B	C	D	A	B	C	D
Bucharest	67	10	27	10	1	0	5	0	2	0	0	0	70	10	32	10
Centre	22	9	10	8	42	7	6	5	9	2	2	0	73	18	18	13
NorthEast	31	6	8	3	30	5	2	2	19	2	1	0	80	13	11	5
NorthWest	28	11	20	10	27	6	3	3	12	1	1	0	67	18	24	13
South	28	10	17	6	41	4	7	0	14	3	3	0	83	17	27	6
SouthEast	28	13	16	10	21	5	5	0	8	5	5	0	57	23	26	10
SouthWest	33	5	13	3	26	1	2	0	17	1	1	0	76	7	16	3
West	25	5	12	8	29	2	10	5	12	1	3	0	66	8	25	13
Total	262	69	123	58	217	30	40	15	93	15	16	0	572	114	179	73

A Petrom; B Rompetrol; C Lukoil; D Mol

Source: Company websites

some tendency to bypass the county town in favour of other large towns, presumably to limit competition: the electrical store Cosmo locates in Hunedoara and Petroşani instead of Deva – also Paşcani rather than Iaşi, while Bârlad is preferred to Vaslui. Banca Românească also prefers Hunedoara to Deva. Cargus operate everywhere but the Road Hauliers Federation only appear in certain cases with the Eurocorridors possibly influential at Alba Iulia and Deva. The average number of Vodafone shops falls to 8.5, compared with 6.0 for the four selected oil companies. However, Petrom's share rises to 53 per cent, indicating a slightly weaker challenge from the competition: 79 stations against Petrom's 89 with the latter particularly strong in Piatra Neamţ, Târgu Jiu, Târgovişte and Vaslui. Table 10.5 summaries the situation over petrol stations and shows the Petrom share rising progressively down the hierarchy as the competition fades: 54.1 per cent in Bucharest and the county towns; 71.8 per cent in other towns and 75.0 per cent in rural areas.

Non-County Towns
Non-county towns in the 30–70,000 group, plus Hunedoara in the 70–150,000 group, record an overall loss of industrial jobs of -85/th, compensated to the extent of 38 per cent: hence the code 3d. This average applies in the specific cases of Sighetul Marmaţiei, Roman and Tecuci, with more compensation at Petroşani (3c) balanced by less at Roşiorii de Vede (3e). A more moderate industrial loss at Odorheiul Secuiesc (2a); Dorohoi, Mangalia and Sighişoara (2c); Curtea de Argeş, Lugoj and Turnu Măgurele (2d); and Feteşti (2f) is balanced by more at Năvodari (4b); Mioveni and Oneşti (4c); Bârlad, Câmpina, Câmpulung, Dej, Făgăraş, Hunedoara,, Medgidia and Paşcani (4c); Lupeni and Turda (4d); Râmnicu Sărat (4e) and Mediaş(4f). As central places all the towns over 40,000 (apart from Medgidia, overshadowed by Constanţa) are well supported: Hunedoara, Roman, Bârlad, Turda, Mediaş, Oneşti, Lugoj, Paşcani, Petroşani, Sighetul Marmaţiei and Tecuci all have substantial hinterlands in addition to their own populations. Occasionally even the special shops appear e.g. Delta Design and Steilmann in the fashionable Black Sea resort of Mangalia. Much the same applies to those with over 30,000: Câmpina, Dej, Făgăraş, Odorheiul Secuiesc, Râmnicu Sărat, Sighişoara, Roşiorii de Vede and Turnu Măgurele (though not all the electrical stores are present). But the Argeş trio of Câmpulung, Curtea de Argeş and Mioveni lose out somewhat to Piteşti (though the locally-based Alpitex is present at Câmpulung) while Dorohoi, Feteşti and Năvodari are constrained by the proximity of Botoşani, Călăraşi and Constanţa respectively; and Lupeni is one of a group of Jiu valley mining towns that look to Petroşani (Petrila, Uricani and Vulcan are all poorly serviced in relation to their population size). However apart from Lupeni all have the services of the Allianz, Ardaf, Asirom, Onmiasig and Unita insurance companies; likewise the banks: RCB, RDB and RSB, as well as Bancpost and Raiffeisen (and most are also served by BT, at least through agencies). But only rarely is there more than one office for each bank, although two to seven shops support Vodafone subscribers (with four the average) and petrol stations average almost three with the Petrom share rising further to 61 per cent. The vast majority also feature, along with the county towns, in the activities of Ramstal whose business is heating, air conditioning and sanitation. Săgeată (2003) has proposed that many of these towns – some of which were county towns in the inter-war period when the counties were

smaller than today – merit an administrative role at the district level that is not currently recognised. His proposals involve Bârlad (Vaslui), Caracal (Olt), Câmpina (Prahova), Câmpulung and Curtea de Argeş (Argeş), Dej and Turda (Cluj), Făgăraş (Braşov), Feteşti (Călăraşi), Hunedoara and Petroşani (Hunedoara), Medgidia (Constanţa), Mediaş (Sibiu), Odorhei (Harghita), Oneşti (Bacău), Râmnicu Sărat (Buzău), Reghin and Sighişoara (Mureş), Roman (Neamţ), Roşiorii de Vede and Turnu Măgurele (Teleorman), Sighetul Marmaţiei (Maramureş) and Tecuci (Galaţi).

Smaller Towns

Smaller towns (15–30,000 population) recorded an overall loss of employment of 58 jobs/ptp during 1992–2002, with a 79/ptp decline in industry compensated by a growth of only 21/ptp in other sectors – hence code 3d again applies, but only marginally. With 59 towns involved it would be tedious to provide a full description. There is great diversity although 20 are in Class 3 for industrial decline compared with 29 in Class 2 and Class 4, while ten are in an extreme position. Cernavodă's code is '0f' indicates a gain in industry and a loss in other sectors (the reverse of the norm) because of the growth of the nuclear power station. There are also three towns in Class 1 with a very small decline in industry: Borşa (1a) has a growth in other sectors greater than the loss in industry while in Blaj and Zimnicea the other sectors have exacerbated the small decline in industry instead of relieving it. And there are six towns in Class 5 where the losses in industry are 120–149/ptp. Gura Humorului sees the loss more than fully compensated for by growth elsewhere, while the compensation in Balş, Fălticeni, Rădăuţi and Târgu Neamţ is less than 50 per cent (5d) and less than 25 per cent in Drăgăşani (5e). As regards services there is general representation by RCB and RSB while in the case of Bancpost, RDB and Raiffeisen two of the three are present on average. In the case of the five insurance companies there are 3.3 of them present on average. Turning to the electrical stores, there are two in each town on average but they tend to cluster in the small towns of Suceava county: Fălticeni, as well as Câmpulung Moldovenesc, Gura Humorului, Rădăuţi and Vatra Dornei (all of which have significant hinterlands quite independent of the county town); likewise two towns in the west of Bacău county (Comăneşti and Moineşti) as well as Adjud, Olteniţa and Târgu Neamţ in Moldavia-Wallachia. Finally a group of towns in Transylvania – Blaj, Caransebeş, Carei, Cugir, Marghita, Sebeş, Târgu Secuiesc and Târnaveni – are also well served and evidently offer considerable spending power.

The towns where all the banks and insurance companies appear are similar to an extent (Adjud, Caransebeş, Carei, Fălticeni, Rădăuţi, Sebeş, Târgu Neamţ, Urziceni and Vatra Dornei) but also Aiud, Gherla, Gheorgheni, Orăştie and Salonta are also favoured. There are 16 Ramstal towns including Brad, Corabia and Şimleu Silvaniei not previously mentioned, while Cargus highlights additionally Brad, Câmpia Turzii, Găeşti and Gheorgheni. Special shops are rare but Alpitex are present at Zimnicea, Delta Design at Rădăuţi and Mondial at Gheorgheni (Ciumani). By contrast there are a number of relatively weak centres, overshadowed by strong neighbours: Baia Sprie (near Baia Mare), Băicoi (Ploieşti), Bocşa (Reşiţa), Borşa (Vişeu de Sus), Breaza (Câmpina), Buftea (Bucharest), Buhuşi (Bacău), Cişnădie (Sibiu), Moreni

(Târgovişte), Ocna Mureş (Aiud), Petrila and Vulcan (Petroşani) and Râşnov and Zărneşti (Braşov). There are no banks other than RCB and RSB present at Băicoi, Borşa, Buhuşi and Petrila (and only one insurance company at Băicoi, Buhuşi and Petrila). There are 2.5 Vodafone shops on average and 1.7 petrol stations with the Petrom share now 64 per cent indicating that the competition is less committed to challenging what was initially a Petrom monopoly. Finally the Săgeată (2003) proposals for county districts involve several towns in this group, a number of which have already been highlighted: Brad (Hunedoara), Calafat (Dolj), Caransebeş (Caraş-Severin), Carei (Satu Mare), Drăgăşani (Vâlcea), Huşi (Vaslui), Olteniţa (Călăraşi), Târnaveni (Mureş), Urziceni (Ialomiţa); also three in Alba (Blaj, Cugir and Sebeş) and four in Suceava county: Câmpulung Moldovenesc, Fălticeni, Rădăuţi and Vatra Dornei. The implication is that these towns have not yet realised their full potential.

The Smallest Towns
The 135 towns with a population below 15,000 have a restructuring code of 3e overall, although the situation is only slightly worse than in the next higher group. As a group they are clearly quite weak (Mihalca 1995; Zamfir & Braghină 2000, 2001). However there is great diversity when individual cases are considered with only 10 towns that reflect the average. On either side there are 28 towns in the 3a-3d bands and 26 for 4a-4f. A further 20 are in Group 1 and 36 in Group 2 with six in Group 5 (Buşteni, Drăgăneşti-Olt, Isaccea, Negreşti-Oaş, Stei and Sulina) and one in Group 6 (Azuga) indicating extremely heavy job losses in industry. There are also seven towns in Class 0f: towns with very little industry under communism where a recent increase in industrial jobs is more than wiped out by losses elsewhere – the opposite to the 'normal' scenario. These towns are Borsec, Hârşova, Negru Vodă, Odobeşti, Sânnicolau Mare, Sovata and Valea lui Mihai. Borsec and Sovata are holiday resorts, while Sânnicolau Mare and Valea lui Mihai have both seen their fortunes transformed through FDI coming across the formerly-closed western frontier.. There is also the one town of Târgu Ocna classified 0a which indicates growth in both industry and orther sectors. Variety also arises in the level of service provision although RSB are present virtually everywhere. Taking Bancpost, Raiffeisen, RCB and RDB there are 197 facilities – some only by ATM or 'bancomat' – roughly 1.5 per town; while the five insurance companies between them provide 1.6 offices in each town.

Vodafone shops are present in all but 22 towns and petrol stations in all but 21 (with Petrom's share now 84 per cent). Electrical stores are provided at Covasna, Întorsura Buzăului and Sinaia, where Mondial are also present. Limited network banks also operate in some small towns: Carpatica serve the resorts of Băile Olăneşti, Buziaş and Tuşnad Băi, but also the towns of Făget, Huedin, Negreşti-Oaş and Târgu Ocna; while Eurom are present at Aleşd, Negreşti-Oaş and Valea lui Mihai; Sanpaolo IMI have offices at Chişineu-Criş, Lipova, Negreşti-Oaş and Valea lui Mihai; and BT agencies or ATMs are available at Aleşd, Beiuş, Chişineu-Criş, Ineu and Rovinari. Cargus pick out Beiuş, Hârlău and Huedin while Ramstal are present in Haţeg, Jibou, Năsăud, Negreşti-Oaş, Orşova, Sânnicolau Mare and Vălenii de Munte. Other small towns with a particularly strong profile are Horezu, Măcin, Strehaia and Târgu Frumos; while Săgeată (2003) sees Oraviţa (Caraş-Severin) and Sulina (Tulcea) having a potential district administrative function. As regards the weaker centres, none

Table 10.6: Development of the urban system 1910–2005

Regn	1910			1948			1989			2005		
	No	Popn	Sh.*	No	Popn	Sh.	No	Popn	Sh.	No	Popn	Sh.#
B-I	1	341.3	83.1	1	1041.8	87.3	2	2056.1	88.7	4	1999.0	90.5
Cen	19	215.7	13.8	21	362.6	19.3	48	1714.7	60.1	57	1515.0	59.9
NE	20	312.1	15.5	31	431.4	18.2	32	1581.6	42.1	45	1624.4	43.4
NW	22	304.6	16.3	27	432.6	19.8	35	1506.8	50.7	42	1458.8	53.1
S	8	242.6	11.6	14	400.9	14.6	43	1418.2	39.3	48	1388.7	41.7
SE	22	326.7	22.2	22	447.2	24.3	33	1637.9	55.0	35	1579.4	55.5
SW	11	149.4	9.6	18	263.8	13.3	32	1049.4	42.8	40	1096.1	47.5
W	18	187.5	12.0	18	336.7	20.1	35	1347.1	61.0	42	1227.5	63.6
Total	119	2079.9	16.3	152	3717.0	23.4	150	12311.8	53.2	313	11879.9	54.9

Figures show the number of towns, the total population (th) and the latter as a percentage of the total population of the region.
After 1910 several towns lost their urban status: Cojocna (NW); Chilia Veche, Ion Corvin, Mahmudia and Ostrov (SE) – also Ocna Sibiului (Cen) until after 1948. Similar demotions occurred after 1948: Falciu, Mihăileni, Ştefăneşti and Vama (NE); Filipeşti Târg (S) and Pleniţa (SW) – also Răcari (S) until after 1989. Several other demotions occurring after 1948 were withdrawn before 1989.
*Regional shares for 1910 are estimates assuming the same regional distribution of the total population as in 1930 (for Bucharest the calculation is based entirely on 1930 figures).
In the absence of any newly-promoted towns after 1989 the figures would be: B-I 88.5; Cen 57.7; NE 40.4; NW 51.3; S 40.3; SE 55.0; SW 44.9; W 60.5; Total 52.9 i.e. a falling urban share.

Source: Statistical Yearbooks

Table 10.7: Village services in Transylvania 1990

County	Commune centres						Other villages						Total
	A	B	C	D	E	F	A	B	C	D	E	F	
Alba	3	7	28	29	0	0	0	0	0	140	165	251	623
Bihor*	0	6	16	11	0	0	0	0	0	134	9	0	176
Bistrița-Năsăud	6	28	16	4	0	0	0	0	4	124	44	2	228
Cluj	4	8	33	29	0	0	0	0	0	238	83	17	412
Hunedoara	1	5	11	26	0	0	0	0	1	171	94	15	324
Maramureş*	1	3	18	16	0	0	0	0	0	118	2	0	158
Mureş	7	17	42	22	0	0	0	0	0	250	68	53	459
Sălaj	5	8	23	18	0	0	0	0	3	194	17	1	269
Satu Mare	1	6	13	6	0	0	0	0	0	76	3	1	106
Sibiu	1	17	12	23	0	0	0	0	0	104	7	0	164
Others#	1	2	5	9	0	0	0	0	0	69	10	0	96
Total	30	107	217	193	0	0	0	0	8	1618	502	340	3015

A Urban standard; B Some high-rank services; C One high-rank or several medium-rank services; D Low-rank services in at least three fields (administration, commerce, education, transport); E Ditto one-two fields; F No services

\# The survey area included small parts of Arad, Braşov, Harghita and Timiş counties

* Small parts of these counties were excluded

Source: Surd & Tomasi 1990

of the banks are present at Aninoasa, Bălan, Beclean, Bereşti, Boldeşti-Scăeni, Brezoi, Bumbeşti-Jiu, Cavnic, Geoagiu, Insuraţei, Nucet, Ocna Sibiului, Ocnele Mari, Ovidiu, Solca, Techirghiol and Uricani – all of these except Brezoi are among the 43 towns where none of the five insurance companies are represented either. Others with particularly limited cover are Darabani, Fundulea, Mihăileşti, Oţelu Roşu, Plopeni and Vlăhiţa.

Rural Areas

Rural areas are not a major concern in this analysis, although it is evident that many communes act as a district centre and during the last century the urban network has expanded by promotion of the more dynamic villages: net figures being 33 during 1910–48; 97 during 1948-89 and 53 since (Table 10.6). Indeed without the promotions since 1989 – swelling the urban population by 439,100 – the urbanisation rate would have fallen from 53.2 per cent in 1989 to 52.9 in 2005 (instead of rising to 54.9 per cent). Interestingly, the rate would have increased in any case in the North West, South and South West while remaining unchanged in the South East; whereas a decline would have occurred in the Bucharest, North East and West regions along with what has occurred in any case in the Central region. Population has of course been declining generally owing to migration abroad, on top of negative rates of natural increase, but there was a significant net urban-rural transfer in the early transition years. Regarding the recent promotions it is worth recalling that one purpose of Ceauşescu's 'sistematizare' was the creation some 350 additional towns as centres for the administration of cooperative and state farms and processing of agricultural commodities. This eminently logical process has therefore operated under the changed conditions. The first post-1989 promotions concerned Baia de Arieş, Făget, Geoagiu, Ghimbav and Teiuş (included in the study as small towns above) but 48 more communes were promoted after the 2002 census and are therefore still treated as villages for this exercise: the largest being Voluntari (29.1th); Popeşti-Leordeni (14.5), Vicovu (14.4), Dăbuleni (13.5), Pecica (13.3), Sântana (13.1); Ştefăneşti (12.9) Flamânzi (12.2), Săcuieni (11.7), Dolhasca (11.3) and Liteni (10.1). Meanwhile Turcanasu (1995–96) has identified dynamic rural centres in Moldavia that could be candidates for urban status in future. Central place functions – considered generally by Ianoş (1994) – include regular markets and numerous businesses established by people in the respective areas (Dobraca 1996,1999) but the survey by Surd & Tomasi (1990) for a large section of Transylvania is much more comprehensive; using a range of six indicators showing that the commune centres attract the bulk of the facilities while at the other extreme the large number of hamlets in the mountains of Alba county have virtually no facilities at all (Table 10.7).

In Figure 10.3 attention has been given to the representation of large companies that profile their networks on websites: mainly the banks – especially RSB and Raiffeisen but also Bancpost, Carpatica, RCB, RDB, Romexterra and Tiriac – insurance companies (especially Asirom, Astrasig and Unita), filling stations and Vodafone shops. 920 communes are represented (33.7 per cent of all communes) of which 767 have one function while 135 have two or three and 18 have four or more. Apart from three in the Bucharest area (especially the rapidly-expanding surburb of Voluntari), the latter include six from the South East: Baia (Tulcea), Băneasa and Mihail Kogălniceanu (Constanţa), Bărăganu (Brăila) and Berca and *Pătârlagele (Buzău); four from the

West: Bozovici (Caraş-Severin) and Gurahonţ, *Pecica and *Sântana (Arad); three from the South West: *Berbeşti (Vâlcea), Izbiceni (Olt) and *Turceni (Gorj); plus one each from the Centre – Bran (Braşov) – and North West – *Săcuieni (Bihor). And since only those asterisked have been promoted to urban status to date there must be some questions about the criteria used for selection especially since 15 counties have not managed to gain any promotions since 1989 even though several of them still have very limited urban systems at present. As percentages of all communes the figures vary regionally with higher figures for Ilfov (51.4 per cent) the South East (43.7 per cent) and Centre (36.5 per cent) than for the West (26.3 per cent), and South West (30.0 per cent); leaving the North East (32.8 per cent), South West (32.2 per cent) and South (34.9 per cent) close to the average. Of course Ilfov is a metropolitan area with a high level of business in some suburban communes; otherwise it could be suggested that a more developed urban system in the Centre and West results in greater cohesion and less need for village services (especially by RSB which is the largest single provider covered by the survey) in comparison with the North East. Figure 10.3 also shows additional communes with potential arising from demographic strength (population over 5,000), non-agricultural functions, proximity to national transport systems and a history of district status in connection with the communist 'raion' (pre-1968) and the 'plasă' of the 1930s.

Conclusion

The progress of transition across Romania is somewhat uneven. The gulf between urban and rural was perpetuated under communism and reinforced early in the transition when land restitution was complemented by heavy redundancies among industrial workers. Commerce has grown and infrastructure is slowly improving although underemployment and poverty has probably been relieved more by emigration (temporarily or permanently) than by domestic measures over employment and welfare. The towns have also experienced substantial unemployment but with compensation through tertiary sector growth particularly evident in the larger towns. But foreign investment – once heavily polarised – is now evening out in relation to available labour and the quality of transport and services. The North East is still relatively poor but in recent years the main towns have been energised by new construction and airport developments. At the same time the initial concentration of growth in the large cities is being moderated as the supermarkets and shopping malls start to arrive in the smaller county towns. But the key cities are still the clear business leaders and it remains to be seen if they will be able to maintain their early lead and realise their potential as metropoles, reinforcing their labour markets by stronger migration currents and managing growth through efficient local government, or if the county towns as a whole – as well as other towns of intermediate size – will be able to benefit through their own enterprise and any constraints that may emerge at the top of the hierarchy.

In the villages there are again great differences in population size and economic potential. While many are potential towns, expanding surburban communities and new settlements to cope with natural disasters (like the new village of Rast – with planning for 700 houses – which followed severe flooding in the Danube valley south of Craiova), at the other end of the scale there are hundreds of small villages with minimal services and a declining population like Topla (in the Mânastiur commune of Timiş county) with 300 people (in 80 houses) in 1930 but only four today (with an average age of 70). The road is suitable only for carts and tractors while services have been non-existent since the historic wooden church was moved to the Banat Museum! And although nominally part of the town of Târgu Cărbuneşti, Rogojeni is isolated (with a total lack of services) by a highly-degraded wire footbridge pending the planned construction of a new bridge that will take light vehicles. However, SAPARD funding has helped to relieve multiple deprivation in the countryside and after the 78,000 new electricity connections since 1989 the final 68,000 households will be supplied by 2010 with funding from the EU as well as bank credits and state/local authority budgets; while a €400mln programme is being rolled out to improve cultural centres. As a result more settlements will gain potential in terms of commuter links with the towns (in the context of travel-to-work or second-home ownership) and opportunity for pluriactivity based on smallholdings and rural tourism; sometimes assisted by a historic building for long hidden from the professionals by its remoteness – such as the church at Geamana in Alba county's Lupşa commune that was recognised only when it was threatened by the rising level of a mining company's decantation lake. The young make money abroad and zero unemployment is reported from Negrileşti (Vrancea) because peasants who worked around Romania with animals under communism can now earn €1,000/month shepherding in the EU as well as the Balkans, Turkey and USA. Meanwhile mobile phones have been a great blessing for the past decade (especially in areas lacking fixed lines), while the churches are still relatively well-distributed and expanding 'bancomat' systems are making it easier for farmers in remote areas to collect their subventions. But Romania also offers the model of a 'European village' managing without any formal services thanks to people who have the expertise to provide 'professional services' on a voluntary basis in the tradition of communality which is everywhere strong and particularly in areas that have literally fought for their interests in the recent past like the villages of Vrancea's Vintileasca commune: a nest ('ciub') of anticommunist partisans in the early post-war years. In such places, where the threatened imposition of apartment blocks has now receded, closure of the local school does not dismay children who then have to walk up to 10 kilometres each way daily to the central village because the roads are unsuitable for minibuses (which have in many cases eased the problems of centralising education) and when ecological disasters force a planned relocation – following landslides in Seciurile village in Gorj county's Roşia de Amaradia commune – the trauma of leaving inspires all manner of reservations over the suitability of the new land and houses. The EU is unlikely to modify overnight the link with the land that gives even the remotest corners of the Carpathians a sense of identity and occupation and it is by no means inevitable that the thousands of villages that Ceauşescu intended to sacrifice on the altar of 'sistematizare' in the 1990s will come to be voluntarily liquidated a generation later.

Postscript

Romania's modernisation tells its own story but it is not entirely unique despite a specific location in Europe, a distinct resource endowment (in which the wealth in cereals, oil and timber has been particularly significant) and a socio-political system giving the monarchy the key role in appointing governments that usually projected the urban-based Liberal Party philosophy of priority for industry in the interest of both national security and relief of rural overpopulation. It was an orientation that became gradually more single-minded with the National-Peasant party's support of foreign capital in the late 1920s (combined with heavy land taxes imposed on its rural constituency) and the harnessing of German technology under Carol II's 'monarcho-fascism'. Despite communism's revolutionary aspects, totalitarianism was in a sense anticipated because the Soviets inherited the fruits of Nazi Germany's penetration of the Romanian economy. Even so, the traditional parties resisted monopoly politics until 1948 and most of the peasants held out against full collectivisation until the 1960s when a significant compromise lay behind the bland declaration of a completed programme: one that never seriously intended to take in the logistically-challenging areas of dispersed mountain settlement where households continued to farm 'independently' albeit with obligations to their local authorities through production programmes. There were other ways in which the centralising ethos of communism fell short of its theoretical totality and it was here that Ceaușescu's extremism was perhaps most apparent in trying to 'mop up' remaining areas of comparative autonomy (most notably through 'sistematizare' applied to rural settlements).

But this book has also been conceived as an in-depth review of a radical post-communist reform project that has emerged from the early years of ambivalence and uncertainty to follow a 'road' every bit as rough and unpredictable as the country's basic transport system is regularly (though somewhat unfairly) portrayed. Setbacks have been frequent and quite demoralising in the case of the initial denial of NATO membership in 1997 after the new Ciorbea government and Constantinescu presidency had staked everything to achieve a favourable outcome. Dealings with the IMF have produced a sort of 'merry go round' where the desired facilities have been compromised by failure to meet the stringent conditions required (although one programme was successfully concluded in 2003). However the Romanian electorate, while certainly polarised between the strongly rural and conservative east and a progressive urban middle class that is strongly reformist in the capital and the Transylvanian metropoles, has not moved far from the centre ground despite the negative campaigning of the nationalist parties while government had avoided major economic crises comparable with the Bulgarian melt-down of 1997, and conservative frustration has rarely boiled over to the extent of the chanting 'down with Bucharest' reminiscent of the 'mineriada' years when Jiu Valley miners regularly took to the streets to peg back the more radical reformers. And if the late 1990s were a 'nightmare' for Romania, with a bitterly contested economic strategy embarrassed by Balkan instability and its discouragement of FDI, the new millennium has been the reverse with greater stability in the region and a surge in investment as well as pragmatism from Brussels with pressure for further reform tinged with generous financial assistance and derogations. Poverty has been eased by improved social security (not least the new pension system launched in 2007 and described as both 'bold' and 'cleverly designed') but more significantly by rising employment and easier travel across Europe so that the young unemployed have found their 'El Dorado' in various other EU countries, especially Italy or Spain.

It is a happy coincidence that the book should be ready to coincide with full membership of the EU that could be seen as a fitting conclusion to a specific 'transition' phase, although accession will not be a panacea for all Romania's modernisation goals. There will certainly be much larger injections of European money, partly through the cohesion funding that a decade ago was supporting the weaker regions of Western Europe. And as one of the EU's poorest countries low labour costs will help maintain the flow of FDI. Yet the benefit will be offset by reduced competitiveness compared with Russia, Ukraine and above-all China; not to mention probable reductions of employment in sectors where substantial productivity gains will be needed. More thought will have to be given to services and above-all tourism which is an outstanding anomaly of transition period in that competitiveness was allowed to slide, even in the case of the Black Sea beaches where Bulgaria made the greater progress: reflecting the problems in industry that provided the key battleground throughout the 1990s until the pain of further down-sizing was balanced by the new jobs generated by FDI. Finally Romania's regional problems must not be overlooked especially in the case of the rural east where the dynamic metropoles of Constanţa, Galaţi-Brăila and Iaşi have not yet energised the surrounding areas, such as Botosani and Vaslui where poverty remains acute. There must surely be more effort – partly through the investment in the Eurocorridors – to ensure that the sort of entrepreneurship evident in Banat (where thousands of Italians are running successful small businesses in clothing and footwear) can be spatially extended in all respects by the next generation of Romanian businessmen.

Bibliography

Abrudan, I.V. 2002, *Cross sectoral linkages in Romanian forestry: final report for FAO* (Brasov: Transilvania University, Faculty of Silviculture & Forest Engineering).

Abrudan, I.V., Blujdea, V., Brown, S. et al. 2003, 'Prototype carbon fund: afforestation of degraded land in Romania', *Revista Pădurilor* 118(1), 5–17.

Abrudan, I.V. & Turnock, D. 1999, 'A rural development strategy for the Apuseni Mountains Romania', *GeoJournal* 46, 319–36.

Agenția Națională pentru Dezvoltare Regională (ANDR) 2000, *Planul national de dezvoltare 2000–2002* (Bucharest: ANDR).

Agenția Națională pentru Dezvoltare Regională 2000b, *Dezvoltarea pentru aderare* (Bucharest: ANDR).

Amelina, M., Chiribuca, D. & Knack, S. 2003, *The Romanian poor in inter-household and community networks* (Bucharest: World Bank).

Anastasoaie, V. & Tarnovschi, D. (eds) 2001, *Proiecte pentru romii din România 1999–2000* (Bucharest: Ministerul Informațiilor Publice, Oficiul Național pentru Romi).

Asay, S.M. 1998, *Family strength in Romania* (Lincoln, Neb.: Graduate College of the University of Nebraska).

Bacon, W. 2004, 'Economic reform', in H.F. Carey (ed.) *Romania since 1989: politics economics and society* (Lanham, Md.: Lexington Books), 373–90.

Badescu, I., Ghinoiu, I. & Buruiana, C. (eds) 2000, *Sociogeografia și etnografia comunităților țărănești: studii de caz Slatioara – un sat de sub Magura – studiu sociologic și etnografic* (Bucharest: Fundația Națională pentru Civilizație Rurală Niste Țărăni/Institutul Național de Cercetare pentru Civilizația Rurală).

Badescu, I., Ghinoiu, I. & Urucu, V. (eds) 2000, *Sociogeografia și etnografia comunităților țărănești: studii de caz Pătârlagele – studiu sociogeografic* (Bucharest: Fundația Națională pentru Civilizație Rurală Niste Țărăni/Institutul Național de Cercetare pentru Civilizația Rurală).

Baga, E. 2004, 'Romania's western connection: Timișoara and Timiș County', in M.Tutur (ed.) *The making of regions in post-socialist Europe: the impact of culture economic structure and institutions: case studies from Poland, Hungary, Romania and Ukraine* (Wiesbaden: Verlag fur Sozialwissenschaften), II, 17–101.

Bălănescu, S., Achim, V. & Ciolte, A. 2002, *Istoria conducerii mineritului a metalurgiei neferoase și prețioase din nord-vestul României: organizare coordonare dezvoltare* (Baia Mare: Editura Gutinul).

Baleanu, V.G. 2000, *In the shadow of Russia: Romania's relations with Moldova and Ukraine* (Camberley: Conflict Studies Research Centre).

Bălteanu, D. 1992, 'Natural hazards in Romania', *Revue Roumaine de Géographie* 36, 47–55.

Bălteanu, D. & Oancea, D.I. 1994, 'Les villes et les risques naturels en Roumanie', in I. Ianos & V. Rey (eds) *Les nouvelles dimensions du changement urbain: le IX-eme colloque franco-roumain de géographie* (Bucharest: Academia Romană Institutul de Geografie, Geographical International Seminars 2), 138–44.

Bălteanu, D., Popescu, C.R., Prapugiciu N. et al. 2003, 'Geographic issues relating to CBC and tourism within the Black Sea-Lower Danube Basin', in Y. Papanicolaou, E. Kutovoy, L. Kavunenko et al. (eds) *The first meeting of the council of presidents of the National Academies of Sciences of BSEC member states: documents and reports* (Kiev: National Academy of Sciences of Ukraine International Centre for Black Sea Studies), 85–109.

Bandacu, D., Moldovan, M., Nichersu, M. & Paun, A. 1993, 'Reconstrucţia ecologică de la ipoteze la realitate', *Analele Ştiinţifice al Institutului Delta Dunării* 2, 267–75.

Barany, Z. 2004, 'Romani marginality and politics', in H. F. Carey (ed.) *Romania since 1989: politics economics and society* (Lanham, Md.: Lexington Books), 255–74.

Bătinaş, R.H. 2000, 'Degradarea calităţii apei râului Arieş ca urmare a diversărilor ape uzate industriale de la exploatarile miniere: Roşia Montană Abrud şi Baia de Arieş', *Geographica Timisiensis* 8–9, 123–33.

Batt, J. 2002a, 'Transcarpathia: peripheral region at the centre of Europe', in J. Batt & K. Wolczuk (eds) *Region state and identity in Central & Eastern Europe* (London: Frank Cass), 155–77.

Batt, J. 2002b, 'Reinventing Banat', in J. Batt & K. Wolczuk (eds) *Region state and identity in Central & Eastern Europe* (London: Frank Cass), 178–202.

Belk, R.W. 1997, 'Romania: consumer desires and feelings of deservingness', in L. Stan (ed.) Romania in transition (Aldershot; Dartmouth), 191–208.

Ben-Ner, A. & Montias, J.M. 1994, 'Economic systems reforms and privatization in Romania', in S. Estrin (ed.) *Privatization in Central & Eastern Europe* (London: Longman), 279–310.

Bennett, G. 1998, 'Guidelines for establishing the Pan-European Ecological Network in Central & Eastern Europe', in P. Nowicki (ed.) *The green backbone of Central & Eastern Europe* (Tilburg: European Centre for Nature Conservation), 183–7.

Boar, N. 1999, 'Turism transfrontalier maramureşean: circulaţie transfrontalieră', *Analele Universităţii din Oradea: Geografie* 9, 76–80.

Boar, N. 2001, 'Impactul reţelei de transport asupra relaţiilor transfrontaliere din spaţiul maramureşean', Comunicări de Geografie 5, 525–30.

Bonciu, F. 1997, Atragerea şi monitorizarea investiţiilor străine directe (Bucharest: Editure Ştiinţifică).

Borcoş, A. & Vîrdol, A. 2001, 'Aspecte metodologice privind ierarhizarea zonelor miniere defavorizate din România', *Revista Geografică* 8, 178–83.

Buga, D. 1996, 'Habitations humaines dans le Massif de Parâng (Carpates Meridionales): le "plai" de Bumbeşti', in G. Niculescu & C. Muică (eds), *Southern Carpathians and Stara Planina (Balkan) Mountains: geographical studies* (Bucharest: Academia Romană Institutul de Geografie, Geographical International Seminars 3), 122–5.

Buza, M., Dimen, L., Pop, G. & Turnock, D. 2001, 'Environmental protection in the Apuseni Mountains: the role of environmental non-governmental organisations' *GeoJournal* 55, 631–53.

Buza, M. & Ianoş, I. 1997, 'Consideraţii geografice privind învăţământul şi publicaţiile în limba minorităţilor naţionale din România', *Geographica Timisiensis* 6, 5–13.

Carey, H.F. 2004a, 'Preface', in H.F. Carey (ed.) *Romania since 1989: politics economics and society* (Lanham, Md.: Lexington Books) xviii–xxiii.

Carey, H.F. 2004b, 'Conclusion: ambiguous democratization?', in H.F. Carey (ed.), *Romania since 1989: politics economics and society* (Lanham, Md.: Lexington Books), 553–618.

Carey, H.F. 2004c, 'Conclusion: ambiguous democratization?', in H.F. Carey (ed.) *Romania since 1989: politics economics and society* (Lanham, Md.: Lexington Books), 553–618.

Carey, H.F. & Eisterhold, C. 2004, 'Introduction', in H.F. Carey (ed.) *Romania since 1989: politics economics and society* (Lanham, Md.: Lexington Books), 1–26.

Cartwright, A. 2000, 'Against decollectivisation: land reform in Romania 1990–2', *Max Planck Institute for Social Anthropology Working Paper 4.*

Cartwright, A. 2003, 'Private farming in Romania: what are the old people going to do with their land?', in C. Hann ed., *The post-socialist agrarian question: property relations and the rural condition* (Munster: Lit.Verlag).

Cavalcanti, M.B. 1992, 'Totalitarian states and their influence on city form: the case of Bucharest', *Journal of Architectural & Planning Research* 9, 275–86.

Cavalcanti, M.B. 1997, 'Urban reconstruction and autocratic régimes: Ceauşescu's Bucharest in its historic context', *Planning Perspectives* 12, 71–109.

Celac, S. 1998, 'Romania: a pivotal country along the Europe to Asia business route', in G. Erdeli & D. Dumbrăveanu (eds) *Romanian-British Geographical Exchanges: Proceedings of the Third Romanian-British Colloquium* (Bucharest: Corint), 13–18.

Chaves, R.A., Sanchez, S., Schor, S. et al. 2001, *Financial markets credit constraints and investment in rural Romania* (Washington DC: World Bank).

Chen, C. 2003, 'The roots of illiberal nationalism in Romania: a historical institutional analysis of the Leninist legacy', *East European Politics & Societies* 17, 166–201.

Chirca, C. & Teşliuc, E.D. 1999, *From rural poverty to rural development* (Bucharest: World Bank).

Chirot, D. 1976, *Social change in a peripheral society: the creation of a Balkan colony* (New York: Academic Press).

Church, G. 1979. 'Bucharest: revolution in the townscape art', in R.A. French & F.E.I. Hamilton (eds) *The socialist city: spatial structure and urban policy* (Chichester: Wiley), 493–506.

Ciotea, F. 1979, 'Aspecte socio-demografice ale navetismului în judeţul Mureş', *Viitorul Social* 8, 106–14.

Ciotea, F. 1980, 'Analiza proiectivă a stabilizării forţei de munca tinere în agricultura', *Viitorul Social* 9, 294–302.

Clement, S. 2000, 'Subregionalism in Southeastern Europe', in S.C. Calleya (ed.) *Regionalism in the post cold-war world* (Aldershot: Ashgate), 71–98.

Coclitu, S. & Bratescu, T. 1996, 'The Romanian Loan Guarantee Fund', in J. Levitski (ed.) *Small business in transition economies: promoting enterprise in Central and Eastern Europe and the Former Soviet Union* (London: Intermediate Technology Publishers), 116–19.

Comisia Naţională pentru Prevenirea şi Combaterea Sărăciei/Programul Naţiunilor Unite pentru Dezvoltare 1998, *Proiectul de Prevenirea şi Combatere a Sărăciei: strategia naţională – recomandări şi soluţii alternative* (Bucharest: CNPCS).

Costachie, S. 1997, 'Socio-demographic characteristics of Romania's gypsy minority', in D. Light & D. Dumbrăveanu-Andone (eds) *Anglo-Romanian geographies: proceedings of the second Liverpool-Bucharest Geography Colloquium* (Liverpool: Liverpool Hope Press), 111–17.

Craiutu, A. 2004, 'Romania: the difficult apprenticeship of liberty 1989–2004', *Woodrow Wilson International Center for Scholars: EES News*, September–October, 5–9.

Creţan, R., Guran-Nica, L., Platon, D. & Turnock, D. 2005, 'Foreign direct investment and social risk in Romania: progress in less-favoured areas', in D. Turnock (ed.) *Foreign direct investment and regional development in East Central Europe and the Former Soviet Union* (Aldershot: Ashgate), 305–48.

Crowe, D.M. 1999, 'The Gypsies in Romania since 1990', *Nationalities Papers* 27, 57–68.

Crowther, W.E. 1988, *The political economy of Romanian socialism* (New York: Praeger).

Dăianu, D. 2001, 'Balkan reconstruction: Romania', *South East European & Black Sea Studies* 1, 203–18.

Dăianu, D. 2002, 'Romania and the European Union', in T.Straubhaar, F-P.Vadean & A.G.W von Czege (eds) *Romania on the path to the EU: labour markets migration and minorities* (Hamburg: Europa-Kolleg Hamburg, Institute for Integration Research Discussion Paper 1/2002), 93–108.

Dăianu, D. 2004, 'Fiscal and monetary policies', in H.F.Carey (ed.) *Romania since 1989: politics economics and society* (Lanham, Md.: Lexington Books), 391–418.

Dăianu, D., Albu, L., Croitoru, L. et al. 2001, *The underground economy in Romania* (Bucharest: Cerope).

Dăianu, D., Voinea, L., Pauna, B. et al. 2001b, *Winners or losers in the process of European integration: a look at Romania* (Bucharest: Romanian Centre for Economic Policy).

Davidson, K.E.K. 2004, 'Conflicts of interest in the restitution and privatisation of housing since the fall of socialism: the case of central Timişoara city – a problem of democracy?', *Europe-Asia Studies* 56, 119–41.

Davidson, K.E.K. 2004, 'Redistributing nationalized housing: impacts on property patterns in Timişoara, Romania', *Eurasian Geography & Economics* 45, 134–56.

Davidson, K.E.K. 2005, 'Geographic impacts of the political: dealing with nationalised housing in Romaia', *Political Geography* 24, 545–67.

Davis, J.R. & Gaburcim A. 1999, 'Rural finance and private farming in Romania', *Europe-Asia Studies* 51, 843–69.

Delepine, S. 2000, 'Populaţia ţigănească a cartierului Ferentari din Bucureşti', *Analele Universităţii de Vest din Timişoara* 9–10, 231–40.

Deletant, D. 1995, 'Central planning as coercion: systematisation', in D. Deletant, *Ceauşescu and the Securitate: coercion and dissent in Romania 1965–1989* (London: Hurst & Co), 294–319.

Dinca, I. 1996, 'Problema golurilor de munte şi a celor forestiere în lanţul neoeruptiv nordic', *Studii şi Cercetări de Geografie* 43, 149–55.

Dobraca, L. 1994, 'Localizarea activităţilor comerciale în Bucureşti: tendinţe actuale', in P. Urdea (ed.) *The First Regional Geography Conference: Geographical Researches in the Carpathian-Danube Space* (Timişoara: Universitatea de Vest din Timişoara, Departmentul de Geografie), 264–89 .

Dobraca, L. 1996, 'Localităţile cu funcţii de loc central generate de activităţile comerciale din Judeţul Prahova', *Geographica Timisiensis* 5, 99–104.

Dobraca, L. 1997, 'Schimbări profilul funcţional al zonei periurbane a Bucureştiului generate de dezvoltarea activităţilor comerciale', *Buletin Geografică* 1(1), 67–73.

Dobraca, L. 1999, 'Embryons urbains en Roumanie: les localités rurales a function de marché', in V. Surd (ed.) *Rural space and regional development* (Cluj-Napoca: Editura Studia), 183–8.

Dobraca, L. & Dobre, S. 2000, 'Tendinţe actuală în organizarea spaţiului geografic în Delta Dunării',*Comunicări de Geografie* 4, 469–76.

Dobrescu, E. 1998, 'Barometer of the Romanian economy', *Romanian Buisness Journal* 5(21), 12.

Dobrescu, E. & Blaga, I. 1973, *Structural patterns of Romanian economy* (Bucharest: Meridiane).

Dogaru, L. 1993, *Satul românesc contemporan* (Bucharest: Centrul de Informare şi Documentare Economic).

Doppler, W. 1994, 'Farming systems approach and its relevance for agricultural development in Central & Eastern Europe', in J.B. Dent & M.J. MacGregor (eds) *Rural and farming systems analysis: European perspectives* (Wallingford: CAB International), 65–77.

Driga, B. & Gâştescu, P. 1997, 'Modificările sistemului circulaţiei apei în depresiunea Roşu-Puiu-Lumina', *Revista Geografică* 4, 38–45.

Drogeanu, P-A., 2000, *Reforma şi lucrărilor publice în România ultimilor ani 1997– 2000* (Bucharest: Editura Universalia/MLPAT).

Dumitrache, L. & Dumbrăveanu, D. 1998, 'Crime perception and its influence on social behaviour: case study of Ferentari estate', in G. Erdeli & D. Dumbrăveanu (eds) *Romanian-British geographical exchanges: proceedings of the Third Romanian-British Colloquium* (Bucharest: Corint), 61–7.

Earle, J.S. & Telegdy, A. 1998, 'The results of mass privatization in Romania: a first empirical study', *Economics of Transition* 6, 313–32.

Earle, J.S. & Telegdy, A. 2002, 'Privatization methods and productivity effects in Romanian industrial enterprises', *Journal of Comparative Economics* 30, 657–82.

EBRD 1999, *Transition report 1999: ten years of transition* (London: EBRD).

Economic Policy Institute & Centre for the Study of Democracy Sofia 2000, 'Bulgaria and Romania', in H. Tang (ed.) *Winners and losers of EU integration: policy issues for Central & Eastern Europe* (Washington DC: World Bank), 98–118.

Eidelberg, P.G. 1974, *The great Romanian peasant revolt of 1907: origins of a modern jacquerie* (Leiden: Brill).

Erdeli, G. 1998, 'The territorial distribution of population and internal migration flows in Romania during the second half of the twentieth century', in G. Erdeli & D. Dumbrăveanu (eds) *Romanian-British geographical exchanges: proceedings of the Third Romanian-British Colloquium* (Bucharest: Corint), 33–40.

Erdeli, G., Tălânga, C. & Popescu, C.R. 2000, 'Development of public services policies in Bucharest', in I. Ianoş, D. Pumain & J.B. Racine (eds) *Integrated urban systems and sustainability of urban life* (Bucharest: Editura Tehnica), 475–86.

Evans, I.L. 1924, *The agrarian revolution in Romania* (Cambridge : Cambridge University Press).

Fischer, M.E. 1989, *Nicolae Ceauşescu: a study of political leadership* (Boulder, Col.: Lynne Rienner).

Florian, V. 1994, *Pluriactivitate şi comportamentul economic al gospodăriilor pluriactive* (Bucharest: IEA).

Floyd, R. 2005, 'For want of rubber: Romania's affair with Firestone in 1965', *East European Quarterly* 38, 485–518.

Freeman, L.A. n.d., *The Ploieşti raid through the lens* (London: Battle of Britain International).

Frucht, R. 2000, 'Danube question', in R. Frucht (ed.) *Encyclopaedia of Eastern Europe from the Congress of Vienna to the fall of communism* (New York: Garland Publishing), 215.

Gallagher, T. 1992, 'Vatra Românească and resurgent nationalism in Romania', *Ethnic and Racial Studies* 15, 570–99.

Gallagher, T. 2005, *Theft of a nation: Romania since commuunism* (London: Hurst).

Gancz, V. & Pătrăscoiu, N. 2000, 'Cartografia ecosistemelor forestiere din România prin mijloace GIS şi de teledetecţie', *Revista Pădurilor* 115(2), 35–40.

Gâştescu, P. 1993, 'The Danube delta: geographical characteristics and ecological recovery', *GeoJournal* 29, 57–67.

Gâştescu, P. 1995, 'Contributions to the coastal zone management of the Romanian sector of the Black Sea', *Revue Roumaine de Géographie* 39, 71–8.

Gâştescu, P. 1996, 'The Danube Delta Biosphere Reserve: present state and management', *Revue Roumaine de Géographie* 40, 27–33.

Gâştescu, P. 1998, 'Bucharest municipality: its periurban zone water supply situation', in I. Iordan (ed.) *Socio-economic changes in the suburban areas of large cities in Romania and Poland* (Bucharest: Academia Romană Institut de Geografie), 41–50.

Gatti, R. 2003, *Poverty and growth in Romania 1995–2002* (Bucharest: World Bank).

Gavrilescu, D. 1994, 'Agricultural reform in Romania: between market priority and the strategies for food security', in J.F.M. Swinnen (ed.) *Policy and institutional reform in Central Europe* (Aldershot: Avebury), 169–209.

Gherănescu, N. 1996, 'The integrated advisory service for private business in Romania', in J. Levitski (ed.) *Small business in transition economies: promoting enterprise in Central and Eastern Europe and the Former Soviet Union* (London: Intermediate Technology Publishers), 135–44.

Ghinea, D. 1993, *Romania: resorts and spas* (Bucharest: Editura Enciclopedică).

Gilberg, T. 1980, 'Romanian agricultural policy in the quest of the multilaterally developed society', in R.A. Francisco (ed.) *Agricultural policies in the USSR and Eastern Europe* (Boulder, Col.: Westview), 137–64.

Golibrzuch, E. 2002, 'Informal activities in rural areas: family situations in farming and day labouring', in R. Neef & M. Stănculescu (eds) *The social impact of informal economies in Eastern Europe* (Aldershot: Ashgate), 149–68.

Goriup, P. 1994, 'Biodiversity ecological investment and sustainable development in the Danube Delta Biosphere Reserve, Romania', *Ecos* 14(1), 45–51.

Goriup, P. (ed.) 1995, *Management objectives for biodiversity conservation and sustainable development in the Danube Delta Biosphere Reserve, Romania* (Newbury: Nature Conservation Bureau).

Government of Romania Ministry of Agriculture & Food 1999, *Rural development in Romania* (Bucharest: EU Phare).

Graf, R. 1997, *Domeniul banatean al StEG 1855–1920* (Reşiţa: Editura Banatica).

Graf, R. 2000, 'Judetul Caraş-Severin: o regiune industrială veche cu un potenţial industrial-cultural şi turistic care asteapta sa fie valorificat', in H. Bonninghausen et al., *Calea fierului din Banat: un proiect de dezvoltarea regională pe baza turismului industrial* (Reşiţa: Editura Graf/Friedrich Ebert Stiftung), 149–61.

Groza, O. 1991–92, 'Paşcani – oraş industrial: trei ani de transiţie – consideraţii de geografie umană', *Lucrările Seminarului Dimitrie Cantemir* 11–12, 171–83.

Groza, O. 1993, 'L'industrie roumaine: entre local şi regional', *Analele Ştiinţifice ale Universităţii A.I.Cuza din Iaşi: Geografie* 38–9, 189–204.

Groza, O. 1994, 'Paşcani: ville industrielle en Roumanie – années de transition', *L'Espace Géographique* 23, 329–41.

Groza, O. 1998, 'Industrie: systèmes économique et territoire', in V. Rey (ed.) *Territoires centre-européens: dilemmas et defies* (Paris: La Decouverte), 184–213.

Groza, O. 1999a, 'Récomposition spatiale des systèmes industriels départmentaux de Roumanie', *Analele Ştiinţifice ale Universităţii A.I.Cuza din Iaşi: Géografie* 44–5, 186–200.

Groza, O. 1999b, 'La déindustrialisation de la Roumanie: une analyse shift et share', *Analele Ştiinţifice ale Universităţii A.I.Cuza din Iaşi: Geografie* 44–5, 201–14.

Groza, O. 1999c, 'Le district industriel: entre concept et realité territoriale – un survol critique de la problématique', *Analele Ştiinţifice ale Universităţii A.I.Cuza din Iaşi: Géografie* 44–5, 215–28.

Guran-Nica, L. 1997, 'Zonele economice libere ale Dunării: favorabilităti şi perspective', *Geographica Timisiensis* 6, 89–103.

Guran-Nica, L. & Turnock, D. 2000, 'A preliminary assessment of social risk in Romania', *GeoJournal* 50, 139–50.

Guvernul României şi Comisia Europeană 1997, *Carta verde: politica de dezvoltare regională în România* (Bucharest: Guvernul României).

Gyulai, I. (ed.) 1998, *The EU and biodiversity* (Brussels: FoEE).

Heller, W. 1998, 'Experiences and assessments of the transformation from private households' point of view: differences between villages', in W. Heller (ed.) 1998, *Romania: migration socio-economic transformation and perspectives of regional development* (Munchen: Sudosteuropa-Gesellschaft, Sudosteuropa Studien 62), 190–204.

Heller, W. 1999, 'The non-agricultural economy in post-socialist Romania: insights and perceptions of national regional and local institutions', *GeoJournal* 46, 199–205.

Heller, W. 2000, 'Socioeconomic transformation in rural Romania through the eyes of experts: demographic and social issues', *GeoJournal* 50, 151–5.

Hitchens, K. 1994, *Rumania 1866–1947* (Oxford: Clarendon Press).

Hunya, G. 1998, 'Romania 1990–2002: stop-go transformation', *Communist Economies & Economic Transformation* 10, 241–59.

Iacob, G. 1981, 'Valorisation des ressources naturelles a principalelor resurse naturale ale Munţilor Maramureşului', *Studii si Cercetări: Geografie* 27, 291–7.

Iacob, G. 1986, 'Le role du Maramureş dans l'économie nationale', *Revue Roumaine de Géographie* 30, 13–19.

Iancu, A. 2000, 'Some problems of the strategy for development and integration into the EU', *Romanian Business Journal* 7(9), 6.

Ianoş, I, 1994, 'Moments critiques dans l'évolution du système urbaine roumain après 1945', in I. Ianoş & V. Rey (eds) *Les nouvelles dimensions du changement urbain: le IX-eme colloque franco-roumain de géographie* (Bucharest: Academia Romană Institutul de Geografie, Geographical International Seminars 2), 19–28.

Ianoş, I. 1994, 'On the central place functions of rural settlements in Romania', *Revue Roumaine de Géographie* 38, 49–57.

Ianoş, I. 1999, 'The impact of transition on the mountain agriculture of Alba county', *Analele Universitatis Bucureşti: Geografie* 48, 49–62.

Ianoş, I., Tălângă, C. & Popescu, C.R. 1989, 'The role and place of centres with inter-communal functions in the territorial development of Romania's industry', *Revue Roumaine de Géographie* 33, 9–15.

Ianoş, I., Tălângă, C. & Ugron, A. 1992, 'Analiza geografică a fostelor resedinţe de judeţ din România', *Studii şi Cercetări de Geografie* 39, 3–10.

Ielenicz, M. & Dumbrăveanu-And one, D. 1997, 'The tourist potential of the Carpathians', in D. Light & D. Dumbrăveanu (eds), *Anglo-Romanian geographies: proceedings of the second Liverpool-Bucharest Geography Colloquium* (Liverpool: Liverpool Hope Press), 59–64.

Ilie, S. 2002, 'Formal and informal incomes of Romanian households', in R.Neef & M.Stănculescu (eds), *The social economy of informal economies in Eastern Europe* (Aldershot: Ashgate), 169–87.

Ionescu, D. 1994, 'Romania adjusting to NATO's Partnership for Peace program', *Radio Free Europe/Radio Liberty Research* 3(9), 43–7.

Ionete, C. & Dinculescu, V. (eds) 2000, *National human development report: Romania 1999* (Bucharest: Romanian Academy for the United Nations Development Project).

Ioraş, F., Muică, N. & Turnock, D. 2001, 'Approaches to sustainable forestry in the Piatra Craiului national park', *GeoJournal* 55, 579–98.

Ipatiov, F. 1996, 'Influenţa poluarii industriale asupra starii de sanitate populaţiei în oraşul Baia Mare', *Studia Universitatis Babes-Bolyai: Seria Geographia* 41, 175–82.

Isărescu, M. 1992, 'The prognoses for economic recovery', in D.N. Nelson (ed.) *Romania after tyranny* (Boulder, Col: Westview), 149–66.

Jackson, M.R. 1986, 'Industrial output in Romania and the historical regions', *Journal of European Economic History* 14, 223–72.

Jigaic, M., Surdu, M., Balica, M. et al. 2002, *Participarea la educaţie a copiilor romi: probleme soluţii actori* (Bucharest: Ministerul Educaţiei şi Cercetări, Institutul de Ştiinţe ale Educaţiei, ICCV, Unicef).

Josan, N. 1997, 'Landslidings impact upon the functionality in the roads of communications in the Apuseni Mountains', *Studia Universitatis Babeş-Bolyai: Seria Geographia* 42, 93–6.

Jowitt, K. 1972, *Revolutionary breakthroughs and national development: the case of Romania 1944–1965* (Berkeley, Calif.: University of California Press).

Karnoouh, C. 2004, 'Multiculturismn and ethnic relations in Transylvania', in H.F. Carey (ed.) *Romania since 1989: politics economics and society* (Lanham, Md.: Lexington Books), 247–54.

Kideckel, D.A. 1982, 'The socialist transformation of agriculture in a Romanian commune 1945-1962', *American Ethnologist* 9, 320–40.

Kim, B-Y. 2005, 'Poverty and informal economy participation in Romania', *Economics of Planning* 13(1), 163–85.

Kligman, G. 1992, 'The politics of reproduction in Ceauşescu's Romania: a case study in political culture', *East European Politics & Societies* 6, 364–418.

Kligman, G. 1998, *The politics of duplicity: controlling reproduction in Ceauşescu's Romania* (Berkeley, Calif.: University of California Press).

Kovacs, C.M. 1996, 'Modèles agroéconomiques et l'homogenité des régions agricoles dans la plaine du Someş', *Studia Universitatis Babeş-Bolyai: Seria Geographia* 41, 153–6.

Lampe, J.R. & Jackson, M.R. 1982, *Balkan economic history 1550–1950: from imperial borderlands to developing nations* (Bloomington, Ind.: Indiana University Press).

Lazaroiu, S., Berevoescu, I., Chiriac, D. & Lazaroiu, A.A. 1999, 'Sărăcia comunitară: harta sărăciei şi studiu de caz', in M.S. Stănculescu (ed.) *Sărăcia în România 1995–1998: coordonate ale sărăciei – dimensiuni şi factori* (Bucharest: UNDP Proiect de Prevenire şi Combatarea a Sărăciei), 127–65.

Leonard, T.M. 2000, 'NATO expansion: Romania and Bulgaria within the larger context', *East European Quarterly* 33, 517–44.

Leşan, M. 2002, 'Cercetări privind instalarea şi dezvoltarea unor specii forestiere în teritoriu poluate situate în zona periurbană a Municipiului Baia Mare', *Revista Pădurilor* 117(1), 1–7.

Light, D., Dumbrăveanu, D. & Asquith, S. 2000, 'Smuggling and the border landscape of southwest Romania', in D. Light & D. Phinnemore (eds) *Post-communist Romania: geographical perspectives* (Liverpool: Liverpool Hope Press), 107–14.

McMahon, P.C. 2005, 'Managing ethnicity: the OSCE and trans-national networks in Romania', *Problems of Post-Communism* 52(1), 15–27.

Maliţa, M. 1999, *Strategia naţională pentru dezvoltarea durabilă* (Bucharest: Editura Nova).

Manuila, S. 1932, *Miscarea populaţiei României* (Bucharest: Editura Institutul Central de Statistica).

Mărginean, I. & Bălasa, A. 2002, *Calitatea vieţii în România* (Bucharest: Editura Expert).

Marin, G. & Schneider, E. (eds) 1997, *Ecological restoration in the Danube Delta Biosphere Reserve, Romania* (Tulcea: DDBRA/WWF).

Maruşca, T. 2002, 'Mountain gradients in support of settlement of natural and economic handicaps in the Romanian Carpathians', in R. Rey & D. Gîţan (eds) *Romanian Carpathians in the International Year of the Mountains* (Câmpulung Moldovenesc: Editura Fundaţiei Culturale Alexandru Bogza), 9–83.

Mehedinţi, M.C. 2000, 'Mediul metropolitan al Municipiului Bucureşti între renaturare şi dezvoltare', *Comunicări de Geografie* 4, 519–24.

Mete, C. 2003, *Labour force participation: unemployment and the poor* (Bucharest: World Bank).

Mete, C., Burnett, N., Teşliuc, E. et al. 2003, *Romania: poverty assessment* (Bucharest: World Bank Report 26169-RO).

Mihai, A. 2001, 'Asociaţia pomiculturilor Dâmboviţeni: capital social şi naţionalitate în acţiunea colectivă', *Sociologie Românească* 3, 194-214.

Mihăiescu, R. & Floca, L. 1999, 'Shifting in environmental problems in the transition period: mountain area Apuseni', in V. Surd (ed.) *Rural space and regional development* (Cluj-Napoca: Editura Studia), 246–51.

Mihăiescu, R. & Haidu, I. 1996, 'Influenta deversărilor urbane asupra calităţii apelor Someşului Mic în aval de Municipiul Cluj-Napoca', *Studia Universitatis Babeş-Bolyai: Seria Geographia* 41, 77–82.

Mihăilescu, V., Nicolau, V., Ghiorghiu, M. et al. 1993, 'Snagov: trei proiecţii asupra sistematizării', *Sociologie Românească* 4(1), 18–32.

Mihalca, D. 1995, 'Integrarea localităţii Făget în sistemul urban al Judeţului Timiş', *Geographica Timisiensis* 4, 129–33.

Misiak, W. 1993, 'The rural areas in Rumania after systematisation experiment: what is the alternative?', *Eastern European Countryside* 1, 57-64.

Mitrache, S., Manole, V., Bran, F. et al. 1996, *Agroturism şi turism rural* (Bucharest: Fax Press/Federaţia Romană pentru Dezvoltare Montană).

Moisei, F., Beres, I. & Coman, I., 2000, 'Destructive effects of human activities', in F. Moisei, N. Boşcaiu, M. Vegh & J. Hamor (eds) 2000, *Munţii Maramureşului: database concerning the establishment of a biosphere reserve* (n.p.: EU Phare), 67–72.

Moldovan, F. & Moldovan, V. 1995, 'Le rôle de l'opération villages roumains dans la réconstruction rurale', *Analele Universităţii de Vest din Timişoara: Geographie* 5, 62–71.

Muică, C. & Bălteanu, D. 1995, 'Relations between landslide dynamics and plant cover in the Buzău Subcarpathians', *Revue Roumaine de Géographie* 39, 41–7.

Muică, C. & Popova, A. 1996, 'Rolul tufărişurilor în conservarea potenţialului natural al mediului', *Studii şi Cercetări de Geografie* 43, 95–9.

Muică, C. & Zăvoianu, I. 1996, 'The ecological consequences of privatisation', *GeoJournal* 38, 207–12.

Muică, N., Nancu, D. & Turnock, D. 2000, 'Historical and contemporary aspects of pluriactivity in the Curvature Subcarpathians of Romania', *GeoJournal* 50, 199–212.

Muică, N., Roberts, L.A. & Turnock, D. 1999, 'Transformation of a border region: dispersed agricultural communities in Braşov county, Romania', *GeoJournal* 46, 305–17.

Nadejde, S. 1999, 'Methodologie d'analyse de l'espace rural selon les critères d'aménagement territoire', in V. Surd (ed.) *Rural space and regional development* (Cluj-Napoca: Editura Studia), 228–30.

Negrescu, D. 1999, *A decade of privatisation in Romania* (Bucharest: Romanian Centre for Economic Policy www.cerope.ro).

Nelson, D.N. (ed.) 1981, *Romania in the 1980s* (Boulder, Col.: Westview).

Nelson, D.N. 1988, *Romanian politics in the Ceauşescu era* (New York: Gordon & Breach).

Nelson, D.N. (ed.) 1992, *Romania after tyranny* (Boulder, Col.: Westview).

Nica, N.A. 1999, 'Disadvantaged areas in the context of rural development policy in Romania', in V. Surd (ed.) *Rural space and regional development* (Cluj-Napoca: Editura Studia), 219–22.

Nicolaescu, T. 1993, 'Privatization in Romania: the case for financial institutions', in D.E. Fair and R.J. Raymond (eds), *The new Europe: evolving economic and financial systems in East and West* (Dordrecht: Kluwer), 101–9.

Niculescu, D. 2004, 'Revigorarea turismul montan', *Revista Geografică* 10, 205–9.

Overy, R.J. 1983, 'Göring's multinational empire', in A. Teichova & P.L. Cottrell (eds), *International business and Central Europe 1918–1939* (Leicester: Leicester University Press), 269–98.

Pal, A. 2000, 'Socioeconomic progress in the Hungarian-Yugoslavian-Romanian border zone: approaches to the Danube-Tisza-Maros-Körös Euroregion', in P. Ganster (ed.) *Cooperation environment and sustainability in border regions* (San Diego, Calif.: Institute for Regional Studies of the Californias/San Diego State University Press), 223–34.

Pal, A. & Nagy, I. 1999, 'The economic relationships of the Hungarian-Romanian border region', in C. Gruia, G. Ianoş, M. Torok-Oance & P. Urdea (eds) *Proceedings of the regional conference of geography: Danube-Criş-Mureş-Tisa Euroregion – geoeconomical space of sustainable development* (Timişoara: West University of Timişoara et al.), 369–85.

Pălăseanu, P. 2000, *Studies of heavy metal contamination in soils from Baia Mare city* (Tampa, Florida: University of South Florida, Department of Environmental Science & Policy, Master's Thesis).

Papadimitriou, D. 2002, *Negotiating the New Europe: the European Union and Eastern Europe* (Aldershot: Ashgate).

Pătroescu, M. & Borduşanu, M. 1999, 'Scenarii restructurare ecologică urbană: specifice ariei urbane şi metropolitane a Bucureştiului', *Analele Universităţi Spiru Haret: Serie Geografie* 2, 147-51.

Pătroescu, M., Cenac-Mehedinţi, M., Osaci-Costache, G. & Rozlowicz, I. 2000, 'Zone arii protejate în Municipiul Bucureşti', *Analele Universităţii de Vest din Timişoara* 9–10, 211–22.

Paul, L.J. 1995, 'Regional development in Central & Eastern Europe: the role of inherited structures external forces and local initiatives', *European Spatial Research & Polily* 2(2), 19–41.

Paun, A., Curelariu, G. & Grigoraş, C. 1994, 'Caracterizarea ecopedalogică a ostrovului Babina în vedere fundamentarii masurilor de ameliorare a starii ecologice actuale', *Analele Ştiinţifice al Institutului Delta Dunării* 3, 275–80.

Petrakos, G. (ed.) 2001, *The development of the Balkan region* (Aldershot: Ashgate).

Pascariu, S. 1997, 'Water preservation strategies and the regional plan for the DDBR', in U.Graute (ed.) *Sustainable development for Central & Eastern Europe* (Berlin: Springer Verlag), 145–62.

Pavel, S. 2001, 'Nivelul de trai în România: o abordare conceptuală', *Geographica Timisiensis* 10, 95–100.

Pearton, M. 1971, *Oil and the Romanian state* (Oxford: Clarendon Press).

Pecsi, K. 1989, 'The extremist path of economic development in Eastern Europe', *Communist Economies* 1, 97–109.

Petrea, R. 2006, *Rural tourism and sustainable development* (Oradea: Editura Universităţii din Oradea).

Petrea, R. & Petrea, D. 2000, *Turism rural* (Cluj-Napoca: Presa Universitară Clujeană).

Phinnemore, D. 1998, 'Romania and the European Union: barriers to membership', in G. Erdeli & D. Dumbrăveanu (eds) *Romanian-British geographical exchanges: proceedings of the Third Romanian-British Colloquium* (Bucharest: Corint), 19–30.

Pogan, G. 2002, 'Providing current and future welfare for communities living in the Apuseni Mountains', in R. Rey & G. Gîţan (eds) *Romanian Carpathians in the International Year of the Mountains* (Câmpulung Moldovenesc: Editura Fundaţiei Culturale Alexandru Bogza), 48–55.

Pomogats, B. 1997, 'The idea of Hungarian autonomy in Transylvania', *The Hungarian Quarterly* 38(147), 3–12.

Popa, I. 2000, 'Sisteme de cartare a zonelor de risc cu doboraturi produse de vânt', *Revista Pădurilor* 115(4), 35–41.

Popa, N. & Junie, A. 2000, 'The geographical national and European position of Timişoara city and its perspectives of development', in N. Popa (ed.) *Regionalism and integration: culture space development* (Timişoara: Editura Brumar), 25–37.

Popescu, C.R. 1994a, 'La megalomanie industrielle et l'évolution des villes roumains', in I. Ianoş & V. Rey (eds) *Les nouvelles dimensions du changement urbain: le IX-eme colloque franco-roumain de géographie* (Bucharest: Academia Romană Institutul de Geografie, Geographical International Seminars 2), 47–54.

Popescu, C.R. 1994b, 'The spatial dimension of Romanian industry during the transition period', *Revue Roumaine de Géographie* 38, 59-64.

Popescu, C.R. 1994c, 'Tipologia industrială a oraşelor româneşti', *Analele Universităţii de Vest din Timişoara: Geografie* 4, 33–43.

Popescu, C.R. 1995, 'Spatial evolution of the Romanian industry during the twentieth century', *Revue Roumaine de Géographie* 39, 21–30.

Popescu, C.R. 1998. 'Reacţii regionale ale industriei în contextual procesului de restructurare', *Revista Geografică* 5, 14–19.

Popescu, C.R. 1999, 'Bucureşti: o metropolă în transiţie – caracteristici demografice', *Revista Geografică* 6, 62–72.

Popescu, C.R. 2000, 'Dinamici recente pe piaţa bucureşteană a forţei de muncă', *Revista Geografică* 7, 6–11.

Popescu, C.R. 2000–2001, 'Specializarea industrială şi riscul social în România: studiu de caz - oraşul textil Buhuşi', *Studii si Cercetări: Geografie* 47–8, 91–9.

Popescu, C.R., Dobraca, L. & Tălângă, C. 1997, Schimbări recente în structura activităţilor de servicii şi industriale în Bucureşti', *Revista Geografică* 4, 14–22.

Popescu, C.R., Neguţ, S., Roznovietchi, I. et al. 2003, *Zonele miniere defavorizate din România: abordare geografică* (Bucharest: Editura ASE).

Popescu, E.N. & Popescu, F. 2001, 'Consideraţii asupra istoriei perdelelor forestiere de protecţie în România 1860–2001', *Revista de Silvicultura* 6(13–14), 103–11.

Radice, E.A. 1985, 'General characteristics of the region between the wars', in M.C. Kaser & E.A. Radice (eds) *The economic history of Eastern Europe 1919–1975: economic structure and performance between the two world wars* (Oxford: Clarendon Press), 23–65.

Rady, M. 1992, *Romania in turmoil: a contemporary history* (London: I.B. Tauris).

Râmniceanu, I. 2004, *Probleme structurale de agriculturii româneşti în perspectiva aderarii la UE* (Bucharest: Institutul European din România).

Resis, A. 1978, 'The Churchill-Stalin "percentages" agreement on the Balkans', *American Historical Review* 83, 368–87.

Rey, R. 1978, 'Perspective ale dezvoltarii complexe a zonelor de munte din România', *Viitorul Social* 2, 355–60.

Rey, R. 1979, *Viitor in Carpati – progres economic civilizaţie socialism: contribuţie la perfectionarea activităţilor economico-sociale ale zonelor montane* (Craiova: Editura Scrisul Românesc).

Rey, R. 1985, *Civilizaţie montană* (Bucharest: Editura Ştiinţifică şi Enciclopedică).

Rey, R. & Gîţan, G. (eds) 2002, *Romanian Carpathians in the International Year of the Mountains* (Câmpulung Moldovenesc: Editura Fundaţiei Culturale Alexandru Bogza).

Rhein, E. 2000, 'European regionalism: where is the European Union heading?', in S.C. Calleya (ed.) *Regionalism in the post cold-war world* (Aldershot: Ashgate), 25–44.

Rizobe, M., Gavrilescu, D., Gow, H. & Mathijs, E. 2001, 'Transition and enterprise restructuring in the development of individual farming in Romania', *World Development* 29, 1257–74.

Ronnas, P. 1982, 'Centrally planned urbanisation: the case of Romania', *Geografiska Annaler* 64b, 143–51.

Ronnas, P. 1984, *Urbanization in Romania: a geography of social and economic change since independence* (Stockholm : School of Economics, Economic Research Institute).

Ronnas, P. 1989, 'Turning the Romanian peasant into a new socialist man: an assessment of rural development policy in Romania', *Soviet Studies* 41, 543–59.

Rosenstein-Rodan, P.N. 1943, 'Problems of industrialization of Eastern and South Eastern Europe', *Economic Journal* 53, 202–11.

Rostas, Z. 2000, 'The Bucharest school of sociology', *East Central Europe* 27(2), 1–17.

Sabiel, E. (ed.) 2000, *Turism integrat: Banat şi Maramureş* (Reşiţa: Editura Inter Graf).

Săgeată, R. 1999, 'Evaluarea impactului generat de posibila revenire la organizarea administrativ-teritorială interbelică asupra sistemului urban din România', *Revista Romană de Geografie Politică* 1(1), 85–92.

Săgeată, R. 2001, Fostele resedinţe de plasi în contextul economico-social actual', *Comunicări de Geografie* 5, 463–9.

Săgeată, R. 2003, 'L'organisation administrative et territoriale de la Roumanie: entre le modèle traditionnel et les realités contemporaines', in R. Creţan & M. Ardelean (eds) *Geographic researches in the Carpathian-Danubian space* (Timişoara: Editura Mirton), 601–10.

Sampson, S. 1981, 'Muddling through in Romania (or: why the mămăligă doesn't explode)' *International Journal of Romanian Studies* 3, 165–85.

Sampson, S. 1984, *National integration through socialist planning: an anthropological study of a Romanian new town* (Boulder, Col.: East European Monographs).

Sandu, D. 1998, *Rural community poverty in Romania* (Bucharest: World Bank).

Sandu, D. 1999, 'Dezvoltarea şi sărăcie în satele României', *Sociologie Românească* 10, 117–38.

Sandu, D. 2003, *Romania rurală de azi: ocupare neagricolă şi navetism* (Bucharest: World Bank).

Sandu, D., Stănculescu, M. & Şerban, M. 2000, *Social assessment for rural development projects: social needs and actions in Romanian villages* (Bucharest: World Bank).

Scărlătescu, V. 1939, 'Comerţul intern', in N. Lupu Kostaky (ed.) *Aspecte ale economiei româneşti* (Bucharest: Consiliul Superior Economic), 175–212.

Shafir, M. & Ionescu, D. 1994, 'Romania: a crucially unsuccessful year', *Radio Free Europe/Radio Liberty Research* 3(1), 122–6.

Shen, R. 1997, *The restructuring of Romania's economy: a paradigm of flexibility and adaptability* (Westport, Conn.: Praeger).

Siani-Davis, P. 2005, *The Romanian revolution of December 1989* (Ithaca, N.Y.: Cornell Univertsity Press).

Sorocovschi, V. 1999, 'Alimentarea cu apă a Câmpiei Transilvaniei', *Studia Universitatis Babeş-Bolyai: Geographia* 44(1), 33–44.

Sotiropoulos, D.A. 2002, *Is South-Eastern Europe doomed to instability?: a regional perspective* (London: Frank Cass).

Stănculescu, M. (ed.) 1999, *Sărăcia în România 1995–1998: coordonate dimensiuni şi factori* (Bucharest: UNDP).

Stănculescu, M. 2002, 'Romanian households between state market and informal economies', in R. Neef, M. Stănculescu, I. Berevoescu & C. Tufiş, *The villages of Romania: development poverty and social capital: updating targeting for Romanian Social Development Fund* (Bucharest: World Bank).

Stewart, M. 1997, '"We should build a statue to Ceauşescu here": the trauma of decollectivisation in two Romanian villages', in S. Bridger & F. Pine (eds) *Surviving post-socialism: local strategies and regional responses in Eastern Europe & FSU* (London: Routledge), 66–79.

Stokes, G. 1987, 'The social origins of East European politics', *East European Politics and Societies* 1, 30–74.

Surd, V. & Tomasi, E. 1990, 'Availability of central facilities in rural settlements of Transylvania', in P. Jordan (ed.) *Atlas of Eastern and Southeastern Europe* (Vienna: Österreichisches Ost- und Sudosteuropa Institut), Sheet 5.2.

Surd, V. & Turnock, D. 2001, 'Romania's Apuseni Mountains: a safeguarding a cultural heritage', *GeoJournal* 50, 285–304.

Swinnen, J.F.M. & Mathijs, E. 1997, 'Agricultural privatisation land reform and farm restructuring in Central & Eastern Europe – a comparative analysis', in J.F.M. Swinnen, A. Buckwell & E. Mathijs (eds) *Agricultural privatisation land reform and farm restucturing in Central & Eastern Europe* (Aldershot: Ashgate), 333–73.

Tăbară, V. 2002, 'Mountain area: problems and opportunity for Romania', in R.Rey & D.Gîţan (eds) *Romanian Carpathians in the International Year of the Mountains* (Câmpulung Moldovenesc: Editura Fundaţiei Culturale Alexandru Bogza), 149–57.

Tălângă, C. 1998, 'Some transport problems in Bucharest's metropolitan area', in I. Iordan (ed.) *Socio-economic changes in suburban areas of large cities in Romania and Poland* (Bucharest: Academia Romană Institutul de Geografie), 55–9.

Teşliuc, C., Pop, L. & Teşliuc, E.D. 2001, *Romania: social protection and the poor* (Bucharest: Polirom).

Teşliuc, C., Pop, L. & Panduru, F. 2003, *Poverty in Romania: profile and trends during 1995–2002* (Bucharest: World Bank).

Teşliuc, E.D., Pop, L. & Florescu, R. 2003, *Protecting the poor and vulnerable* (Bucharest: World Bank).

Thomas, C. 1999, 'Waste management and recycling in Romania: a case study of technology transfer in an economy in transition', *Technovation* 19, 365–71.

Thomka, A. 2005, 'The informal economy and the viability of small family farms in Romania', *East European Countryside* 11, 89–109.

Tismaneanu, V. 1990, 'Understanding National Stalinism: Romanian communism in hostorical-comparative perspective' (Washington, D.C.: Wilson Center, European Institute, East European Program Occasional Paper 25).

Toma, L. & Mathijs, E. 2004, 'Stated environmental preferences in a Romanian rural community', *Post-Communist Economies* 6, 215–27.

Tsantis, A.C. & Pepper, R. 1979, *Romania: the industrialization of an agrarian economy under socialist planning* (Washington DC: World Bank).

Turcănasu, G. 1995–96, 'Aşezări rurale evoluante din Moldova: premise a completării reţelei urbane regionale', *Lucrările Seminarului Geografic Dimitrie Cantemir Iaşi* 15–16, 183–97.

Turnock, D. 1986, *The Romanian economy in the twentieth century* (London: Croom Helm).

Turnock, D. 1990, 'City profile: Bucharest', *Cities : International Journal of Urban Policy & Planning* 7, 107–18.

Turnock, D. 1994, *Regional development in the new Eastern Europe with special reference to Romania* (Leicester: Leicester University Social Sciences Faculty Discussion Papers in Geography G94/1).

Turnock, D. 1997, *The Romanian Carpathians in transition: human resources and development potential in the context of national demographic trends* (Leicester:

University of Leicester Faculty of Social Sciences Discussion Papers in Geography G97/1).

Turnock, D. 1999a, *Path dependency and sustainable rural tourism in the Romanian Carpathians* (Leicester: University of Leicester Department of Geography Occasional Paper 41).

Turnock, D. 1999b, 'Sustainable rural tourism in the Romanian Carpathians', *Geographical Journal* 165, 192–9.

Turnock, D. 1999c, 'Romania', in D. Turnock & F.W. Carter (eds) *The states of Eastern Europe: II South-Eastern Europe* (Aldershot: Ashgate), 195–246.

Turnock, D. 2001a, 'Railways and economic development in Romania before 1918', *Journal of Transport Geography* 9, 137–50.

Turnock, D. 2001b, 'Cross-border conservation in East Central Europe: the Danube-Carpathian complex and the contribution of the World Wide Fund for Nature', *GeoJournal* 55, 655–81.

Turnock, D. 2002a, 'Prospects for sustainable rural cultural tourism in Maramureş, Romania', *Tourism Geographies* 4, 62–94.

Turnock, D. 2002b, 'The Carpathian ecoregion – a new initiative for conservation and rural tourism: the case of Maramureş', *Journal of Tourism* 5(1), 21–39.

Turnock, D. 2002c, 'Romania', in F.W.Carter & D.Turnock (eds) *Environmental problems of East Central Europe* (London: Routledge), 366–95.

Turnock, D. 2003, 'The poverty problem in rural Romania: approaches to sustainable development in the Carpathians', *Studia Universitatis Babeş-Bolyai: Geographia* 48(2), 89–102.

Turnock, D. 2007, *Restructuring the Romanian economy: a study of transition 1990–2006* (Cheltenham: Edward Elgar).

Urucu, V. 1998, 'Satul-model Dioşti după şase decenii', *Revista Romană de Sociologie* 9, 271–82.

Vasile, I. 1998, 'Geographical distribution of the drying phenomenon in Romania's forests', in G. Erdeli & D. Dumbrăveanu (eds) *Romanian-British geographical exchanges: proceedings of the Third Romanian-British Colloquium* (Bucharest: Corint), 199–203.

Velcea, V. 1998, 'Natural and man-induced hazard factors in the southern Carpathians', in G. Erdeli & D. Dumbrăveanu (eds) *Romanian-British geographical exchanges: proceedings of the Third Romanian-British Colloquium* (Bucharest: Corint), 195–8.

Verdery, K. 1971, *National ideology under socialism: identity and cultural politics in Ceauşescu's Romania* (Berkeley, Calif.: University of California Press).

Verdery, K. 1983, *Transylvanian villagers: three centuries of political economic and ethnic change* (Berkeley, Calif.: University of California Press).

Verdery, K. 1995a. 'Caritas and the reconceptualisation of money in Romania', *Anthropology Today* 11, 3–7.

Verdery, K. 1995b, 'Faith hope and Caritas in the land of the pyramids: Romania 1990–1994', *Comparative Studies in Society and History* 37, 625–69.

Verdery, K. 2003, *The vanishing hectare: property and value in post-socialist Transylvania* (Ithaca, N.Y.: Cornell University Press).

Vlad, S. & Popescu, C.R. 1993, 'Evoluţia comerţului bucureştean ca urmare a trecerii la economia de piaţa', *Analele Univsităţii Timişoara* 2, 189–96.

Voiculescu, C. 2002, 'Construcţii identitare la rromi din Sângeorgiu de Mureş', *Sociologie Românească New Series* 1–2, 100–25.

Weiner, R. 2004, 'Romanian bilateral relations with Russia and Hungary', in H.F. Carey (ed.) *Romania since 1989: politics economics and society* (Lanham, Md.: Lexington Books) 485–502.

Wortthelet, D. (ed.) 1997, *Au pays des villages roumains* (Bruxelles: Opération Villages Roumains).

Young, S. 2001, *Romanian regional economic development 1945–1995* (Nottingham: Nottingham Trent University Ph.D. thesis).

Zamfir, D. & Braghină, C. 2000, 'Locul localităţilor componente în evoluţia demografică a oraşelor mici din România', *Comunicări de Geografie* 4, 423–7.

Zamfir, D. & Braghină, C. 2001, 'Consideraţii geografice privind ierarhizarea oraşelor mici din România', *Comunicări de Geografie* 5, 539-44.

Zinnes, C.E. 2004, 'The environment in transition', in H.F. Carey (ed.) *Romania since 1989: politics economics and society* (Lanham, Md.: Lexington Books), 439–57.

Index

administration 15, 18, 24, 27, 36, 47, 52, 56, 64, 67, 69, 101, 104, 109, 112–13, 182, 187, 240–41, 257 see also civil service; economic/social policy
agriculture 1–2, 6–7, 10–11, 15, 18, 21–4, 29–31, 35–6, 41, 47–50, 56, 65, 69–70, 76, 81, 88, 91–2, 96–8, 105, 112–15, 118–21, 124, 128, 139–40, 147, 171–203, 214–15, 221, 229, 239–40 see also farms and livestock etc.
aircraft see aviation
airports/air transport 20, 57, 60–1, 73, 154, 205–6, 208–9, 217, 220–28, 266
Alba/Alba Iulia 2, 27, 41–8, 68, 84, 99, 111, 134–6, 160, 177–80, 185–6, 211, 220, 226–8, 231, 237, 239–47, 251, 258–62, 267
Albania/Albanians 70, 74, 77–9, 82–4, 171, 225
Alexandria 68, 142, 247, 252, 256–8
Antonescu, I. 20, 29, 31, 87
arable farming 2, 17–19, 29, 176, 182, 188–94 see also cereals
Arad 17, 21, 25–7, 41–7, 57–8, 68–9, 84, 111–12, 136, 147, 157–8, 160, 164–8, 186–9, 194, 201, 209–12, 223–7, 231, 239–44, 247–9, 252, 256, 266
Argeş 25, 41–8, 58–60, 68, 110, 134–6, 184, 231, 249–51, 260–61
armaments 10, 20, 28–9, 33, 80–81, 128, 142, 159, 221, 245
armed forces xviii, 3–4, 10, 15, 32, 71–3, 80, 101, 118
artisans 9, 24
Austria 39, 63, 78, 124, 154, 158, 160–64, 185, 203, 220, 227–8, 247–9 see also Habsburg Empire
autarky 15, 18, 21, 24, 29–31, 38–40, 93, 127–8, 134, 173, 192–4
automotive industry 39, 57, 114–16, 134, 137, 142, 159, 167, 172, 194, 251

autonomy 4, 8, 14, 17, 31–3, 47, 75, 82–7, 90, 95–8, 102, 137, 141, 229, 269
aviation 28, 56, 72–5

Bacău 41–8, 53–4, 68, 118, 124, 134–6, 141–5, 158–60, 165, 201–2, 223–7, 231, 237, 242–3, 247–50, 261
backwardness/backward regions 9, 11–12, 40, 66, 70, 135, 172
Baia Mare 11, 25, 28, 38–9, 54, 59, 65, 68, 84, 110, 137–9, 141, 187, 189, 212, 223, 225, 227, 237–8, 247, 250–58
Balkans xvii, 1, 4, 66, 69, 72–9, 93, 118, 208, 219, 267, 270 see also named Balkan states
Banat xvii, 3, 11, 18, 21–3, 27, 59, 75–7, 117, 141–3, 150, 160–61, 187–9, 192–4, 231, 250, 254–5, 267
banking 7–8, 11, 22, 63, 70, 95–102, 105–6, 110–14, 117–25, 139, 143–5, 162–3, 173, 198, 201, 209–12, 223, 234, 253, 257–62, 265–7
bankruptcy 96–8, 105, 109, 121, 124, 163–5, 173, 194, 212
Bărăgan 2, 15, 189
Băsescu, T. xviii, 65, 69–70, 74, 80–81, 87, 93, 119–25
Bessarabia 3–4, 14, 17, 20, 23, 25, 27, 31, 63
Bihor 41–8, 53, 65, 68, 111, 115, 136, 142, 152, 186–7, 211, 231, 266
Bistriţa/Bistriţa–Năsăud 11, 25, 41–8, 58, 68, 84, 136–7, 184–7, 195, 212, 226, 231, 237, 242, 247, 252–3, 256–8
Black Sea 2–3, 13–14, 20–21, 24, 34, 51, 57–64, 69–73, 79–80, 99, 117, 183, 205–9, 212, 216–18, 224, 238, 242–3, 246–9, 270
Botoşani 11, 25, 41–8, 53, 68, 106, 110–11, 136, 164, 187–9, 200, 233, 231, 250–52, 256–60, 270
Brăila 11–15, 25–6, 41–8, 50, 68, 128, 134–6, 166, 189, 193, 205, 213,

free trade/zones 1, 10, 166, 209, 213–16,
218–20, 229
freight/freight rates 10, 205–7, 210–11, 218,
226–7, 244
frontier/frontier cooperation 4, 13, 21, 57,
64–5, 67–9, 73, 76–9, 208–9, 220,
227–9, 239, 248, 262
fruit 2, 9, 15, 23, 27, 49, 175–6, 182–4,
195–6
fuels see energy and named fuels
furniture 39–40, 91, 114, 125, 128–30, 134,
238, 245, 258

Galați 11, 14–15, 25–6, 35–7, 40–47, 53, 73,
68, 90, 98, 107, 111, 116, 125, 136,
142, 148, 150–51, 160, 187, 189,
205, 212–17, 226–8, 231, 240, 248,
251–2, 254–6, 261, 270
GDP 95, 98, 101–2, 104, 108–9, 112, 170
Germans/Germany xviii, 3–4, 6–7, 14,
17–18, 20, 28–9, 31, 39, 57, 64, 72,
76–8, 81–7, 90–92, 103, 115, 118,
143, 147, 160–69, 185, 196–7, 201,
218–20, 224–8, 238, 243–6, 269
Gheorghiu-Dej, Gh. 31–2, 40
Giurgiu 11, 15–17, 41, 68, 78, 134–6, 165,
187, 203, 211–13, 219–20, 231, 242,
247, 251–3, 256–8
globalisation 66, 70, 93, 116, 127–8, 135, 200
Gorj 41–8, 68, 111, 134–6, 158, 231, 251,
265–7
government 5, 7–8, 17, 62, 65–7, 70–71, 77,
82, 94, 101–6, 109, 125–8, 171, 181,
182, 185–7, 192, 197–8, 211, 221–3,
229, 269
Greece/Greeks 72, 74, 77–9, 82–4, 116–18,
125, 146, 150, 159, 188, 212, 227

Habsburg Empire xviii, 1, 3–4, 6–11, 13–15,
18, 76
handicrafts 9–10, 15, 34, 56, 108, 110–11,
182–4, 186, 239, 242
Harghita 7, 41–8, 68, 87, 118, 136, 142, 174,
177–80, 185, 231, 243, 248, 261
health 6, 15, 22–4, 34, 52, 61, 65, 75, 87,
89–91, 93, 118, 123, 138–9, 149–51,
182, 244

heavy industry 35, 45, 116, 127 see
also chemicals, engineering and
metallurgy
hotels 13, 61, 97, 107, 128, 215, 233, 238,
242–5
housing xvii, 4, 27, 35, 39, 51, 56, 59–60,
77, 87–91, 146, 158, 160, 181–3,
228, 267, 232–4, 240–47
Hunedoara 2, 9–13, 28, 41–8, 68, 111,
135–6, 158, 161–3, 186–8, 228, 231,
241, 246, 257–8, 260–62
Hungarians/Hungary 3–4, 6–7, 11–13, 17,
21–2, 28–9, 32–4, 39, 62–4, 69–85,
117, 138–9, 148–50, 160, 167–73,
179, 192–3, 211–14, 218–20, 225,
239, 247, 250
hydropower 11, 13, 20, 39, 51, 57, 77, 80,
218, 221

Ialomița 41–8, 68, 89, 134–6, 193, 231, 249,
262
Iași 9–11, 17–18, 21–3, 37, 41–7, 53, 57,
60, 68, 74, 80–4, 89, 107, 110–11,
124, 136, 149–50, 156–60, 164–6,
189, 212, 220, 224–6, 231–2, 237,
240–49, 252, 256–60, 270
ideology xviii, 6, 22, 38, 63 see also
communism, socialism etc.
Ilfov 41–8, 56, 68, 158, 231
Iliescu, I. xviii, 85–6, 93–101, 112–18, 126,
127
IMF 32–4, 66, 101–3, 112–14, 122–5, 269
immigration see migration
imperialism 3, 14 see also named powers
imports/import substitution 9–10, 19–21,
34–5, 65, 94–6, 102–4, 109, 112–14,
120–23, 135, 142, 150–51, 159,
165–8, 188–90, 192, 194–8, 201,
212–20
income 5, 94, 125, 172–4, 179, 181
independence xviii, 1, 3, 7–8, 28, 32, 35, 50,
61, 80, 173, 208, 269
industrial growth/industry xvii, 1–2, 6–29,
32, 35–46, 59, 67, 70, 86, 92–100,
127–68, 173–4, 177, 182, 185–7,
212, 215, 234, 238, 242–3, 255,
261–2, 269–70 see also named
sectors
industrial park 165, 212, 229, 238–45

For Product Safety Concerns and Information please contact our EU representative GPSR@taylorandfrancis.com Taylor & Francis Verlag GmbH, Kaufingerstraße 24, 80331 München, Germany